JUDGES
OF THE
SUPREME COURT
OF INDIA

1950–1989

JUDGES
OF THE
SUPREME COURT
OF INDIA

1950–1989

GEORGE H. GADBOIS, JR

OXFORD
UNIVERSITY PRESS

Oxford University Press is a department of the University of Oxford.
It furthers the University's objective of excellence in research, scholarship,
and education by publishing worldwide. Oxford is a registered trademark of
Oxford University Press in the UK and in certain other countries.

Published in India by
Oxford University Press
2/11 Ground Floor, Ansari Road, Daryaganj, New Delhi 110 002, India

First Edition published in 2011
Oxford India Paperbacks 2018

ISBN-13: 978-0-19-946936-9
ISBN-10: 0-19-946936-9

Typeset in Goudy Old Style 11/14
by Sai Graphic Design, New Delhi 110 055
Printed in India by Replika Press Pvt. Ltd.

To My Son
Keith Allen Gadbois
1960–1983

Contents

PART TWO

A Collective Portrait

Acknowledgements

This book could not have been written without the assistance of the judges. I am profoundly appreciative of their willingness to make time available to meet and talk with me. Every interview request was granted. They treated me with unlimited kindness and hospitality. They made this the most enjoyable research project I have ever undertaken.

Generous financial support from the American Institute of Indian Studies made this project possible. I am deeply indebted to it and to the New Delhi support staff. Thanks are due also to the University of Kentucky Research Foundation.

On three occasions my host was the Indian Law Institute, and on another the Institute of Constitutional and Parliamentary Studies. The staff of these institutes was wonderfully hospitable, both professionally and personally.

My indebtedness to my wife Judy, for everything, can never be adequately expressed.

India's Judicial Elite

For a Supreme Court often described as the most powerful in the world,[1] it is perplexing that so little attention has been paid to who its judges have been. Where did they come from and why, how, and by whom were they chosen to be Supreme Court (hereafter SCI) judges? What manner of people have they been? Where were they born and what were the circumstances of their birth—their social and economic backgrounds, their father's occupation, their religion and, if Hindu, their caste? How did they spend their formative years? Were they the first in their family history to practise law, to become a judge, or were they the most recent member of a family where practising law was a family tradition? What was the nature of their higher education? What was the nature of their career before being chosen for appointment to the SCI? What life experiences, professional and otherwise, socialized them? All of us are shaped by our backgrounds and life experiences, but these matters have not been deemed important enough to attract much interest.

---

[1] Rajeev Dhavan, *Justice on Trial: The Supreme Court Today* (Allahabad: A.H. Wheeler & Company, Ltd., 1980), p. 1. Dhavan is one of very few Indian scholars to pay some attention to the backgrounds and careers of the judges. In addition to this book, see his *The Supreme Court of India: A Socio-Legal Critique of its Juristic Techniques* (Bombay: N.M. Tripathi Pvt. Ltd., 1977); and, with Alice Jacob, *Selection and Appointment of Supreme Court Judges: A Case Study* (Bombay: N.M. Tripathi Pvt. Ltd., 1978). Brief profiles of the 1973–81 judges are found in Vijay K. Gupta, *Decision Making in the Supreme Court of India* (Delhi: Kaveri Books, 1995).

This book attempts to do three things. The first is to provide a brief biographical essay for each of the ninety-three[2] men (all were males) who served on the Court from 1950 through mid-1989. The second attempts to account for why they, rather than others, were chosen—the selection criteria employed and, to the extent possible in a furtive selection environment, identify those who selected them. The third is to paint a collective portrait of them, paying particular attention to changes in the background characteristics of the judges over the four decades. This book is best described as a reference book—a who's who of the ninety-three judges, an account of why, how, and by whom they were selected, and finally, a description of the similiarities and differences among them, and the changes over the two generations.

Biographical data are very difficult to locate in India. There is no tradition of judges leaving behind autobiographies or memoirs. Only a half-dozen did. Nor is there any tradition of judicial biographies. There are about the same number of them if one is most generous in defining biography. The most recent collection of life sketches of judges of which I am aware was published nearly eighty years ago.[3]

---

[2] Two others served as *ad hoc* judges. Article 127 of the Constitution provides that the Chief Justice of India (CJI), with the consent of the president after consultation with the high court chief justice, may request that a high court judge 'attend the sittings' of the SCI. This could be done 'should [there] not be a quorum of the Judges of the Supreme Court available to hold or continue any session of the Court. ...' The only two high court judges ever appointed in this manner were Ramachander Naik and Khalil-ul-Zamaan Siddiqui, the chief justice and most senior associate judge of the old Hyderabad High Court. They sat with SCI judge M.C. Mahajan on a special bench in Hyderabad for a few months in 1950 to dispose of about 400 Urdu language cases pending before the Privy Council of Hyderabad which ceased to exist after the Constitution became operative. After those cases were resolved, they returned to their high court. I have chosen, as most others have, to treat them as 'borrowed' high court judges rather than SCI judges.

[3] *Indian Judges: Biographical & Critical Sketches* (Madras: G.A. Natesan & Company, 1932), reprinted in 1988 as *Eminent Indian Judges* (Delhi: Mittal Publications).

After this manuscript was completed, *Indian Judges: Yogesh Kumar Sabharwal, V.R. Kirshna Iyer, K.S. Hegde, Radhabinod Pal, Hans Raj Khanna, Chief Justice of India, James Fitzjames Stephen, Mahadev Govind Ranade, Abdur Rahim, Abbas Tyabji, C.K. Thakker, B.N. Srikrishna, V.M. Tarkunde* (BooksLLC: Memphis, TN, USA, 2010) was published. Information is provided for 112 individuals, not all of whom were judges. Thirty-five are former SCI judges, and sixteen of these served during the 1950–89 years. The entries are from Wikipedia, a web-based encyclopaedia. The reader is warned that '[t]he publisher makes no representation or warranties with respect to the accuracy or completeness of this book,' and the reader is invited to go to the online edition (http://en.wikipedia.org/wiki/Category:Indian_judges and suggest changes, last accessed 3 October 2010).

The press has not provided readers with anything more than the appointee's name and the high court from which he was promoted. News of appointments take up no more space than the daily weather forecast and it is not uncommon for names to be misspelled. Their retirements and deaths are only rarely noted by the national press.

The SCI maintains files containing some biographical information about each judge, provided by the judge. Though this is not available to the public, I was given access to it. Occasionally useful are the 'full court references' delivered following the death of a judge. They are published in the official *Supreme Court Reports* (hereafter SCR) but are seen by few because lawyers and scholars use the more promptly published *All India Reporter* (hereafter *AIR*) and *Supreme Court Cases* (hereafter *SCC*). The SCI's official website was of some value.[4] Of little use was the frequently updated *Judges of the Supreme Court and the High Courts*.[5] Very few of the who's who collections included judges. All the above sources were not immune from errors. Biographical information in the public domain was replete with inaccuracies.

The essays embrace their entire lives. Their post-SCI years are included because less than a half dozen went into full retirement after reaching the mandatory retirement age of sixty-five and because for some, their post-court activities can be considered as important a part of their lives as their usually brief tenures on the SCI. Some are remembered more for their post-superannuation activities than their years on the bench.

The contents of the biographical essays were gathered in the only way they could be—from conversations with the judges. Sixty-eight were alive when this study was conducted in 1983 and 1988, and I had the opportunity to meet with all except four.[6] For the deceased judges, I met or corresponded with widows and children or with other relations, and with close friends and associates. Every interview request was granted. They ranged from forty-five minutes to ten hours spread over several days.

Prior to each interview and after scouring every available source, I prepared a draft essay. The interviews were semi-structured—errors in the drafts were corrected and the missing materials added. Most of the judges

---

[4] www.supremecourtofindia.nic.in (last accessed October 2010).

[5] New Delhi: Department of Justice of the Ministry of Law and Justice.

[6] K.C. Das Gupta and J.R. Mudholkar were too ill to meet. My schedule and P.N. Shinghal's never coincided. J.S. Verma, the last of the CJI R.S. Pathak era judges, was appointed in mid-1989, a few months after I had returned home. Biographical information about both him and Shinghal was gathered via correspondence. Both K. Subba Rao and J.M. Shelat were interviewed in 1970.

had things other than biographical matters they wanted to talk about, with the result that many of the interviews were really wide-ranging conversations. Most were conducted in New Delhi. The author travelled throughout the country to meet the others.

The biographical essays are written in who's who form. Each can be read independently of the others. They are, of course, no substitute for full ones, but one need not apologize for providing the first collection of brief biographies of the first two generations of SCI judges.

The second objective is to account, as far as was possible, for their selection to be an SCI judge—to answer the questions of why and by whom they were chosen. These important questions were very difficult—in many instances impossible—to answer because the entire selection process is secret. Selection decisions are made behind closed doors. At no stage does the public participate.

It is necessary at the start to clarify the language of appointments. An SCI judge must be an Indian citizen and must have served for at least five years as a high court judge, or have been for at least ten years a high court advocate, or be, 'in the opinion of the President, a distinguished jurist'.[7] The executive appoints every judge and is accountable for every appointee. The official announcement is in the form of a warrant of appointment issued by the president acting on the advice of the prime minister. A judge's tenure begins when he is sworn in by the CJI. But the selection of those who become judges is a very different matter. Constitutionally, the CJI must be consulted by the executive before an appointment can be made. Proposals that his concurrence be required were explicitly rejected by the Constituent Assembly, the members of which wrote the Constitution.

Virtually all evidence compels one to conclude that, in practice, more during the first twenty years than the second, the CJI in fact initiated the names of most of those who were approved by the executive. For many years, accounts of the selection and appointment process credited or debited the executive with the judges who were chosen. Only later was the often pivotal role of the CJI recognized by scholars and acknowledged by the executive. The selection of others was initiated by the executive, but even in those instances, the executive usually stated that every appointee was 'recommended' by the CJI. The latter never publicly protested the use

[7] Art. 124 (3), *The Constitution of India as modified up to the 1st August 1977.* (New Delhi: Government of India, Ministry of Law, Justice and Company Affairs.)

of that term even when he neither nominated the person nor wanted him. The language of appointments is clouded further when every CJI said that, regardless of where the name came from, he was *responsible* for all appointees during his stewardship.

That CJIs were responsible for appointees during their tenures was stated very emphatically by P.B. Gajendragadkar, CJI from 1964 to 1966. He wrote that

ultimately in the matter of appointments to the Supreme Court, the Chief Justice alone is responsible. ...[8] As Chief Justice, it was my privilege to recommend to the Union Government the names of persons I wanted to be appointed as my colleagues. This is a very important power and every wise Chief Justice must take care to exercise this power after deep and mature deliberation freely, independently and without favour or fear. I claim that I did observe this principle both in appointments I actually made and those which I refused to make.[9]

There were eighteen CJIs during the four decades. Seven had died before this study commenced. The appointment of judges during their watches was discussed with the remaining eleven.[10] From B.P. Sinha (1959–64) through R.S. Pathak (1986–9), I met with all except the deceased Gajendragadkar. All, some more so than others, were willing to talk about those appointed during their reigns, the selection criteria employed, and their own and the executive's role. Revealed were some fascinating stories about why and by whom some judges were chosen.

The fact that the CJIs of the 1950s were not alive meant that for most of the appointees of those years, the identity of the selectors and the selection criteria could not be determined with confidence. Twenty-four associate[11] judges served during that decade. The eight who were alive were interviewed, the eldest being Vivian Bose, aged ninety-two and appointed in 1951. Each was certain that he was the choice of the CJI. Some were less certain about one or two of their colleagues.

---

[8] P.B. Gajendragadkar, *To the Best of My Memory* (Bombay: Bharatiya Vidya Bhavan, 1983), p. 98.

[9] Ibid., pp. 179–80.

[10] A twelfth, K. Subba Rao, was interviewed in 1970, but his recommendations of C.A. Vaidialingam and K.S. Hegde were not part of that conversation. According to both those judges, however, they were definitely the choices of Subba Rao.

[11] The term 'associate' rather than the archaic 'puisne' will be used throughout. The terms 'advocate' and 'lawyer' are used synonymously.

Mainly because the CJIs were unanimous in saying that they were responsible for every appointee during their tenures, and agreed that for better or worse those appointees were part of their legacies, the biographical essays for the ninety-three judges are grouped according to who was the CJI when they became an SCI judge. Thus, there are eighteen 'courts', beginning with the Kania Court and concluding with the Pathak Court.[12]

Arranging the biographical essays in this manner serves other important purposes. In particular, it permits consideration of the political contexts. Contextual changes can have a bearing upon who is appointed. The context when Jawaharlal Nehru was Prime Minister and Govind Ballabh Pant was Home Minister[13] was very different than the context after Mrs Gandhi's landslide election victory in 1971 and the arrival in her cabinet of Minister of Steel and Mines S. Mohan Kumaramangalam and Law Minister H.R. Gokhale.

Grouping the judges in this manner also enables one to compare the selection criteria employed by each CJI. There was not a fixed set of criteria. Thus, the Sikri Court (1971–3) discusses the men appointed during his stewardship, the political contexts and imperatives of the day, the relative roles of the executive and Sikri, and the real or apparent selection criteria employed.

The associate judges were asked who they believed initiated their appointments—the CJI or the executive. There were only a few instances where their accounts and the CJIs were not the same. Associate judges were often reluctant to acknowledge that their name was advanced from the executive side. Being chosen by the executive was considered less deserving than if his name was advanced by the CJI.

An attempt was made to write each of the CJI Court sections so that, like the biographical essays, it can be read independently of the others. This effort was not entirely successful, for while the biographical sketches easily stand alone, a succeeding CJI's role in the selection process was often affected by things his predecessor had done, and problems of too much repetition arose. A partial solution was to include in the glossary definitions

---

[12] Because no fresh appointees joined the SCI during the tenures of B.K. Mukherjea and J.C. Shah, there were actually sixteen courts as that term is being used here. The month-long tenure of J.C. Shah was important for who he tried but failed to get appointed.

[13] Until 1971, the home minister's portfolio included the appointment of judges. Thereafter, this became the responsibility of the law minister.

of some terms—the supersession, Emergency, and some decisions (such as *Kesavananda*) are prime examples—so that an event or decision need be defined or explained in the text only once.

When a judge spoke off-the-record—and this was not often—those requests were, of course, honoured. This occasionally meant that important material could not be used here. The judges trusted me and I have not knowingly betrayed that trust. I have also deemed some on-the-record matters inappropriate to include. The CJI who described one of the appointees during his tenure as 'the low point of SCI appointments' is not identified nor is the name of the appointee.

When individuals are named, it was occasionally a delicate matter whether or not to include some materials. Examples are the identities of nominees not accepted by the CJI or by the executive. Delicate also is identifying the nearly two dozen senior advocates and high court judges who declined invitations to become SCI judges and the real or apparent reasons why. Should the patrons who lubricated the paths of some who reached the SCI be named? Should the half-dozen who acknowledged going to England to seek acceptance into the highly competitive and prestigious Indian Civil Service (hereafter ICS), were unsuccessful, remained in England until called to the bar, and later became SCI judges, be identified? This book is not intended to be an exposè. I have endeavoured to use good taste, though some readers will find some of the contents better left unwritten.

Only rarely do decisions of the SCI find a place here. Almost equally rare is mention of the purported social and economic philosophy of a judge. Exceptions are when the judge carried his views as a badge of pride and was well known for these views. Very rarely is an evaluative observation made about the quality or importance or contributions of a judge. Some were giants who will be remembered a century from now. Others are blips on the radar screen, sidebars to the history of the SCI, likely to be recalled only by the closest of court watchers. All, however, are members of the Indian judicial elite and deserving of attention. Because each of the CJIs said he was responsible for every appointment during his watch, there are occasions where the failures and successes of a CJI in seeing his choices appointed are subjected to some assessment.

The forty years are divided into two periods—from 1950 to 1970 and from 1971 to 1989. There are several reasons why this has been done. Among them is that the executive, after largely conceding to the CJI the power to select judges during the first twenty years sought after 1970, to retrieve some of that power. Thereafter, the selection power was shared between the CJI and the executive and the selection criteria underwent some changes. Secondly, twenty years can fairly be considered a generation, and this delineation allows one to compare the backgrounds of the first generation judges with the second. The last[14] of the judges who received his high court appointment before the British departed retired from the SCI in 1970.

The biographical essays, many of which contain content that differs from what others have reported, are likely to provoke relatively little disagreement or controversy. Some readers will find some of their contents minutiae that will test their patience, but when faced with the decision to include or exclude, I usually chose the former. Where sources other than the interviews were utilized, factual errors in them may have been repeated here. The final results are inevitably incomplete, uneven, and despite going to extraordinary lengths to be accurate, surely include mistakes of commission or omission. Where the full citations of publications are missing, the dates of various events not provided, and other relevant information missing as well, such simply could not be located. The full name of each judge and its spelling is rendered as he preferred. States of birth are according to 1980s boundaries. Interviews are usually cited only once in each essay—there is no need to litter them with multiple citations.

There will be disagreement over the identities of the alleged initiators and other actors in the selection of some of the judges. The secrecy of the process is fertile ground for different accounts of the principals involved in appointments. Some of these accounts may well be correct. This is particularly the case with alleged patrons. Some differing accounts of why a particular judge was selected may be correct because I was misinformed, felt compelled to withhold information, or was simply wrong. After the first decade, the initiator could almost always be identified but the selection criteria were not always known or were incomplete. There are occasions when the criteria were inferred. I have no illusions that the questions of why and by whom each judge was selected are correct in every instance. This is the first attempt to connect the dots between a potential nominee and his ultimate appointment. It is the first, not the last word. Much more remains to be done.

[14] M. Hidayatullah.

It is likely that some will question the veracity of some of what is found here. I have relied almost entirely upon what the CJIs and associate judges have told me.[15] I believe that there is little reason to question the truthfulness of almost everything I was told. I do suspect, however, that some were less active in the struggle for Independence and played less pioneering roles during the early years of the legal aid movements than they reported, and that one, perhaps two of the CJIs may have exaggerated his role in the selection of judges appointed during his stewardship.

An effort has been made to include in each biographical essay a complete listing of each judge's publications, including official reports he prepared. Except, for space constraints, only publications longer than forty pages are included and, for the same reason, the names of the endowment, memorial, and other lectures that were published have been omitted. The best source for the titles of books and official reports is the United States Library of Congress online catalog.[16]

The post-retirement activities of some of the judges who were on the SCI or otherwise alive in 1989 are incomplete. An effort was made in 2009 via correspondence to update their essays but this was not entirely successful.[17] Much post-1989 material was gathered from the Internet and the Indian press.

It bears emphasizing that this book covers only the SCI's first four decades. Thus, there is no need to repeat 'until 1990'. All the changes in the backgrounds of the judges and the selection process after 1989—and there have been significant ones—are beyond the boundaries of this book.

Much of the material in this book no one else has, nor ever will. The author is aware that this imposes upon him an immense amount of responsibility. The elephantine gestation period, though otherwise inexcusable, is partly a consequence of poor health which compelled premature retirement from the university.

---

[15] Ashoke K. Sen, Law Minister from 1957 to 1966 and 1984 to 1987, was the only law minister interviewed. Efforts were made to interview others and all were agreeable, but those interviews never took place.

[16] www.loc.gov/. In 2010, the Library of Congress holdings included eighty-four publications of V.R. Krishna Iyer. The National Law School of India University library (www.nls.ac.in/) in the same year held twenty-six.

[17] Thirty-six letters were written to the retired living judges and to the families of those who died after 1989. The sixteen responses enabled me to bring those biographical essays up to date.

Part One

EIGHTEEN COURTS AND NINETY-THREE JUDGES

I

The Kania Court (1950–1)

What would become the Kania Court began to take shape on 20 June 1946, the date of both Sir Srinivasa Varadachariah's retirement and Sir H.J. Kania becoming a Federal Court judge. Kania was fifty-five and, with fifteen years as a Bombay High Court judge, was second in seniority. A year later there were two personnel changes in quick succession. On 9 June, Sir S. Fazl Ali replaced Sir Muhammad Zafrullah Khan who, the day before had opted for Pakistan and resigned. Less than a week later and just two days before national Independence, Chief Justice Sir William Patrick Spens resigned, leaving only Kania and Fazl Ali on the Court. Kania became the first Indian CJI on 14 August 1947.

The Government of India Act 1935, had provided for a chief justice and as many as six associate judges, but the strength of the Federal Court from 1937 to 1947 never exceeded three, including the CJI. Having decided only 135 decisions and rendered only four advisory opinions during its entire existence, three were sufficient.[1] The transition from the Federal Court to the SCI was seamless—Kania on 26 January became the first CJI under the 1950 Constitution and the five other Federal Court judges became SCI judges. The authorized strength of the Court at this time was eight, including the CJI. After the appointments of N. Chandrasekhara Aiyar in 1950 and Vivian Bose in 1951, the Court reached its full strength.

[1] George H. Gadbois, Jr, 'The Federal Court of India: 1937–1950', *Journal of the Indian Law Institute*, 6 (April–September, 1964), pp. 253–315. The 135 figure is through January 1950.

There might not have been a Kania Court. M.C. Setalvad wrote that in early 1946 he was asked by the law secretary if he would accept a Federal Court judgeship. 'He also told me that Spens would retire in 3 or 4 years, and I would succeed him as Chief Justice. I told him that I was already 61, and would myself retire in four years and was not therefore interested.'[2] When Kania became CJI first in 1947 and again in 1950, there was no convention in place that the most senior judge would become the CJI. There had been an incident in 1943 that touched upon this matter. As Sir Maurice Gwyer, the Federal Court's first chief justice was on the threshold of retirement, the viceroy announced that his replacement was Spens. Gwyer objected because his views on his replacement were not ascertained. He felt strongly that Varadachariar, the most senior associate judge, should have been his replacement.[3]

Later, just three days before Kania was to become CJI under the 1950 Constitution, Nehru expressed irritation about comments Kania had made on a file dealing with making permanent several Madras High Court additional judges.[4] Kania made what Nehru considered 'unjudicial [sic] and indeed improper' observations about Bashir Ahmed, a Muslim, and wrote to Home Minister Sardar Vallabhbhai Patel expressing doubts about whether Kania should become CJI. Patel went ahead with Ahmed's appointment, but not before telling Kania that the failure to confirm Ahmed's appointment might be regarded as communal.[5]

[2] Motilal C. Setalvad, My Life: Law and Other Things (Bombay: N.M. Tripathi Pvt. Ltd., 1971), p. 103.

[3] Kuldip Nayar (ed.) Supersession of Judges (New Delhi: India Book Company, 1973). K.S. Hegde, Crisis in Indian Judiciary (Bombay: Sindhu Publications Pvt. Ltd., 1973), pp. 34–5. Nayar cited 'some lawyers'. Hegde cited an article by B. Shiva Rao in The Hindu dated 21 July 1973. Granville Austin repeats this account in Working a Democratic Constitution: A History of the Indian Experience (New Delhi: Oxford University Press, 1999), p. 135. Although supporting evidence is lacking, it is quite conceivable that Gwyer was no less upset that he was being replaced by an Englishman.

[4] An additional judge is one appointed for a period not exceeding two years if there is an increase in the business of a high court. The practice became that most permanent high court judges began as additional judges.

[5] Austin, Working a Democratic Constitution, pp. 125–6. Austin's source for Nehru's letter to Patel, and Patel's reply, both dated 23 January 1950, is Durga Das (ed.), Sardar Patel's Correspondence, 1945–1950, 10 vols (Ahmedabad: Navajivan Publishing House, 1973), vol. 10, p. 378. Austin added that 'Patel also wrote that some indiscretions by a chief justice have to be tolerated, "but, on the whole, I think I have been able to manage him." Kania's petty-mindedness "is a trait not uncommon with some heads of the judiciary who feel that they have the sole monopoly of upholding its independence,"'

Returning to Kania's Federal Court appointment, Bombay had not been represented since Sir Mukund Ramrao Jayakar was appointed to the Judicial Committee of the Privy Council in 1939. Setalvad and Kania had been close friends for decades, and he is widely believed to have been instrumental in Kania's appointment.[6]

Fazl Ali's appointment was not unexpected. He was the most senior Muslim judge in the country, aged sixty, had spent nineteen years on the Patna High Court, and in 1943 became the first Indian to become its chief justice. Moreover, according to his son, the Nehru and Fazl Ali families were well acquainted.[7] Kania's role in the selection of Fazl Ali could not be ascertained.

The first to join the Federal Court during Kania's stewardship was M.P. Sastri of the Madras High Court. Aged fifty-eight when he was sworn in on 6 December 1947, he was third in seniority at Madras. Both the then chief justice and the next most senior were Englishmen. His appointment meant that Madras regained representation after Varadachariar's retirement.

The warrants of the appointments of M.C. Mahajan and B.K. Mukherjea were issued on the same day. According to Mahajan's account, Kania in July 1948 had inquired about his interest in a Federal Court judgeship: '... I want at least two more judges for the Federal Court and I am considering your name. ... I should like to know if you like [sic] to be considered ...'[8] Mahajan replied in the affirmative, and Kania wrote in September, saying that 'he had recommended my name and there was nothing further to write till he knew that the names he had submitted had gone through.'[9] Soon Kania wrote again, saying 'Everything has passed through as intended.'[10] He accepted Kania's invitation, but his chief justice, Dewan Ram Lal, wanted that appointment himself and had Nehru's support.[11] The Chief Justice of

---

Austin, p. 126, fn. 9, citing Durga Das, vol. 10, p. 379. A more complete account of this incident is found in A.G. Noorani, 'The Prime Minister and the Judiciary', in James Manor (ed.), Nehru to the Nineties: The Changing Office of Prime Minister of India (Vancouver: University of British Columbia Press, 1994), pp. 94–114, 99–100.

[6] Setalvad, My Life, pp. 68, 180.

[7] Interview with S.M. Fazal Ali on 24 April 1983 in New Delhi.

[8] Mehr Chand Mahajan, Looking Back: The Autobiography of Mehr Chand Mahajan, Former Chief Justice of India (Bombay: Asia Publishing House, 1963), p. 191.

[9] Ibid., pp. 191–2.

[10] Ibid., p. 192. Mahajan recalled that he took the oath of office on 1 October but the official records indicate that the correct date was the 4th.

[11] Mahajan, Looking Back, pp. 191–2.

India and the Home Minister, Sardar Patel, were of a different opinion and eventually I was appointed.'[12] Mahajan was fifty-eight and the first Federal Court judge from Punjab when he was sworn in on 4 October 1948.

B.K. Mukherjea also received his invitation to become a Federal Court judge from Kania.[13] The first Bengali to serve on the Court, he was fifty-seven when he was sworn in on 14 October. He had served on the Calcutta High Court for twelve years, and was second in seniority when the chief justice was Sir Arthur Trevor Harries. Although Mukherjea had much more high court service than Mahajan, Mukherjea's arrival in Delhi was delayed, meaning that Mahajan became senior to Mukherjea. This seemed of little consequence at this time, but following Kania's death, Sastri, the most senior associate judge, became CJI. If the convention of the seniormost becoming CJI can be dated from then, because he was sworn in ahead of Mukherjea, Mahajan became CJI following Sastri's retirement in 1954. He would not have become CJI otherwise.

Nearly sixteen months would pass before S.R. Das, at age fifty-five, joined the Federal Court on 20 January 1950, one week before the SCI succeeded the Federal Court. Although a second consecutive Bengali, and having been a member of the Calcutta bench for seven years, he came to the Federal Court from the East Punjab High Court for, in 1949 Patel, believing there was a need for a chief justice from the outside, persuaded Das to accept transfer to Simla as that court's chief justice.

The first to be sworn in after the commencement of the Constitution was N. Chandrasekhara Aiyar, who had retired from the Madras High Court in 1948. When he joined the SCI on 23 September 1950, he was nearly sixty-three. Another thirty years would pass and sixty more SCI judges would be appointed before anyone older would reach the Court.[14] Because of his advanced age, his appointment was the most unusual of the Kania years.

The final member of the abbreviated Kania regime was Vivian Bose, sworn in on 5 March 1951. A Christian, Bose was nearly sixty when he arrived in Delhi. He had served fifteen years on the Nagpur High Court,

---

[12] Ibid., p. 192.

[13] Interview with Mukherjea's son, Amiya Kumar Mookerji, a retired Calcutta High Court judge, on 29 June 1983 in Calcutta.

[14] Baharul Islam, appointed in 1980, was a few weeks older than Chandrasekhara Aiyar.

the last two as its chief justice. Bose recalled that the invitation came directly from Kania.[15]

At least one to whom Kania extended an invitation declined. M.C. Chagla, Kania's former junior colleague on the Bombay High Court, wrote that 'Kania offered me a judgeship of the Federal Court. ... I declined the offer because I thought I was doing more useful work as Chief Justice of Bombay. ...'[16] Chagla wrote that this invitation was extended in 1950. Born in 1900, he was no older than fifty at this time. Had he accepted the offer, and if being the seniormost associate judge would determine who would become CJI, he would have been the next in line for the chief justiceship no later than S.R. Das's retirement in 1959, three years earlier had he reached Delhi ahead of Das, and would have had a very long tenure as CJI. Chagla wrote that when Kania died, Setalvad urged Nehru to appoint him as CJI, and Nehru 'seemed agreeable'. But when the sitting judges '... threatened to resign if the seniority rule was not followed ... the Government yielded to the threat.'[17]

The above points to the conclusion that Kania was a very active participant in the process of identifying the high court judges he wanted appointed. How many of the six who joined the Court during his watch were initiated by him cannot be determined. The best guess is that Kania was a party to each appointment, perhaps the decisive one, but Patel's role should not be overlooked. Kania apparently was the first to approach a prospective nominee and after the decision was made he was the conveyer of the formal invitation. Because there were only about one hundred high court judges during these years, Kania was most likely familiar with most, or all, of the six. The inherited tradition was that the home minister was responsible for appointments to the higher judiciary, and the limited evidence available points to Patel, a powerful figure during these transitional years, taking this responsibility seriously. Following Patel's death at the end of 1950, C. Rajagopalachari became home minister, and was holding that post when

[15] Interview with Bose in Bangalore on 21 June 1983.

[16] M.C. Chagla, *Roses in December: An Autobiography with Epilogue*. Eighth enlarged edition (Bombay: Bharatiya Vidya Bhavan, 1978), p. 171. Apparently, an SCI judgeship was not offered to any other Bombay High Court judge at this time. With Kania as CJI, Setalvad as the first attorney general, and C.K. Daphtary the nation's first solicitor general, all from Bombay, the SCI, in its formative years, was strongly influenced by the traditions and culture of the Bombay High Court and bar.

[17] Chagla, *Roses in December*, p. 171.

Vivian Bose was appointed. The only evidence of Nehru's involvement in these appointments was his reservations about the Mahajan appointment and about Kania becoming CJI, but it is likely his involvement went beyond that. It is perplexing, given the extent to which the Constituent Assembly wrestled over devising a method of selecting judges, that the names of Sastri, Mahajan, and Mukherjea, all appointed during their deliberations, were never mentioned.

At the time of their appointments, the average age of the first eight judges was 58.6.[18] All had been senior high court judges, their tenures averaging 10.7 years. Three had been chief justices, and three others were the most senior associate judges. Five of them came from the three presidency high courts of Bombay, Calcutta, and Madras. The remaining three represented Patna, Punjab, and Nagpur. There were nine high courts during these years. That the United Provinces, the most populous in the country, was not represented with a judge from the Allahabad High Court is surprising. The high courts of Orissa and Assam had been created only in 1948.

In terms of geography, the east was represented by Das and Mukherjea, the west by Kania and Bose, the south by Sastri and Chandrasekhara Aiyar, and the north by Fazl Ali and Mahajan. Men from the four corners of the country were brought together and, for some, this was their first exposure to judges from other regions.

All except Mukherjea were the offspring of privileged or at least economically comfortable families. The fathers of four (Kania, Sastri, Mukherjea, and Chandrasekhara Aiyar) were Sanskrit scholars, and the fathers of four (Fazl Ali, Mahajan, Mukherjea, and Chandrasekhara Aiyar) had been lawyers. There were lawyers in the extended family backgrounds of Kania, Das, and Bose. Only Sastri was the first lawyer in his family. Three (Fazl Ali, Das, Bose) were London-educated barristers, the others having received all their education in India.

Of the six Hindus, three (Sastri, Mukherjea, and Chandrasekhara Aiyar) were brahmins. Although the caste pedigrees of Hindu high court judges at this time are not available, it is very likely that half were brahmins. Fazl Ali, without minimizing his sterling credentials was the likely choice because he was a Muslim. Bose was a Christian, but unlikely to have been selected mainly for that reason. So, among a group as small as eight, the three largest

[18] For the six who were Federal Court judges, their age at the time of that appointment has been used.

religions were represented. Particularly in terms of religion and region, this first bench was a truly diverse and assimilative institution.

Although Kania's death in November 1951 cut short his tenure by four years, in the judges who comprised the first bench, he left a significant legacy. Four of them would follow him as CJIs and serve throughout the first decade. When he died, the strength of the Court fell to six, for the vacancy that arose when Fazl Ali retired six weeks earlier had not yet been filled. Kania had, however, persuaded Fazl Ali to return to the bench a month later under the terms of Article 128.[19]

1. Harilal Jekisondas Kania (1950–1)

Sir H.J. Kania was born into a middle-class family at Surat, Surat district, Gujarat on 3 November 1890. He was the son of Jekisondas Kania, a professor of Sanskrit and later principal of Samaldas College at Bhavanagar in what was then Saurashtra state. Kania received his BA degree from that little known college in 1910. In 1912, he received the LLB from Government Law College, Bombay, followed by an LLM. After further studies, he began his practice at the Bombay High Court in 1915. He married the daughter of Sir Chunilal V. Mehta, a prominent lawyer, businessman, and politician who served for some time as a member of the executive council of the Governor of Bombay. Kania's grandfather had been a revenue officer in Gujarat. An elder brother, Hiralal J. Kania, whose son M.H. Kania[20] would become an SCI judge in 1987, was also a lawyer and together they represented the first generation of this family to enter the law profession.

During his early years at the bar, he was the acting editor of the *Indian Law Reports*. In 1930, he served four months on the Bombay High Court as an acting judge. In June 1931, he was appointed an additional judge and continued as such until March 1933.[21] He then returned to the bar until

---

[19] Article 128 of the Constitution provides that the CJI, with the permission of the retired SCI judge and with the previous consent of the President of India, may ask the retiree to return to the Court for a designated period. The usual reason is that the SCI is short-handed.

[20] Assistance with this essay was provided by M.H. Kania, interviewed on 23 April 1988 in New Delhi.

[21] Seniority on a high court is determined by the date continuous service commences, so his service as an acting and additional judge was not considered.

June 1933 when, at age forty-two, he accepted appointment as a permanent judge.[22] He remained on the Bombay bench for the next thirteen years. In 1939, he accepted the additional task of serving as chairman of the Bombay Disturbances Inquiry Commission, and in 1943 he was knighted.

As Bombay's Chief Justice Sir John Beaumont was approaching retirement age in 1943, Kania was the most senior associate judge and as such in line to become the first Indian to hold that position. But Beaumont and Kania had had a falling out in 1942 and he refused to recommend Kania.[23] Sir Leonard Stone superseded him and became chief justice. From May to September 1944, and from June–October 1945, Kania did serve as acting chief justice.

On 20 June 1946, the same day that Sir Srinivasa Varadachariar retired, Kania, then fifty-five, became a judge of the Federal Court. This appointment was strongly supported by Stone who felt that an injustice had been done when Kania was denied the Bombay chief justiceship.[24] On the eve of national Independence, Spens resigned and Kania, on 14 August 1947, became the first Indian chief justice of the Federal Court. In the same year, he also served as the Indian representative on an arbitral tribunal created to settle some differences between India and Pakistan.

When the Federal Court was replaced by the SCI on 26 January 1950, Kania became the SCI's first chief justice. Aged fifty-nine at this time, he was expected to lead the Court for nearly six years, but he died of a heart attack on 6 November 1951, three days after turning sixty-one.

---

[22] An acting judge was appointed if a sitting judge was by reason of absence or any other reason unable to perform his duties.

[23] Motilal C. Setalvad, *My Life*, p. 56. Setalvad writes that Beaumont, the Bombay chief justice since 1930, had an anti-Indian bias and wanted his successor to be an Englishman. Governor Sir Roger Lumley wanted an Indian to be appointed and persuaded Beaumont to offer the post to Setalvad, who was then the Bombay Attorney General. Setalvad declined the offer because he felt that Kania should become chief justice, pp. 68–9. For more, see Chagla, *Roses in December*, pp. 132–3, and K.M. Munshi, *Bombay High Court: Half a Century of Reminiscences* (Bombay: Bharatiya Vidya Bhavan, 1963), p. 40. Chagla became Bombay's first Indian chief justice in 1947, by which time Kania was serving on the Federal Court.

[24] Setalvad, *My Life*, p. 82, and interview with H.M. Seervai on 3 November 1988, in Bombay.

2. Saiyed Fazl Ali (1950–1, 1951–2)

Sir S. Fazl Ali was born on 19 September 1886 at Varanasi, Varanasi district in Uttar Pradesh into a prominent and wealthy Muslim family. He was the son of Saiyed Nazir Ali, a lawyer who practised in Varanasi. Fazl Ali's family must have had law in its genes, for this Fazl Ali represented the seventh consecutive generation of lawyers. The family tradition continued with his son, S.M. Fazal Ali,[25] following his father to the SCI a generation later.

Educated at Muir Central College, Allahabad, he graduated at the top of his class, earning the BA degree in 1907. He went to England to prepare for the ICS examinations. Unsuccessful, he read law at London's Middle Temple, passed the bar final examination in the first class, and was called to the bar in 1912.[26]

Upon his return to India, he began his law practice at the district courts in Chapra, Bihar in 1912. Practising at that level was unusual for a barrister as was the fact that he specialized in criminal cases. Very few who would reach the SCI had prior experience with criminal cases. In 1924, he moved his practice to the Patna High Court, that court having been created in 1916. At age forty-one, in April 1928, Fazl Ali was appointed to that high court. In 1938, he was acting chief justice for a short period, and on 19 January 1943[27] and at age fifty-six, he was the first Indian to be become chief justice at Patna. Although due to retire in September 1946, the central government extended his tenure by one year, something that could be done during the colonial period.

Fazl Ali was called upon frequently to resolve difficult and often delicate disputes. He was deputed by the Bihar government to settle industrial disputes at Jamshedpur and in April 1946, near the end of his high court career, he was appointed chairman of the Royal Indian Navy Mutiny Inquiry Commission. In September 1947, because of his reputation for impartiality

[25] Assistance with this essay was provided by his son, interviewed on 23 April 1983 in New Delhi. The latter chose a different spelling of his surname to avoid confusion with his father's.

[26] In London, Fazl Ali became acquainted with his future SCI colleague Vivian Bose, for the latter was also called to the bar from Middle Temple a year later. Jawaharlal Nehru, in London at the same time, was called to the bar from Inner Temple in 1913.

[27] On this same day, B.P. Sinha, later CJI and a former junior of Fazl Ali, was sworn in as an additional judge at Patna. B.P. Sinha discusses Fazl Ali's life and career in *Reminiscences and Reflections of a Chief Justice* (Delhi: B.R. Publishing Corporation, 1985), pp. 36–7 and 188–90.

towards persons of all communities, religious and otherwise, he was appointed a member of the Calcutta Disturbances Inquiry Commission, which had been established to investigate the widespread communal killings in Calcutta.

On 9 June 1947, he was appointed to the Federal Court to fill the seat which had become vacant a day earlier when Sir Muhammed Zafrullah Khan opted for Pakistan. Aged sixty at this time, and with nineteen years of high court experience, more than any other high court judge would ever bring to the SCI, he was among the most senior, if not the seniormost, high court judge in the country. He was the last of the judges appointed to the Federal Court before the departure of the British. Shortly after joining the Federal Court, Fazl Ali, in September 1947, was one of the five members of the Indian delegation to the second session of the United Nations General Assembly, where he was elected chairman of the Fifth Committee of the Assembly for that session.[28]

When the Federal Court was replaced by the SCI, Fazl Ali became a charter member. He was sixty-three by this time and, on 19 September 1951 was the first to reach retirement age. But it was a very brief retirement, for CJI Kania asked him to return under the terms of Article 128 and he was back on the court on 15 October. His judicial career concluded on 30 May 1952. His SCI tenure was only about twenty-eight months, but his combined high court, federal court, and SCI tenures were twenty-four years.

He was knighted in 1941. Later he received an LLD (*honoris causa*) from Aligarh Muslim University and in 1956 he was awarded the Padma Vibhushan, the nation's second highest civilian honour.

Fazl Ali remained very active after leaving the SCI. Indeed, retirement was followed by a highly visible second career as an administrator. He had left the Court just before the beginning of the summer vacation in 1952 because he had been asked by Prime Minister Nehru to become the Governor of Orissa. This provoked a minor controversy confined mainly to legal circles because he was still serving on the SCI when the appointment was announced, and over the propriety of a former judge becoming a state governor.[29] Fazl Ali served as Orissa's governor until early

---

[28] Because of the communal frenzy that followed Independence and Partition, Setalvad wrote that Fazl Ali '... had to be brought, I was told, to the Delhi airport dressed in Hindu garb, so that he might be safe from attack by the Hindu mob.' Setalvad, *My Life*, p. 114.

[29] Setalvad, *My Life*, pp. 190–1. Not until the early 1990s, when M. Fathima Beevi

1954, when he resigned to accept Nehru's request that he take on one of the most important administrative posts of that time—the chairmanship of the States Reorganization Commission. Shortly after that assignment was completed,[30] Nehru's high regard for him was demonstrated still again when he was named Governor of Assam on 15 May 1956. This was probably the most demanding governorship of the day because of the unrest in the Naga and other tribal areas of the Northeast Frontier Agency. As governor he was in charge of the Northeast Frontier Agency and acted at his own discretion. Though suffering from cancer for several years, he continued as governor until his death on 22 August 1959, at age seventy-two.

3. Mundakulathur Patanjali Sastri (1950–4)

M.P. Sastri, the first judge appointed to the Federal Court after British rule ended, was born in Madras, Tamil Nadu, on 4 January 1889. His father, Krishna Sastri, was the senior Sanskrit pandit at Pachaiyappa's College in Madras. M.P. Sastri was the first member of his family to enter the legal profession.[31]

He received his BA degree from Pachaiyappa's College in about 1910, and won the Godavari Sanskrit scholarship. After teaching briefly at the high school level, Sastri, in about 1912, earned the BL degree from Madras Law College.

He enrolled as an advocate of the Madras High Court in 1914. Early in his career, he gained a reputation of having special expertise in tax law, particularly in the complicated types of tax cases involving Chetty clients.[32] Shortly after the enactment of the Income-Tax Act, 1922, the central government acknowledged his expertise by appointing him Standing Counsel to the Commissioner of Income Tax, a post he held until he was appointed a judge.

---

was appointed governor of Tamil Nadu, was another former SCI judge appointed a state governor.

[30] *Report of the States Reorganization Commission* (Delhi: Manager of Publications, 1956).

[31] Interview with his nephew, M.S. Krishnamurthy Sastri, on 25 June 1983 in Madras City.

[32] V.C. Gopalratnam, *A Century Completed (A History of the Madras High Court): 1862–1962* (Madras: Madras Law Journal Office, c. 1962), p. 227.

On 15 March 1939, at age fifty, Sastri became a judge of the Madras High Court, replacing his close friend Sir Srinivasa Varadachariar who had been appointed to the Federal Court. Nearly nine years later on 6 December 1947, by which time he was third in seniority, he became a member of the Federal Court. Fifty-eight at this time, he filled the seat vacant after the resignation of Chief Justice Spens a few months earlier. Sastri served during the remainder of the Federal Court's existence.

Older than CJI Kania, he could not have anticipated becoming CJI. But when death removed Kania from the bench on 6 November 1951, Sastri, the most senior associate judge, was named acting chief justice on 7 November. There was then no convention that an outgoing CJI be replaced by the most senior associate judge but Sastri was confirmed as CJI. After having presided over the Court for twenty-six months, he reached retirement age on 4 January 1954.

He had become pro-chancellor of Delhi University in 1953, and continued to hold that post until 1956. An accomplished Sanskrit scholar, he served as chairman of the Central Sanskrit Board from 1959 until his death, and headed the Kendriya Sanskrit Vidyapeeth Society at Tirupati, Tamil Nadu. He was active with the Delhi branch of the International Law Association, served as chairman of the Airlines Compensation Commission which dealt with matters concerning the nationalization of airlines, and was a member of the board of directors of the Press Trust of India. From 22 July 1958 to 20 April 1962, he was a nominated member of the Madras Legislative Council. At the time of his death on 16 March 1963 at age seventy-four, he was an active member of the executive council of Banaras Hindu University.

4. Mehr Chand Mahajan (1950–4)

On 23 December 1889, M.C. Mahajan was born into a wealthy family of Mahajan Sahukars in the village of Tikka Nagotra in Kangra district, which was then part of Punjab but is in today's Himachal Pradesh. He described his family as 'a conservative money-lending, shop-keeper class',[33] and

---

[33] Mehr Chand Mahajan, Looking Back, p. 53. Mahajan is also the subject of a biography by Vidya Dhar Mahajan, Chief Justice Mehr Chand Mahajan (Lucknow: Eastern Book Company, 1969). Most useful in the latter is the reproduction of nine of M.C. Mahajan's speeches and writings. Having sired 16 children, Mahajan was irrefutably without peers among SCI judges.

himself as a zamindar.[34] His childhood was most unusual. Agnatic kinsmen, who coveted his father's wealth, conspired with the village astrologers who said that he was born at a moment when the stars were in such malignant conjunction that his father would die as soon as he saw the face of his son.[35] He was, thus, exiled to live with a poor Rajput family who raised him to the age of seven and thereafter lived with relatives for the next five years. Not until the age of twelve did his father see his face. His father, Brij Lal Mahajan, looked after his large landholdings and also practised law in Dharamsala as a *mukhtar*.[36] M.C. Mahajan, after he finished high school, was licensed to practise as a mukhtar, and during his college years did so.[37]

After receiving a BA (honours) in history from Government College, Lahore, Mahajan began work towards an MSc in chemistry. His father, however, persuaded his then only surviving son to switch to law, and he earned the LLB from the University Law College, Lahore, in 1912, finishing second in the law examinations. He started practising law with his father at Dharamsala in 1912 and, two years later, he began his own practice at the district courts at Gurdaspur. In October 1918, he moved again, this time to the Lahore chief court, which the next year became the Lahore High Court, where he would remain for nearly three decades.

During these years, he became involved in a wide variety of activities. While in college, he converted 'from an orthodox Hindu of the old style to a zealous Arya Samajist'[38] and, in 1919, began a lifetime association with the Arya Samaj's D.A.V. (Dayanand Anglo-Vedic) College Trust and Managing Committee, serving as its president from 1938 to 1943. First in Gurdaspur and later in Lahore, he was active in the Indian National Congress and attended the Congress meetings at Calcutta and Amritsar. From 1922 to 1931 he served as a part-time lecturer at the University Law College. In 1930, he accepted an appointment as the legal advisor to the Maharaja of Chamba. From 1934 to 1943, he served as a director of the Punjab National Bank which had been started by the D.A.V. College Society. From 1938 to

---

[34] Mahajan, *Looking Back*, p. 137.

[35] Ibid., p. 3.

[36] An inferior class of lawyers who had no formal training and could practise only in the lower courts.

[37] Samuel Schmitthener, 'A Sketch of the Development of the Legal Profession in India', *Law & Society Review*, vol. III, nos 2 and 3 (November 1968–February 1969), pp. 337–82, especially pp. 363 and 371.

[38] Mahajan, *Looking Back*, p. 21. The Arya Samaj is a Hindu reform movement which seeks social reform coupled with Hindu revivalism.

1943, he was president of the Lahore High Court bar association. An avid agriculturist and horticulturist throughout his life, he was a member of the Punjab Fruit Development Board and, in 1945 was elected president of the All-India Fruit Producers Association.

In November 1942, Mahajan was offered a Lahore High Court additional judgeship, but declined, holding off for a permanent appointment. That came the following year and, at age fifty-three, he took the oath of office on 27 September 1943.[39] In 1946 he served as a member of the Royal Indian Navy Mutiny Inquiry and, in 1947, he served on the Punjab (Radcliffe) Boundary Commission.

Following the departure of the British and the partitioning of the subcontinent, he continued as a judge of the new East Punjab High Court at Simla. He was not there long, for on 18 September 1947, at the invitation of the Maharaja of Jammu and Kashmir and the urging of Union Home Minister Sardar Patel, he agreed to serve as Prime Minister of Jammu and Kashmir. He took over as prime minister on 15 October, just a few days before the invasion by Pakistan tribesman, and held that post until 6 March 1948, when Sheikh Abdullah replaced him. As prime minister, Mahajan had to juggle being loyal to the Maharaja and to India's national interests as defined by Prime Minister Nehru. This meant occasional prickly relations with Nehru—Mahajan wrote that at one point Nehru 'flew into a rage' at him.[40] They differed particularly over the role of Sheikh Abdullah. He held this post during the Maharaja's accession to India, thus playing a key role in one of modern Indian history's most significant political events.[41]

A few days after leaving Kashmir, Mahajan accepted an offer from the Maharaja of Bikaner to become his constitutional adviser. Three months later, on 10 June 1948, and upon the expiry of the eight months leave Patel had negotiated, he returned to the high court. During these months, Mahajan resisted Patel's urging that he go to Assam as chief justice, declined

---

[39] Daya Kishan Mahajan, his eldest son, served as a judge of the Punjab and Haryana High Courts, retiring as chief justice in 1974. In March 1988 the latter's son, C.K. Mahajan, was sworn in as a judge of the Delhi High Court. See Rema Nagarajan, 'Three Generations of Judges', The Hindustan Times, 2 March 1998.

[40] Mahajan, Looking Back, p. 277. See also the Maharaja's son, Karan Singh's Heir Apparent: An Autobiography (New Delhi: Oxford University Press, 1982), p. 55.

[41] Mahajan must have considered this Kashmir sojourn his finest hours, for his autobiography devotes three times more space to it than the twenty-four pages he spent recalling his years on the Federal and Supreme Courts.

appointment as chief justice of the United States of Rajasthan, and declined the Maharaja of Patiala's invitation to serve as his advisor.[42]

Mahajan had hardly settled back to his high court duties when Federal Court Chief Justice Kania inquired about his interest in a Federal Court judgeship.[43] Five years after he joined the Lahore High Court, he was sworn in as a Federal Court judge on 4 October 1948 at age fifty-eight.

In late 1950, Mahajan spent several months in Hyderabad, heading a bench which disposed of nearly 400 cases which had been transferred to the SCI from the Nizam's Privy Council, which had lapsed after the 1950 Constitution came into force. Chosen for this task by CJI Kania because of his knowledge of Urdu, Mahajan sat with two members of the Hyderabad High Court, Chief Justice Ramachander Naik and associate judge Khalil-ul-Zamaan Siddiqui, who were appointed *ad hoc* judges of the SCI.[44] Later he would head another bench of the SCI in Kashmir to decide the cases that had been transferred from that state's Privy Council to the SCI.[45]

On 4 January 1954, upon the retirement of CJI Sastri, Mahajan became the third CJI. His tenure lasted less than a year, for he reached retirement age on 22 December.

After leaving the Court, Mahajan rejected offers to become vice-chancellor of Allahabad, Punjab, and Banaras Hindu Universities, preferring to continue his long association with the Arya Samaj's D.A.V. College Trust and Managing Committee of which he again became president in 1955.[46] He also remained actively involved with Punjab University; he had been a member of the executive councils of Punjab University in Lahore from 1940 to 1947, of East Punjab University from 1947 to 1950, and of the University of Delhi during his SCI years. After retirement, he also served as a member of the Banaras Hindu University Enquiry Committee. He was elected dean of the faculties of commerce and law at Punjab University which, in 1948, had conferred upon him an honorary LLD. In 1961–2, at the request of the

---

[42] Mahajan, *Looking Back*, pp. 179, 188, and 191.

[43] Ibid., p. 191.

[44] Ibid., pp. 201–2. See also P. Jaganmohan Reddy's account in M.V.K. Sivamohan, (ed.) *Law & Society: Lectures and Writings of Justice P. Jaganmohan Reddy* (Delhi: Ajanta Publications, 1986), pp. 49–50.

[45] Mahajan, *Looking Back*, p. 211.

[46] After his death, the Mehr Chand Mahajan D.A.V. College for Women was established in Chandigarh in his memory.

Punjab government and the Union Ministry of Home Affairs, he chaired the Punjab Police Commission.

Well known for his voracious capacity for work, he served as a director of Delhi Cloth and General Mills, as a member of the Camp College Enquiry Commission set up to meet the needs of Punjab refugees, and served as a trustee of several institutions, including the Dewan Bishan Trust, the Lala Barru Shah Trust, and the Sir Ganga Ram Trust Hospital. He did some arbitration work as well, and wrote that occasionally 'I have given legal advice to persons seeking my help.'[47]

Mahajan is remembered most for what is invariably referred to as the Mahajan Commission Report.[48] In October 1966, shortly after Indira Gandhi became prime minister, he was appointed a one-man commission to recommend solutions to settle contentious boundary disputes which followed the reorganization of the states along linguistic lines, the most controversial of which was Maharashtra's claim to Belgaum city. Mahajan rejected Maharashtra's claim, leaving Belgaum in Karnataka, and this dispute continues to fester today.

On the occasion of his retirement from the SCI, his colleagues hosted a farewell dinner in his honour. Mahajan said that in retirement he was going to '... assume the role of agitator, because it seems to me that nothing succeeds in this country more than agitation.'[49] And agitate he did. He often spoke out in speeches and newspaper articles against corruption, provincialism, parochialism, and communalism.[50] He emphatically opposed the reorganization of states along linguistic lines. His major concern was the unity and integrity of the nation, and this was reflected in his belief that India's federal system should be scrapped and replaced by a centralized, unitary system. He believed certain policies of Nehru were wrong, and told him so.[51]

---

[47] Mahajan, *Looking Back*, p. 233. Some believe that he was the first retired judge to engage in what would later be termed 'chamber practice'.

[48] *Report of the Commission on Maharashtra, Mysore, and Kerala Boundary Disputes*, 2 vols (Delhi: Manager of Publications, 1967). See also *Memorandum on Maharashtra-Mysore Border Dispute to the Commission on Maharashtra-Mysore-Kerala Boundary Disputes, 1967*: *Supplementary Memorandum on Maharashtra-Mysore Border Dispute* (Bombay, 1967).

[49] 'Retirement of Shri Mehr Chand Mahajan, Chief Justice of India: Judges' Farewell Dinner' [1955] *SCR*, pp. i–viii, especially p. vi.

[50] Some of these are reprinted in his autobiography and V.D. Mahajan's biography.

[51] Mahajan, *Looking Back*, pp. 226–9.

Virtually everyone who spoke of Mahajan was unable to resist describing aspects of him. Hidayatullah described him as a 'colourful personality.'[52] G.D. Kholsa, a fellow judge at Lahore and Simla, wrote that he was 'the most forceful personality' on the Punjab High Court, 'a judge who inspired awe if not affection.'[53] B.K. Mukherjea, who succeeded him as CJI, described him as 'an extremely lovable person ..., a strong personality ..., generous, warm-hearted ..., [of] vivacious temperament..., his hospitality is almost proverbial.'[54] M.C. Setalvad described him as 'rough and brusque, characteristic of the hill areas of Punjab to which he belonged ...', and that 'his industry was phenomenal'.[55]

Shortly after submitting the Mahajan Commission Report, he died on 12 December 1967 at age seventy-seven.

5. Bijan Kumar Mukherjea (1950–6)

B.K. Mukherjea's family home was Nabadwip in West Bengal, but his birth on 15 August 1891 took place in Hooghly, Hooghly district, at the home of a maternal uncle, as per the Bengali tradition.[56] He was the eldest son of Rakhal Das Mukherjea, a Sanskrit scholar who was also a practising lawyer at the Chinsura–Hooghly district courts. His father was more the former than the latter and the family enjoyed high social status but little economic security. Mukherjea was one of a very small number of SCI judges born in what can be termed humble economic circumstances. He had to struggle and can be described as a self-made man.

Mukherjea earned five degrees. He received a BA in Sanskrit and history from Hooghly College in 1912 and an MA in history from Calcutta University in 1914. In the same year, he earned the BL from University Law College, followed by an ML earned at the same institution in 1916. An interest in international law led to a dissertation entitled *Problems of Aerial*

---

[52] Foreword to V.D. Mahajan's *Chief Justice Mehr Chand Mahajan*, p. iii.

[53] G.D. Khosla, *Memory's Gay Chariot: An Autobiographical Narrative* (New Delhi: Allied Publishers Pvt. Ltd., 1985), p. 145.

[54] Mukherjea, 'Retirement of Shri Mehr Chand Mahajan', [1955] *SCR*, pp. i–viii.

[55] Setalvad, *My Life*, pp. 152, 203.

[56] Mukherjea was a widower since 1920. His only child, Amiya Kumar Mookerji, followed in his father's footsteps and served as a judge of the Calcutta High Court from 1969 to 1980. I interviewed Justice Mookerji in Calcutta on 29 June 1983.

Law, which earned him a Doctor of Law degree in 1923 from Calcutta University. These years of study were filled with many honours. He won gold medals by finishing first in his BL and ML examinations, and also won the Anath Deb Research Prize.

He began the practice of law as an advocate of the Calcutta High Court at age twenty-two on 9 January 1914. Although in time he would enjoy a successful practice, at the beginning he had a difficult time and to meet expenses he became a part-time lecturer at the University Law College, earning Rs 100 per month. Two decades later, in 1934, he was appointed junior government pleader. After briefly officiating as senior government pleader, he was appointed an additional judge of the Calcutta High Court on 9 November 1936. Aged forty-five then, this appointment was made permanent on 3 July 1939. In 1947, he served on the Bengal (Radcliffe) Boundary Commission.

After twelve years on the Calcutta bench, by which time he was second in seniority, CJI Kania invited Mukherjea to join the Federal Court. On 14 October 1948, at age fifty-seven, he became the first Bengali member of that Court, ending an association with the Calcutta High Court that had spanned a third of a century.

On 23 December 1954, upon CJI Mahajan's retirement, Mukherjea became the fourth CJI. Soon, however, his health began to fail and in late 1955 he was compelled to be on leave for several months. He was to have served as CJI until August 1956, but declining health forced him to resign on 31 January 1956.

By virtually all accounts, Mukherjea was among the most brilliant and scholarly of SCI judges. His *The Hindu Law of Religious and Charitable Trusts*[57] revealed his extensive knowledge of Hindu law and became a widely read classic. Mukherjea was also named a fellow of Calcutta University. An acclaimed student of Sanskrit, the titles of Bidyaranjan and Saraswati were conferred upon him by the Bangiya Bibhuda Janani Sabha of Nabadwip,

---

[57] Calcutta: Eastern Law House, 1952. By 1983, this acclaimed work had been published in its fifth revised edition, now titled *B.K. Mukherjea on The Hindu Law of Religious and Charitable Trusts*. Two of these revised editions were done by retired SCI judges, the third by T.L. Venkatarama Ayyar in 1962, and the fourth by P.B. Gajendragadkar in 1979. United States Supreme Court Justice, William O. Douglas, was the author of *We the Judges: Studies in American and Indian Constitutional Law from Marshall to Mukherjea* (Garden City, New York: Doubleday and Company, Inc., 1956). B.K Mukherjea was the Mukherjea in this felicitous title.

a prominent seat of Sanskrit education. He also served as the president of the Bengal Sanskrit Association, and was active in a number of Calcutta literary and cultural organizations, including the Gita Sava and the Sahitya Parishad. His other interests were as diverse as English poetry and the promotion of the Boy Scouts movement in Bengal.

On 22 February 1956, three weeks after his worsening heart ailment had compelled him to resign from the SCI, Mukherjea died at age sixty-four.

6. Sudhi Ranjan Das (1950–9)

S.R. Das, a scion of a prominent and wealthy family, was born in Calcutta, West Bengal on 1 October 1894. His father, Rakhal Chandra Das, was the licensing officer for the Calcutta Corporation. S.R. Das's younger brother, Prafulla Ranjan Das, was a judge of the Patna High Court, and another brother was a barrister who practised at the Calcutta High Court. Other members of his extended family included Deshbandu Chittaranjan Das, a major figure in Bengal politics and the Indian National Congress, J.R. Das who was a judge of the high court of Rangoon, and Satish Ranjan Das who held the post of Advocate General of Bengal and later as the law member of the Viceroy's Executive Council. S.R. Das's only daughter, Anjana, was a lawyer and the wife of Ashoke K. Sen, a leader of the Indian bar who was also the union law minister from 1957 to 1966 and again from 1984 to 1987.[58]

Das earned his BA in English Literature in 1915 from Bangabasi College, Calcutta. He then journeyed to England where he received an LLB from University College, London in 1918, and was called to the bar from Gray's Inn the same year. He obtained a first class first in the LLB examinations, and was among the first Indian students to earn that honour. Upon his return to India he joined the Calcutta High Court bar in 1919. During the first few years of his practice he was also a part-time lecturer at the Calcutta University Law College.

After twenty-three years at the bar, and at age forty-eight, Das joined the bench of the Calcutta High Court as an additional judge on 1 December 1942. He was confirmed as a permanent judge on 11 November 1944. In 1949, Union Home Minister Sardar Patel prevailed upon Das to accept

[58] I interviewed Ashoke K. Sen in New Delhi on 27 December 1988.

transfer to Simla and, on 19 January 1949, he became chief justice of what
was then the East Punjab High Court.[59] In the same year, the Government
of India appointed Das as the Chairman of the High Court Arrears
Committee, which offered suggestions to reduce the increasing backlog of
cases in the high courts.

On 20 January 1950, a week before the SCI replaced the Federal Court,
Das became the final appointee to the latter. Only fifty-five when he arrived
in Delhi, Das would serve on the SCI throughout its first decade. In
1951–2, he also served as chairman of the All-India Bar Committee, the
report of which began the process of establishing a nationally unified bar.[60]
Because of the illness of CJI Mukherjea, Das, then the most senior associate
judge, served as acting CJI from 5 September to 31 October 1955, and
from 1 December until 31 December 1955. Mukherjea resigned effective 31
January 1956, and the following day, six months earlier than anticipated,
Das became the fifth CJI. He served in that capacity for more than three and
one-half years, until his retirement on 1 October 1959. With his retirement,
the last of the original judges had departed.

Immediately after leaving the bench, he became vice-chancellor of Visva
Bharati University at Shantiniketan and held that position until 1965. This
was a homecoming for him, for he had received his early education at the
Tagore School and was one of Rabindranath Tagore's favourite students.[61]
In 1961, he accepted the appointment as chairman of a commission, set up
after the agitation carried on by Master Tara Singh and the Akali Dal, which
conducted an inquiry into the grievances of the Sikh community.[62] In 1963,
he served as the one-man commission, established by the Union Home
Ministry, which investigated allegations of corruption and misuse of power
against Chief Minister Pratap Singh Kairon of Punjab, who lost his office

---

[59] Under the 1935 Government of India Act, a high court judge could not be
transferred without his consent. The 1950 Constitution does not protect a judge from
non-consensual transfer, but a convention of transfer only with consent continued until
1976.

[60] *Report of the All India Bar Committee* (Delhi: Manager of Publications, 1953).

[61] This according to A.K. Sarkar, whom I interviewed on 28 June 1983 in Calcutta.
Sarkar was not, as some sources say, a former student of S.R. Das, but did 'devilling' in
Das's chambers after he had been called to the bar. Devilling was an English practice
under which new entrants in the profession joined the chambers of a successful lawyer
to learn the work first-hand.

[62] *Punjab Commission, 1961: Report* (New Delhi: Manager of Publications, 1962).

as a result of Das's findings.[63] From 1962 to 1965, he was a member of the University Grants Commission and, in 1964-5, he served as vice president of the Indian Council for Cultural Relations. He was also, in the late 1960s, chairman of the board of trustees of *The Statesman* newspaper. He was honoured with the LLD (*honoris causa*) from three universities—Allahabad, Calcutta, and Visva Bharati, and was named a fellow of London's University College. Earlier in his career, Das was the editor of both the third and the fourth editions of *Mulla on the Transfer of Property Act, 1882.*[64]

After more than a decade of vigorous and often demanding post-retirement activities, he wound down in the 1970s but remained active in the Brahmo Samaj social reform movement. His long and distinguished career ended when he died at age eighty-two on 16 September 1977.

7. Nagapudi Chandrasekhara Aiyar (1950–3, 1955–6)

N. Chandrasekhara Aiyar was born on 25 January 1888 at Vellimalia, in the Chittoor district of Andhra Pradesh. His father, Nagapudi Kuppaswamya Garu, was apparently a lawyer but was more widely known for his Telugu and Sanskrit learning and scholarship. Chandrasekhara Aiyar received his BA in English literature and Sanskrit from Madras Christian College in about 1907 and his BL from the Madras Law College in about 1909.[65]

He was twenty-two when he began his law practice at the Madras High Court in 1910. Seventeen years later, in July 1927, he joined the Madras judicial service. His first appointment was as Madras city civil judge. In December of the same year, he became a district and sessions judge and during the next fourteen years was posted in several districts of the Madras presidency. In July 1941, at age fifty-three he was appointed an additional judge of the Madras High Court, was confirmed as a permanent judge in 1954, and retired on 24 January 1948.

[63] *Commission of Inquiry on Certain Allegations Against Pratap Singh Kairon, Chief Minister of Punjab, 1963—Report* (Delhi: Manager of Publications, 1964).

[64] Calcutta: Eastern Law House, 1949 and 1956.

[65] An interview in Madras on 24 June 1983 with C.R. Pattabhi Raman, who knew Chandrasekhara Aiyar well, was a member of Parliament from 1957 to 1967 and minister of state for law from 1965 to 1967, was helpful in gathering biographical information.

Later in 1948, he was appointed as one of India's representatives on the Indo-Pakistan Boundary Disputes Tribunal. In 1949, he was appointed a member of the All-India Industrial (Bank Disputes) Tribunal.

He was nearly sixty-three when he was sworn in as an SCI judge on 23 September 1950. The first to be appointed after the Constitution came into effect, he was also the first to have risen from the subordinate judiciary. After twenty-eight months of SCI service, Chandrasekhara Aiyar reached retirement age on 25 January 1953. However, when CJI Mukherjea fell ill in 1955, he recommended that Chandrasekhara Aiyar be recalled under the terms of Article 128 of the Constitution. He agreed to return for the periods of 5 September–31 October 1955, and from 1 December 1955–11 May 1956. When he left the Court for the last time, he was sixty-eight.

During his second retirement he served as chairman of the First Delimitation Commission from January 1953 to August 1955. After retiring a third time, he was appointed in 1956 as chairman of the Second Delimitation Commission which dealt with revisions of legislative district boundaries necessitated by the reorganization of states in that year.

Chandrasekhara Aiyar was well known for his knowledge of both Sanskrit and English literature. He edited the eleventh edition of *Mayne's Treatise on Hindu Law and Usage*,[66] and he was one of the joint editors of Bhavan's Book University Series. He also played an important role in the establishment of Vivekananda College in Madras.

He died on 31 March 1957, at age sixty-nine.

8. Vivian Bose (1951–6, 1957–8)

Vivian Bose was born in Ahmedabad, Gujarat, on 9 June 1891, but his family had close ties with the Central Provinces and Berar. Bose considered Nagpur his home. He was the son of Lalit Mohan Bose, an engineer employed by the government who was posted in Ahmedabad when Bose was born. He was the grandson of Sir Bipin Krishna Bose, a Bengali who had come to Nagpur in 1874. Sir Bipin, a lawyer, was a prominent figure in the Nagpur and Central Provinces civic, educational, cultural, and political scenes. A philanthropist as well, he was the founder of Nagpur University.

---

[66] Madras: Higginbothams, 1950.

Knighted in 1909, he was a member of the Viceroy's executive council. An uncle, J. Mitra, was a judge of Nagpur's judicial commissioner's court.

Bose was the first Christian and the only Eurasian[67] to serve on the SCI. He married an American, whose father, Dr John R. Mott, won the Nobel Peace Prize in 1946.[68] Having an Indian father, an English mother, and an American wife, Bose jokingly described himself as a 'mongrel'.[69]

At age fifteen, Bose went to England for the remainder of his education. After completing secondary education at Dulwich College, he received his BA (honours) and his LLB from Pembroke College, Cambridge University in 1913, and was called to the bar from Middle Temple the same year.

He returned to India in 1913. He was twenty-three when he began practising law at Nagpur, where he was to spend the next thirty-eight years. He practised before the then judicial commissioner's court, for the Nagpur High Court was not created until 1936. From 1924 to 1930, in addition to his law practice, he served as first principal of the Nagpur University College of Law which had been started by his grandfather. In 1930, he was appointed government advocate[70] and Standing Counsel to the Government of the Central Provinces and Berar. From 1931 to 1934, he twice officiated as Additional Judicial Commissioner.

Bose's interests ranged far beyond law. He was the founder of the Boy Scouts organization in the Central Provinces and Berar, and served as its secretary from 1921 to 1934, provincial commissioner from 1934 to 1937, and for distinguished service he was awarded the Kaiser-i-Hind Medal in 1936. He was also active in the volunteer mounted infantry and the Nagpur rifles from 1913 until appointed to the Nagpur bench. In 1933, he was a member of the team that represented India in the riflery competition of the Calcutta Cup and was awarded a medal for the highest individual score in the British Empire. Motoring was another passion—in 1933, without a driver and with his wife and nineteen-month-old son, he drove over poor

---

[67] Not an Anglo-Indian, for Article 366 (2) of the Constitution defines an Anglo-Indian as '... a person whose father or any of whose other male progenitors in the male line is or was of European descent. ...'

[68] A Methodist layman, social worker, and leader of the Young Men's Christian Association.

[69] I interviewed Bose, then age ninety-two, at Bangalore on 21 June 1983. More about Bose was learned from his daughter, Mrs Leila Powar, in whose home Bose spent his final years, and from Ms Julie Mott, Bose's American grand niece.

[70] This post then was the equivalent of today's advocate general and meant being next in line for a seat on the bench.

roads from Nagpur to London. In 1956, he did the reverse trip. Among his other lifelong hobbies were photography and magic, particularly stage illusions.[71]

On 9 January 1936, when he was forty-four, Bose was appointed one of the original members of the newly created Nagpur High Court. After thirteen years as an associate judge he became chief justice on 20 February 1949. While on the Nagpur bench, he chaired the Bilaspur Commission of Inquiry dealing with election malpractices in 1938, and headed the Hill Investigation Tribunal in 1940.

When he was nearly sixty and on the threshold of retirement and, with fifteen years of service on the Nagpur Bench, one of the most senior high court judges in the nation, CJI Kania invited him to become a member of the SCI. Bose was sworn on 5 March 1951, becoming the final member of the original bench. Although he reached retirement age on 9 June 1956, the next year he was asked by CJI S.R. Das to return under the terms of Article 128. This second instalment of Bose's tenure on the SCI began on 9 September 1957 and continued until 30 September 1958.

In May 1958, before his second departure from the court, the union government appointed him chairman of a board of inquiry to investigate charges against senior officers of the finance ministry who had been implicated earlier by Bombay Chief Justice M.C. Chagla.[72] The latter's inquiry into this 'Mundhra Scandal' was a major event which rocked Parliament and resulted in the resignation of Finance Minister T.T. Krishnamachari.[73] Angered by Bose's follow-up report which concluded that the government's dealings with Mundhra were a *quid pro quo* for Mundhra's donation of money to the Congress party, Prime Minister Nehru said Bose was 'lacking in intelligence'. Nehru quickly wrote a very gracious letter of apology to Bose saying that, under the stress of work he had been careless

---

[71] For an affectionate account of Bose's life by his former junior colleague at Nagpur, and later CJI, M. Hidayatullah, see chapter XV ('Justice Vivian Bose') in A Judge's Miscellany (Bombay: N.M. Tripathi, Pvt. Ltd., 1972), pp. 143-9. See also Justice K.K. Mathew's felicitation of Bose on the occasion of his 85th birthday, AIR 1975 Journal, pp. 9-12.

[72] Report of the Commission of Inquiry into the Affairs of the Life Insurance Corporation of India (Delhi: 1958).

[73] For an excellent account, including Bose's role, see Setalvad, My Life, pp. 267-94.

with his words, was very sorry, and asked Bose's forgiveness. Bose responded with equal grace and style.[74]

Later in 1958, Bose headed what is referred to either as the Dalmia–Jain Commission of Inquiry, or simply the Bose Inquiry Commission. This was another much publicized investigation which concerned alleged improprieties of wealthy industrialists V.H. Dalmia and Shanti Prasad Jain.

Very active with the International Commission of Jurists, he served as its president from 1959 to 1966, visiting more than two dozen countries in that capacity. From 1959 to 1962, he served as national commissioner of the Bharat Scouts and Guides which, by then, he had been associated with for more than four decades. In his eighties, he and his wife took to the fields of legal and cultural anthropology and studied nomadic tribes in the Nagpur area.

The record reveals that during his Nagpur years he was a freedom fighter from the bench, particularly holding the British to a higher standard in the preventive detention cases. On the SCI he dissented more than any other judge, and these dissents, all but one solo, revealed his antipathy toward what he believed were deprivations of civil liberties and other abuses of power.

A soft-spoken and shy man, Bose is a member of virtually everyone's all-star team of SCI judges. A superb craftsman of the English language, M.C. Setalvad recalled that Sastri '... when he was Chief Justice, telling me that whenever the Judges had to put forward their views in elegant language, the task was entrusted to Vivian Bose.'[75]

When he died on 29 November 1983 at age ninety-two, the last remaining link with the Court's original bench was broken.

[74] Bose shared this correspondence with me. Though very upset at losing his friend and confidant Krishnamachari as a result of Chagla's report, and being angry with Bose's follow-up report, a few months later he chose Chagla to be India's ambassador to the United States, and Bose would soon be tapped for another important investigation. These are among many illustrations of Nehru's respect for the judiciary. By the 1970s, it became increasingly common for retired SCI judges, whose decisions had upset the Congress (I), to receive no post-retirement invitations from the government to serve on commissions of inquiry and the like.

[75] Setalvad, My Life, p. 165.

II

The Sastri Court (1951–4)

Following the death of Kania, for the first time in post-Independence India, a new CJI had to be chosen. Had Kania not died on 6 November 1951 there would not have been a Sastri Court, for Sastri would have reached retirement age nearly two years before Kania. Article 126 of the Constitution provides that when the office of CJI falls vacant, '...the duties of the office shall be performed by such one of the other Judges of the Court as the President may appoint ....' So, any of the then six sitting associate judges could have been named acting CJI. There was no convention in place that the most senior associate judge would be named acting or permanent CJI. But Sastri, who was the most senior associate judge, was appointed by the president a day after Kania's death 'to perform the duties of Chief Justice of India ...'[1] It fell to the executive to decide who the next CJI would be.

What happened during the weeks before Sastri was confirmed is the stuff of legend—stories handed down for generations and popularly believed to have historical basis, although not verifiable. Components of the legend are that Nehru was not averse to overlooking Sastri and considered appointing a less senior judge or an outsider. There are conflicting accounts about who Nehru preferred, but all agree that it was not Sastri. Some believe that Nehru preferred M.C. Chagla, a man he had great respect for, and who was at this time chief justice of the Bombay High Court. Others are certain his choice was B.K. Mukherjea, at this time third in seniority on the SCI,

---

[1] [1951] SCR Memoranda page. I have been unable to locate the exact date when Sastri was confirmed as CJI. No date was found in the SCI's official records.

but his son said his father said it was nothing more than a rumour which had gained a lot of currency over the years.[2] Still others believed that Prime Minister Nehru preferred S.R. Das, fourth in seniority, because he would be CJI for nearly the remainder of the 1950s.

Every published source does agree about what happened next. All six associate judges are said to have threatened to resign if Sastri's seniority was overlooked and he was not made permanent. The only mention of this threat is found in Chagla's autobiography. He wrote that M.C. Setalvad urged Nehru to make him the new CJI, but 'It transpires that the judges of the Supreme Court threatened to resign if the seniority rule was not followed, and the Government yielded to the threat.'[3] Lingering questions about its veracity notwithstanding, thus was born what would quickly become the convention of the CJI being 'selected' solely on the basis of being next in line. Sastri would ultimately be confirmed as CJI but only after more than six weeks had passed.[4]

Not without interest is the fact that Sastri is the only former CJI, and an 'accidental' one at that, whose native tongue was Tamil and who's entire high court career was spent on the Madras High Court.[5] Thirty-five more, through to K.G. Balakrishnan (2007–10), have followed Sastri as CJI, but none of them was a Tamil-speaking judge who had come to the SCI directly from the Madras High Court and would become CJI.

The SCI that Sastri inherited comprised six judges, himself included, plus Fazl Ali, who had reached retirement age a few weeks earlier but who

---

[2] Interview with A.K. Mookerji in Calcutta on 29 June 1983.

[3] M.C. Chagla, *Roses in December: An Autobiography with Epilogue* (Bombay: Bharatiya Vidya Bhavan, 1978), p. 171. Mahajan, on the SCI at this time, and the only one who left behind an autobiography, wrote not a word about any threat to resign.

[4] 'Legal Causerie', *The Hindustan Times*, 23 December 1951, p. 4, reported that 'It is expected that he will be confirmed in his appointment.'

[5] K. Subba Rao, who would become CJI in 1966, had earlier served on the Madras High Court. But he was a Telugu speaker and when the Andhra High Court was created in 1954, he became its first chief justice. He was chief justice of the Andhra Pradesh High Court when he was promoted to the SCI in 1958. One explanation for why no other judge appointed to the SCI from the Madras High Court became CJI is that the average age at the time of high court appointment at Madras was higher than that at other high courts. While there was some variation among the high courts concerning the age considered appropriate for appointment—the middle forties was the all-India average—the norm at the Madras High Court was about five years higher. By the time they were sufficiently senior to be promoted to the SCI, they were usually older than most appointees from elsewhere and reached retirement age before becoming senior enough to be named CJI.

had agreed to extended duty under the terms of Article 128. Four judges were appointed during Sastri's twenty-six month stewardship. During his entire tenure, Dr Kailash Nath Katju was the Union Home Minister. The first two, sworn in on 8 September 1952, were sixty-one year-old Ghulam Hasan, recently retired from the Lucknow bench of the Allahabad High Court, and fifty-eight-year-old N.H. Bhagwati, an eight-year veteran of the Bombay High Court where he was third in seniority.[6] The former was the Muslim replacement for Fazl Ali, who had left the SCI for the last time as the summer vacation began in May. Hasan may have had more high court service than the few other Muslim judges who remained in India after Partition. Whether there was a Muslim seat on the SCI at this juncture is a matter of definition. During the first decade of the Federal Court when there were just three judges, one was always a Muslim. Fazl Ali was the third of these and Hasan was the next SCI appointee after Fazl Ali's departure.

Bhagwati filled the Bombay seat, vacant since Kania's death. Because of the closeness of Setalvad to the prime minister, it is tempting to believe that Bhagwati was boosted by him, and perhaps by Chagla, considered by many as the most distinguished high court chief justice in the nation. Both knew him well from their long association together at Bombay. Whether Sastri had earlier met Hasan or Bhagwati is unknown.

Six months later, on 9 March 1953, B. Jagannadhadas, aged fifty-nine and the chief justice of the Orissa High Court[7], arrived in Delhi. He and the then President of India, Rajendra Prasad, had been in the same jail together during the Freedom Movement. Sastri, of course, would have known Jagannadhadas from their decades together in Madras. The only retirement during Sastri's tenure was that of Chandrasekhara Aiyar. Jagannadhadas, though at Orissa when elevated, had spent three decades with Chandrasekhara Ayer at Madras, and was the replacement for him.

[6] Many believe that Bhagwati was sworn in first, but this is not the case. Throughout the SCI's history, in most cases when more than one appointment is made on the same day, the swearing in order is determined by the amount of high court seniority the appointees have. Because the Oudh chief court had the status of a high court, Hasan had more seniority than Bhagwati. With the most senior associate judge becoming CJI, the swearing in order can be very important. In this instance, the order was irrelevant for both Hasan and Bhagwati who would have reached retirement age before S.R. Das retired as CJI in late 1959.

[7] Orissa has not been fertile ground for the recruitment of SCI judges. Not until Ranga Nath Misra, thirty years later, was another Orissa High Court judge appointed to the SCI.

The final appointee during Sastri's years was T.L. Venkatarama Ayyar, aged sixty, who just a month earlier had retired from the Madras High Court. He joined the SCI on 4 January 1954, the day after Sastri retired, so Sastri was able to fill his own vacant seat. Sastri, of course, would have known Venkatarama Ayyar also from their Madras days.

Striking about these Sastri appointees was their advanced age, the average being 59.7. Not until the Bhagwati Court, more than three decades later, were older men appointed. All had high court experience but averaged only 6.5 years, less than the appointees of any other CJI, ranging from less than two and one-half years to eleven. Because neither Jagannadhadas nor Venkatarama Ayyar had served five years as high court judges, they qualified for their SCI appointment because they had been for '... at least ten years an advocate of a High Court...'[8] Only Jagannadhadas had been a high court chief justice. Both of these Sastri appointees, because they were relatively elderly when they arrived in Delhi, and because S.R. Das's tenure as CJI did not end until late 1959, would not later become CJIs.

Sastri's quartet was an all-India group, representing the four major regions of the nation. Of the three Hindus, two were brahmins. All four had received all their education in India. Three were from middle-class backgrounds, the exception being Bhagwati's humble beginnings. Only Jagannadhadas came from a family of lawyers. The fathers of the others, who were the first in their families to enter the legal profession, ranged from a pashmina shawls' dealer to a Sanskrit scholar and a school teacher.

When Sastri's twenty-six -month tenure as CJI ended with his retirement on 3 January 1954, he bequeathed to his successor, M.C. Mahajan, an SCI at its full strength of eight judges.

9. Ghulam Hasan (1952–4)

G. Hasan, the Court's second Muslim judge, was born on 3 July 1891 in Amritsar, Punjab. He was the son of Ghulam Nabi Baksh, a pashmina shawls' dealer whose roots were in Kashmir, but who had migrated to Amritsar. Hasan received his BA degree from Khalsa College in Amritsar in about 1912. Shortly thereafter, he moved to Uttar Pradesh, and received

[8] Art. 124 (3) (b), Constitution of India.

his LLB from Allahabad University in about 1915. He was the first college graduate and first lawyer in his upper middle-class family.[9]

He began practising law at the district courts of Hardoi on 7 August 1917, at age twenty-six. On 19 August 1922, he enrolled as an advocate of the Allahabad High Court, but practised at Lucknow, where he would remain for nearly thirty years. On 16 April 1928, he enrolled as an advocate of the Oudh Chief Court in Lucknow.

In August 1940, at age forty-nine, Hasan was appointed a judge of the Oudh Chief Court, which had the status of a high court, and six years later, became that court's chief judge. On 25 July 1948, the Oudh Chief Court was merged with the Allahabad High Court and Hasan, then fifty-seven, was absorbed as a senior judge of that court. However, he never served on the Allahabad bench and remained in Lucknow as a member of what became the Lucknow bench of the Allahabad High Court. During most of 1949, at the request of the union government, he served as chairman of the Dargah Khwaja Sahib (Ajmer) Inquiry Commission. When he reached retirement age on 3 July 1951, he was third in seniority among the Allahabad High Court judges.

During his years in Lucknow, Hasan was active in a variety of educational, social, cultural, and political activities. From 1922 to 1934, he served as a part-time professor of Mohammedan Law at Lucknow University and, for some time, was also a member of that university's executive council. Later he served as a member of Aligarh Muslim University's executive council. In the 1940s, he served as chairman of the United Provinces branches of the Indian Red Cross and the St. John's Ambulance Brigade. In 1947, in recognition of this humanitarian work, he was awarded knighthood of the Order of St. John of Jerusalem. He also served as president of the board of governors of the La Martineri College for Boys and the La Martineri School for Girls. From 1937 to 1939, he served as a member of the United Provinces legislative assembly, elected as an independent.

Shortly after retiring from the high court, Hasan was appointed a member of the All-India Labour Appellate Tribunal and was serving in that capacity when, at age sixty-one, he was sworn in as a member of the SCI on 8 September 1952.

[9] His wife Aisha was the daughter of M.A. Ghani, who retired as a district judge in the United Provinces. His daughter, Nishat Rahman, would later practise law in Lucknow. Both of them were helpful in providing information about Hasan when I interviewed them in Srinagar on 24 June 1988.

Hasan died at age sixty-three on 5 November 1954, after serving for only twenty-six months.

10. Natvarlal Harilal Bhagwati (1952–9)

N.H. Bhagwati was born on 7 August 1894 at Ahmedabad, Gujarat.[10] Unlike the vast majority of SCI judges whose families were financially comfortable, Bhagwati was born into a family of modest means.[11] His father, Harilal Bhagwati, was a school teacher in Baroda state, earning about Rs 50 per month. Bhagwati not only achieved both professional success and financial security himself, but several of his children achieved great distinction in their chosen fields.[12]

Bhagwati began his higher education at Baroda College before moving to Elphinstone College in Bombay, where he received the BA (honours) degree in Sanskrit in 1914, and an MA in economics in 1917. In 1918, he received the LLB from Government Law College, Bombay, becoming the first lawyer in his family. He stood first in the BA examinations, winning the Bhau Daji Prize, the Dhirajlal Mathurdas Scholarship, and the Senior Daxina Fellowship. In the LLB examinations, he stood first in the first class and won the Sir Kinloch Forbes Gold Medal and Prize, the Judge Spencer Prize, and the Sir Mangaldas Nathubhai Legal Scholarship.

After having finished first in the advocates examination in 1921, he commenced a thirty-one year association with the Bombay High Court. At age fifty, after twenty years in private practice, he was appointed an additional judge of that high court on 27 August 1944, and was confirmed as a permanent judge on 17 February 1946.

While at the bar and on the bench at Bombay, Bhagwati was closely associated with higher education matters, particularly educational reform and administration. From 1929 to 1931, he served as a part-time professor of law at the Government Law College. He was a member of the Bombay

---

[10] Most of the first generation judges, including H.J. Kania, Bhagwati, and J.C. Shah, who came to the SCI from the Bombay High Court were not Maharashtrians by birth, but Gujaratis.

[11] Some of this biographical material was provided by his son, P.N. Bhagwati, in an interview in New Delhi on 20 April 1983.

[12] Among his seven children, P.N. Bhagwati became CJI, and Jagdish N. Bhagwati holds a prestigious chair in economics at Columbia University, New York, USA.

bar council in 1943. After joining the high court, he was a member of the senate (1947) and syndicate (1948) of Bombay University, and also vice-president of the Law College's board of visitors in 1948. In 1949, he was the representative of Bombay University on the Bombay Legal Education Reforms Committee. From 1949 to 1951, he served as acting vice-chancellor of Bombay University and, in 1950, was chairman of the university's reorganization committee. In 1949, he was named chairman of the Bombay state legal aid committee, one of the earliest efforts in India addressing the issue of legal aid for the poor.[13]

At age fifty-eight, and after eight years on the Bombay bench, by which time he was third in seniority, he was sworn in as an SCI judge on 8 September 1952. Shortly after his arrival on the SCI, Delhi University benefited from his higher education expertise when he was appointed a member of its executive council. While on the SCI, he edited the second edition of *Sir Dinshah Mulla's Law of Insolvency*.[14] Earlier he had translated V.L. Mehta's *Cooperative Movement* into Gujarati.

Bhagwati reached retirement age on 7 August 1959, after nearly seven years on the SCI. His retirement from public life lasted just a few months, for he accepted the vice-chancellorship of Banaras Hindu University on 16 April 1960, returning to the field of higher education which, if not his first love, was the main avocation of his life. Given the turmoil at that university before his arrival, it must have been one of the most demanding vice-chancellor posts in the country. By the time his tenure ended six years later, stability had been restored.

That assignment completed, he returned to Ahmedabad and went into full retirement. He died there at age seventy-five on 7 January 1970.

---

[13] *Report of the Committee on Legal Aid and Legal Advice in the State of Bombay*, 1949, usually referred to as the 'Bhagwati Committee' report, was described as 'perhaps the most informed study that has been produced so far in India on this subject' in the *Fourteenth Report* of the Law Commission, vol. I (*Reform of Judicial Administration*), p. 588. See also, B.N. Gokhale, *The Story of the High Court of Judicature at Bombay after Independence* (Nagpur: The Maharashtra Law Journal, 1963), pp. 88–9.

[14] Bombay: N.M. Tripathi Pvt. Ltd., 1958.

11. Bachu Jagannadhadas (1953–7)

B. Jagannadhadas[15] was born at Berhampur, Ganjam district, Orissa, on 27 July 1893. The law profession was a tradition in his middle-class family. His father, Narisimha Rao, his grandfather, and an elder brother were lawyers.

He earned the BA (honours) degree in 1914 from Presidency College, Madras. Two years later, he received his BL from Madras Law College and in 1918, earned an ML from the same institution. He stood first in the first class in the BL and ML examinations and was awarded the L.C. Miller Medal, the Gold Medal in Hindu Law, and the Sir T. Muthuswami Aiyar Scholarship.

In 1917, at age twenty-four, Jagannadhadas began practising law at Berhampur, and the next year he enrolled as an advocate of the Madras High Court, and remained in Madras for the next thirty years. In 1920, he declined an invitation to become a *munsif*. From 1943 to 1948, he was a member of the Madras bar council.

He joined the Indian National Congress in 1921 and for the next quarter century was active in the Freedom Movement. From 1938 to 1943, he was a member of the Madras corporation, having won election as a Congress candidate. His participation in the 1942 Quit India Movement resulted in him spending the September 1942 to June 1944 period in jail.

Jagannadhadas was active in a number of educational and social reform organizations, including the Gandhi Seva Sangh, the Harijan Seva Sangh, the Hindi Prachar Sabha, the Thakar Bapa Vidyalaya, the Madras Mahajan Sabha, and the Andhra Mahasabha. From 1936 until he left Madras in 1948, he served as director of the Harijan Industrial School at Kodabakam.

Orissa was separated from the Madras presidency in 1936 and when the Orissa High Court was inaugurated in 1948, Jagannadhadas was among its original members, and was designated the seniormost associate judge.[16] This appointment came rather late in his career—on 26 July 1948, a day before he turned fifty-five. He became chief justice on 30 October 1951. From 1948 to 1953, he was a member of the senate and dean of the faculty of law at Utkal University.

---

[15] Many sources render his surname as Das, but he preferred Jagannadhadas. His son, B. Parthasarthi, was interviewed on 12 July 1983 in New Delhi.

[16] The *Cuttack Law Times*, vol. 34, 1968, pp. 54–7 wrote that his long friendship with Congress party leaders 'helped him in being elevated to the Bench in 1948.' A cousin, P.V. Rao, was also a judge of the Orissa High Court.

At age fifty-nine, and with slightly less than five years of high court service, he was sworn in as a judge of the SCI on 9 March 1953.[17]

On 8 September 1957, nearly a year before he would have retired from the SCI, Jagannadhadas resigned to accept appointment as chairman of the Second Pay Commission, and continued in that capacity until 1959.[18] He remained in New Delhi and, from 1960 to 1963, he served as the executive chairman of the recently established Indian Law Institute.

He died on 30 May 1968 at age seventy-four.

12. Tirunelveli Lakshmanasuri Venkatarama Ayyar
(1954–8, 1961–2)

T.L. Venkatarama Ayyar was born on 25 November 1893 in Tinnevelly, Tinnevelly district, in Tamil Nadu into a middle-class family rich in South Indian brahmin heritage and culture. It was not a family with any tradition of association with the legal profession and Venkatarama Ayyar was the first lawyer in the family.[19] His father, Mahamahopadhyaya M. Lakshmana Suri, was a prominent Sanskrit scholar and author who taught Sanskrit at St. Peter's College in Thanjavur and later at Pachaiyappa's College in Madras City, where he was a colleague of M.P. Sastri's father.

After starting at Pachaiyappa's College, he received his BA degree in 1914 from Madras Christian College and, two years later, acquired the BL degree from Madras Law College, winning the Bashyam Ayyangar Gold Medal for finishing first in the BL examination in Hindu Law. While pursuing his legal education, he taught Sanskrit and Indian history at Madras Christian College. Venkatarama Ayyar was a cultured man of letters and a scholar with wide-ranging interests. He was an accomplished student of the Sanskrit language, literature, and drama, and was widely acclaimed as a musicologist for his knowledge of Carnatic music, a passion throughout his life, and for

[17] Having served less than five years on the high court, he qualified for appointment by virtue of having been a high court advocate for at least ten years. Constitution, Art. 124(3)(b).

[18] *Report of the Commission of Inquiry on Emoluments and Conditions of Service of Central Government Employees, 1957–1959* (New Delhi: Ministry of Finance, 1959).

[19] I interviewed his son, T.V. Balakrishnan, in Madras, on 25 June 1983. A useful short biography of Venkatarama Ayyar is found in V.C. Gopalratnam, *A Century Completed: A History of the Madras High Court, 1862–1962* (Madras: Madras Law Journal Office, 1962), pp. 248–52.

which he was awarded the prestigious title of Sangeeta Kalanidhi in 1944 by the Madras Music Academy.

He joined the Madras High Court bar at age twenty-three in 1917 and practised law there for the next thirty-four years. The most unusual aspect of his professional career was the fact that he was fifty-seven when he accepted appointment to the high court on 7 July 1951. B.P. Sinha, a colleague of his on the SCI, wrote that 'his elevation to the Bench of the Madras High Court came very late because he was born of a Brahmin family.'[20] No one before or since Venkatarama Ayyar reached the SCI after getting such a late start as a high court judge. After just twenty-eight months on the Madras bench, he reached retirement age on 24 November 1953.

Six weeks later, on 4 January 1954, he was sworn in as an SCI judge, filling the vacancy created the day before by Sastri's retirement. He spent about five and one-half years on the SCI, but his tenure was divided into three parts. He served nearly five years before reaching age sixty-five on 25 November 1958. CJI Sinha asked him to return as a retired judge from 1 March to 30 April 1961, and again from 20 December 1961 until 6 May 1962. Nearly sixty-eight and a half then, no one earlier or since was a judge at that age.

A modest and unassuming man, Venkatarama Ayyar has been acclaimed by colleagues and scholars as among the most brilliant to have served on the nation's highest tribunal. He is remembered particularly for his extensive knowledge of American constitutional law which was frequently cited in the early years when Indian constitutional law was in its infancy.

Less than a month after retiring from the SCI, he was appointed for a three-year term as chairman of the reconstituted Law Commission, beginning the tradition of retired Supreme Court judges 'owning' that post, for every Law Commission chairman since then, except for the 1968–71 period, has been a retired SCI judge. He served in this capacity from 20 December 1958 to 19 December 1961.

Writing and his passion for Carnatic music occupied his last years, although he did serve on two commissions. In 1967, he served as a one-man commission of inquiry which investigated charges made against former Congress party ministers in Bihar, including the chief minister. In the same year, he was appointed chairman of the Pay Commission for Reserve Bank

[20] B.P. Sinha, *Reminiscences and Reflections of a Chief Justice* (Delhi: B.R. Publishing Corporation, 1985), p. 74.

of India staff—the former a state level one and the latter appointed by the union government. He was elected a fellow of the central board of the Sangeet Natak Academy in 1964, served as a member of the board of music and board of examiners in music for Madras University, and was the teacher of several Carnatic musicians who would achieve eminence. He authored *The Life of Muthuswami Dikshitar*, a biography of a leading Carnatic music composer.

After leaving the SCI, he edited revised editions of several law publications. These included *Mulla on the Code of Civil Procedure*, 3rd edition (Bombay: N.M. Tripathi Pvt. Ltd., 1965); *Mulla on the Code of Criminal Procedure*, 13th edition, 2 vols (Bombay: N.M. Tripathi Pvt. Ltd., 1965-7); *Mulla on the Key to Indian Practise: Being a Summary of the Code of Civil Procedure*, 4th and 5th editions (Bombay: N.M. Tripathi Pvt. Ltd., 1966 and 1968); *Mulla on the Code of Civil Procedure (Student's Edition)*, 10th edition (Bombay: N.M. Tripathi Pvt. Ltd., 1972); and *Field's Law of Evidence in India and Pakistan*, 10th edition, six vols (Allahabad: Allahabad Law Publishers, 1973). He also edited and revised the second edition of B.K. Mukherjea's classic *Hindu Law of Religious and Charitable Trusts* (Calcutta: Eastern Law House, 1962). In 1970, his *The Evolution of the Indian Constitution* was published by the University of Bombay.

Venkatarama Ayyar died on 2 January 1971, at age seventy-seven.

III

The Mahajan Court (1954)

M.C. Mahajan was in his sixty-fifth year when he became CJI on 4 January 1954. Like Sastri, he would not have become CJI had Kania not died. Mahajan's tenure spanned almost all of that year, ending with his retirement on 22 December. There is no evidence that the government considered bypassing him because he would be CJI for such a short time, or because of the sometimes difficult relations he had with Prime Minister Nehru when he was the prime minister of Jammu and Kashmir. Indeed, there seems to have been at least a tacit acceptance by the executive that seniority would determine who would become CJI, though surely some questioned the wisdom of the nation's highest court being led by three different CJIs in one calendar year. According to M.C. Setalvad, Mahajan believed so strongly that he was entitled to follow Sastri—that seniority would be the sole determining factor—that he said he would resign if not appointed.[1] He was informed by Home Minister Dr K.N. Katju on 27 November 1953, well in advance of Sastri's retirement date, that he would be the next CJI.[2]

Inheriting an SCI at full strength, and with no retirements on the 1954 calendar, Mahajan anticipated filling only his own vacancy. But in early November, G. Hasan, the occupant of the Muslim seat died, giving Mahajan

[1] M.C. Setalvad, *My Life: Law and Other Things* (Bombay: N.M. Tripathi Pvt. Ltd., 1970), p. 189–90.
[2] Mehr Chand Mahajan, *Looking Back: The Autobiography of Mehr Chand Mahajan, Former Chief Justice of India* (Bombay: Asia Publishing House, 1963), p. 209.

the opportunity to fill this vacancy. The only account of the events of the next few weeks comes from an interview with B.P. Sinha in 1983.[3] Both Mahajan and Sinha wrote autobiographies, but neither wrote a word about what transpired after Hasan's death; Mahajan's autobiography makes no mention of Sinha or S.J. Imam, and Sinha's doesn't mention Imam either.

According to Sinha, Mahajan quickly decided to recommend that he, then the chief justice at Nagpur, be appointed to fill the Hasan vacancy, and that Imam, the chief justice at Patna and the most senior Muslim judge in the country, replace Mahajan when he retired the next month. Nehru became involved in this matter and expressed the view that Imam should replace Hasan—that another Muslim should replace Hasan. Nehru knew Imam for his family had long been prominent in Congress politics in Bihar. Mahajan had met Sinha during an official visit to Nagpur. He may not have met Imam. He discussed with his colleagues his desire that Sinha be appointed before Imam. According to Sinha, at this time recommendations communicated to the government were based on consensus among the judges and they were never rejected. There was no disagreement among Mahajan's colleagues concerning the appointments of Sinha and Imam but some felt that because it was the Muslim seat that was vacant, Imam should arrive first. Ultimately, Mahajan's wishes gained the support of the majority of the judges. He then communicated this consensus to Nehru, and he reluctantly agreed.[4]

Given Mahajan's expectation that seniority on the SCI would determine who would become CJI, the one sworn in first would become CJI following S.R. Das's retirement in 1959 and would have a very lengthy tenure.[5] If it was Imam, he would be CJI for five and one-half years, and Sinha would not become CJI. Because the latter was sworn in first, he would serve as CJI for fifty-two months and Imam for fifteen months. Sinha, then fifty-five, was

---

[3] In New Delhi on 17 July.

[4] Another actor in this decision may have been President of India, Dr Rajendra Prasad. Sinha had known Prasad, a fellow Bihari, since he was a teenager. He devoted an entire chapter of his autobiography to his long association with Prasad, is effusive in his praise throughout and, on p. 70 has referred to him as 'my old friend and benefactor'.

[5] A similar situation, but without the communal aspect, arose nearly two decades later. Before they reached the SCI in the early 1970s, both Y.V. Chandrachud and P.N. Bhagwati were viewed as destined to be appointed to the SCI. The one who arrived in Delhi first would enjoy a very long tenure as CJI. Although slightly less senior, Chandrachud was the first appointed and served as CJI for seven and a half years. Bhagwati followed him, and served as CJI for only seventeen months.

sworn in on 3 December, and Imam, fifty-four, took his oath a few weeks later, on 10 January 1955. So Mahajan, although his tenure as CJI was very brief, left a significant legacy, one that may have affected the history of the SCI.

Events of this nature cannot be interpreted without knowing the motives of the actors. But it was the Muslim seat that was vacant when Sinha was appointed, and one of the later Muslim SCI judges said that 'all Muslims know that Imam should have been appointed before Sinha'.

The careers of Sinha and Imam ran along almost parallel lines. Close to the same age, both were from Bihar and both began practising law at the Patna High Court in 1922. Imam would win the advocate general post, while Sinha was a step behind as assistant government advocate. Both were forty-three years old when appointed to the Patna bench, but Sinha got there a few months earlier than Imam. Sinha widened the all-India seniority gap when he became chief justice at Nagpur in 1951. Imam remained at Patna and became chief justice there in 1953.

Their social and economic backgrounds were as different as their professional careers were similar. Sinha was a rather rustic, home-grown, and locally educated product of Bihar from a traditional background, was the first member of his Rajput family to receive a higher education, and was the first to achieve success in the modern sector. Imam's antecedents for generations were prominent members of Bihar's legal, social, and political elite. Before he began his law practice as a barrister, Imam had spent about half of his life in England receiving a liberal western education. He was, thus, a hybrid, a product of two cultures, and possessed the cosmopolitanism that comes with such a privileged background.

The legal and judicial careers of these two men, so closely parallel for more than four decades, ended on the same day. Debilitating illness prevented Imam from succeeding Sinha as CJI, and both left the SCI on 31 January 1964, Sinha's last day as CJI. Because the Imam appointment had been decided upon before Mahajan retired, he is credited with it. When he left office, the SCI was at full strength.

13. Bhuvaneshwar Prasad Sinha (1954–64)

B.P. Sinha was born on 1 February 1899 at Ghazipur in Ghazipur district, Bihar, into what he described as 'a relatively well-to-do family' whose business was 'money-lending, agriculture and landlordism'.[6] His surname was in fact Singh, but Patna University listed it as Sinha, and he left it that way.[7] His father, Kashi Nath Singh, was a small-scale zamindar, but considered himself a saint with curative powers and spent years wandering about the country rather than managing the family properties, with the result that the family's wealth was nearly depleted before Sinha began his higher education. He was the first university graduate in his family but not the first to practise law, for an uncle who, though lacking formal education, was a pleader in a district court.

Sinha commenced his higher education in Patna in 1915 and received his BA (honours) in history from Patna College in 1919. He next pursued both an MA, again in history, and the BL simultaneously, earning the former degree in 1921 and the latter from Governmernt Law College, Patna in 1922. He ranked first in both the BA and MA examinations, and won the Shrimati Radhika Sinha gold medal for standing first in history at the BA level. During the course of his life he gained a reputation for proficiency in the Persian language and poetry.

On 15 December 1922, at age twenty-three, he began practising law at the Patna High Court, the latter having been spun off from the Calcutta High Court in 1916. In August 1935, he was appointed government pleader, which according to the conventions of that time, put him on track for appointment to the high court. In 1940, he was promoted to the post of assistant government advocate and was serving in that capacity when, at age forty-three, he was sworn in as an additional judge of the Patna High Court on 6 January 1943. He was confirmed as a permanent judge on 6 December 1943. Sinha's son and grandson would later serve on the Patna High Court. Rameshwar Prasad Sinha served from 1973 to 1982, and grandson, Bisheshwar Prasad Singh, was appointed in 1987. The latter was appointed to the SCI in 2001 and retired in 2007.

During his early years at the bar, Sinha taught part-time at the Government Law College from 1926 to 1935. During 1932–51, he served as a member of the senate of the faculty of law and of the board of examiners in law at Patna University. He was also a member of the court of Banaras Hindu

[6] B.P. Sinha, *Reminiscences and Reflections of a Chief Justice* (Delhi: B.R. Publishing Corporation, 1985), pp. 5, 11.

[7] Interview on 17 July 1983 in New Delhi. Sinha was the first SCI judge I had the pleasure of meeting. A Duke University graduate student at the time, I was granted an interview with him on 14 February 1963 in New Delhi.

University. Just before he left Patna he spent much of 1950 as chairman of a state-level commission of inquiry which dealt with a threatened strike in the sugar industry. In the same year, he declined an offer to go to the Assam High Court as chief justice.[8]

After spending thirty-six years in Patna, the last eight on the Patna bench, Sinha, then fifty-two, and at the urging of Union Home Minister Sardar Patel, agreed to be transferred to the Nagpur High Court as its chief justice, assuming this post on 24 February 1951. Earlier a decision had been made to replace Vivian Bose, the Nagpur chief justice whose appointment to the SCI had been gazetted, with a chief justice from elsewhere. By this time Sinha had reason to believe that the then Bihar government, because of caste considerations, was not going to agree to him, a Rajput, becoming chief justice at Patna.[9] Sinha wrote that neither the bar nor the judges at Nagpur were pleased that an outsider was brought in as chief.[10]

After nearly four years at Nagpur, where he succeeded in improving the working conditions and salaries of the subordinate judiciary, he was sworn in as a judge of the SCI on 3 December 1954. Age fifty-five at this time, he spent just over nine years on the SCI, a little more than half of those years as an associate judge and the remaining fifty-two months as CJI. He became the sixth CJI on 1 October 1959 and reached retirement age on 31 January 1964. Only Y.V. Chandrachud would serve longer than Sinha as CJI.

While CJI, he served as pro-chancellor of Delhi University and also played a major role in founding the Indian Law Institute, serving as its executive chairman briefly after leaving the SCI. He received the LLD (*honoris causa*) from Patna University in 1960, and from Bhagalpur University and Vikram University, both in 1962.

After leaving the SCI, Sinha remained in Delhi, but unlike most retired judges, he accepted few post-retirement assignments. He served on no commissions of inquiry or tribunals. During the 1960s, he conducted a number of arbitrations at the request of the SCI and other arbitrations at the request of private parties, usually quarrelling businesses or families. During his remaining years, blind during many of them, Sinha, a deeply religious man during all of his adult life, devoted most of his time to spiritual pursuits. He died on 12 November 1986 at age eighty-seven.

[8] Sinha, *Reminiscences*, pp. 40–1.

[9] Ibid., pp. 39–42. In Sinha's words, 'Unfortunately, Bihar is notorious for its indulgence in caste distinctions ...' p. 39.

[10] Ibid., pp. 46–7.

14. Syed Jafer Imam (1955-64)

S.J. Imam, the first SCI judge born in the twentieth century, was born into a wealthy and aristocratic Muslim family on 18 April 1900 in Patna, Bihar.[11] Imam's antecedents had long been prominently involved in law and politics. His great-grandfather had been a district judge, and his grandfather and father were lawyers. Law was in the family genes, and Imam came to the law almost as a matter of biological necessity. His father was Sir Ali Imam, a member of the viceroy's executive council, was a major force in the creation of Bihar as a separate province, and played a prominent role in Congress politics and the nationalist movement. The Imam family had close ties with the Nehru family. His uncle, Hasan Imam, also a lawyer, was briefly a judge of the Calcutta High Court, and was also a well-known figure in the nationalist movement. A younger brother, S. Naqui Imam, served as a judge of the Patna High Court.[12]

Imam was privileged to receive an elegant and cosmopolitan education. When very young, he travelled to England and attended prestigious public schools before enrolling at Trinity College, Cambridge University, from which he received his BA in about 1921 and LLB in about 1922. He was called to the bar from Middle Temple on 26 January 1922.

Returning from England, he was twenty-one when he enrolled as an advocate of the Patna High Court in March 1922. He specialized in criminal law—one of the few future SCI judges with that background. He was only thirty-two when he was appointed assistant government advocate in 1932, a post he held until 1939. In 1942, he was named Advocate General of Bihar. From that threshold and at age forty-three, he was appointed to the Patna bench in October 1943. A decade later, on 3 September 1953, he became the Patna chief justice and served in that capacity until he was sworn in

[11] Helpful in providing biographical information was correspondence with Begum Aziza Imam, S.J. Imam's sister-in-law, in October 1983. Also of assistance were discussions with former SCI judges S.M. Fazal Ali, N.L. Untwalia, and L.M. Sharma, all from Bihar, each of whom knew Imam.

[12] According to Theodore P. Wright ('Kinship Ties Among the Muslim Elite in India Since Independence', an unpublished paper presented at the annual meeting of the Association for Asian Studies, Chicago, USA, 1978), the Imam family tree reveals that many of the Muslim judges were related, closely or distantly, and often by marriage. Among the Muslims who have served on the SCI, the list includes S. Fazl Ali, Imam, M. Hidayatullah, M. Hameedullah Beg, and S.M. Fazal Ali. Several others in this family tree served on the Calcutta or Patna High Courts.

as an SCI judge on 10 January 1955. At that time he was the most senior Muslim judge in the country and, at age fifty-four, the youngest man to date to be appointed to the SCI.

Following Sinha's retirement on 31 January 1964, Imam was the next in line for the chief justiceship. He was to have been India's first Muslim CJI and hold that post for nearly fifteen months. Debilitating illness prevented this from happening. Among his colleagues was M. Hidayatullah, who later described Imam as having suffered 'a succession of strokes, resulting in deprivation of speech, and who could not even finish a sentence which he began because his speech centres were affected. And I am sure his memory and powers of concentration were also gone.'[13] But Imam wanted to become CJI. M.C. Setalvad wrote that thought was given to taking the steps provided in the Constitution to secure Imam's removal from office.[14] Prime Minister Nehru had to become involved in this sad and delicate situation. He was concerned about how Pakistan would react to superseding the first Muslim to be in line for the chief justiceship.[15]After medical experts from the All-India Institute of Medical Sciences reported to Nehru that Imam was no longer in full control of his mental faculties, Nehru gently persuaded Imam to resign from the SCI, effective the same day that Sinha retired. On 21 October 1963, more than three months in advance of Sinha's retirement date, the home ministry, without any explanation of why or any mention of Imam, announced that P.B. Gajendragadkar, the next in line after Imam, would follow Sinha as CJI.[16]

Imam returned to Patna and died there on 30 November 1965, at age sixty-five.

[13] 'Unjustified Departure from Settled Convention', in N.A. Palkhivala (ed.), A Judiciary Made to Measure (Bombay: M.R. Pai, 1973), pp. 9–15, especially p. 13. Imam's illness is discussed also by Gajendragadkar, To the Best of My Memory, pp. 158–9, and Setalvad, My Life: Law and Other Things, pp. 507–8.

[14] Setalvad, My Life, p. 508.

[15] Interview with Sinha, 17 July 1983 in New Delhi. Also, interview with Hidayat-ullah, 3 June 1983.

[16] The Hindustan Times, 23 October 1963.

IV

The Mukherjea Court (1954–6)

Sixty-three and the most senior associate judge when he replaced Mahajan on 23 December 1954, Mukherjea was to have been CJI for nineteen months. But soon his health began to fail and in late 1955, he was on leave for four months. While on leave, S.R. Das served as acting CJI, and N. Chandrasekhar Aiyar returned in the retired judge capacity. Mukherjea's declining health resulted in his resignation on 31 January 1956. The Court was at full strength when he took over and there were no retirements during his brief tenure. Had he served his full term, he would have had the opportunity to select a replacement for only Vivian Bose.

V

The Das Court (1956–9)

S.R. Das, the last of the six men who comprised the SCI at its beginning in 1950, served as CJI for forty-four months.[1] The Das years were marked by many changes in personnel. He inherited a Court composed of seven permanent judges, including himself, plus the recalled Chandrasekhar Aiyar.

He became CJI on 1 February 1956; shortly thereafter and at his initiative, the strength of the Court was increased from eight to eleven judges.[2] There were vacancies to fill every year. Ten new judges, including some of the most distinguished in the SCI's history, joined the SCI during his watch. He also persuaded the retired V. Bose to return for the 1957–8 year.

His first appointee was S.K. Das, the fifty-seven-year-old chief justice at Patna. This appointment broke new ground, for he was a career ICS officer without a law degree or barrister credentials. Until this appointment, there had been opposition from most of the judges to an ICS judge being promoted to the SCI.[3] The two Das's had known each other for many years,

[1] Not included in this figure is the four months he was acting CJI when Mukherjea was ill. Only Y.V. Chandrachud, B.P. Sinha, and A.N. Ray had longer tenures as CJI.

[2] The Supreme Court (Number of Judges) Act of 1956. An increased workload dictated this expansion and the additional judges permitted the SCI to function in three or four divisions.

[3] Sinha, *Reminiscences and Reflections of a Chief Justice*, Delhi: B.R. Publishing Corporation, pp. 73–4, wrote that CJI Kania was of the view that ICS judges were not fit to be SCI judges. Both Gajendragadkar, *To the Best of My Memory*, Bombay: Bharatiya Vidya Bhavan, pp. 97–8, and Setalvad, *My Life: Law and Other Things*, Bombay: N.M.

mainly through their common membership in the Brahmo Samaj.[4] The first to join the Court after Mukherjea's resignation, he was sworn in on 30 April 1956. Both of these, like S.R. Das himself, were Bengalis, so Das can be considered Mukherjea's replacement.

S.K. Das was the third consecutive appointee from the Patna High Court. Never again were there three consecutive appointees from the same high court. But this seems coincidental for, after the decision was made to appoint an ICS judge, Das, being the most senior in the country, was the likely choice. The previous appointee, Imam, was the most senior Muslim judge in the nation when the court needed a Muslim judge, and Sinha had preceded Imam.[5]

After V. Bose retired in June, P.G. Menon, second in seniority on the Madras High Court, was sworn in on 1 September 1956. At nearly sixty he was the eldest of the Das class. He had been considered for the Court in 1953 but that vacancy was filled by Jagannadhadas. And Venkatarama Aiyar, four years his junior when they were colleagues on the Madras High Court, had reached the SCI nearly three years before him. Menon was the fourth appointee and first non-brahmin from the Madras High Court, and the SCI's first Keralite.

The three new judgeships were filled in 1957. The first to arrive was J.L. Kapur, sworn in on 14 January. He was fifty-nine and fifth in seniority on the Punjab bench. Das knew Kapur well, for he was the chief justice of the then East Punjab High Court when Kapur was appointed to that court. After a two-year hiatus, Punjab was again represented on the SCI.

Three days after Kapur took his seat on the Court, the fifty-five-year-old P.B. Gajendragadkar, fourth in seniority on the Bombay High Court, was sworn in. He was the first of a string of five young men appointed in succession, each of whom would later rise to the chief justiceship and most of whom would be ranked among the towering figures of the SCI. The third to come up via the Bombay High Court, he was the first Maharashtrian by birth and brought the Bombay representation to two for the first time.

Tripathi Pvt. Ltd., 1971, pp. 342–3, wrote that Sastri was also opposed to service judges being brought to the SCI, and that the succeeding CJIs shared that view.

[4] Later the two families would become related through marriage. Interview with S.K. Das, New Delhi, 18 October 1988.

[5] Four (the other was Fazl Ali) of the first fifteen SCI judges came from the Patna High Court, but only three (Vaidyanthier Ramaswami in 1965, N.L. Untwalia in 1974, and L.M. Sharma in 1987) of the next seventy-eight. So, while it seemed by 1956 that Bihar was fertile ground for locating talent for the Court, this was not the case thereafter.

The final member of this trio was A.K. Sarkar, fifty-five and sixth in seniority at the Calcutta High Court. Das earlier had offered this seat to P.B. Chakravartti, the then chief justice of the Calcutta High Court and the first Indian to serve as such, but he declined the invitation.[6] Das and Sarkar had been close friends for more than a quarter century. At the beginning of his career in 1930, Sarkar had worked as a junior in Das's chambers. Das had recommended Sarkar at the same time as Kapur and Gajendragadkar, but his appointment wasn't gazetted until 7 February. No earlier SCI appointee had less high court seniority, and some of the superseded Calcutta judges protested to home minister G.B. Pant.[7] Sarkar was ultimately sworn in on 4 March. With his arrival in Delhi, the Calcutta High Court representation returned to two.

Almost a year would pass before Das's sixth appointment and, in the meantime, Menon died. His replacement was K. Subba Rao, aged fifty-five and the then chief justice of the recently created Andhra Pradesh High Court. Earlier he had spent twenty-eight years associated with the Madras High Court as an advocate and judge. He was sworn in on 31 January 1958, so rather quickly after the 1956 reorganization of states, a judge from one of the new high courts was on the SCI. Because both were South Indians, and both had served on the Madras High Court, we can assume that Subba Rao replaced Menon.

On 11 August 1958, two weeks after Jagannadhadas retired, K.N. Wanchoo, fifty-five, the second appointee from the ranks of the ICS, arrived on the SCI from the Rajasthan High Court, where he was the chief justice. If he had not met him earlier, Das would have become acquainted with Wanchoo when he testified before the Law Commission, of which Wanchoo was a member. Obviously Wanchoo was not a regional replacement for Jagannadhadas. But the Orissa and Rajasthan High Courts had much in common. Both were recently established, both small, and both were located in states that then, and even today, seemed to be viewed from Delhi as politically less important than many other states. There would not be another appointee from Orissa until R.N. Misra in 1983 and, of

---

[6] P.B. Chakravartti, 'Appointment to the Supreme Court', *Calcutta Weekly Notes*, LXXIII (1 September 1969), clv. He wrote here that he was offered an SCI seat 'and I even received a telegraphic communication that the President had approved my appointment. But, before such selection and appointment, I had not been consulted as to whether I was willing to go and when the intimation came to me, I declined it for reasons which need not be stated here'.

[7] Interview with Sarkar on 28 June 1983 in Calcutta.

our ninety-three, only two more came to the SCI from Rajasthan, P.N. Shinghal in 1975 and J.S. Verma in 1989, and only the former was a native of Rajasthan. So, perhaps, the vacancy filled by Wanchoo could be termed a small or new court one. And because the first twenty-five years of Wanchoo's career had been spent in Uttar Pradesh before moving to Rajasthan, he was viewed more likely as an Allahabad High Court appointee than a Rajasthan one.

The third and final 1958 appointee was the youngest appointed to date, the fifty-two-year-old M. Hidayatullah, then the chief justice of the Madhya Pradesh High Court, who was sworn in on 1 December, just a week after Venkatarama Ayyar retired.[8] Hidayatullah's memoirs provide a fascinating account of the events leading up to his appointment. In late 1957, while attending a high court chief justices conference in New Delhi, CJI Das asked him whether he'd be interested in becoming the chief justice at Calcutta. Hidayatullah responded that he was not interested.[9] Later, Ashoke K. Sen,[10] the Union Minister of Law, was more specific about the reasons behind Das's query:

He suggested that I would swap places with K.C. Das Gupta, who would then be brought to the Supreme Court, and I would become Chief Justice of the Calcutta High Court. He added that I would get a chance when Justice Imam retired. This meant that I was to get what had till then become a Muslim seat in the Supreme Court. I rejected the proposal outright. I told him that I could give my reply in writing rejecting the offer of a Supreme Court Judgeship in the room of Imam. He kept quiet. Later I came to the Supreme Court before Das Gupta and was thus a second Muslim Judge. I was, so to speak, a Muslim judge appointed out of turn.[11]

A year would pass before Hidayatullah received the invitation from Das. He heard from several sources that Das had proposed his name earlier, before Subba Rao and Wanchoo were appointed.[12] 'Later, I learnt that Government

---

[8] Hidayatullah recalled that it was Venkatarama Ayyar 'in whose room I was appointed.' *My Own Boswell* (New Delhi: Arnold-Heinemann Publishers (India) Pvt. Ltd., 1980), p. 200. Bose, Hidayatullah's former colleague at Nagpur, had left the Court a few weeks earlier, but he had been serving as an Article 128 judge, meaning that his departure did not create a vacancy.

[9] Hidayatullah, *My Own Boswell*, p. 181.

[10] He was CJI Das's son-in-law.

[11] Hidayatullah, *My Own Boswell*, pp. 181–2.

[12] Ibid., p. 190. When Hidayatullah was appointed, Das 'was almost apologetic that I had joined the Court so late', p. 196. Had Hidayatullah been appointed before Subba Rao and Wanchoo, neither would have served as CJI, and the course of Indian constitutional law would very likely have been different.

had asked for two more names, when my name was sent up, and although I was the first I was pushed down to the last place.'[13] One can only speculate why he was not appointed earlier. His age must have been a factor—even when he arrived in 1958 he was the youngest ever appointed.[14] That there was a Muslim on the Court was a factor. Hidayatullah refused to wait for Imam's scheduled retirement in 1965, and then become the occupant of the Muslim seat; he didn't like that label. He wanted to be selected on his own merits and not because he was a Muslim. Had his appointment been delayed until Imam was gone, he would not have become CJI later.[15]

K.C. Das Gupta, the fifty-nine-year-old Calcutta High Court chief justice and the first from the ranks of the ICS to reach that post, was sworn in on 24 August 1959. Das, of course, knew him well from their days together on the Calcutta court. Das Gupta was the first chief justice from one of the presidency high courts to accept appointment to the SCI.[16]

The tenth and final appointee during Das's stewardship was J.C. Shah, fifty-three and second in seniority on the Bombay High Court. Although his swearing in occurred on 12 October 1959, a dozen days after Das retired, there is no doubt that he was selected by Das. According to both Sinha, who succeeded Das as CJI, and Shah himself, it was Das who extended the invitation shortly before his retirement.[17] Sinha had concurred with Das's choice of Shah. According to Shah, the two had not earlier met. He was the Bombay replacement for Bhagwati who had reached retirement age

[13] Hidayatullah, My Own Boswell, pp. 190–1.

[14] And the third youngest ever, after P.N. Bhagwati and Y.V. Chandrachud.

[15] J.C. Shah, appointed in 1959, would have succeeded Wanchoo in 1968, and served as such beyond Hidayatullah's retirement date.

[16] Earlier, Chief Justices P.V. Rajamannar of the Madras High Court and M.C. Chagla of the Bombay High Court, and Chakravartti of Calcutta, had declined invitations. Forty-two of our ninety-three judges had been high court chief justices. Thirty-six came from the Bombay, Calcutta, and Madras High Courts, but only three more were chief justices—D.P. Madon of Bombay, A.N. Sen of Calcutta, and P.S.G. Kailasam of Madras. S. Mukharji's stepping stone was as Calcutta's acting chief justice, but an acting one is still an associate judge. Those who declined did so for a variety of reasons, including personal and family illnesses, juniors appointed earlier, and reluctance to leave the glamour of a prestigious post to become the most junior SCI judge.

[17] Interview with Sinha in New Delhi on 17 July 1983, and with Shah on 3 November 1988 in Bombay. Had Sinha not concurred, he could have withdrawn the Shah nomination after replacing Das. According to Shah, his appointment was gazetted 'almost immediately after the retirement of Chief Justice'. Correspondence with the author dated 27 May 1983.

two months earlier and Das Gupta was the Calcutta replacement for Das himself.

During Das's tenure, the landmark *Fourteenth Report* of the Law Commission was published, and among its observations was that there was a '... general impression, that now and again executive influence exerted from the highest quarters has been responsible for some appointments to the Bench. It is undoubtedly true, that the best talent among the Judges of the High Courts has not always found its way to the Supreme Court.'[18] Home Minister Pandit Pant, who held that portfolio throughout CJI Das's tenure, responded in Parliament to this charge: '... since 1950, seventeen Judges have been appointed to the Supreme Court and every one of these Judges was nominated and recommended by the Chief Justice of India. ... To say that the Judges that have been recruited there have just been thrust on the Court by somebody else is against the facts and is absolutely incorrect.'[19] Seventeen includes eight appointees of the Das era. Pant did not say whether any of Das's nominees were not accepted by the government. How many of the Das era appointees were in fact selected by him simply cannot be ascertained, but some believe that one, perhaps two, were not. Das had some acquaintance with nearly all before they were appointed. The high court judicial fraternity was small then—130 judges in 1957.[20]

Pant had urged CJIs to extend invitations to leading advocates.[21] Das did offer judgeships to at least two but both declined. These were H.M. Seervai and Lal Narayan Sinha. Seervai, then the Advocate General of Maharashtra, received his invitation in November 1957.[22] He was fifty at this time and, had he accepted, he would have followed Sarkar as CJI in 1966 and retired in 1971. Subba Rao, Wanchoo, Hidayatullah, and Shah

[18] Law Commission of India, *Fourteenth* Report, I, p. 34.

[19] *Lok Sabha Debates*, 2nd Series, 7th Session, XXVIII (1959), 20 March 1959, col. 7521.

[20] B.N. Datar, minister of state in the ministry of home affairs, told Parliament that on 1 January 1957 there were 130 high court judges, and on 1 January 1960 the total was 182. *Lok Sabha Debates*, 2nd Series, 10th Session, 1960, XLIII, 27 April 1960, cols 14144–236, especially 14223.

[21] Sinha, *Reminiscences*, pp. 175–6.

[22] Interviews with Seervai on 3 and 6 November 1988 in Bombay.

would not have become CJIs.[23] When invited in 1958,[24] L.N. Sinha was fifty-one and serving as the Advocate General of Bihar.

The most striking difference between the judges appointed during Das's watch and those appointed before and after was their relative youth. The median age of the first fourteen was fifty-eight and four were sixty or older. The median age of Das's ten was 55.8—their average age was 56.6 years—and none were in their sixties. Das himself was fifty-five when he joined the SCI and he may have looked for men who were also comparatively young. Largely because of their ages and the order of their appointments, six of them would serve as CJI during the 1964-71 years. With an average of 10.6 years of high court experience, their relative youth did not mean that they had less high court experience than earlier appointees, and five had been high court chief justices.

In terms of geographic representation there were some departures from past practice but, in the main, earlier recruitment patterns continued. Five of these men came from the three presidency high courts. But the Court Das left was without a direct representative from the Madras High Court, for Menon died shortly after his arrival in Delhi, and was replaced by Subba Rao, whose initial high court appointment was at Madras, but who was a Telugu speaker who came to Delhi from the Andhra Pradesh High Court. Punjab, with the arrival of Kapur, reclaimed a seat vacant since Mahajan's retirement, and Bihar gained a third representative with the appointment of S.K. Das. Finally, the three states created as a result of the 1956 reorganization of states—Andhra Pradesh, Rajasthan, and Madhya Pradesh—saw their first representatives reach the SCI. Noteworthy is the absence of a judge appointed from the Allahabad High Court, but Wanchoo had served on that court before his transfer to Rajasthan. So Das left a nearly perfectly geographically balanced Court—three from the east, three from the west, and two each from the north and south.

Nine of the ten judges were Hindus, and Hidayatullah increased the Muslim representation to two for the first time. After Bose's retirement,

[23] Three decades later, Seervai wrote that had he accepted the invitation and become CJI, '... the tragedy of Golaknath would never have occurred [but] one Judge could not do much, and I honestly believed that I had made a larger contribution to the development of Constitutional Law by my book than I could ever have done by being a Judge of that Court.' *High Court of Judicature at Bombay: Post-Centenary Silver Jubilee, 1862-1987* (Bombay, Government Central Press, 1988), 'Judgments: Need for Clarity and Accuracy', pp. 48-52, especially p. 50.

[24] Interview with his son, L.M. Sharma, 24 April 1988 in New Delhi.

another Christian would not be appointed until K.K. Mathew in 1971. When Das took over, the five Hindu judges included two brahmins and three non-brahmins. Of the nine Hindus Das selected, seven were non-brahmins as was Das himself. Of the ten Hindus from Kania through Sinha's appointment, six were brahmins. So, in caste terms, the social composition of the Court was reversed during Das's stewardship.

In terms of paternal occupation, another and more universal measure of social status, there were also some noteworthy changes. Whereas sons of Sanskrit scholars and lawyers were often appointed before 1956, of the Das men, only Gajendragadkar was the son of a Sanskrit scholar and only three were the offspring of lawyers. The fathers of five spent their careers in government service. The fathers of only two or three of the first fourteen had held positions in government service.

Four of his appointees were India-educated advocates, and four were barristers (Sarkar was both). ICS judge Das Gupta was a barrister; the other two appointees from the ICS were neither lawyers nor barristers. Of the first fourteen judges, only four were barristers, including Das himself, so coincidentally or not, barristers were more likely to reach the Court. Das left a more cosmopolitan Court, for six of his team, including the ICS officers, had received some of their education in England. The fact that the first ICS officers were appointed was a significant change during the Das years.[25]

According to all accounts, the Das Court was marked by uncommon collegiality and congeniality among the brethren. Das had earned the respect and esteem of his colleagues.[26] At the retirement dinner in his honour, and following his successor's affectionate farewell speech, Das revealed the friendly atmosphere of the Court when he offered warm and amusing comments about each of his brethren. These merit quotation in full:

[25] Another barrier that fell during the Das years was that, upon his recommendation, the first woman was appointed to a high court. This was Anna Chandy, appointed to the Kerala High Court in 1959. V.R. Krishna Iyer claims at least partial credit for this breakthrough appointment, for he said that he initiated this recommendation when he was serving as Kerala's law minister. Interview in New Delhi on 25 June 1983. Another thirty years would pass before the first female—M. Fathima Beevi—would be appointed to the SCI in 1989.

[26] Hidayatullah wrote, 'I do not think any Chief Justice was so universally loved and admired', My Own Boswell, p. 196. Gajendragadkar, in To the Best of My Memory, p. 133, wrote that 'In the time of S.R. Das, the atmosphere in the court was very friendly'.

We have been, indeed, a very happy family. There is my successor-designate. He relieves us from the monotony of our Court work by quoting couplets from Urdu and Persian poets and our minds are immediately refreshed. Then we have brother Imam, all the time trying—but never succeeding—to convince the advocate that his arguments are entirely useless. Then comes my friend S.K. Das. He is there all the time cutting jokes and pulling our legs using chaste language and very apt quotations, many of which are not fit for the Presidential ear. Then comes my brother Kapur. When an argument is in full swing, he distinctly remembers that there is a decision, either of the House of Lords or of the Privy Council, which is pat on the point under discussion, but unfortunately that decision he cannot, for the moment, lay his hands on and all the members of the Bar appearing in the case cannot find it till the case is over. Then comes my learned brother, Gajendragadkar. His heart is literally bleeding for the under-dogs, and unless the bleeding can be stopped, the under-dogs will soon become the top dogs. My brother Sarkar has been an onlooker on the highway of life. He attends dinners but does not eat; he sees other people eat. He has joined many bridal processions but has not married. But I do not know whether he will change his mind. Then we have brother Subba Rao, who is extremely unhappy because all our fundamental rights are going to the dogs on account of some ill-conceived judgments of his colleagues which require reconsideration. There is brother Wanchoo. Sometimes, when it is said that U.P. is not represented in this Court we point our finger to brother Wanchoo, and when it is said that Rajasthan is not represented, there is brother Wanchoo. He has the best of both worlds. Then we have brother Hidayatullah. He has given us three Gospels: Stroud's Judicial Dictionary, Wilson's Glossary and Words and Phrases by some author whose name I forget. I do not know when he will produce the fourth Gospel. Last but not least is my brother K.C. Das Gupta. He is a dark horse, and it is too early to appraise his merit.[27]

When Das departed on 1 October 1959, he brought the Court's first decade to a close, and bequeathed to incoming CJI Sinha a Court operating at its full strength of eleven members.

15. Sudhanshu Kumar Das (1956–63)

S.K. Das was born on 3 September 1898 at Patna, Bihar into an upper middle-class Bengali family. He was the son of Rajkumar Das, a member of

[27] Quoted from 'Speeches Delivered at a Farewell Dinner in Honour of Shri S.R. Das, the Retiring Chief Justice, on 30 September 1959, in the Supreme Court Building'. [1959] SCR, pp. vii–xvi, especially, pp. xv–xvi. Shah was not mentioned, because he had not yet been sworn in.

the Bengal provincial educational service who served as a secondary school headmaster in various places in the old Bengal presidency. S.K. Das was the first member of his family to be involved in the administration of justice.[28]

He received a BA (honours) in history from Presidency College, Calcutta, in 1920, standing second in the university—second only to the acclaimed writer Nirad C. Chaudhuri. Later that year, he travelled to England and enrolled in the MA course in history at the London School of Oriental Studies, the purpose of which was preparation for the ICS examination. He was successful in August 1921 and then spent his probationary year at the University of London, where he taught the Bengali language while attending classes in Indian history, the Indian Penal Code, the Code of Criminal Procedure, and the Hindi language.

After becoming an ICS officer on 30 October 1922, he was assigned to the then province of Bihar and Orissa and was posted first in Cuttack as an assistant magistrate and collector. From that beginning on the first step of the ladder, Das, over the next thirty-four years, would rise to the SCI holding, as he moved along, virtually every post open to a judicial officer. During the 1920s, he worked not only as a judicial officer, but also held executive and revenue posts. In 1929, he underwent six months of judicial training, and served first as a munsif, then as a subordinate judge and next as an additional district and sessions judge. While serving in the latter capacity in Bihar, in 1930, he took six months leave, returned to England, and joined Gray's Inn to study for the bar examination. He passed the examinations in constitutional and criminal law, but had to return to India before he could complete the dinners' requirement and take the final examination. Unable to return to England later, Das was never called to the bar.

In July 1933, he was promoted to district and sessions judge and posted at Chhapra. In 1937, he served as the legislative secretary to the first Congress ministry in Bihar. He next held the post of labour commissioner and from 1939 to 1941 he served as registrar of the Patna High Court—the first Indian to serve in that capacity. From March 1941 to March 1944, he held the post of judicial secretary and legal remembrancer.

On 4 November 1944, he was appointed to the Patna High Court as a temporary judge. Early the next year at age forty-six and without any interruption of service he was named an additional judge. Confirmation as a permanent judge came on 12 January 1948. In 1950, he served as

---

[28] The author interviewed him twice in New Delhi—on 14 May 1983 and 18 October 1988.

chairman of the jury committee of Bihar. On 10 January 1955, after more than a decade on the Patna bench and following Imam's departure for the SCI, Das became chief justice. While serving in that capacity, he conducted a judicial inquiry into the police firing on students in Patna, a major event in Bihar at that time.

During his years in Patna, Das was much involved in that city's cultural and social life, and played a major role in the establishment of the Academy of Music, Dance and Drama. A sports enthusiast throughout his life, he started a cricket club during his Chhapra days and had tennis courts built in Patna, both at his own expense.

Das was sworn in as an SCI judge on 30 April 1956. At age fifty-seven, he was the first member of the ICS and the first without either a law degree or barrister credentials to reach the nation's highest court. He was probably the most senior ICS high court judge in the country at that time. While Das was serving on the Court, Prime Minister Nehru requested CJI Sinha to assign a judge to investigate allegations made against K.D. Malaviya, then the Union Minister of Mines and Fuel. Sinha selected Das for this delicate assignment.[29] This was the first time that a sitting SCI judge conducted an inquiry concerning charges made against a union minister, and Malaviya ultimately resigned. During his tenure on the SCI, Das was also selected to be a member of the Indian delegation at meetings of the Afro–Asian legal consultative committee held in Sri Lanka in 1960 and Japan in 1961.

Over forty years after taking up his first ICS assignment, Das retired from the Court on 3 September 1963. In 1964, he served as chairman of the dearness allowance inquiry commission for central government employees.[30] In 1965, he chaired the inquiry into the Dhori colliery disaster. He spent some three years as the arbitrator in a dispute between the government of India and the Jessop Company concerning the value of shares purchased by the government. He also served as a director of the central board of the State Bank of India for about five years and as a member of the executive council of Banaras Hindu University. In 1970, he was offered the vice-chancellorship of that university but declined for health reasons. He began enjoying full

[29] See 'S.K. Das Commences Investigation of Serajuddin Affair', *The Times of India*, 13 May 1963. This was a confidential or private inquiry to establish the facts of the case, not an inquiry conducted under the Commissions of Inquiry Act. Das's conclusions were essentially an advisory opinion for the prime minister.

[30] S.K. Das, *One-Man Independent Body to Enquire into the Question of Dearness Allowance Payable to Central Government Employees, 1964 Report* (Delhi: Ministry of Finance, Manager of Publications, 1965).

retirement in the late 1970s and devoted much of his remaining time to his nearly lifelong involvement with the Brahmo Samaj movement.

Das was the nation's longest living judicial statesman and the last link with the SCI of the 1950s when he died on 22 October 1994 at the age of ninety-six.

16. Parakulangara Govinda Menon (1956–7)

P.G. Menon,[31] born on 10 September 1896 at Parakkulangara, Palghat district, Kerala, was the son of Vaiyannath Kunhunni, a wealthy landowner connected with the Zamorin of Calicut.[32] He received his BA from Presidency College, Madras, in about 1917, and his BL from Madras Law College in about 1919. His eldest brother, B. Narayana Menon, was the first lawyer in the family and retired as a subordinate judge.

On 19 September 1920, P.C. Menon enrolled as an advocate of the Madras High Court, where he would spend the next thirty-six years. Having acquired a reputation for expertise in criminal law, he was appointed crown prosecutor in 1940. He was serving in that capacity when, from April to September 1946, he was in Tokyo serving as the chief Indian prosecutor at the International Tribunal for the Far East, where Japanese accused of war crimes were prosecuted. On 28 July 1947, at age fifty, he became a member of the Madras High Court as an additional judge. Confirmation as a permanent judge followed a few months later.

Well known for his extensive knowledge of Hindu law, he authored the chapters on the Marumakkathayam and Aliyasantana branches in the tenth edition of *Mayne's Treatise on Hindu Law and Usage*.[33] For many years he was the chief examiner and chairman of the board of studies for the ML examinations at Madras Law College.

After nearly a decade on the Madras bench, by which time he was the most senior associate judge and just a few days short of age sixty and mandatory retirement, he was sworn in as an SCI judge on 1 September

[31] Not to be confused with another P. (Panampilli) Govinda Menon, who was Union Law Minister from 1967 to 1968.

[32] Of assistance in providing information about his background was his son, M. Sankaranarayanan, whom I interviewed in Bangalore on 21 June 1983.

[33] S. Srinivasa Iyengar (ed.), *Mayne's Treatise on Hindu Law and Usage* (Madras: Higginbothams, 1938).

1956. Not in good health when he arrived in Delhi—he had suffered from diabetes for many years—he died on 16 October 1957 at age sixty-one after serving for only thirteen months.

17. Jeevan Lal Kapur (1957–62)

J.L. Kapur was born into an affluent family on 13 December 1897 at Chiniot, Jhang district, in what is today Pakistan. His father, L. Bhagwan Das Kapur, was a wealthy landowner and a lawyer who practised at Dera Ismail Khan in the North-West Frontier Province.

He received his higher education both in India and in England. He received a BA in mathematics and physics from Government College, Lahore in 1917, and a second BA (Tripos in mathematics, natural sciences, and law) in 1920 from Magdalene College, Cambridge University. In 1921, he was awarded an LLB from Magdalene College and in 1922 he was called to the bar from the Inner Temple.[34] During his years in England, he was active with various socialist groups.

Returning to India, Kapur enrolled as an advocate of the Lahore High Court on 13 June 1922 and quickly became very active in the Indian National Congress in Lahore. In 1930, he was jailed for participating in the Salt Satyagraha. During the 1930s and 1940s, he frequently defended, free of charge, Congress activists, including Jayaprakash Narayan, who were being prosecuted by the British for political offences. He was also active in the trade union movement and from 1926 to 1947 he was vice-president and president of the Punjab Postman's Union. In 1938, Kapur served as a member of the Bannu Raid Inquiry Commission. Early in his career, he authored a book entitled *Law of Adoption in India and Burma*.[35]

Kapur left Lahore following Partition and shifted his law practice to the new East Punjab High Court located in Simla. In December 1947, he was appointed to the Federal Public Service Commission. After resigning from that post in April 1949, he returned to private practice at Simla. Within a matter of just a few weeks, on 6 June 1949, Kapur, then fifty-one, was appointed to the East Punjab High Court as an additional judge.

[34] Some sources indicate that Kapur received an MA from Cambridge University, but it was a conferred and not an earned degree. Other judges, including M. Hidayatullah, acquired Cambridge MA degrees the same way.

[35] Calcutta: Eastern Law House, 1933.

Confirmation as a permanent judge came on 26 July 1949. A generation later, in 1970, his son, Dalip Kumar Kapur, was appointed to the Delhi High Court and served there until 1986, the last year as chief justice.[36]

After some seven and one-half years on the high court, by which time he was the fifth most senior member of the Punjab bench, Kapur was selected to serve on the SCI. He was fifty-nine when he was sworn in on 14 January 1957 and reached retirement age on 13 December 1962.

Kapur was a man of many commissions. A year before he left the Court he was appointed chairman of the Fourth Law Commission and served two terms, from December 1961 to December 1967. He also chaired two successive Delimitation Commissions, from 1963 to 1966. He served as chairman of the Exodus of Minorities from East Pakistan Commission during this same period. From 1965 to 1969 he headed the inquiry commission which re-examined the murder of Mahatma Gandhi.[37] So for part of this period, he served simultaneously on three different commissions. Finally, from about 1969 to 1970, Kapur served as chairman of the Bharat Sevak Samaj Inquiry Commission.

He continued to be active in the 1970s, conducting arbitrations, and providing free legal advice to war widows and retired soldiers. Active in the Arya Samaj for many years, he served a three-year term as chairman of the D.A.V. College managing committee. He also held the position of president of both the Devan Chand Trust and the Lahore Hospital Society. Near the end of his life, he completed a revision of *Pollock and Mulla on Indian Contract and Specific Relief Acts*.[38] Kapur had never really retired when, at age eighty-four, he died on 14 October 1982.

18. Pralhad Balacharya Gajendragadkar (1957–66)

P.B. Gajendragadkar was born in comfortable economic circumstances on 16 March 1901 at Satara, Satara district in Maharashtra. His family traced its ancestry to court pandits of the Satara Chhatrapatis and, for at least six generations, this orthodox brahmin family had been well

[36] I interviewed Justice D.K. Kapur in New Delhi on 5 July 1983.
[37] *Report of Commission of Inquiry into Conspiracy to Murder Mahatma Gandhi* (New Delhi: Ministry of Home Affairs, 2 vols, 1970).
[38] Tenth edition (Bombay: N.M. Tripathi Pvt. Ltd., 1986), published posthumously in 1986. In 1972, he had edited the ninth edition.

known for producing Sanskrit scholars and educators. His father was Balacharya Gajendragadkar, a Sanskrit scholar–teacher and owner of large landholdings. Gajendragadkar was not quite the first lawyer in his family, for an elder brother, K.B. Gajendragadkar, began practising law at Satara just ahead of him.

After attending Karnataka College in Dharwar for two years, in 1920 he proceeded to Pune where he continued his education at Deccan College. Both his BA (first class honours) in 1922 and his MA (first class) in 1924 were in English and Sanskrit. His LLB was earned at the Indian Law Society's Law College in Pune in 1926. He was named a Dakshina Fellow when he received his BA degree. When he received the MA, he won the Gokuldas Jhala Vedanta Prize for ranking first among those who wrote a paper on the Vedanta in Sanskrit, and was awarded the Bhagwandas Purshottamdas Scholarship for securing the first rank in Sanskrit. His passion for Sanskrit and Hindu law continued throughout his life.

He was twenty-five when he enrolled as an advocate of the Bombay High Court on 25 August 1926. Three months passed before he received his first brief and he gave serious consideration to accepting an offer to become a professor of English at Karnataka College.[39] When briefs started coming, he remained in Bombay and began prospering as a lawyer. Nineteen years later, on 6 March 1945 and at age forty-three, he became an additional judge of the Bombay High Court and was confirmed as a permanent judge on 1 March 1947.[40] After nearly twelve years on the Bombay bench, by which time he was fourth in seniority, Gajendragadkar was invited to join the SCI. He was fifty-five when he was sworn in on 17 January 1957.

During his three decades in Bombay, he participated in a variety of social reform, educational, and cultural activities. Early in his career he taught part-time at the Government Law College and served as editor of the *Hindu*

[39] Much of the material in this biographical essay comes from Gajendragadkar's memoir, *To the Best of My Memory*. Published after his death in 1981, it was completed by his son-in-law, Raghavendra A. Jahagirdar, who was a Bombay High Court judge from 1976 to 1990. Vidya Dhar Mahajan's *Chief Justice Gajendragadkar: His Life, Ideas, Papers and Addresses*, published in 1966 (New Delhi: S. Chand & Co.), contains some biographical information but is largely a praise-filled tribute. Useful biographical information is found in G.L. Chandavarkar, A.N. Kothare, and D.N. Marshall (eds), *Law, Society and Education* (Bombay: Somaiya Publications Pvt. Ltd., 1973), a felicitation volume.

[40] M.C. Chagla claims that it was upon his recommendation to Bombay Chief Justice Sir Leonard Stone that Gajendragadkar was appointed. Chagla, *Roses in December*, p. 134.

Law Quarterly. His proficiency in Sanskrit was evident early when he edited the text of Nanda Pandit's *Dattaka Mimamsa*, which he later translated into English. Well known for his expertise in Hindu law, he lectured often on this topic at various universities. He served for some time as dean of the faculty of law and a member of the syndicate at Bombay University. In 1953 and again in 1954, he was president of the Maharashtra Social Reform Conference. He also served as president or chairman of a number of other organizations, among these the Shikshan Prasarak Mandali and the Indian Law Society, both in Pune, and the Swastik League, the Sameeksha Trust, and the Maharshi Karve Satkar Samiti in Bombay.

Before he arrived in Delhi in 1957 Gajendragadkar had national name recognition because of the attention attracted by the report he made in 1955 when he was chairman of the Bank Award Commission.[41] Usually referred to as the Gajendragadkar Award, it vindicated V.V. Giri, who had resigned earlier as union labour minister in protest against the modification of the Shastri award for bank employees. The Gajendragadkar Award also contributed to his growing reputation of having pronounced pro-labour views.[42]

Gajendragadkar spent just over nine years on the SCI. When he arrived in Delhi, he anticipated replacing S.J. Imam as CJI on 18 April 1965 and holding that post for less than a year. Imam's poor health led to his resignation and Gajendragadkar became the seventh CJI on 1 February 1964. His stewardship lasted just over two years, until he retired on 16 March 1966.

During his SCI tenure, Gajendragadkar was one of its true workhorses. He participated in 993 decisions reported in the official *Supreme Court Reports*, hundreds more than any of his predecessors. Although he was surrounded by colleagues who dissented frequently, Gajendragadkar never once wrote a dissenting opinion.[43] Whereas K. Subba Rao, whose SCI

[41] *Report of the Bank Award Commission, Bombay, July 1955* (Delhi: Manager of Publications, 1955).

[42] Chief Justice S.R. Das, at the farewell dinner in his honour, jocularly said of Gajendragadkar: 'His heart is literally bleeding for the under-dogs, and unless the bleeding can be stopped, the under-dogs will very soon become the top dogs.' 'Speeches Delivered at a Farewell Dinner in Honour of Shri S.R. Das, the Retiring Chief Justice, on September 30, 1959' [1959] *SCR*, pp. vii–xvi, especially p. xvi.

[43] See George H. Gadbois, Jr, 'Indian Judicial Behaviour', *Economic and Political Weekly* (January 1970), pp. 149–66. See also H.M. Seervai, *The Position of the Judiciary under the Constitution of India* (Bombay: University of Bombay, 1968), p. 76. J.C. Shah would later surpass Gajendragadkar's participations in decisions. It will surprise many

tenure coincided with Gajendragadkar's, was the Court's greatest dissenter with forty-three dissenting opinions, Gajendragadkar was the Court's greatest assenter.

Less than a week after his career as a judge ended, another began when he became vice-chancellor of Bombay University, a post he held until 1971.[44] Serving in that capacity allowed ample time for other assignments and, during the same five-year period, he spent considerable time in Delhi and elsewhere as chairman of seven commissions or committees, more than any earlier or subsequent judge. He chaired the Dearness Allowance Commission constituted by the ministry of finance in 1966-7,[45] the National Commission of Labour from 1966 to 1969,[46] the Jammu and Kashmir Commission of Inquiry from 1966 to 1968,[47] and the Banaras Hindu University Inquiry Commission in 1968-9.[48] After leaving the Bombay University vice-chancellorship, he took on his most significant post-retirement activity when Prime Minister Indira Gandhi appointed him as chairman of the Sixth Law Commission of India,[49] and, from 1971 to 1977, served two terms. In 1972, Gajendragadkar chaired the Indian Council of Agricultural Research Institute Inquiry Commission. Earlier he had headed a committee which looked closely at legal education at Delhi University.[50]

There were many other post-retirement assignments. Obviously a man with an extraordinarily high energy level he remained very active in a

---

that V.R. Krishna Iyer, during his seven plus years on the court also never wrote a dissenting opinion, but most of his concurring opinions were thinly disguised dissents. See George H. Gadbois, Jr, 'The Decline of Dissent on the Supreme Court, 1950–1981', in Ram Avtar Sharma (ed.), *Justice and Social Order in India* (New Delhi: Intellectual Publishing House, 1984), pp. 235–59, especially, p. 251.

[44] At about the same time, he was offered the vice-chancellorship of Rajasthan University and Banaras Hindu University. Gajendragadkar, *To the Best of My Memory*, p. 231.

[45] *Report of the Dearness Allowance Commission on the Question of Adequacy of the Dearness Allowance Admissible to the Central Government Employees as from 1st December 1965* (Delhi: Manager of Publications, 1966).

[46] *National Commission of Labour, 1966 Report* (Delhi: Manager of Publications, 1969), 2 vols.

[47] *Report of the Gajendragadkar Commission* (Jammu: Ranbir Government Press, 1969).

[48] *Report of the Banaras Hindu University Inquiry Committee* (New Delhi: Government of India: Ministry of Education and Youth Services, 1969).

[49] Both this chairmanship and the Bombay University vice-chancellorship were honorary, meaning without salary.

[50] *Report of the Commission on the Re-organization of Legal Education in the University of Delhi* (Delhi: 1964).

variety of social reform and educational activities. He was a member of the University Grants Commission in the late 1960s, and was director and later chairman of the Press Trust of India from 1966 to 1970. In 1971, he was appointed a member of the committee of experts on the application of conventions and recommendations of the International Labor Organization in Geneva, serving until 1977. From 1975 to 1979, he was the chancellor of the Gandhigram Rural Institute in Tamil Nadu. At various times he was a member of the senates of Bombay, Delhi, and Banaras Hindu Universities. A member of the Asiatic Society in Bombay from 1933 until his death, he served as its president from 1966 to 1971.

Gajendragadkar's memoirs reveal that he enjoyed his many friendships with those holding high political office, both during and after his years on the SCI. According to Kuldip Nayar, Prime Minister Gandhi considered Gajendragadkar for the presidency of India in 1974, but feared that 'he might turn out to be too legalistic.'[51] His tenure as Law Commission chairman embraced both the 1973 supersession and the entire 1975–7 Emergency. The fact that he did not speak out against these events, including the Forty-Second Amendment which sharply reduced the powers of the SCI, led to some criticism. Gajendragadkar later expressed regret about choosing to remain silent during the Emergency: 'When I left Delhi on retirement as Chairman of the Law Commission I felt very sorry and said that to some extent I had to remain content as a passive observer of things that were happening to the judiciary.'[52]

Gajendragadkar's legacy includes many publications. They include The Hindu Code Bill (Dharwar: Karnatak University, 1951), Law, Liberty, and Social Justice (Bombay: Asia Publishing House, 1965); Jawaharlal Nehru: A Glimpse of the Man and His Teachings (Nagpur: Nagpur University, 1967); The Imperatives of Indian Federalism (Bangalore: Institute of Science, 1968); Kashmir: Retrospect and Prospect (Bombay: Bombay University Press, 1967); The Constitution of India: Its Philosophy and Basic Postulates (Bombay: Oxford University Press, 1969); Research on Gandhian Thought (Bombay: Khadi and Village Industries Commission, 1969); Secularism and the Constitution of India (Bombay: Bombay University Press, 1971); The Indian Parliament and the Fundamental Rights (Calcutta: Eastern Law House, 1972); The Philosophy of National Integration: Its Broad Imperatives (Delhi: National Publishing House, 1974); Indian Democracy: Its Major Imperatives (Bangalore: B.I. Publications,

---

[51] Kuldip Nayar, India After Nehru (Delhi: Vikas Publishing House, 1975), p. 257.
[52] Gajendragadkar, To the Best of My Memory, p. 328.

1975); and *Law, Lawyers, and Social Change* (New Delhi: National Forum of Lawyers and Legal Aid, 1976). He and P.M. Bakshi edited the fourth edition of *B.K. Mukherjea's Hindu Law of Religious and Charitable Trusts* (Calcutta: Eastern Law House, 1979). Upon returning to Bombay in the late 1970s he served as general editor of *The Ten Classical Upanishads* project for the Bharatiya Vidya Bhavan, the first volume of which was published in 1981.

He was awarded the Padma Vibhushan in 1972 and received an honorary LLD from Karnataka University. Gajendragadkar died at age eighty on 12 June 1981.

19. Amal Kumar Sarkar (1957–66)

A.K. Sarkar was born on 29 June 1901[53] at Dhaka, then in the Bengal presidency and today the capital of Bangladesh. His father, Kali Kumar Sarkar, was a civil judge in the district courts. His grandfather, although he held no formal law degree, was a magistrate in Calcutta who dealt with criminal offences. An elder brother was a solicitor at the Calcutta High Court.

He was educated in Calcutta and London. He received his BA degree from Scottish Church College, Calcutta University in 1923, and his LLB from that university's law college in 1927. He enrolled as a vakil of the Calcutta High Court on 22 September 1927, but immediately proceeded to England to earn credentials as a barrister. On 28 January 1929, he was called to the bar from Lincoln's Inn.

Upon returning, Sarkar enrolled as an advocate of the Calcutta High Court on 9 January 1930. At first he worked as a junior[54] in the chambers of S.R. Das who would later, when CJI, initiate Sarkar's appointment to the SCI. After nineteen years at the bar, and at age forty-seven, he was appointed a temporary judge of the Calcutta High Court on 25 January 1949. Confirmation as a permanent judge came on 23 January 1950.

After eight years on the Calcutta bench, when he was fifty-five years of age and sixth in seniority, he was sworn in as an SCI judge on 4 March 1957. Nine years later, Sarkar became the eighth CJI on 16 March 1966. His tenure was only fourteen weeks and on 29 June he reached retirement age.

[53] Supreme Court and Ministry of Law records list his birth date as 30 June, but the 29th is correct. Interview with Sarkar in Calcutta, on 28 June 1983.

[54] Sarkar had not been, contrary to what some believe, a student of Das's.

A noteworthy feature of Sarkar's years on the Court is that he wrote more separate opinions than any other judge in the Court's history. He wrote a total of sixty-nine—thirty-eight dissenting opinions and thirty-one separate opinions concurring with the outcome.[55]

Shortly after leaving the Court, Sarkar served from 1966 to 1967 as chairman of an inquiry commission which investigated some controversial steel transactions. Following the storming of Parliament in November 1966 by *sannyasis* and others who demanded that the slaughter of cows be banned, Sarkar headed the Committee on Cow Protection which dealt with the question of whether the killing of cows should be prohibited. This committee was terminated before its work was completed. From 1967 to 1968, he headed an inquiry commission which looked into issues concerning the Council of Scientific and Industrial Research. Later, he accepted appointment as a one-man commission of inquiry which examined questions concerning several large industrial companies. This particular investigation lasted several years until its work was terminated by the Janata government when it came to power in 1977. Simultaneous with the work of the latter commission, he was the arbitrator in a dispute between several public sector corporations concerning the supply of coal.

In 1978, he returned to Calcutta and went into complete retirement. One of two bachelors[56] who served on the SCI, he died on 29 December 1993 at age ninety-two.

20. Koka Subba Rao (1958–67)

K. Subba Rao was born at Rajahmundry, East Godavari district, Andhra Pradesh on 15 July 1902 into a prominent and wealthy family. Born into one judicial family, he married into another. Remarkably, the combined families produced three chief justices. Subba Rao's father, K. Subrahmaneswara Rao Naidu, was a leading member of the Rajahmundry bar. His maternal grandfather, M. Venkata Ratnam Naidu, also had been a lawyer at Rajahmundry. Subba Rao's father-in-law, P. Venkataramana Rao, served from 1935 to 1942 as a judge of the Madras High Court and from 1943 to 1948 as chief justice of the Mysore High Court. The latter's son,

---

[55] Gadbois, 'Indian Judicial Behaviour', p. 151. K. Subba Rao, with fifty-seven, ranks second.

[56] The other was A.P. Sen.

Subba Rao's brother-in-law, P.V. Rajamannar, served from 1948 to 1961 as the first Indian chief justice of the Madras High Court.[57]

Subba Rao earned his BA from Government Arts College, Rajahmundry, in 1923 and the BL from Madras Law College in 1925. He enrolled as an advocate of the Madras High Court on 13 December 1926. In 1933, he joined the subordinate judiciary as a *munsif* but resigned after six months and returned to the Madras bar, where he practised in partnership with Rajamannar.[58] During his years at the Madras bar, Subba Rao served as a member of the bar council and as secretary of the advocates' association.

Twenty-two years after entering the law profession, and shortly after his brother-in-law began his long tenure as chief justice at Madras, Subba Rao was appointed a judge of the Madras High Court on 22 March 1948 when he was forty-five years of age. Soon after the state of Andhra came into being in 1953, Subba Rao on 5 July 1954 was sworn in as the first chief justice of the Andhra High Court located at Guntur. While there, he served also as chancellor of Sri Venkateswara University from 1954 to 1955. With the integration of Telengana and Andhra and the formation of the state of Andhra Pradesh, the high courts of Andhra and Hyderabad merged, and the new Andhra Pradesh High Court was located at Hyderabad. Subba Rao became its first chief justice on 1 November 1956.

Fifteen months later he was sworn in as an SCI judge on 31 January 1958, at age fifty-five. After eight and a half years of moving up the seniority ladder, he became the ninth CJI on 30 June 1966.

After nine months as CJI and three months before reaching retirement age, Subba Rao, by nature a rather quiet and soft-spoken man who shunned publicity and had never participated in politics, accepted the invitation of the leader of the opposition in Parliament, Minoo Masani, to become the United Opposition's candidate for the presidency of India. He resigned

---

[57] Rajamannar, whose tenure as chief justice at Madras paralleled that of Chagla at Bombay, was offered an SCI judgeship by CJI Sastri in about 1953, but declined the offer because he felt it was more important to look after his aged father. Had Rajamannar accepted the invitation, he would have served as CJI from 1959 to 1966. See Challa Kondaiah, 'Late Dr P.V. Rajamannar', *AIR 1980 Journal*, pp. 3–6. I interviewed Subba Rao in Bangalore on 24 March 1970, and later his widow, Mrs K. Parijatham Subba Rao, on 23 June 1983, also in Bangalore. Some biographical material is found in V.D. Mahajan, *Chief Justice K. Subba Rao: Defender of Liberties* (New Delhi: S. Chand & Co., 1967), pp. 1–26. See also T.V. Subba Rao, *Constitutional Development in India: Contribution of Justice K. Subba Rao* (New Delhi: Deep & Deep Publications, 1992).

[58] One of the juniors Subba Rao drew into his chambers was C.A. Vaidialingam, whom Subba Rao would bring to the SCI when he was CJI.

from the SCI on 11 April 1967, accepted the nomination the next day and overnight became a national figure. This was the first time an SCI judge had resigned to enter the political arena and this action generated a good deal of controversy and criticism, most of it focusing on the propriety of an SCI judge entering politics. The election was the first time there was a real contest for the presidency. Subba Rao was defeated by the Congress Party nominee, Dr Zakir Hussain, but he received 44 per cent of the electoral college vote. In earlier presidential elections, the Congress candidate had never received less than ninety-seven per cent of the vote.

During Subba Rao's nine years on the court, he acquired a reputation as an uncompromising champion of the Constitution's Fundamental Rights, particularly property rights. He wrote forty-two solo dissents,[59] more than any other judge before or since, almost all in support of the private party's claim against various government actions. One can select almost randomly from Subba Rao's judgments and find him describing and defending the Fundamental Rights as 'inviolable', 'transcendental', 'inalienable', 'paramount', and 'sacrosanct'. He was the Court's most outspoken critic of what he perceived as the ravage and pillage of civil liberties and property rights by the government. CJI Das, at the farewell dinner in his honour, speaking humorously but accurately, said Subba Rao '... is extremely unhappy because all our fundamental rights are going to the dogs on account of some ill-conceived judgments of his colleagues which require reconsideration.'[60] Some judgments were indeed reconsidered during Subba Rao's brief tenure as CJI, the landmark *Golaknath*[61] decision, which he must have considered his greatest triumph and most significant legacy, being the best illustration.

After leaving the Court, Subba Rao spent much of his time speaking out and writing, mainly about the Constitution and, predictably, about the

[59] Gadbois, 'Indian Judicial Behaviour', pp. 149–66. Dissenting opinions have never been common on the SCI and since the early 1970s have become increasingly rare. Gadbois, 'The Decline of Dissent on the Supreme Court, 1950–1981', in Ram Avtar Sharma (ed.), *Justice and Social Order in India* (New Delhi: Intellectual Publishing House: 1984), pp. 236–59. Subba Rao neither dissented nor was in the minority as chief. CJIs can avoid being in the minority for they construct the benches.

[60] 'Speeches Delivered at a Farewell Dinner in Honour of Shri S.R. Das, the Retiring Chief Justice, on September 30, 1959' [1959] *SCR*, pp. vii–xvi, especially p. xvi.

[61] I.C. *Golaknath v. State of Punjab* [1967] 2 *SCR*, pp. 762–948. For a perceptive and provocative account of Subba Rao's (and V.R. Krishna Iyer's) contributions to creative judicial thinking on the SCI, see Fali S. Nariman, 'The Judiciary and the Role of the Pathfinders' [1987] 3 *SCC (Journal)*, pp. 1–17. The author interviewed Nariman on 16 July 1983 in New Delhi.

Fundamental Rights, warning of governmental interference in the economy and infringements upon civil liberties. Unlike most of his predecessors, Subba Rao, after retirement, was not asked to serve on any commissions of inquiry, nor was he offered other government appointed posts. When the 1973 supersession of J.M. Shelat, K.S. Hegde, and A.N. Grover occurred, Subba Rao was among three former CJIs who spoke out at a public meeting in Bombay in criticism.[62] After the Emergency was declared by Mrs Gandhi in 1975 it was no surprise that Subba Rao turned his energies towards attacking that event.[63]

Among the many publications of Subba Rao are *Fundamental Rights under the Indian Constitution* (Madras: University of Madras, 1966); *Property Rights under the Constitution* (Bombay: Forum for Free Enterprise, 1968); *The Philosophy of the Indian Constitution* (Bangalore: Advocates Association, 1969); *Conflicts in Indian Polity* (Delhi: S. Chand & Co., 1970); *The Indian Federation* (Poona: University of Poona, 1970); *Some Constitutional Problems* (Bombay: University of Bombay, 1970); *Man and Society* (Bangalore: Bangalore University, 1971); *The Indian Federal System* (Madras: Institute for Techno-Economic Studies, 1972); *Social Justice and Law* (New Delhi: National Publishing House, 1974); and *Caste and Creed under the Indian Constitution* (Bombay: Bharatiya Vidya Bhavan, n.d.).

Osmania University in 1968 and Bangalore University in 1972 honoured Subba Rao by conferring upon him the LLD (*honoris causa*). One of Subba Rao's last activities, during 1975 and 1976, was serving as chairman of a committee appointed by Bangalore University to recommend improvements in the University Law College degree courses.

On 6 May 1976, during the middle of the Emergency, he died at age seventy-three.

21. Kailash Nath Wanchoo (1958–68)

K.N. Wanchoo, a Kashmiri brahmin whose family migrated to Gwalior state about 200 years earlier, was born on 25 February 1903, at Mandsaur,

---

[62] Subba Rao, 'The Supersession of Judges: The Price of Executive Interference', in Palkhivala (ed.), *A Judiciary Made to Measure*, pp. 30–5. The other two were M. Hidayatullah and J.C. Shah.

[63] See, for example, Subba Rao, 'Constitutional Despotism', *Swarajya* (Annual Number 1975), 6, pp. 42–4, 47–8.

Mandsaur district, Madhya Pradesh. His family enjoyed high social status but was of modest means. His father, Pandit Pirthi Nath Wanchoo, started in government service as a clerk and retired as the superintendent agent of the governor-general's office in Lahore. There were no lawyers in his family history and Wanchoo was the first to become a judge.

After receiving his BA from Muir Central College, Allahabad in 1923, he passed into the ICS by examination in India.[64] He then proceeded to England for the two years of ICS training, and there attended Oxford University's Wadham College. He received no formal legal education beyond the mainly criminal law portions of the ICS training programme.

Returning to India at age twenty-three, his career began on 22 October 1926 when he was assigned to the then United Provinces, his first posting being as an assistant magistrate and collector. In October 1930, he was appointed officiating sessions and civil judge and in October 1933, he was promoted to officiating district and sessions judge. In September 1937, he was confirmed as a district and sessions judge and served as such in several United Provinces districts.

On 17 February 1947, at age forty-three, he became an acting judge of the Allahabad High Court, filling in for another ICS judge who was on leave. This appointment was continuous, and Wanchoo was confirmed as a permanent judge on 12 December 1947. After four years on the Allahabad bench, Wanchoo's twenty-five years of service in Uttar Pradesh ended when he agreed to be transferred to become chief justice of the then Part B High Court of Rajasthan, effective 2 January 1951. After the reorganization of the states, he was reappointed as chief justice of the new Rajasthan High Court on 1 November 1956.

During the course of his eleven-year career as a high court judge, Wanchoo served on several commissions and committees. From 1950 to 1951, he served as chairman of the United Provinces judicial reforms committee.[65] In January 1953, the Nehru government which had bowed to the Telengana agitation and announced that steps were being taken to form a separate state of Andhra carved out of the state of Madras, called upon Wanchoo to head the commission to investigate and make recommendations concerning the administrative and financial implications of the new state,

---

[64] A brother, Niranjan Nath Wanchoo, was also an ICS officer. The author interviewed Wanchoo on 24 May 1983 in New Delhi.

[65] *Report of the Uttar Pradesh Judicial Reforms Committee, 1950–1951* (Allahabad: Superintendent of Printing and Stationary, 1952).

and to suggest steps to implement safeguards for the Telengana region. This very difficult assignment revealed the confidence Nehru had in Wanchoo, but was considered by some an unusual assignment for a high court judge and resulted in some controversy in legal circles over the propriety of judges being called upon to perform tasks having little to do with their judicial backgrounds.[66] In 1954, Wanchoo was the sole member of the Indore Firing Inquiry Commission which investigated the police firing upon students in Indore.[67] In early 1955, he was named chairman of the Dholpur Succession Case Commission. In September 1955, his high stature in the community of judges was confirmed when he was selected as one of the two high court judges[68] appointed to the first post-Independence Law Commission, chaired by M.C. Setalvad, the work of which culminated in the comprehensive and landmark *Fourteenth Report*.[69]

After completion of that assignment in 1958 Wanchoo was promoted to the SCI. He was sworn in on 11 August 1958 when he was fifty-five. Nearly nine years after he arrived in Delhi he was in line to become CJI in July 1967 when Subba Rao was to reach retirement age. When the latter unexpectedly resigned on 11 April, Wanchoo was named acting chief justice the same day. On 24 April, he was sworn in as India's tenth CJI. Wanchoo has the distinction of being the only ICS officer and the only non-lawyer to hold the highest judicial office in the land. Although Subba Rao's resignation served to increase Wanchoo's expected tenure as CJI he held the post for only ten months and retired on 25 February 1968. During his decade on the SCI he participated in 1,006 reported decisions, more than any of his predecessors.

Shortly after leaving the Court, he was appointed by the ministry of railways to serve as chairman of the Railway Accidents Inquiry Committee, a post he held from 3 April 1968 to 31 August 1969.[70] Also in 1968, he was appointed chairman of the board of arbitration of the labour ministry

[66] *Calcutta Weekly Notes*, LVII (1953), p. 43. The results of this commission are found in *Inquiry into Financial and Other Implications Relating to the Creation of the New Andhra State, 1952: Report* (New Delhi: Ministry of Home Affairs, 1953).

[67] *Report on the Indore Firing Incidents* (Indore, 1954).

[68] The other was Bombay High Court Chief Justice M.C. Chagla.

[69] *Reform of Judicial Administration*, 2 vols (New Delhi: Ministry of Law, Government of India, 1958). According to CJI Pathak, who delivered the full court reference following Wanchoo's death, Home Minister G.B. Pant considered Wanchoo for the chairmanship of this commission before M.C. Setalvad was chosen.

[70] *Report of the Railway Accidents Inquiry Committee*, 2 vols (New Delhi: Ministry of Railways, 1970).

and held that post until 1975. In 1970, he returned to Andhra Pradesh as chairman of a committee dealing with difficult issues, particularly the matter of providing safeguards for the Telengana people in the matter of public employment, which had precipitated widespread agitation in the Telengana region of Andhra Pradesh. In 1970-1, he was chairman of the Direct Taxes Inquiry Committee, better known as the Black Money Inquiry Commission, which looked into the problem of tax evasion, hidden currency, and other forms of undisclosed assets.[71] In 1974-5, he was the sole member of the commission of inquiry which looked into corruption charges made against some West Bengal government ministers. In the mid-1980s, when he was in his eighties, he was still active, serving as the sole arbitrator in a dispute between the Indian Oil Corporation and the Thakur Shipping Company, a task he had begun in 1974.

In 1967, Wanchoo was awarded the LLD (*honoris causa*) from Agra University. After over sixty years of distinguished service to his nation, he was eighty-five when he died on 14 August 1988.

22. Mohammed Hidayatullah (1958–70)

M. Hidayatullah, one of the only two judges whose tenure on the SCI spanned three decades,[72] was born on 17 December 1905 in the town of Betul, Betul district, Madhya Pradesh. His was a prominent, modern, cultured, upper class, and financially comfortable Muslim family. His father, Khan Bahadur Hafiz Mohammed Wilayatullah, a widely respected Urdu poet, was in provincial government service. After retiring as a deputy commissioner and district magistrate, Wilayatullah turned to politics and won the provincial Muslim seat in the central legislative assembly. Hidayatullah's grandfather, Moonshi Kudrutallah, though without formal training in law, was a pleader who practised in Varanasi, and who later moved the family to Bhopal. Hidayatullah's family roots were in Madhya Pradesh but he spent many of his early years in Nagpur after his father was posted there. The family had a strong literary tradition to which Hidayatullah added in large measure.

[71] *Direct Taxes Inquiry Committee: Final Report* (New Delhi: Ministry of Finance, 1972).
[72] J.C. Shah was the other one. I interviewed Hidayatullah on 3 and 17 June 1983 in New Delhi and on 4 November 1988 in Bombay.

He received his BA degree in English, history, and Persian from Morris College, Nagpur in 1926, where he held the Phillips Scholarship and won the Malak Gold Medal. He went to Cambridge with plans to become either a physician or a professor of English but his father persuaded him to study law. In 1930, he received another BA (honours) from Trinity College,[73] where he opted for the Tripos in English, English literature, and law. Also in 1930, he was called to the bar from Lincoln's Inn. In 1929, he served as president of the Indian Majlis, an interdenominational organization of Indians.

Upon his return from England, Hidayatullah, on 19 July 1930, enrolled as an advocate and began his law practice at what was then the Nagpur judicial commissioner's court of the Central Provinces and Berar, which would become the Nagpur High Court in 1936. Recognition of his abilities came quickly. When only thirty-six, he was appointed government pleader on 12 December 1942. On 2 August 1943, he was appointed advocate general, the youngest in the country, and served in that capacity until he became a judge in 1946. During these same three years, he was a member of the Nagpur bar council and served as chairman of the school code committee and the court fee revision committee. From 1932 to 1935, and again from 1943 to 1946, he was a member of the Nagpur municipal corporation. From 1943 to 1945, he was a member of the Nagpur improvement trust. He taught jurisprudence and Mohammedan law and was an extension lecturer in English literature at Nagpur University from 1934 to 1943, and from 1951 to 1955 was dean of the University's College of Law. From 1934 to 1943, he was a member of the University's executive and academic councils. He was also a member of the law faculties of Aligarh, Saugar, and Vikram Universities during the 1954-8 years. He was very active with the Madhya Pradesh Bharat Scouts and Guides, serving as chief commissioner

[73] Hidayatullah's two brothers also graduated from Trinity College. His eldest brother, M. Ikramullah, served in the ICS and, following Partition, went to Pakistan where he rose to the post of foreign secretary. His other brother, Ahmadullah, served as secretary of the Indian Tariff Board. A great deal of information about Hidayatullah's family is found in his memoirs, My Own Boswell (New Delhi: Arnold-Heinemann Publishers, 1980). Other sources I have used include official and other versions of his biographical data, particularly Bio-Data of Mr Hidayatullah (c. 1988, cyclostyled), and full court references in his memory, delivered by CJI M.H. Kania [1992] Supp.1 SCR, pp. iv-xiv), and Bombay High Court Chief Justice P.D. Desai [1992] 4 SCC (Journal), pp. 10-12.

from 1950 to 1953 and vice-president of the national council of the Bharat Scouts and Guides from 1950 to 1952.

At age forty and on 24 June 1946, he was appointed an acting judge of the Nagpur High Court. This appointment was continuous and he was made a permanent judge on 13 September 1946. Some eight years later, on 3 December 1954, he became chief justice at age forty-eight, the youngest high court chief justice in the country. Following the reorganization of the states, the Nagpur High Court became a bench of the Bombay High Court, and Hidayatullah, on 1 November 1956, became chief justice of the newly established Madhya Pradesh High Court at Jabalpur.

On 1 December 1958, he was sworn in as an SCI judge. At age fifty-two, he was the youngest appointed up to that time and the third youngest ever.[74] If merit was the primary criterion, it was not a question of would he be appointed, but when.

In his tenth year on the Court, amid speculation that he might be superseded,[75] and upon the retirement of Wanchoo, Hidayatullah became the nation's eleventh CJI on 25 February 1968. His tenure as chief spanned nearly three years. From 20 July to 24 August 1969, following the death of President Zakir Hussain and the resignation of acting president V.V. Giri, he served as acting president.[76]

Hidayatullah reached retirement age on 17 December 1970, just a day after he wrote the majority opinion in the controversial *Privy Purses*[77] decision, which rejected a presidential order abolishing the titles, privileges, and privy purses of the former princes. A few days later, Mrs Gandhi dissolved Parliament and called the first mid-term elections in the nation's history. He had spent almost a quarter century as a high court and SCI judge, longer than any other SCI judge up to that time.

After leaving the Court, he moved to Bombay, where his son and his wife's family resided, and remained there until 1979. His financial situation

[74] P.N. Bhagwati was fifty-one when he reached the Supreme Court. Both Hidayatullah and Y.V. Chandrachud were fifty-two, but the latter was slightly younger.

[75] Hidayatullah, *My Own Boswell*, p. 217.

[76] As acting president, it fell to Hidayatullah to assent to the Bank Nationalization Act. Because of his involvement in that legislation, he recused when its constitutional validity was decided by the SCI in 1970.

[77] *Madhav Rao Scindia v. Union of India* [1971] 3 SCR 9. On p. 266 of his memoirs he implies that this decision may also have cost him Mrs Gandhi's government's endorsement for a seat on the World Court which, in 1972, went to Dr Nagendra Singh.

precarious after his years as a judge, he engaged in chamber practice, providing legal advice for a fee.[78] His clients included domestic parties, foreign interests, and state governments. He also conducted a number of arbitrations.

Unlike most judges who had retired earlier, Hidayatullah served on no commissions of inquiry after leaving the Court, nor did he hold any other government appointed positions. No assignments of this nature were offered to him by Mrs Gandhi's government. His reputation as a judge willing to stand up to the government probably resulted in his name being placed near the bottom of the list of retired judges who might be called upon for commission or otherwise official assignments. His strong criticism[79] of the 1973 supersession added to his reputation as a critic of Mrs Gandhi's government.

After the Janata government came to power in 1977, he was offered about half a dozen different commission assignments, including the Law Commission and the Maruti Commission, but he turned down all of them. Not once in his career did he serve on a commission of inquiry. It was his view that the regular courts should deal with most issues taken up by commissions of inquiry.

He wrote that 'Three times after I retired as Chief Justice of India I declined to run [for President of India] even at the instance of Mr Jaya Prakash Narain, Mrs Gandhi, and the entire opposition. This was when Fakhruddin Ali Ahmed, Sanjiva Reddy, and Giani Zail Singh were elected.'[80] He did agree to become vice-president in 1979, after the collapse of the Janata government and the dissolution of the Lok Sabha preceding fresh national elections. He was elected unopposed and unanimously for the five-year term beginning on 31 August 1979. From 6 October to 31 October 1982, when President Zail Singh went to the United States for heart surgery, he again served as acting president. When his term ended on 30 August 1984, he returned to Bombay. Although most vice-presidents had moved up to the presidency, Mrs Gandhi had returned as prime minister and he

---

[78] Such work has been criticized as inappropriate for retired judges, but since 1970 has become increasingly common.

[79] 'Unjustified Departure from Settled Convention', in Palkhivala (ed.), A Judiciary Made to Measure, pp. 9–15.

[80] 'Some Reflections and Recollections', a speech delivered at Nagpur on the occasion of the celebration of the 125th anniversary of the High Court of Bombay on 28 September 1987. Offprint from an unidentified journal, pp. 73–9, especially p. 78.

was not nominated. No other citizen of India has served as CJI, presiding officer of the upper house of Parliament, and acting president of the nation.

During his retirement years, Hidayatullah continued to write and pursue his passion for literary matters. Before leaving the Court, he had written *Democracy in India and the Judicial Process* (New York and Bombay: Asia Publishing House, 1966); *The South-West Africa Case* (New York, Bombay and London: Asia Publishing House, 1967); *Mulla's Principles of Mahomedan Law*, 16th edition, co-edited with R.K.P. Shankardas (Bombay: N.M. Tripathi Pvt. Ltd., 1968); the 17th edition in 1972, and, co-edited with his son Arshad, the 18th edition in 1985 and 19th edition in 1990, *Judicial Methods* (New Delhi: National Publishing House, 1970); *Parliamentary Privileges, the Press and the Judiciary* (Bombay: Asia Publishing House, 1969); *A Critical Study of Ahmad Raza's Urdu Poetry* (Madinah, Saudi Arabia: Al Madinah Printing & Publishing Company, in Urdu, 1976); *U.S.A. and India* (Nagpur: All India Reporter, 1977); *Fifth and Sixth Schedules to the Constitution* (Gauhati: Ashok Publishing House, 1979); *My Own Boswell: Memoirs of M. Hidayatullah* (New Delhi: Arnold-Heinemann, 1980); *Right to Property and the Indian Constitution* (Calcutta: Calcutta University, and New Delhi: Arnold-Heinemann, 1983); and *Taqrir-o-Tahir*, (in Urdu, 1983).

He was editor-in-chief of *Constitutional Law of India* (New Delhi: Bar Council of India Trust and Arnold-Heinemann)—vol. I was published in 1982 and vol. II in 1986. He edited, with V.R. Manohar, the 17th and 18th editions of *Ratanlal and Dhirajlal's Law of Evidence* (Nagpur: Wadhwa and Company, 1987 and 1992). He was the editor, with R. Deb, of *Ratanjlal & Dhirajlal's Indian Penal Code*, 26th edition (Nagpur: Wadhwa and Company, 1987, and 27th edition, 1990). He was the editor with S.P. Sathe of *Ratanjlal and Dhirajlal's Code of Criminal Procedure*, 13th edition (Nagpur: Wadhwa and Company, 1987) and 14th edition in 1992; and, with Y.R. Rao, *Soonavala's The Supreme Court on Code of Criminal Procedure, 1950–1990: Being an Analysis of the Decisions of the Supreme Court during the Last Four Decades*, 3rd edition (Nagpur: Wadhwa and Company, 1991); and editor with V.R. Manohar and Avtar Singh of *Ratanlal and Dhirajlal's The Indian Penal Code*, 28th edition (Nagpur: Wadhwa and Company, 1991).

He also published five collections of speeches, memorial lectures, biographical sketches, convocation addresses, literary, education, arts, and literature pieces. The first four were entitled *A Judge's Miscellany* (Bombay: N.M. Tripathi Pvt. Ltd., 1972), Second Series (Bombay: N.M. Tripathi Pvt. Ltd., 1979), Third Series (New Delhi: Arnold-Heinemann, 1982), and

Fourth Series (Bombay: N.M. Tripathi, Pvt. Ltd., 1984). The final one was *Miscellanea: The Pick of the Four Judge's Miscellanies and Later Writings* (Bombay: N.M. Tripathi Pvt. Ltd., 1988).

Over the years, Hidayatullah held many offices, was a member of many organizations in a wide range of fields, and was the recipient of many honours. After retirement, he resumed devoting time to important positions in higher education. He served as chancellor of Delhi and Punjab Universities from 1979 to 1984, of Jamia Millia Islamia from 1969 to 1985, and Hyderabad University from 1986 to 1990.

He served as president of the following: International Law Association (India Branch) from 1968 to 1970; the Indian Law Institute (ILI) from 1968 to 1970;[81] the Inns of Court Society from 1968; the Indian Society of International Law from 1969 to 1970; the Indian Red Cross Society from 1982 to 1984; the Bombay Natural History Society, the Honour of the Inns of Court Society (India); and the Commonwealth Society of India.

He was the chairman, member, or was otherwise associated with the following: the International Institute of Space Law (Paris) beginning in 1966; of the International Council of Former Scouts and Guides (Brussels) from 1966; the executive council of the World Assembly of Judges from 1967; the British International and Comparative Law Association from 1982; the Legal Education Committee of the Bar Council of India; the Independent Commission on International Humanitarian Issues from 1982 to 1984; the World Association of Orphans & Abandoned Children (Geneva); the Hunger Project of the U.S.A. (India Chapter); and the India Islamic Cultural Center (New Delhi).

Other activities in a wide range of fields to which he gave his time, energy, and leadership skills included being chief scout of the Boy Scouts Association of India, advisor to the Council for World Peace Through Law, associate member of the Royal Academy of Morocco, vice-president of the Heritage Fund of Lincoln's Inn, patron of the fund appeal for Fitzwilliam

---

[81] As president of the ILI, Hidayatullah headed the editorial committee of the *Journal of the Indian Law Institute*. Upendra Baxi was joint editor and was required to present the contents of each quarterly issue to the committee. Baxi affectionately recalled that 'He was very prompt; within a week the material of about three hundred pages came back, with scribbles on the margin, and encirclings of grammatical/syntax errors. I was astonished that a Chief Justice of India had the time and patience to participate in copy-editing of a learned journal!' 'Remembering Justice Hidayatullah' [1993] 1 SCC (*Journal*), pp. 13–15, especially p. 14.

College (Cambridge University), patron-in-chief of the Schizophrenic Research Foundation (India), patron of the Commonwealth Society of India, patron of Former Scouts and Guides in India, and settler of the Jawaharlal Nehru Cambridge University Trust from 1983.

He was the recipient of many honours and awards, including the Order of the British Empire in 1946; Boy Scouts Silver Elephant award (the highest Scouts and Guides award); the War Service Badge in 1948; Honorary Bencher of Lincoln's Inn in 1968; Bronze Medal for Gallantry in 1969;[82] Medallion and Plaque of Merit Philconsa (Manila) in 1970; Knight of Mark Twain (USA) in 1971; Order of the Yugoslav Flag with Sash in 1971; Shiromani award in 1986; Architects of India award in 1987; the Dashrathmal Singhvi Memorial award from Banaras Hindu University; and honorary membership of Bharatiya Vidya Bhavan in 1991.

He received more than a dozen honorary degrees—LLDs from the University of the Philippines in 1970; Ravishankar University in 1970; Rajasthan University in 1975; Banaras Hindu University in 1980; Kashmir University in 1983; Berhampore University in 1983; Punjab University in 1985; Nagpur University in 1985; and Agra University in 1987. Honorary DLitt degrees were bestowed on him by both Kakatiya University and Bhopal University in 1982. Delhi University awarded him an honorary DCL in 1984. After his death, the M. Hidayatullah National Law University was established at Raipur, in Chhattisgarh.

Sajid Zaheer Amani's *Justice Hidayatullah on Commercial Laws* was published in 1982 (Delhi: Deep & Deep Publications Pvt. Ltd., 1982). Abdul Hamid's two volume *Constitutional Law: A Profile of Justice M. Hidayatullah* was published in 1992 (Jaipur: Printwell and Rupa Books).

Hidayatullah lived a truly rich and fulfilling life. A cultured and scholarly man, he had a lifelong love for learning and was knowledgeable in such diverse fields as philosophy, poetry, literature, politics, art, history, and law. He had a particular love for literature and language, and was at home with Sanskrit, Urdu, Persian, Bengali, French, Latin, Hindi, and, of course, the King's English. He was a gentleman of high culture, an embodiment of old world style, and had a dignified bearing. But he was an unpretentious person with a wide circle of friends and acquaintances, each of whom, it seemed, he

---

[82] This was a Bharat Scouts and Guides Association award, and was presented to Hidayatullah by President Zakir Hussain for overpowering an assailant who had entered the courtroom and attacked and wounded Justice A.N. Grover with a knife. Hidayatullah, *My Own Boswell*, pp. 217–23.

could find time to meet even on short notice. He was as comfortable with children as with heads of state and he was in possession of a charming sense of humour, often poking fun at himself. A very cosmopolitan figure who represented India with great distinction at functions in at least two dozen countries, he was at the same time truly Indian in culture. He was a genuine secularist, a respecter of all religions, a product of India's composite culture. Hidayatullah married a Hindu, Pushpa Shah, and theirs was one of the most widely admired Hindu–Muslim marriages. He was an extraordinarily active man with an enormous capacity for work and other activities. When in his mid-seventies and serving as vice-president, he found time to play golf virtually every morning at 6:30.

Active literally until the end, just three days before his death, as chairman of the advisory council of the Jamanlal Bajaj Foundation, he handed out its annual awards for social work.[83] After his death on 18 September 1992 at age eighty-six, the then CJI, M.H. Kania, put it well when he said, 'He was perhaps the last of the great generation of Judges who were held in awe and respect combined with affection by the entire Bar.'[84]

23. Kulada Charan Das Gupta (1959–65)

K.C. Das Gupta was born into a middle-class family on 3 January 1900 at Kalia village in today's Bangladesh. He was the son of Annada Charan Das Gupta, who was in government service.[85]

He received a BA (honours) degree from Presidency College, Calcutta, in 1920 where he earned a first class first in economics. He then proceeded to Cambridge University's Magdalene College where he received a double first in the economics tripos while earning another BA degree in 1923. Although Cambridge did not formally rank candidates within the first class, Das Gupta was regarded as the top student of his class. An MA followed in 1924. Years later, he took leave from his post as a district and sessions judge, returned to England, and was called to the bar from Gray's Inn in 1938. He was the first lawyer in his family and was probably also the first university graduate.

[83] 'He lived a full life until the end', *The Times of India*, 20 September 1992.

[84] 'Full Court Reference in Memory of the Late Chief Justice M. Hidayatullah' [1992] *Supp*. 1 SCR, pp. iv–xiv, especially p. vii.

[85] Das Gupta was too ill to meet with me in 1983. His son, A.K. Dasgupta, was helpful in providing biographical information. Correspondence dated 19 March 1984.

After passing the ICS examinations in England, his career began on 25 October 1923. Unlike the most ICS officers who preferred serving on the executive side, he opted for a judicial career. He began as an assistant magistrate and collector and subdivisional officer in the province of Bengal. In July 1925, he was promoted to joint magistrate and deputy collector. In 1929, he was promoted to officiating district and sessions judge. He became an additional district and sessions judge in October 1932 and was confirmed as a district and sessions judge in December 1934. After serving for eight years in this capacity in several districts, in 1942 he was promoted to the post of registrar of the appellate side on the Calcutta High Court, becoming the first Indian to hold that post.

Although there was resistance from the legal community which considered ICS officers as civil servants,[86] Das Gupta was appointed an acting judge of the Calcutta High Court on 13 May 1948, at age forty-eight. This appointment was continuous and he was confirmed as a permanent judge on 11 February 1949. A decade later, advancing seniority brought him to the top, and he was fifty-eight when he became chief justice on 12 October 1958. This marked the first time an ICS judge was not passed over for the Calcutta High Court chief justiceship.

Das Gupta's tenure as Calcutta chief was brief for he accepted appointment to the SCI less than a year later. When he was sworn in on 24 August 1959, he was fifty-nine. His expertise in the field of economics was well known, but his colleagues found that he was equally at home quoting both Greek philosophers and Sanskrit literature.

He retired on 3 January 1965. A day before he left the SCI, he was named chairman of the Commission to Inquire into Monopolies and Concentration of Wealth, a task he completed later that year.[87] He was offered other posts and commission assignments but his wife died shortly after he left the Court and he returned to Calcutta and accepted no other work.

Das Gupta died on 14 February 1987, at age eighty-seven.

---

[86] When Das Gupta was appointed, the *Calcutta Weekly Notes* wrote that 'As our readers are very well aware, we are opposed on principle to the appointment of civil servants to High Court judgeship. We are very firmly of opinion that High Court Judges should, except in the most unusual instances, be appointed from among practising members of the Bar'. Quoted by Attorney General K. Parasaran in [1987] 2 *SCR*, pp. iv–x, especially p. vi.

[87] *Report of the Monopolies Inquiry Commission, 1964–1965*, 2 vols (Delhi: Manager of Publications, 1965).

24. Jayantilal Chhotalal Shah (1959–71)

J.C. Shah was born into a middle-class family on 22 January 1906 at Ahmedabad, Ahmedabad district, Gujarat. His father was Chhotalal A. Shah, who spent his life in service to the former princely state of Danta in Gujarat, retiring as the Dewan.[88]

Shah began his higher education at Gujarat College in Ahmedabad in 1922, and then transferred to Elphinstone College, Bombay, where he earned the BA (honours) degree in mathematics in 1926. He commenced his legal education at the Government Law College, Bombay but transferred to the Sri Lallubhai Shah Law College in his home town after it was founded in 1927, and received the LLB in 1928. He was both the first graduate and first lawyer in his family.

On 28 September 1928, at age twenty-two, he enrolled as an advocate of the Bombay High Court but spent his first five years of law practice at the Ahmedabad district court before settling in Bombay in 1933. His stature at the bar was underlined in 1948 when he was appointed special public prosecutor, assisting C.K. Daphtary, the Advocate-General of Bombay, in the Mahatma Gandhi murder trial at Red Fort in Delhi.

Shortly after the completion of that trial, Shah, on 1 March 1949 and at age forty-three, became a judge of the Bombay High Court. His appointment was initiated by chief justice M.C. Chagla. Shah had been a student of his in the 1920s.[89] While serving on the high court, the union government in 1958 appointed him chairman of the Kerala and Madras Food Poisoning Cases Inquiry Commission.[90]

After just over a decade on the Bombay bench by which time he was the seniormost associate judge,[91] Shah was selected for the SCI. When he was sworn in on 12 October 1959, he was only fifty-three years of age, among

[88] Interviews with Shah in Bombay on 2 April 1983 and 3 November 1988. An interview with Shah is found in Harish Bhanot, 'I have been looking for grain in mounds of chaff', The Overseas Hindustan Times, 1 November 1986, p. 9.

[89] M.C. Chagla, Roses in December, pp. 166, 340.

[90] Report of the Kerala and Madras Food Poisoning Cases Enquiry Commission (New Delhi: Government of India, Ministry of Health, 1958).

[91] As Chagla was leaving the Bombay chief justiceship in 1958, he recommended to Chief Minister Y.B. Chavan that Shah replace him as chief justice. But an ICS judge, H.K. Chainani, was then the next in line and there had never been a service judge as chief justice. Chavan felt that passing over Chainani might offend the Sindhi community, and Chainani became chief justice. Chagla, Roses in December, pp. 169–70.

the half a dozen youngest ever appointed to the SCI. Had he not gone to the SCI, he likely would have become the first chief justice of Gujarat High Court when it was established in 1960.

While serving on the SCI in 1966, Shah was made chairman of the Punjab Boundary Commission, the report of which contributed to the birth of the state of Haryana and the designation of Chandigarh as a union territory. In 1969, he was appointed Chairman of the High Court Arrears Committee. From 20 July to 24 August 1969, when Hidayatullah was acting president of India, Shah served as acting CJI.[92]

On 17 December 1970 following Hidayatullah's retirement, Shah became the twelfth CJI. Because he was on the threshold of mandatory retirement, his tenure was only thirty-five days.[93] His last day in Court was 21 January 1971.

When Shah retired, incoming CJI S.M. Sikri made the observation that Shah had 'outworked every other Judge'.[94] That compliment is factually accurate for no other judge, before or after, participated in more reported cases or wrote as many opinions. During his eleven years on the SCI, Shah participated in 1,520 decisions reported in the *Supreme Court Reports*. A distant second was Wanchoo with 1,006. Shah wrote in excess of 600 judgments, far more than any other judge. He usually had his opinions completed a few hours after the hearings. Indeed, no one deserves the 'workhorse' or 'iron man' label more than Shah. His passion in life was the

---

[92] In 1970, Shah was the subject if an impeachment proceeding, the first and only one directed at an SCI judge until the 1990s. A dismissed public servant, O.P. Gupta, published a pamphlet attacking Shah, accusing him of dishonesty because of comments he had allegedly made about him during oral argument in a 1969 case. Gupta had political friends, and S.M. Joshi, a Samyukta Socialist Party member of Parliament (MP), introduced an impeachment motion which alleged that Shah was biased against Gupta. The motion was signed by nearly 200 MPs representing most political parties. CJI Hidayatullah intervened and convinced Lok Sabha Speaker G.S. Dhillon that the matter was entirely frivolous. Many of those who had signed the motion withdrew their signatures, Dhillon disallowed the motion and the matter ended. Materials relating to this incident are found in the Shah file in the offices of *The Times of India*, New Delhi. Hidayatullah discusses this incident in *My Own Boswell*, p. 263, as does N.A. Palkhivala in 'The Supreme Court Judgment in the Judges' Case', *Journal of the Bar Council of India*: 'Special Number on Higher Judiciary', vol. IX (2), 1982. Gupta was later sentenced to imprisonment for contempt in *C.K. Daphtary v. O.P. Gupta* [1971] *Supp. SCR*, p. 76.

[93] Only K.N. Singh's eighteen-day tenure in 1991 was shorter.

[94] *The Times of India*, 21 January 1971. See also Palkhivala's tribute to Shah, 'Chief Justice J.C. Shah', in *We the People: India: The Largest Democracy* (Bombay: Strand Book Stall, 1984), pp. 292–5.

law. During his long career as a high court and SCI judge, he had few other interests and remained aloof from educational, cultural, social, and other off-the-bench activities.

After retiring, he returned to Bombay and continued his work on the High Court Arrears Committee which meant visiting every high court. He completed that report in 1972.[95] In 1972, his *The Rule of Law and the Indian Constitution* (Bombay: N.M. Tripathi, Pvt. Ltd., 1972) was published. In 1975, he was appointed to the board of *The Statesman* and became its chairman in 1977. His primary activity was chamber practice, mainly in the areas of company and taxation law, which kept him busy until nearly the end of his life. In 1973, Shah was among the few retired SCI judges who spoke out against the government after the supersession, terming that action 'a remarkable piece of political skullduggery'.[96] Two years later he spoke out in criticism of the Emergency at a meeting sponsored by the Citizens for Democracy.[97]

After his work on the High Court Arrears Committee was completed, it was not unexpected that he was not offered any other official assignments through the remainder of Mrs Gandhi's first regime. But, in late 1977, after the coming to power of the Janata coalition, he accepted the chairmanship of the most important and most delicate post-Emergency commission, known by all as the Shah Commission, the task of which was to determine the extent to which Mrs Gandhi and her aides had abused authority and power during the 1975–7 Emergency. This commission's hearings attracted not just national attention but international as well. The three volumes *Report of the Shah Commission of Inquiry*[98] was completed the following year. Shah is probably better known for this report than for his twenty-two year career as an SCI and high court judge. This report was never acted upon and copies were withdrawn from circulation after Mrs Gandhi returned to power in 1980.

---

[95] *Report on Arrears in High Courts* (New Delhi: Controller of Publications, 1972).

[96] 'Improper Exercise of Executive Power', in Palkhivala (ed.), *A Judiciary Made to Measure*, pp. 16–19, especially p. 16.

[97] Chagla, *Roses in December*, pp. 494, 496, and Kuldip Nayar, *The Judgement: Inside Story of the Emergency in India* (New Delhi: Vikas Publishing House, 1977), p. 94.

[98] The full citation is *Shah Commission of Inquiry, Interim Report I, Interim Report II, and Third and Final Report* (Delhi: Controller of Publications, 1978). Published separately was *Memorandum of Action taken on the First and Second Reports of the Commission of Enquiry Headed by Justice J.C. Shah* (New Delhi: Controller of Publications, 1978).

In 1980, Shah inaugurated the National Convention of Lawyers for Democracy, a group composed of prominent lawyers who protested the Gandhi government's proposal to change to a presidential system and reduce the powers of the judiciary. In 1981, he was the president the Bombay branch of the People's Union for Civil Liberties. In 1984, he edited the 10th revised edition of *Ramaiya's Guide to the Companies Act*.[99]

He died on 4 January 1991, at age eighty-four.

[99] In collaboration with K.K. Desai and J.L. Jain (Nagpur: Wadhwa and Company, 1984).

VI

The Sinha Court (1959–64)

P.B. Sinha became CJI on 1 October 1959. Only Y.V. Chandrachud would have a longer tenure than Sinha's fifty-two months. In personnel terms, the Sinha years were the most stable the SCI has ever experienced. He had nothing to do with this for most of the judges he inherited were relatively young men. There were just two retirements—J.L. Kapur in December 1962 and S.K. Das in September 1963.

Shortly after he became CJI, he persuaded a skeptical Prime Minister Nehru that more judges were needed to cope with an increased workload and increase of cases in arrears. Nehru told Sinha that he was under the impression that the judges didn't work very long hour hours.[1] In 1960, the Court's strength was increased from eleven to fourteen judges.[2] These new judgeships were filled quickly in 1960 and there was not another appointment during Sinha's remaining forty months. The only other personnel activity during his tenure was the recall of the retired T.L. Venkatarama Ayyar, who returned from 1 March to 30 April 30, 1961 and from 20 December 1961 to 5 May 1962. Counting Sinha's own retirement on 31 January 1964 and Imam's resignation the same day, there were four vacancies during the Sinha years. The strength of the SCI, which had reached fourteen in 1960, had fallen to ten when he retired.

---

[1] B.P. Sinha, *Reminiscences and Reflections of a Chief Justice* (Delhi: B.R. Publishing Corporation, 1985), pp. 165–7.

[2] The Supreme Court (Number of Judges) Amendment Act, 1960.

R. Dayal, sworn in on 27 July 1960, was the most senior associate judge on the Allahabad High Court. Fifty-nine, he was on the threshold of retirement. He was the fourth from the ICS to reach the SCI and all four were serving together in the early 1960s. He was also the first to reach the SCI directly from the Allahabad bench.[3] According to Sinha, Home Minister Pandit Pant preferred V. Bhargava, an Allahabad judge also, but Sinha prevailed.[4] Frequently in Patna to visit his daughter, Dayal and Sinha were well acquainted.[5]

N. Rajagopala Ayyangar had reached retirement age from the Madras High Court eight months before he became an SCI judge on the same day as Dayal. There is some evidence that his name may have come up earlier. According to Hidayatullah, there was speculation that he was considered for the seat Hidayatullah gained in November 1958.[6] Even earlier, just prior to the appointment of P.G. Menon in 1956, Rajagopala Ayyangar may have been a candidate for that seat.[7] Because this was a recently created judgeship, he technically replaced no one. Sinha said that the SCI needed a Madras judge because the Madras High Court had been unrepresented since Venkatarama Ayyar's November 1958 retirement.[8]

J.R. Mudholkar, the last of this threesome, sworn in on 3 October 1960, was fifty-eight and the seniormost judge of the Bombay High Court. He and Sinha were well acquainted because Mudholkar, before moving to the Bombay High Court in 1956, had been a member of the Nagpur High Court throughout Sinha's tenure there as chief justice. Sinha said that he used to discuss SCI and high court appointments with President Rajendra Prasad from time to time—those two, both Biharis, were long-time friends. Prasad raised questions about Sinha's recommendation of Mudholkar, but after Sinha reminded him that Mudholkar's father was once president

[3] After the Oudh chief court was amalgamated with the Allahabad High Court in 1948, Hasan was absorbed but remained on the Lucknow bench of that court.

[4] Sinha, *Reminiscences and Reflections of a Chief Justice*, pp. 175–6. Pant ceased being home minister in March of 1961. Thereafter, Sinha would have dealt with Lal Bahadur Shastri from 5 April 1961 to 10 April 1962, followed by Gulzari Lal Nanda who served as home minister throughout the remainder of Sinha's tenure.

[5] Interview with Dayal in New Delhi, 2 June 1983.

[6] M. Hidayatullah, *My Own Boswell* (New Delhi: Arnold-Heinemann Publishers, 1980), p. 191.

[7] This was Rajagopala Ayyangar's belief. Interview in Madras, 25 June 1983.

[8] This was the understanding of *The Law Weekly* (*Madras*) which reported in its 1959 issue that he did fill the seat vacated by Venkatarama Ayyar, p. 124.

of the Indian National Congress, Prasad was satisfied.[9] The appointment of Mudholkar brought the strength of the SCI to its new full strength of fourteen.

As CJI, Sinha maintained a watchful eye over the high courts. He held conferences of high court chief justices every year and visited all the high courts at least once. He claimed credit for the age of retirement of high court judges being raised from sixty to sixty-two, though he had argued in favour of age sixty-five, and was of the view that age seventy for both high court and SCI judges could be justified.[10] He paid close attention to the recommendations he received for high court appointments, agreeing to most, but rejecting some. It was during his stewardship that three young rising stars received Sinha's approval for high court appointments. These were R.S. Pathak at age thirty-seven at Allahabad, P.N. Bhagwati at age thirty-eight at Gujarat, and Y.V. Chandrachud at age forty at Bombay.

Among those whose appointments he refused to agree to was Mohan Kumaramangalam's to the Madras High Court. Kumaramangalam was then the Advocate General of Madras and had been recommended by the Madras High Court chief justice. According to Sinha, Pant initially supported Kumaramangalam's appointment. In Sinha's words,

I wrote a strong note opposing this proposal chiefly on the ground that Mr Mohan Kumaramangalam was well-known to have very pronounced political views in favour of communism. I said it in my note to the Government of India that I was opposed to the appointment not on the ground that he was a communist in his views but on the very general ground that any lawyer who is well-known to the public to have pronounced views on matters political, of any complexion, should not be appointed a Judge in any Court, because I said, such persons would not command universal respect for their judicial integrity and impartiality. ... I am happy to say that the Prime Minister and the Home Minister who were chiefly concerned with such appointments, appeared to have agreed with my viewpoint and that appointment was not made.[11]

Whereas the Das Court appointees were noteworthy for their relative youth, Sinha's were notable for their advanced age. Both the average and median ages of his three appointees was 59.7. When Sinha retired on 31 January 1964, seven of the Das appointees were still on the SCI. Sinha's

[9] Interview with Sinha.

[10] Sinha, *Reminiscences and Reflections of a Chief Justice*, pp. 86–7. The Constitution (Fifteenth Amendment) Act, 1963, increased the retirement age of high court judges to sixty-two.

[11] Sinha, *Reminiscence and Reflections of a Chief Justice*, p. 167.

three would be gone by mid-1966. This does not mean that they had unusually lengthy high court careers, for the average here is 10.6 years, exactly the same as Das's men. None of them had been chief justices of their high courts. In terms of regional representation, three of the four who left the Court were Biharis, leaving Patna unrepresented. The Bombay High Court gained a second representative with Mudholkar, Rajagopala Ayyangar restored representation of the Madras High Court, and Dayal became the north's sole representative after Kapur's retirement. All three were Hindus, two of whom were brahmins, while the Hindus who retired were all non-brahmins. So the Court was 40 per cent brahmin when Sinha left. The Muslim representation fell to one with Imam's departure. Two of the three received some of their education in England, one of whom was a barrister and the fathers of all three were lawyers.

When Gajendragadkar replaced Sinha he inherited a Court composed of only nine associate judges. Why did the Court atrophy to this extent? Sinha did not comment on this matter in his autobiography, but wrote that on the eve of his retirement no writ petitions or other constitutional matters were pending longer than six months, implying that the Court did not need fourteen judges.[12] Wanchoo confirmed this, saying that there were not enough cases pending by the mid-1960s to require more than eleven judges.[13] The SCI actually remained at a *de facto* strength of eleven for most of the 1960s until it returned to fourteen when Hidayatullah was CJI.[14] Sinha was the first retiring CJI who did not leave a replacement for himself.

25. Raghubar Dayal (1960–5, 1966)

R. Dayal was born on 26 October 1900 in Delhi. He was the son of Bhairon Dayal who was a pleader at the Muzaffarnagar district courts. A number of Dayal's antecedents were members of the legal profession, including an

[12] Sinha, *Reminiscences and Reflections of a Chief Justice*, p. 177. Appeals from the high courts were pending much longer. During the 1960s the number of cases pending at the end of each year rose from 2,319 in 1960 to 7,104 in 1970. Rajeev Dhavan, *The Supreme Court Under Strain: The Challenge of Arrears* (Bombay: N.M. Tripathi Pvt. Ltd., 1978), p. 43.

[13] Interview with Wanchoo in New Delhi, 24 May 1983.

[14] Most of the judges who were on the Court during the 1960s thought that eleven was the full sanctioned strength of the Court.

uncle who was a pleader at Meerut and another uncle who practised in Delhi.[15] Yogeshwar Dayal, a close relative, would serve on the SCI from 1991 to 1994.

He earned the BSc degree in 1921 from Muir Central College in Allahabad, and the MSc two years later from the same institution. Dayal passed the ICS by examination in India in 1923, then proceeded to England and joined Sidney Sussex College,[16] Cambridge University. Upon completing his probationary training, he returned to India and became an officer of the ICS on 26 January 1925, beginning thirty-five years of service in increasingly senior posts in Uttar Pradesh. After serving as an assistant magistrate for six months, he was a joint magistrate until 1932. He served as a sessions and civil judge in 1932–3, then as a district and sessions judge from 1933 to 1946. From 20 March to 19 April 1946, he served as an acting judge of the Chief Court at Oudh.

On 22 July 1946, when he was forty-five, Dayal was appointed to the Allahabad High Court as an acting judge. This appointment was continuous and he was confirmed as a permanent judge on 17 March 1947. He spent fourteen years on the Allahabad bench, by which time he was the most senior associate judge. During brief periods in 1957 and 1959, he served as acting chief justice.

On the eve of the mandatory retirement age, he was promoted to the SCI. Aged fifty-nine at this time, he was sworn in on 27 July 1960 and retired on 26 October 1965. The next year, because of vacancies on the SCI and because illness prevented Justice P.S. Raju from attending Court, Dayal returned from 4 April to 7 May at the request of CJI Sarkar, and again from 8 August to 10 September at the request of CJI Subba Rao.

In retirement, Dayal, from 1967 to 1969, served as chairman of the Commission of Inquiry on Communal Disturbances which investigated communal incidents in several north Indian cities.[17] In 1970, he became chairman of the Third Central Pay Commission. Upon completion of that report[18] in 1973, Dayal fully retired. He died on 28 July 1991, at age ninety.

---

[15] Interview on 2 June 1983 in New Delhi.

[16] He did not attend regular classes because there were separate arrangements for ICS probationers.

[17] *Report of the Commission of Inquiry on Communal Disturbances*, 6 vols (New Delhi: Manager of Publications, 1968–70).

[18] *Report of the Third Central Pay Commission*, 4 vols (New Delhi: Ministry of Finance, 1973).

26. Narisimha Rajagopala Ayyangar (1960–4)

The last of the judges born in the nineteenth century, N. Rajagopala Ayyangar[19] was born in comfortable circumstances on 15 December 1899 in Vennar Bank, Thanjavur district, Tamil Nadu. The first lawyer in his family was his father, R. Narisimha Ayyangar, who spent his career as a member of the subordinate judiciary and retired as a district judge in Madurai district.

Rajagopala Ayyangar earned four degrees. He received a BA (honours) from Presidency College, Madras in 1920. This was followed by the BL from the Madras Law College in 1922, where he ranked first in the first class. In 1924, he received both an MA from Presidency College and an ML and Gold Medal from Madras Law College.

He enrolled as an advocate of the Madras High Court in 1925. In 1928, he became a junior partner of Sir Alladi Krishnaswami Ayyar, a doyen of the Madras bar. This partnership continued until 1945 when he began an independent practice. In the mid-1930s, he authored *The Government of India Act, 1935.*[20]

He was fifty-three when he was appointed an additional judge of the Madras High Court on 23 November 1953 and was confirmed as a permanent judge the following year. During his high court years, he served on two important commissions. In 1955–6, at the request of T.T. Krishnamachari, the then Union Minister for Commerce and Industry, he served as Chairman of the Central Government Commission which recommended revisions in the law of trade and merchandise marks.[21] From April 1957 to September 1959, on leave from the high court for much of this time, he chaired another central government committee to recommend revisions in the law governing patents. His report[22] would form the basis for the Patents Act of 1970.

Shortly after the completion of that task, he retired from the Madras bench. The invitation to join the SCI came some seven months later.

---

[19] Although his surname is rendered as Ayyangar in many places, including the *SCR*, he preferred Rajagopala Ayyangar. Interview in Madras on 25 June 1983.

[20] Madras: Madras Law Journal Office, 1937.

[21] *Report on Trade Marks Law* (Delhi: Manager of Publications, 1957).

[22] *Report on the Revision of the Patents Law* (Delhi: Manager of Publications, 1959). For an extensive analysis of the committee's recommendations and the legislative history of this legislation, see Rajeev Dhavan, Lindsay Harris, and Gopal Jain, 'Whose Interest? Independent India's Patent Law and Policy', *Journal of the Indian Law Institute*, vol. 32, no. 4 (October–December 1990), pp. 429–77.

Because of the two commission reports and the fact that he had practised before both the Federal Court and the SCI, he was not an unknown figure in Delhi. He was sworn in on 27 July 1960 at age sixty. His tenure on the SCI was brief, with retirement coming on 15 December 1964.

He remained in New Delhi for the next fifteen years. At the request of the Jammu and Kashmir government, he served from 1965 to 1967 as a one-man commission to look into charges of misconduct against Bakshi Ghulam Mohammed, a former prime minister of that state.[23] From 4 May 1968 to 31 December 1975, he was Chairman of the Press Council of India.[24] During these years he also spent some time at the request of the central government arbitrating a dispute between the Indian Oil and Natural Gas Commission and a French company. He eschewed chamber practice but often provided free legal advice to the poor.

Another post-retirement activity, a labour of love, was the construction of a temple in New Delhi which he started building in 1967 and saw completed in 1979. After persuading his friend T.T. Krishnamachari, then the union finance minister, to provide the land, he raised the funds for the construction of the Sri Venkataswara Mandir (Balaji Mandir). When that task was completed, he retired to Madras in 1979.

He died on 8 November 1984, at age eighty-four.

27. Janardhan Raghunath Mudholkar (1960–6)

J.R. Mudholkar was born into a prominent family on 9 May 1902 at Pune, Pune district, Maharashtra. His father was Rao Bahadur R.N. Mudholkar, a lawyer who acted briefly as an additional judicial commissioner at Nagpur but was much better known as a wealthy industrialist and politician. He was president of the Bankipore session of the Indian National Congress in 1912 and later was president of the first Legislative Council under the Montague–Chelmsford Reforms.

In 1919, at age seventeen, Mudholkar went to England where he remained for eight years. He received the BA in 1923 and the LLB in 1925 from Sidney Sussex College, Cambridge University. Also in 1925, he was called to the Bar from Lincoln's Inn.

[23] *Report of the Bakshi Ghulam Mohammed Commission of Inquiry* (Srinagar, 1967).
[24] On 31 December 1975, Prime Minister Indira Gandhi abolished it.

Upon returning, he enrolled as an advocate on 26 June 1925, and began his law practice at the Amravati district courts. In 1929, he moved his practice to the judicial commissioner's court at Nagpur, then the highest court in the Central Provinces and Berar. He served as secretary of the first bar council of the Nagpur High Court after the latter was established in 1936 and, for several years, was a member of the executive committee of the high court bar association.

On 22 September 1941, at age thirty-nine, he left private practice to become a district and sessions judge. This was the first such direct appointment made in the Central Provinces and Berar.

From 1 April 1948 to 20 June 1948, he served as chairman of the commission of inquiry which looked into various matters relating to the newspaper industry. Earlier he served as the chairman of a commission which investigated industrial disputes. Both these inquiries were conducted in the Central Provinces and Berar.

From 21 June to 5 October 1948, Mudholkar served as an acting judge of the Nagpur High Court. On 11 November 1948, at age forty-six, he was appointed an additional judge and was confirmed as a permanent judge on 21 October 1949. Following the reorganization of states on 1 November 1956, the Nagpur High Court became a bench of the Bombay High Court, and Mudholkar, a Marathi, moved to Bombay where he remained until the call came from the SCI.

Mudholkar was the seniormost associate judge at Bombay—for a brief period in September and October 1960 he had acted as chief justice—when he left for the SCI. He was fifty-eight when he was sworn in on 3 October 1960. On 3 July 1966, he resigned and became the first chairman of the Press Council of India the following day. On 1 March 1968, he resigned from that post over a difference in principle between him and M. Chalapathi Rau, then a very influential journalist.

From 3 May to 30 September 1968 he conducted an inquiry into allegations made against H.K. Mahtab, a former chief minister of Orissa.[25] From October 1968 to October 1969, after the Congress party returned to power in Bihar, he was a one-man commission which inquired into charges of corruption against former Bihar chief minister M.P. Prasad Sinha and

---

[25] *Report of Justice J.R. Mudholkar, Special Judge for Inquiries* (Government of Orissa, 1968).

thirteen of his United Front ministers.[26] In 1972, he served as a one-man tribunal under the Mineral Development Corporation (Acquisition) Act. His Tagore Law Lectures were published as *Press Law* in 1975.[27]

Mudholkar died on 27 June 1983, at age eighty-one.[28]

---

[26] *Report on the Charges against Fourteen ex-United Front Ministers* (Patna, 1970).
[27] Calcutta: Eastern Law House, 1975.
[28] He was too ill to be interviewed.

VII

The Gajendragadkar Court
(1964–6)

When P.B. Gajendragadkar arrived on the Court in 1957 he anticipated becoming CJI on 17 April 1965, following the retirement of S.J. Imam. His expectation was an eleven-month tenure. Imam's poor health, however, resulted in his resignation effective 31 January 1964. Gajendragadkar learned on 21 October 1963 that he would succeed Sinha and become CJI on 1 February 1964. Nehru was prime minister when his twenty-five month tenure began but by the time he retired both Nehru and his successor, Lal Bahadur Shastri, had died and Mrs Gandhi had begun her long tenure as prime minister. There is no evidence that these changes at the top had any bearing upon the appointments made during his tenure.[1] Gajendragadkar had nine colleagues when he became CJI. There were three retirements (N. Rajagopala Ayyangar in December 1964, K.C. Das Gupta in January 1965 and R. Dayal in October of 1965) and five new appointments during his regime. Before he made each recommendation, he sought and received the concurrence of his most senior colleague, K.N. Wanchoo.[2]

The first appointee was S.M. Sikri, the fifty-five-year-old Advocate General of Punjab, sworn in on 3 February 1964. Sikri was a significant appointment, for he was not only the first to come directly from the bar

[1] Gulzari Lal Nanda was home minister throughout Gajendragadkar's tenure.
[2] Interview with K.N. Wanchoo, 24 May 1983 in New Delhi.

but was the youngest of the Gajendragadkar's group and would later have a relatively long tenure as CJI. Because Sikri was a familiar figure at the SCI, Gajendragadkar was well-positioned to assess his qualifications.

The events that preceded Sikri's appointment went back nearly four years, and both Sinha and Gajendragadkar wrote about them. Because there is no other such detailed account concerning the selection of any other judge, what they wrote bears repeating here.

Sinha did not want anyone appointed directly from the bar. But Home Minister Pant had told Parliament that the government was considering appointing to the SCI a lawyer without prior high court experience. Sinha wrote:

... [H]e did so wrongly because it should be only the seasoned Judges who should be ordinarily brought on to the Bench of the Supreme Court where more complicated questions of law and Constitution generally arise for determination. I had told Pantji that it would be very difficult to get practising lawyers of the right calibre and character to be recruited direct to the Bench of the Supreme Court, unless he had in view to promote politicians and not competent lawyers to the Bench of the Supreme Court irrespective of their standing at the Bar. I further told Pantji that knowing as I did that practising lawyers at the Bar whom I thought fit to be raised to the Bench of the Supreme Court, would not accept the offer, I did not like to make the offer myself. But I gave a list of 8 or 9 names any one of whom could be approached by Pantji directly or through the State Governments concerned. The result of Pantji's efforts in this behalf was that none of the names I had given him except one would even look at the proposal. Only Mr. S.M. Sikri, the Advocate-General of Punjab who was rich enough to make a great deal of sacrifice could be available.[3]

Gajendragadkar's account is very different. He wrote that after joining the SCI in 1957:

I had been talking to all my colleagues, and the Chief Justice in particular, that on the Bench of the Supreme Court there should be one judge who was recruited directly from the Bar. The idea did not catch [at] first, but later S.R. Das saw that it would be a good plan to get a lawyer as a judge of the court and Sinha readily agreed. Attempts were therefore made to persuade Seervai, Palkhivala and Lal

---

[3] B.P. Sinha, *Reminiscences and Reflections of Chief Justice* (Delhi: B.R. Publishing Corporation, 1985), pp. 175–6. Sinha repeated much of what is found in this book when I interviewed him on 7 July 1983. The 'eight or nine' he referred to were all state advocates general. Sinha's conversations with Pant occurred no later than March 1961 when Pant died. During the remainder of his tenure, Sinha would have dealt with Home Ministers Lal Bahadur Shastri and G.L. Nanda.

Narayan [Sinha] from Patna, but all of them refused. I did not however despair. In course of time, I found that S.M. Sikri ... would be a good choice.[4]

Sinha, about to retire as CJI, had not 'readily agreed' to Sikri being appointed, but asked Gajendragadkar to invite Sikri to join the two of them for tea.[5] Sinha extended the offer, Sikri accepted, and joined the SCI two days after Gajendragadkar became CJI. Normally a nominee of an outgoing CJI in the pipeline is credited to that CJI. But clearly Sinha didn't want Sikri and the latter's appointment must be attributed to Gajendragadkar's efforts. Sikri agreed that his appointment was the result of Gajendragadkar's efforts.[6]

R.S. Bachawat, the court's first Marwari and, after fourteen years the second most senior judge on the Calcutta High Court, was sworn in on 7 September 1964 at age sixty. Gajendragadkar had not earlier met Bachawat

[4] P.B. Gajendragadkar, *To the Best of My Memory* (Bombay: Bharatiya Vidya Bhavan, 1983) pp. 152–3. H.M. Seervai said that the invitation he received came from CJI S.R. Das in November 1957. He was fifty at this time. Had he accepted then, he would have followed Sarkar as chief in 1966 and retired in 1971. Subba Rao, Wanchoo, Hidayatullah, and Shah would not have become CJIs. Seervai was certain that Palkhivala received an invitation in 1961 when Sinha was CJI. If Seervai's recollection was accurate, Palkhivala's invitation came from Pant. (Interviews with Seervai, 3 and 6 November 1988 in Bombay.) Palkhivala was then forty-one. Had he joined the court then, he would have served as CJI from 1971 to 1985. That Lal Narayan Sinha was invited in 1958 was confirmed in an interview on 24 April 1988 in New Delhi, with his son, L.M. Sharma, who would be appointed to the Court himself in the 1980s. M.C. Setalvad, aware that Gajendragadkar had been urging that a member of the bar be appointed, suggested to him that S.V. Gupte, who at the time was Additional Solicitor General of India, be invited. 'He [Gajendragadkar] asked whether it would be right for him, a Maharashtrian, to recommend the appointment of another Maharashtrian. I said I saw no objection if the person recommended was a competent person. At his suggestion, I asked Gupte if he would accept the appointment, but he declined for personal reasons.' M.C. Setalvad, *My Life: Law and Other Things* (Bombay: N.M. Tripathi Pvt. Ltd., 1970), p. 508.

[5] Gajendragadkar, *To the Best of My Memory*, pp. 153–4.

[6] Interview on 6 May 1983 in New Delhi. Sinha and Gajendragadkar disagreed over other important matters as well. Sinha believed it was useful to hold annual conferences of high court chief justices; Gajendragadkar believed they were a waste of time and held none when he was CJI. Sinha wanted a code of conduct for high court judges to be drawn up; Gajendragadkar 'summarily rejected the idea'. The two had very different ideas about the mission of the recently created Indian Law Institute and Gajendragadkar prevailed. Sinha felt strongly that Delhi needed a high court but Gajendragadkar didn't agree. Sinha was in favour of transferring high court judges but Gajendragadkar 'vehemently opposed such transfers'. See Sinha, *Reminiscences and Reflections of Chief Justice*, pp. 89–92, and 144. Sinha's memoirs were published after Gajendragadkar's death.

but had been impressed with his judgments and heard good reports about his ability and character.[7] Gajendragadkar had not sought Bachawat's consent to be appointed to the SCI; he learned of his selection from the newspapers. Bachawat's arrival in Delhi brought the Calcutta representation up to three, but Das Gupta would retire four months later.

On 4 January 1965, Vaidyanathier Ramaswami, sixty years of age and the fifth from the ICS, was sworn in. He was the most senior of the Gajendragadkar selections, having spent seventeen years on the Patna High Court, almost nine of which as its chief justice. His arrival in Delhi meant that Patna was again represented. Before recommending him, Gajendragadkar travelled to Patna to meet him.[8]

His fourth appointee, sworn in on 20 October 1965, was P.S. Raju, the chief justice of the Andhra Pradesh High Court. At fifty-seven, he was in line to succeed Sikri as CJI for a few months in 1973 but he died shortly after he arrived in Delhi. Gajendragadkar had come to know him during a visit to Hyderabad. This appointment increased the Andhra Pradesh representation to two.

J.M. Shelat, the fifty-seven-year-old chief justice of the Gujarat High Court, was sworn in on 24 February 1966, three weeks before Gajendragadkar retired. He was the first appointee after Mrs Gandhi became prime minister. Until he moved to the Gujarat High Court when it was created in 1960, Shelat and Gajendragadkar were colleagues on the Bombay High Court. Shelat was the first from the Gujarat High Court to reach the SCI. When appointed, he was not in line to become CJI but after Raju's death he anticipated a brief stint as CJI after Sikri's retirement. Appointed on the eve of Gajendragadkar's retirement, he can be considered the replacement for Gajendragadkar.

Gajendragadkar continued the balanced regional representation on the Court. Two of his appointees were from the east,[9] and one each from the north, south, and west. When he retired, the high courts of Calcutta and Bombay had two representatives each but there was none from the Madras

---

[7] Gajendragadkar, *To the Best of My Memory*, pp. 180–1. He had also sought the counsel of Das Gupta, who endorsed Bachawat.

[8] Gajendragadkar, *To the Best of My Memory*, p. 170, and interview with Ramaswami in Bangalore on 22 June 1983.

[9] Although Ramaswami was born in Tamil Nadu, his entire thirty-six year career before being appointed to the SCI was spent in Bihar, hence his identification as being from the east.

High Court. Nor was an Allahabad replacement for Dayal appointed. The most recently created high court, Gujarat, gained its first representative. Lengthy experience and high court seniority apparently were important considerations for Gajendragadkar. Three of the four from the high courts were chief justices and Bachawat was second in seniority at Calcutta. They averaged thirteen years of high court experience, more than the norm, and their average age was 58.1 years, about the norm, and two of them were in the queue to become CJIs in the early 1970s. Although Gajendragadkar had received all his education in India, he showed no preference for judges with educational experiences similar to his own, for four of his selections were barristers. This meant that seven of the eleven judges on the Court when he retired were barristers. Never again would the Court have a majority of barrister judges.

All five were Hindus, two (Ramaswami and Shelat) of whom were brahmins. Another Muslim was not appointed to replace Imam, so Hidayatullah became the occupant of the Muslim seat. In terms of paternal occupation, two were from modern professions (a physician and an engineer), two were businessmen, and one was an agriculturist/landowner.

When Gajendragadkar's tenure ended on 16 March 1966, he left the court at the *de facto* full strength of eleven—his successor Sarkar and ten associate judges.

28. Sarv Mittra Sikri (1964–73)

S.M. Sikri was born in privileged circumstances on 26 April 1908 in Lahore, Pakistan. His father, Dr Nihal Chand Sikri, was a prominent and wealthy Lahore physician. He wanted his son to study medicine and Sikri tried that for a short time,[10] but ultimately earned his BA in economics and politics from Trinity Hall, Cambridge University, in 1929. The next year he was called to the bar from Lincoln's Inn, becoming the first lawyer in his family.

Upon his return from England, he set up law practice in 1930 at the Lahore High Court. During his early years at Lahore, he taught part-time at the University Law College. Following Independence and Partition, he moved his practice to the East Punjab High Court at Simla. Known for his

---

[10] He joked that he gave up medicine because that required him to be in a laboratory until 6 p.m., too late for him to pursue his passion for tennis. Interview, 6 May 1983 in New Delhi. A second interview was conducted on 17 October 1988.

interest in international law, he was appointed by the union government in 1947 as the alternate representative to the United Nations Committee on Codification and Development of International Law. In 1949, he was appointed Assistant Advocate General of Punjab. In the same year, he served as legal advisor to the Ministry of Works, Mines and Power, advising particularly on the Indo-Pakistan dispute over the Indus River. During this period, he was also a director of the Saraswati Sugar Syndicate, Ltd. His expertise in income tax law led to his appointment in 1950 as Standing Counsel to the Central Government Income Tax Department and he served in that capacity until 1963.

On 2 July 1951, he was appointed Advocate General of Punjab, a post he would hold for thirteen years until his appointment to the SCI. From 1955 to 1958, he was a member of the first law commission of independent India. He began an association of more than three decades with the Sir Ganga Ram Hospital in 1956, serving first as a trustee and later as its chairman. In 1955, he was a member of the International Law Association's committee on rivers. In 1963, in his capacity as Advocate General, he appeared before the Das Commission of Inquiry which investigated allegations of corruption and misuse of power against Punjab Chief Minister Pratap Singh Kairon. Sikri also represented India at a number of international conferences, including the Law of the Seas Conference in Geneva in 1958, the World Peace Through Law Conferences at Tokyo in 1961 and 1963, and the Accra Assembly in 1962. From 1971 to 1973, he would serve as president of the Indian branch of the International Law Association.

On 3 February 1964, at age fifty-five, Sikri was sworn as an SCI judge, the first to be appointed directly from the bar without any high court grooming. He was a well known figure at the SCI, for over the years he had appeared before it on many occasions, both as advocate general and as an attorney for private parties.[11] In the 1950s, he had been offered a Punjab High Court judgeship, but had declined because the offer had not come 'early enough', meaning that he would have reached retirement age before gaining enough seniority to become chief justice.[12] When he accepted the SCI offer, he knew that he would became CJI barring changes in the seniority convention.

[11] There are, or were, some inter-state differences in the rules governing advocates general taking private briefs. When Sikri first became advocate general, having a concurrent private practice was not permitted in Punjab but later that rule was changed.

[12] Interview, 6 May 1983.

Nearly seven years later and by then the most senior associate judge, Sikri became the CJI on 22 January 1971. There were rumours that he would be superseded, and he received official word that he would become CJI only two days before Shah's retirement. Twenty-seven months later, he retired on 25 April 1973.

After leaving the SCI, Sikri remained busy with chamber practice and as an arbitrator of various disputes at the request of state governments and private parties. Until the Janata government replaced Mrs Gandhi's Congress (I) in 1977, no commissions of inquiry or other official assignments had come his way. This was hardly surprising, for he had been in the majority in *Kesavananda* and had been openly critical of the supersession.[13] From 1978 to 1980, he served as chairman of the Railway Accidents Inquiry Committee, and simultaneously as chairman of the Jammu and Kashmir Commission of Inquiry from 1979 to 1980. He also served as a member of the University Grants Commission. He was president of the Citizen's Justice Committee, a private group created in late 1984 which conducted an investigation of the anti-Sikh riots that followed the assassination of Mrs Gandhi.

An avid golfer, he could be found at the Delhi Golf Club almost every day until Parkinson's disease so debilitated him that playing golf was no longer possible.[14] He died at age eighty-four on 24 September 1992.

29. Ranadhir Singh Bachawat (1964–9)

R.S. Bachawat, the first member of the Marwari[15] community to reach the SCI, was born at Azimganj, Murshidabad district in West Bengal on 1 August 1904.[16] His ancestors had migrated to Calcutta from western India

[13] Kuldip Nayar, 'An interview with former Chief Justice S.M. Sikri: Consequences of Supersession', in Nayar (ed.), *Supersession of Judges*, New Delhi: India Book Company, 1973, pp. 130–6.

[14] In a letter to the author dated 28 April 1988 he wrote, 'I used to change for golf in the Supreme Court on working days and go directly to the Club after Court hours. This caused some misgivings in official circles. Mrs Indira Gandhi once mentioned this to me. I replied that "There are twenty-four hours in a day and spending two hours on the golf course still leaves 22 hours for other things." She merely smiled and said "Well I suppose that depends on how you regulate your schedule."'

[15] The author interviewed Bachawat on 30 June 1983 in Calcutta.

[16] This birth date is incorrect. He told me that he was actually born on 18 July 1907. His date of birth was changed by his parents when he was thirteen. Had he matriculated

about 300 years earlier. The Bengalis considered him a Marwari, and the latter considered him a Bengali. His father, Prasana Chand Bachawat, was a prosperous merchant.

He received a BA in mathematics from St. Xavier's College, Calcutta University, in 1925, where he won the Bankim Behari Sen Gold Medal, the Sarveswara Purna Chandra Gold Medal, and the Jubilee Post-Graduate Scholarship. Two years later, he received an MA in economics from Calcutta University. He then went to England where he earned the LLB from the University of London in 1931 and, in the same year, was called to the bar from Inner Temple. He was the first lawyer in his family.

Bachawat enrolled as an advocate of the Calcutta High Court in 1931, and remained in the environs of that court for the next thirty-three years. After nineteen years of private practice, he was forty-five when he was appointed a judge, the first Marwari, of the Calcutta High Court on 23 January 1950. Fourteen years later, at which time he was second in seniority, he was sworn in as an SCI judge on 7 September 1964, at age sixty. Retirement removed him from the court on 1 August 1969.

Earlier, on 10 April, he had been named by the union government as chairman of the Krishna and Godavari Water Disputes Tribunal, and he took up that assignment immediately. His work on this tribunal, a delicate task which involved resolving disputes regarding the sharing of water among five states, was not completed until eleven years later.[17] He returned to Calcutta in 1980 and engaged in some chamber practice. Drawing upon his expertise in arbitration and commercial law, his *Law of Arbitration*[18] was published in 1983.

Bachawat died on 12 June 1986, at age eighty-one.

---

at that age, he would have had to wait until age sixteen to move on to the next level of schooling. His correct date of birth was no secret. See, for example, *The India Who's Who 1979–1980* (New Delhi: INFA Publications, 1980). Because both the Calcutta High Court and the SCI used the 1904 date, it is used here.

[17] Completed earlier was *The Report of the Krishna Water Disputes Tribunal, with Decision in the Matter of Water Disputes regarding the Interstate River Krishna and the River Valley thereof, between 1. the State of Maharashtra, 2. the State of Karnataka, 3. the State of Andhra Pradesh, [and] Parties to the Dispute until 19th April 1971, 4. the State of Madhya Pradesh, 5. the State of Orissa*. 4 vols. (Controller of Publications, New Delhi, 1974). Subsequently, there was the *Further Report of the Krishna Water Disputes Tribunal under Section 5 (3) of the Inter-State Water Disputes Act, 1956* (New Delhi: The Tribunal, 1976). The final decisions concerning the Godavari River were announced by the tribunal in 1980.

[18] Calcutta: Law Reports Pvt. Ltd, 1983. There have been at least four revised editions of this standard work. See K.K. Venugopal, *et. al.*, *Justice Bachawat's Law of Arbitration &*

30. Vaidyanathier Ramaswami (1965–9)

V. Ramaswami[19] was born into a modern and economically secure family on 30 October 1904 at Kattanagaram, Tanjore district, Tamil Nadu. His father, S. Vaidyanathier, was in government service, retiring as a district board engineer.[20]

He earned his BA in chemistry and physics from Presidency College, Madras in 1924. Having encountered a brilliant professor of physical chemistry from Allahabad at a seminar in Madras, he decided to go to Allahabad University to study under him, and there Ramaswami earned an MSc in 1926. He earned a first class honours in both the BA and MSc examinations.

He then went to England to study for the ICS examinations and was successful in 1928. Upon his return, he joined the ICS on 9 October 1929 and was assigned to the province of Bihar and Orissa, where he would spend the next thirty-six years. His first assignment, which he held from 9 December 1929 to 29 June 1933, was as assistant magistrate and collector posted first in Cuttack, then Ranchi. On 30 June 1933, he began serving as secretary to the Orissa committee and reforms officer. This was a central government committee which dealt with the question of creating the province of Orissa. From 21 November 1933 to 24 February 1936, he held the post of joint magistrate. In March of 1936, he was appointed officiating district and sessions judge. In 1938, by which time he was a district and sessions judge, he returned to England on leave to study law at Balliol College, Oxford University. The onset of World War II compelled him to return to India and resume his official duties before earning the law degree. He was also enrolled in the Inner Temple at that time but because of the war was not called to the bar until 1944 when the examination was conducted in India. He was the first member of his family to have formal credentials in law.

From 1939 to 1946, he was a district and sessions judge in Shahabad and Bhagalpur. On 11 November 1946, he was appointed registrar of the Patna

---

Conciliation, including Commercial, International & ADR, fourth edn, revised and enlarged (Nagpur: Wadhwa and Company, 2005).

[19] He must not be confused with another V. (Veeraswami) Ramaswami, who was the subject of a protracted controversy which included an impeachment proceeding when he served as a judge of the SCI from 1989 to 1994.

[20] Interview on 22 June 1983 in Bangalore.

High Court and held that post until, at age forty-three, he was appointed an additional judge of the Patna High Court on 1 November 1947. He was confirmed as a permanent judge on 28 October 1948. On 30 April 1956, at age fifty-one, he became the chief justice. After serving in that capacity for nearly nine years, he was one of the most senior, if not the most senior, high court judge in the country.

On 4 January 1965, after more than seventeen years of high court experience and at age sixty, he was sworn in as a judge of the SCI. Retirement came on 30 October 1969. Before he left the bench, the union government announced his appointment as chairman of the Narmada Inter-State Water Disputes Tribunal, the mandate of which was to adjudicate disputes between Gujarat, Madhya Pradesh, Maharashtra, and Rajasthan relating to the sharing of the Narmada River. This task would last a full decade. His report,[21] which contains an elaborate discussion of interstate water law, was completed in December 1979. Ramaswami, then age seventy-five, and having completed fifty years of public service, went into full retirement and settled in Bangalore, where he died on 30 September 1996, at age ninety-one.

31. Penmetsa Satyanarayana Raju (1965–6)

P.S. Raju was born on 17 August 1908 into a middle-class family at Ajjaram, west Godavari district in Andhra Pradesh. He was the son of P. Rama Bhadra Raju, an agriculturalist and landowner. Raju was the first university graduate and first lawyer in his family.[22]

He earned his BA in about 1928 from Maharaja's College, Vizianagaram and his law degree from Madras Law College in 1930. In September of that year, he enrolled as an advocate of the Madras High Court and, during his

[21] The Report of the Narmada Water Disputes Tribunal, with its Decision, in the Matter of Water Disputes regarding the Interstate River Narmada and the River Valley thereof between 1. the State of Gujarat, 2. the State of Madhya Pradesh, 3. the State of Maharashtra, 4. the State of Rajasthan, 5 vols (New Delhi: The Tribunal, 1978), and Further Report of the Narmada Water Disputes Tribunal under section 5(3) of the Inter-State Water Disputes Act, 1956: In the Matter of Water Disputes regarding the Inter-state River Narmada and the River Valley thereof between 1. the State of Gujarat, 2. the State of Madhya Pradesh, 3. the State of Maharashtra, 4. the State of Rajasthan, 2 vols (New Delhi: Controller of Publications, 1980).

[22] Interview with his son P. Srirama Raju, then the registrar of the Andhra Pradesh High Court, on 20 June 1983 in Hyderabad. Additional information about Raju's career is found in the 1954 and 1965 issues of the Andhra Law Times.

early years at the bar, was closely associated with P. Satyanarayana, later a Madras High Court judge, and with T. Prakasam who would later become the chief minister of Andhra. During these years, he was a reporter for the *Andhra Law Times*. While at the bar, Raju acquired a reputation as an expert on land tenure law and was the author of a Telugu language book on the Madras Agriculturist Debt Relief Act, 1938. On 15 July 1950, after twenty years of private practice, he was named the government pleader for the Madras Presidency. A prestigious post at that time, it was a stepping stone to the high court. Simultaneously, he served as state counsel for Madras from 21 December 1951 to 26 November 1953, and was in charge of litigation involving the government of India. When the state of Andhra was created in 1953, Raju continued as government pleader.

On 1 November 1954, at age forty-six, he was appointed to the Andhra High Court. Following the reorganization of states in 1956, he became a judge of the Andhra Pradesh High Court. After more than a decade as an associate judge, he was appointed acting chief justice on 23 November 1964 and permanent chief justice on 30 December 1964.

Less than a year later, on 20 October 1965, Raju was sworn in as a judge of the SCI. Age fifty-seven at that time, he was in line to follow S.M. Sikri as CJI for a few months. But Raju's tenure was much shorter. He had been in poor health before coming to Delhi, suffering from untreatable diabetes. Three months after arriving in Delhi, he suffered a cerebral hemorrhage. He went on leave on 5 February and never returned to the bench. He was fifty-seven when he died on 20 April 1966, exactly six months after he arrived on the SCI.

32. Jayendra Manilal Shelat (1966–73)

J.M. Shelat was born into an upper middle-class family on 16 July 1908, in the town of Umreth in Kaira district, Gujarat. He was the son of Manilal Shelat who was a businessman and the sixth generation of a family of bankers.[23] Shelat was the first lawyer in his immediate family but two elder cousins preceded him in the legal profession.

In 1928, he earned a BA (honours) in English language and literature from Elphinstone College, Bombay. He then proceeded to England where

[23] His official given name is incorrectly listed as Jayashankar. Correct is Jayendra, but he preferred simply J.M. Shelat. Interview with Shelat on 8 August 1970, New Delhi, and correspondence on 21 April and 3 June 1983.

he enrolled in King's College, a constituent of the University of London. In 1931, he received second BA from that institution where he majored in history and political science. During these years, he also attended lectures delivered by the eminent Professor Harold Laski of the London School of Economics and Political Science. Shelat enrolled in London University's Institute of Historical Research and earned an MA degree in 1933. The focus of his post-graduate work was the American Constitution. His MA thesis was entitled 'The Creation of the U.S. Senate'. Simultaneously, he was studying law and, in 1933, became a barrister of the Inner Temple.

Upon his return to India, he enrolled as an advocate of the Bombay High Court on 18 August 1933. When his mentor Dr K.M. Munshi was jailed as a Satyagrahi, Shelat filled in as editor of Munshi's weekly, *Social Welfare*. After fifteen years in private practice, on 1 September 1948 and at age forty, he was selected to be one of the first four judges of the newly established city civil and sessions court of Greater Bombay. On 14 October 1954, he was promoted to principal civil and sessions judge. The next step in his judicial career was appointment as an additional judge of the Bombay High Court on 6 January 1957 when he was forty-eight. He was confirmed as a permanent judge on 24 November 1957.

When Bombay state was bifurcated and the state of Gujarat created in 1960, Shelat, on 1 May, became one of the first judges of the new High Court of Gujarat in Ahmedabad. When the chief justiceship fell vacant, Shelat, then the most senior associate judge and after serving briefly as acting chief justice, became the permanent chief justice on 31 May 1963. Promotion to the SCI came three years later, on 24 February 1966. Fifty-seven at this time, Shelat was the first Gujarat High Court judge to reach Delhi.

Seven years later, Shelat was the most senior associate judge of the SCI and, according to the seniority convention, was to succeed S.M. Sikri as CJI. But on 25 April 1973, the day after the SCI handed down the *Kesavananda* decision, Prime Minister Indira Gandhi shocked the nation by passing over Shelat and naming A.N. Ray as the new CJI. Had Shelat become CJI,[24] he would have presided over the court for only a few weeks, for the court's summer vacation began on 6 May, and Shelat's sixty-fifth birthday was on 16 July. Shelat's response to his supersession was to announce his

[24] Had P.S. Raju not died, he would not have been in line to follow Sikri as CJI and Shelat would have reached sixty-five before Raju retired. Shelat briefly (28 August–9 September 1972) served as acting CJI.

resignation immediately, with effect from 30 April. During his years on the court, Shelat participated in all the landmark decisions of his era and, from the government's perspective, was on the wrong side in the *Golaknath, Bank Nationalization, Privy Purses,* and the *Kesavananda* decisions.

His quarter century as a judge at three levels having ended abruptly, Shelat returned to Ahmedabad and commenced chamber practice in both Ahmedabad and Bombay and served as an arbitrator as well. He was offered no official assignments by Mrs Gandhi's government nor did he expect any.[25] When the Janata government came to power in 1977, Shelat was appointed chairman of the Seventh Finance Commission, and completed that work the following year.[26]

A lifelong student of the history of the Mughal period and English literature, Shelat was among the more scholarly SCI judges. His publications included *Akbar: A Historical Biography,* 2 vols (Bombay: Bharatiya Vidhya Bhavan, 1959); *Ibadat Khana: Its Impact on the Religious Policy of Akbar, The Tragedy of Shah Jahan* (Surat: Chunilal Gandhi Vidyabhavan, 1960); *The Spirit of the Constitution* (Bombay: Bharatiya Vidhya Bhavan, 1967); *Secularism: Principles and Application* (Bombay: N.M. Tripathi Pvt. Ltd., 1972); and *Historical Aspects of the Concept of Sovereignty.* For decades, he was closely associated with the Bharatiya Vidhya Bhavan and was one of its trustees during his retirement years. He was also chairman of Bhavan's Gujarat Kendra. Earlier, he was a trustee of Bombay's Hansraj Morarji Public School. His final project was serving as editor of the fourteenth edition of *Mulla on the Code of Civil Procedure, Act V of 1908* (Bombay: N.M. Tripathi Pvt. Ltd.). He had completed volume I in 1981, and II in 1983. Volume III carries Shelat's name but was completed after his death by B.J. Divan in 1989.

Shelat died on 1 November 1985, at age seventy-seven.

---

[25] He contributed a brief essay, 'The Explanations', critical of the supersession, to Kuldip Nayar (ed.), *Supersession of Judges* (New Delhi: India Book Company, 1973), pp. 42–5.

[26] *Report of the Seventh Finance Commission* (Delhi: Controller of Publications, 1979).

VIII

The Sarkar Court (1966)

Nine years after he arrived on the SCI, A.K. Sarkar became CJI on 16 March 1966. His was the briefest stewardship to date, just three and a half months, for he reached retirement age on 29 June and, during half of those days, the court was closed for the summer vacation. Despite his short tenure and the fact that he was the first new CJI after Mrs Gandhi became prime minister, the seniority convention was routinely applied and Sarkar learned he would succeed Gajendragadkar a few weeks earlier.[1]

Sarkar inherited a court at its *de facto* full strength of eleven and no personnel changes were expected. But P.S. Raju, who had been ill and on leave since early February, died on 20 April. Earlier in April, Sarkar had persuaded R. Dayal to return to fill in for Raju until the court's summer recess. Near the end of Sarkar's tenure, J.R. Mudholkar announced that he would be resigning from the court effective 3 July to become the Press Council's first chairman. It would be left to the next CJI to fill that vacancy. But it did fall to Sarkar to set in motion two fresh appointments, one to replace Raju and the other for his own replacement.

His two choices were V. Bhargava and G.K. Mitter. Although neither was sworn in until after Sarkar had retired and the summer vacation had ended, because Sarkar initiated both appointments they are credited to him. Sarkar had consulted with K. Subba Rao, who would succeed him, and the latter

[1] Interview with Sarkar on 28 June 1983, in Calcutta.

gave his approval to both men. Both received word of their nomination in mid-April.

Bhargava, sixty, the last of the ICS judges, and the chief justice of the Allahabad High Court and one of the most senior judges in the nation, was sworn in on 8 August. He was the replacement for Dayal, also from Allahabad, who was the most recent retiree. This nomination was approved routinely and quickly before Sarkar's retirement and Bhargava was sworn in when the Court returned from vacation.

Mitter, a few days short of sixty, was fourth in seniority on the Calcutta High Court. His nomination was not quickly approved. Mitter and Sarkar had been friends for many years and colleagues at the bar and on the Calcutta bench. Sarkar's recommendation of Mitter raised concerns of cronyism in government circles and the Calcutta Chief Justice D.N. Sinha wanted the seat himself and complained in writing to both the West Bengal chief minister and union Home Minister Gulzari Lal Nanda.[2] The latter discussed this matter with Sarkar, but he stood firm and Mitter was ultimately approved, but not until late August after Sarkar was gone and Subba Rao was the CJI. Mitter was sworn in on 29 August, and must be considered the Calcutta replacement for Sarkar. Raju was not replaced by another appointee from the south, leaving Subba Rao as the south's sole representative.

Sarkar's two appointees are noteworthy because of their lengthy high court experience, the average being 15.4 years, more than the choices of any previous CJI. They were also older than the norm, averaging 60.2 years of age. Bhargava was a brahmin and Mitter a non-brahmin, and the parents of both worked in the modern sector, as was by now increasingly common, one a teacher, the other a lawyer.

Counting Bhargava and Mitter, Sarkar passed on to Subba Rao a court operating at the *de facto* full strength of eleven. If education abroad is a significant indicator of cosmopolitanism, this was the most cosmopolitan group ever for all, except Subba Rao and Shah, had studied in England.

---

[2] Interviews with Sarkar and Mitter, both on 28 June 1983, in Calcutta.

33. Vashishtha Bhargava (1966–71, 1971)

V. Bhargava, the last of the appointees from the ranks of the ICS and the last without a law degree or barrister credentials to serve on the SCI, was born on 5 February 1906 at Allahabad in Uttar Pradesh. His background can be described as newly middle-class. His grandfather was an illiterate villager and his father, Chhotey Lal Bhargava, was a teacher in government service.[3]

He earned two degrees in physics—a BSc (honours) from Ewing Christian College in Allahabad in 1927 and an MSc the following year from Allahabad University. In 1929, he went to England and successfully competed in the ICS examinations. After completing his probationary year at the London School of Oriental Studies, he became a member of the ICS on 10 October 1930 when he was twenty-four.

He was assigned to the United Provinces cadre where he would spend the first thirty-six years of his career. From 1930 to 1935, Bhargava served first as an assistant magistrate and collector, then as joint magistrate. He was a civil and sessions judge in 1936–7. Next was promotion to officiating district and sessions judge, which was made permanent in 1940. As Independence approached and many English ICS officers were leaving India, Bhargava was persuaded in 1947 by the then Chief Minister G.B. Pant, to shift from the judicial side of the ICS to the executive side and accept the post of additional commissioner for food and civil supplies. He held that post for about six months and, in 1948, returned to the judicial side as judicial secretary and legal remembrancer for the United Provinces.

On 1 August 1949, at age forty-three, he was promoted to the Allahabad High Court as an additional judge and was confirmed as a permanent judge on 24 January 1950. In 1958–9, he functioned as a one-man commission of inquiry to investigate a police firing in Allahabad. After more than sixteen years as an associate judge, including periods during 1961–4 when he was acting chief justice, he became Allahabad's chief justice on 25 February 1966.

Bhargava was sixty, and the first native son of Uttar Pradesh, when he was sworn in as an SCI judge on 8 August 1966. While on the Court, he

---

[3] Interview on 31 May 1983 in New Delhi. An uncle was a lawyer who practised in the Allahabad district courts.

served as chairman of the committee on Telengana Surpluses in 1969.[4] He reached retirement age on 5 February 1971 but, at the request CJI Sikri and without interruption, remained on the SCI under the terms of Article 128 until the Court's term ended on 7 May 1971.[5]

From September 1971 to February 1974, he served as chairman of the Sugar Industry Enquiry Commission.[6] From 1977 to 1978, he was a one man commission of inquiry into the alleged murder of Naxalites by the police in Andhra Pradesh.[7] On several occasions he served as an arbitrator, one of which was a major dispute between 155 sugar companies and the State Trading Corporation. In 1982, at the request of the chancellor of Delhi University, he investigated alleged malpractices in the conduct of entrance examinations for the MBBS and MD/MS courses.

Bhargava died on 20 August 1985, at age seventy-nine.

34. Gopendra Krishna Mitter (1966–72, 1972–3)

G.K. Mitter was born on 24 September 1906 at Muzaffarpur, Muzaffarpur district, Bihar into a financially comfortable family. His maternal grandfather, B.N. Basu, was a lawyer and politician and his own father, Apurba Krishna Mitter, was an advocate who practised at the Muzaffarpur district courts from 1900 to 1934. Two elder brothers were also lawyers and one of his own sons was a fourth generation lawyer who declined an invitation to join the Calcutta High Court in 1983.[8]

Mitter was educated in India and England. In 1926, he received the BSc in science with honours in chemistry from Patna University. He then went to England where he attended courses at University College London in 1926-7. He considered getting a degree in engineering but decided there

---

[4] *Report of the Committee on Telengana Surpluses* (Delhi: Manager of Publications, 1969).

[5] Hidayatullah had retired in December 1970 and Shah followed in January. Had Bhargava left the bench in February, the SCI would have been left with only eight associate judges.

[6] *Report of the Sugar Industry Enquiry Commission, 1974* (New Delhi: Ministry of Agriculture, 1974).

[7] There is a discussion of the controversy surrounding this inquiry in Arun Shourie, *Institutions in the Janata Phase* (Bombay: Popular Prakashan Private, Ltd., 1980), pp. 165-8, 184.

[8] Interview with G.K. Mitter on 28 June 1983, in Calcutta.

would be better opportunities in being a lawyer. He was called to the bar from Lincoln's Inn in 1930.

Upon returning, he enrolled as an advocate of the Patna High Court in April 1931, but practised with his father at the district courts at Muzaffarpur until December 1934. He then moved his practice to the Calcutta High Court. Eighteen years later, at age forty-six and on 24 November 1952, Mitter was appointed to that court as a permanent judge.

After nearly fourteen years on the Calcutta bench, at which time he was fourth in seniority and fifty-nine, he was sworn in as an SCI judge on 29 August 1966. He reached retirement age on 24 September 1971 but at the request of CJI Sikri, and with no break in service, he continued on the court under the terms of Article 128 until the 1971–2 term ended on 7 May 1972.

After returning to Calcutta, he served often as an arbitrator or umpire in disputes between private companies, and between such companies and the union or state governments at the request of the SCI or the Calcutta High Court. From May 1973 to August 1974, he served as a one-man commission of inquiry appointed by the government of Orissa to investigate alleged irregularities in the granting of licenses for the collection of *kendu* leaves. In 1973, the central government appointed him chairman of the Committee on the Protection of Cows. The work of this committee continued for several years until the Janata Government came to power, when it was abruptly dissolved in May 1977 on the ground that no finding regarding a ban on the slaughter of cows was necessary.

Mitter died on 5 March 1989, at age eighty-two.

IX

The Subba Rao Court (1966–7)

Because the SCI was in summer recess when he succeeded Sarkar on 30 June 1966, K. Subba Rao's tenure as CJI began virtually unnoticed. His departure from the Court the following year was quite another matter. He left not by the usual route, retirement, but by his surprise resignation to become the United Opposition's candidate for president of India. When he jumped into the political arena on 11 April 1967, he became a national figure overnight. Never before had a judge resigned to enter politics.

Before he assumed the chief justiceship, Subba Rao had acquired a reputation in judicial and political circles as a vigorous champion of Fundamental Rights, particularly the right to property and for writing opinions critical of a variety of government policies and actions. Yet there were no rumours that Mrs Gandhi's government, by then in power for close to six months, considered placing anyone else in the centre chair.

With the retirement of Sarkar and the previously announced departure of J.R. Mudholkar four days later, Subba Rao inherited a court composed of only eight judges, himself included. But the appointments of V. Bhargava and G.K. Mitter were in the pipeline and Sarkar had secured the concurrence of Subba Rao for both.[1] Bhargava was sworn in on 8 August, and Mitter on 29 August, leaving only the Mudholkar vacancy to fill. Subba Rao's first personnel action was to request R. Dayal to return for a second

---

[1] Interview with Sarkar on 28 June 1983, in Calcutta.

stint in the retired judge capacity; he was on board on 8 August when the new term commenced.

Only the appointment of C.A. Vaidialingam, fifty-nine and third in seniority on the Kerala High Court, can be credited to Subba Rao. Sworn in on 10 October 1966, he was the first to come to the SCI from the Kerala High Court. Subba Rao and Vaidialingam had been friends and associates for a third of a century, dating back to their days together in Madras.[22] Surely this long friendship was a factor in Subba Rao's selection of Vaidialingam, though the latter's credentials were impeccable. He arrived in Delhi just in time to participate in the *Golaknath* case, and when the six-to-five decision was announced, Vaidialingam was with Subba Rao in the majority.[3] The vacancy Vaidialingam filled was that created by Mudholkar's resignation.

The only other vacancy during the remainder of Subba Rao's tenure was that to be created by his own scheduled retirement in July 1967. Earlier that year, two major events had taken place. Firstly, in February, Subba Rao had led the majority in handing the government a defeat in the *Golaknath* case. Reversing the direction of constitutional interpretation since 1950, the majority ruled that in the future, Parliament would have no authority to abridge or take away any of the Fundamental Rights. *Golaknath* was the most significant constitutional law decision in the Court's history up to that time. Secondly, and almost simultaneously, the fourth national elections had returned the Congress party to power but with a much reduced majority.

Subba Rao's resignation came some six weeks later. Just a few days earlier, and with the concurrence of incoming CJI K.N. Wanchoo,[4] Subba Rao sent over to Home Minister Y.B. Chavan the recommendation that K.S. Hegde be his replacement. A few months earlier, he persuaded him to

---

[2] Interview with Vaidialingam on 25 May 1983, in New Delhi.

[3] *I.C. Golak Nath v. State of Punjab* (1967) 2 SCR 763. Dr V.A. Seyid Muhammad, a member of Parliament, in his *Our Constitution for Haves or Have-nots?* (Delhi: Lipi Prakashan, 1975, pp. 115–16), after mentioning the long standing friendship, wrote that

Golak Nath's case is the first case in which Justice Vaidyalingam sat as a Judge of the Supreme Court and it is with his support that the majority of one was obtained. These are facts. If one were to adopt the objectional [sic] method of Mr Palkhivala, one could easily say that Justice Vaidylingam was deliberately and intentionally brought over to the Supreme Court to get support to Subba Rao's points of view.

Muhammad's book was written in response to N.A. Palkhivala's *Our Constitution, Defaced and Defiled* (New Delhi: Macmillan, 1975).

[4] Wanchoo interview, New Delhi, 24 May 1983.

come to Delhi as the first chief justice of the Delhi and Himachal Pradesh High Court. Both men understood that this transfer was a step toward appointment to the SCI.[5] The timing of the Hegde nomination could hardly have been worse and the government surely had good reason to be reluctant to approve Subba Rao's final act as CJI. In Hegde's favour, though, was his lengthy association with the Congress party (twice he had been elected to the Rajya Sabha with Congress support), which may have led the government to believe that he would be sympathetic to the Congress. But there was no response from the government before Subba Rao's departure. Although Hegde became an SCI judge three months later, his appointment cannot be credited to Subba Rao. He bequeathed to K.N. Wanchoo a court one short of its *de facto* strength of eleven.

35. Chittur Anantakrishna Iyer Vaidialingam (1966–72, 1972–3)

C.A. Vaidialingam was born in Madras, Tamil Nadu, on 30 June 1907 into a prominent and wealthy family. He was the eldest son of Rao Bahadur Sir C.V. Anantakrishna Iyer, whose distinguished career as a lawyer and judge included holding the posts of government pleader and advocate general for the Madras Presidency, judge of the Madras High Court and, following his retirement from the latter, chief justice of the Travancore–Cochin High Court. Vaidialingam was born in Madras because his father practised law there. But his father's birthplace was in Chittur in present day Kerala. Thus, Vaidialingam was a product of both Malayalam and Tamil culture—he spoke Malalayam while growing up in Madras but considered Madras to be his home.[6]

Like most of the South Indian judges of his generation, he attended Presidency College, Madras, where he earned his BA in history and economics in 1928, and Madras Law College where he received his BL in 1930. After completing an apprenticeship year in the chambers of P. Venkataramana Rao, who would become K. Subba Rao's father-in-law and later a Madras High Court judge, he enrolled as an advocate of the Madras

---

[5] Interview with Hegde in Nitte, Karnataka, on 14–15 November 1988.
[6] Interviews in New Delhi on 25 May 1983 and 24 October 1988. Both officially and by personal preference, his name was rendered C.A. Vaidialingam.

High Court on 13 August 1931. Soon thereafter, he became associated in a law practice with Subba Rao and P.V. Rajamannar as his partners.

On 25 November 1953, he was named government pleader for Madras and ex-officio government pleader for the central government, positions he would occupy until 25 March 1957. At that time, there was only one government pleader. It was a prestigious position and a stepping stone to the advocate generalship and then to the high court bench. During his Madras years, he was elected to three terms (1948, 1950, and 1955) as a member of the bar council. In 1956, he was appointed the amicus curiae counsel before the Ariyular Railway Accident Inquiry Commission. He also provided an endowment for Madras bar council lectures, endowed a women's and children's ward in the government hospital in Chittur, and served as a vice-president of the Society for the Protection of Children in Madras.

When the state of Kerala was created in 1956, the Kerala High Court's first chief justice claimed Vaidialingam as a Keralite and urged him to become associated with it either as a judge or as the state's advocate general. He initially demurred on the grounds that his roots were really in Madras and he was in line for a Madras High Court judgeship. But because of the growing anti-brahmin attitudes in Tamil Nadu, he felt that he may not receive a Madras High Court appointment even though his long-time associate and friend, P.V. Rajamannar, was the chief justice. The Kerala chief justice kept pressing him to accept a judgeship and even enlisted the assistance of Vaidialingam's father and urged him to prevail upon his son to accept the Kerala offer. He could not resist his father's wishes and, at age forty-nine, he was sworn in as a permanent judge on 26 March 1957.

After nearly a decade on the Kerala bench, by which time he was third in seniority he was called to the SCI by CJI Subba Rao. Sworn in on 10 October 1966 at age fifty-nine, he was the first from the Kerala High Court to become an SCI judge.

Vaidialingam reached retirement age on 30 June 1972. By this time, the *Kesavananda* litigation was on the horizon and CJI Sikri, needing in addition to a minimum of thirteen judges for that case a few other judges to handle all other court business, asked Vaidialingam to return in the status of a retired judge. He returned for the 23 October 1972–6 May 1973 period.

Vaidialingam was the only member of the SCI whose tenure spanned all of the momentous judicial and political events of the 1967–73 years. These included the 1967 and 1971 national and the 1972 state elections, the

Golaknath, *Bank Nationalization*, and *Privy Purses* decisions (on all of which he was in the majority), the split of the Congress party in 1969, the victory over Pakistan in the 1971 war, the arrival of S. Mohan Kumaramangalam and G.K. Gokhale in the Cabinet in 1971, the *Kesavananda* decision, and the supersession following that decision.

After leaving the Court, Vaidialingam remained in Delhi, but unlike most retired judges who engaged in chamber practice, he felt strongly that this was an inappropriate activity for a retired judge. He was a judge of the old school and his values were those of an earlier era. He believed that a judge should speak only in his judgments from the bench. Until the early 1980s, he did serve as an arbitrator in a number of disputes at the request of the union government, state governments, and private parties. It was a testimonial to his reputation for integrity and scrupulous non-involvement in politics of any stripe throughout his career that he was asked, in 1979, by the Morarji Desai government to serve as a special judge to investigate charges made in Parliament against the family members of Prime Minister Desai and Home Minister Charan Singh. He submitted his report in 1980, but by that time Mrs Gandhi and the Congress (I) was back in power. So as not to appear vindictive, Mrs Gandhi did not act upon Vaidialingam's findings. His last investigation was into allegations made by a professor and others against the vice-chancellor of Jawaharlal Nehru University. During these years, he was also active in the Government Legal Aid Clinic in Delhi. Only after reaching the age of seventy-eight did he fully retire from such post-retirement activities.

He died on 28 December 1989, at age eighty-two.

X

The Wanchoo Court (1967–8)

K.N. Wanchoo, the only member of the ICS and the only judge without a law degree or status as a barrister to reach the nation's pinnacle judicial post, served as CJI for ten and a half months—from K. Subba Rao's resignation on 11 April 1967—until his own sixty-fifth birthday on 25 February 1968. Had Subba Rao not resigned, his tenure would have been three months shorter. Immediately following Subba Rao's resignation, he was named acting CJI and was sworn in as CIJ on 24 February.[2] There was no thought of superseding him.[1]

Before resigning Subba Rao had, with Wanchoo's concurrence, recommended that his replacement be K.S. Hegde, who had recently been transferred from the Mysore High Court to become the chief justice of the Delhi and Himachal Pradesh High Court. Wanchoo was led to believe, and so informed Hegde, that Home Minister Y.B. Chavan and Prime Minister Indira Gandhi had cleared his name, but no official notification followed. Wanchoo inquired several times about the delay, went to see Mrs Gandhi to ask why formal approval of Hegde had not been announced, and went so far as to tell her that he would resign if Hegde's nomination wasn't approved.[2]

The day before the SCI returned from its summer vacation on 17 July, the Court's case list was delivered to Hegde. His name was not on it but there was an entry that said 'new judge.' That afternoon, the home ministry

---

[1] Interview with Wanchoo in New Delhi on 24 May 1983.
[2] The Wanchoo interview and the 1988 interview with Hegde.

informed him that he should get the medical certificate within an hour.[3] He did so and learned that evening that his appointment had been notified. Hegde, fifty-eight, was sworn in on 17 July. The three month delay was most likely the result of Subba Rao casting his lot with the opposition. It is possible that, had not Wanchoo pressed so emphatically, Hegde may not have been appointed. Hence, Wanchoo must be credited with the Hegde appointment.

As Wanchoo approached retirement, he recommended A.N. Grover as his replacement. Grover was fifty-five and third in seniority on the Punjab and Haryana High Court. Wanchoo had met Grover more than a decade earlier when the first law commission, of which Wanchoo was a member, co-opted Grover to assist the commission's inquiries in Punjab.[4] This nomination was approved quickly and Grover was sworn in on 12 February 1968.

With the appointment of Hegde, Mysore gained its first representative on the Court and Grover increased the Punjab representation to two. Wanchoo bequeathed to incoming CJI Hidayatullah a Court at its full *de facto* strength of eleven judges. The SCI's regional diversity continued—nine states were represented, with Calcutta and Punjab each having two judges. Both Hegde and Grover were non-brahmins, reducing the brahmin contingent to four. Their average of ten years of high court experience was below the norm, as was their average age of fifty-seven. Both could look forward to a spell as CJI—Hegde for eleven months and Grover for thirty-two.

36. Kawdoor Sadananda Hegde (1967–73)

K.S. Hegde was born on 11 June 1909 at Kawdoor, a small village in the South Kanara district[5] of Karnataka. His father, Subbayya Hegde, was a prosperous farmer in a feudal environment.[6] His family was very traditional, little touched by modern ways. Hegde was the first in his family to graduate from college and the first lawyer in the family.

[3] The Wanchoo and Hegde interviews.
[4] Interview with Wanchoo, and with Grover on 24 May 1983 in New Delhi. See also, Law Commission of India, *Fourteenth Report I*, (New Delhi: Ministry of Law, Justice, and Company Affairs, Government of India Press, 1980), pp. 6–7.
[5] Renamed Dakshina Kannada district.
[6] Interviews with Hegde on 11 May 1969 and 13 January 1980 in New Delhi, 22 June 1983 in Bangalore, and 14–15 November 1988 in Nitte, Karnataka.

After two years at St. Aloysius College in Mangalore, he enrolled in the three-year honours programme at Presidency College, Madras, where, in 1933 he earned both a BA (honours) and an MA, both in economics, history, and politics. He received a BL with distinction from the Madras Law College in 1935.

He enrolled as an advocate of the Bombay High Court in December 1935 but did not practise there. There was a one year apprenticeship requirement at Madras but not at Bombay. His father had recently died and he needed to start earning. He practised from 1935 to 1940 at a *munsif*'s court at Karkala near his birthplace. He then shifted his practice to the district courts in Mangalore where he would remain for the next fourteen years. While in Mangalore, he served as government pleader and public prosecutor from September 1947 to November 1951.

Hegde joined the Indian National Congress in 1935. He was secretary of the student's union at Aloysius College and president of the student's union at Presidency College, both offices associated with the Congress. During his Mangalore years, he became secretary of the district Congress committee in 1941. In 1951, he resigned the posts of government pleader and public prosecutor in order to become more active in Congress politics. On 3 April 1952, he was elected to the Rajya Sabha for a two-year term and was re-elected on 3 April 1954 for a full six-year term. In 1954, he went to New York as the alternate Indian delegate to the United Nations General Assembly. During these years, he was also a member of the Railway Corruption Enquiry Committee and of the governing body of the Indian Council of Agricultural Research.

While in the Rajya Sabha, he was offered the post of deputy home minister by Home Minister Pandit Pant. He declined that invitation mainly because he had a large family to support and six children to educate,[7] and felt compelled to continue his law practice when the Rajya Sabha was not in session. He was also offered the chairmanship of the Law Commission with cabinet rank but declined because he believed it would be wrong to hold both legislative and executive posts.

Hegde had been involved in preparing the draft of the States Reorganization Act and Pant, impressed by his legal knowledge, told him that he would make an excellent high court judge. But Pant pointed out that only service judges had been appointed to a high court without

---

[7] A son, N. Santosh Hegde, was an SCI judge from 8 January 1999 to 16 June 2005.

having practised before a high court. To gain such experience, Hegde began practising at the Madras High Court in 1955 and, after the reorganization of states in 1956, the Mysore High Court.

Midway through his second Rajya Sabha term, Pant offered Hegde a permanent judgeship on the Mysore High Court. He resigned from the Rajya Sabha and took the oath of office on 26 August 1957 at age forty-eight. Nine years later, he agreed to become the first chief justice of the recently constituted Delhi and Himachal Pradesh High Court.[8] This offer had been extended first by CJI Gajendragadkar in early 1966 when plans to create a new high court were being made, but Hegde was then hesitant to leave Bangalore. When the offer was extended a second time by then CJI Subba Rao, Hegde was amenable and was sworn in at Delhi on 31 October 1966. Both Gajendragadkar and Subba Rao had earlier observed Hegde on the Mysore bench.

Hegde was not to remain long on the Delhi High Court for he was sworn in as an SCI judge on 17 July 1967 at age fifty-eight. He looked forward to serving as CJI for about one year, from 16 July 1973 when J.M. Shelat would reach retirement age, until his own retirement on 11 June 1974. During his years on the court, Hegde acquired a reputation for his voracious appetite for work and the speed with which his opinions were produced. He also acquired a reputation for being increasingly strident in his opposition, often expressed quite bluntly, to various government policies which were litigated before the Court, particularly matters of special interest to Prime Minister Gandhi after the Congress party split in 1969.

His tenure on the Court ended abruptly in April 1973. The day after the *Kesavananda* judgment was handed down on 24 April, the government announced that A.N. Ray, fourth in SCI seniority, was the new CJI. Hegde was among the superseded trio and, on 26 April, he announced his resignation, effective 30 April. There is little doubt that Hegde was the main target of the supersession, with Shelat and A.N. Grover being secondary victims.[9] Kuldip Nayar reported that 'Kumaramangalam told me: "we ... could not let Hegde become Chief Justice. Hegde was the Congress (Organization) man ... He was a brilliant Judge though of a different

[8] Himachal Pradesh gained its own high court in 1971.

[9] Another reason for the supersession is believed by some to get V.R. Krishna Iyer on the SCI. Hegde, J.M. Shelat, and A.N. Grover had persuaded Sikri to refuse to accept Krishna Iyer in 1972. Shelat was senior to Hegde and had to be bypassed to get to Hegde. Grover had to be superseded also in order to give A.N. Ray the chief justiceship.

philosophy. We simply could not have him".'[10] Nayar added that 'Hegde was also the topic of discussion at the Political Affairs Committee meeting. It was noted that he had always taken an anti-government stand and might, if made Chief Justice, prove to be an impediment in the way of "progressive" legislation'.[11]

The past of no SCI judge prior to Hegde had been so openly and prominently associated with the Congress party but, by the late 1960s, he had become disenchanted with it. He rejected the party's policies in *Privy Purses, Bank Nationalization,* and *Kesavananda.* Shortly after he was superseded, Hegde wrote:

Ever since the Congress split in 1969, several important Communists have entered the ruling party ... to capture the Congress from within and to pervert our Constitution. The various steps taken by our Government since the 1971 election bear testimony to the enormous influence wielded by the Communists. An independent judiciary and the guaranteeing of human rights to the citizens are incompatible with the Communist system. For all practical purposes the Congress horse is now being ridden by the Communists. An ex-communist was the main spokesman on behalf of the Government before the Lok Sabha when the question of supersession of judges came up for consideration.[12]

Following his resignation, Hegde returned to Bangalore and built a lucrative chamber practice. The supersession, followed by the declaration of the Emergency in 1975, brought him back into the political arena. He was the convener of the Sangharsh Samiti in Karnataka, an anti-Emergency movement started by J.P. Narayan, and travelled around South India speaking out against the Emergency.

In the 1977 national election Hegde, contesting as the Janata candidate,

---

[10] Kuldip Nayar, 'The 13th Chief Justice', in Nayar (ed.), *Supersession of Judges,* pp. 9–41, especially p. 15. A.N. Ray was actually the fourteenth. S. Mohan Kumaramangalam, a close advisor to Prime Minister Indira Gandhi, though holding the steel and mines portfolio, was the principal defender of the supersession. The Congress (O) was the product of the 1969 Congress party split in opposition to what became Mrs Gandhi's Congress (I).

[11] Nayar (ed.), *Supersession of Judges,* p. 15. See also Granville Austin, *Working a Democratic Constitution: A History of the Indian Experience* (New Delhi: Oxford University Press, 1999), p. 281.

[12] K.S. Hegde, 'A Dangerous Doctrine', in Nayar (ed.), *Supersession of Judges,* pp. 46–53, especially, pp. 52–3. Hegde's anti-communism ran deep and, long before the supersession, there was no love lost between him and Kumaramangalam, the 'ex-communist' referred to by Hegde whom he had known for many years, dating to their Madras days. Interview with Hegde, 14–15 November 1988.

won election to the Lok Sabha from the Bangalore South district, defeating Congress (I) candidate K. Hanumanthaiah, a former chief minister and union minister of railways. He was one of just two Janata candidates to win in Karnataka.

In the Lok Sabha, he was first appointed chairman of the Committee of Privileges. Following N. Sanjiva Reddy's resignation as Lok Sabha speaker, Hegde, on 21 July 1977, was unanimously elected to succeed him,[13] and held that post until Mrs Gandhi returned to power in January 1980.[14] While speaker, he led Indian parliamentary delegations to many Commonwealth and other international conferences.

He did not contest the 1980 national election and returned to the small village of Nitte, close to his birthplace, where he lived in a small cottage. He served occasionally as an arbitrator when asked to do so by the SCI and private parties, but did not resume chamber practice, believing that would not be appropriate by a former speaker. He did remain active in politics. From 1980 to 1986, he was one of the vice-presidents of the Bharatiya Janata Party and thereafter a member of its executive council. The 1984 national election, following the assassination of Mrs Gandhi, found Hegde, then seventy-five, again seeking a Lok Sabha seat from Karnataka. Standing as the BJP candidate, he was defeated by the Congress (I) candidate.

Hegde had spent the first two decades of his career practising law near his roots, and he spent most of the last decade of his life giving back to his roots. Dakshina Kannada district was an economically backward area of Karnataka. He founded the Nitte Education Trust in 1979, which created nearly two dozen institutions aimed at improving the quality of life of the poor in the Dakshina Kannada and Udupi districts. Through his efforts, primary, secondary, professional schools and colleges, hospitals, and other institutions were built. After his death, the Justice K.S. Hegde Law College, the Justice K.S. Hegde Institute of Management, the Justice K.S. Hegde Charitable Hospital, and the Justice K.S. Hegde Medical Academy came

[13] According to BJP leader L.K. Advani who, in 1977, was the Information and Broadcasting Minister, he recommended to Prime Minister Morarji Desai that Hegde be the party's nominee for the presidency of India. Desai, however, chose Sanjiva Reddy. See 'Hegde could have been President', blogs Advani, CoastalDigest.com dated 10 July 2010, quoting from blog.lkadvani.in.

[14] In the late 1970s, with M. Hidayatullah having been elected Vice-President of India, which meant serving as chairman of the Rajya Sabha, both houses of Parliament were being presided over by former SCI judges.

into existence. Through his efforts, the entire region was transformed from backwardness to modernity. Announced annually is the Justice K.S. Hegde Charitable Foundation Award.

His career was a remarkable one, more varied than any other SCI judge. He had been a member of Parliament, first of the Rajya Sabha, later the Lok Sabha, an alternate Indian delegate to the United Nations, a judge of the Mysore, Delhi and Himachal Pradesh High Courts and later the SCI, Speaker of the Lok Sabha and, finally, a philanthropist. He spent half of his life (1930-57 and 1973-90) openly active in politics first in the Congress party, later in opposition to it.

He was the author of *Directive Principles of State Policy in the Constitution of India* (Delhi: National Publishing House, 1972), and *Crisis in Indian Judiciary* (Bombay: Sindhu Publications, 1973). In 1978, he received an LLD (*honoris causa*) from Kyung-Hee University, Republic of Korea.

Hegde was eighty when he died on 24 May 1990.

37. Amar Nath Grover (1968–73)

A.N. Grover was born on 15 February 1912 at Shwebo in Burma.[15] His father, Girdharilal Grover, was an engineer in government service posted in what was then British Burma. When he was five, the family returned to its roots in Punjab and his father established what would become a large construction business.

He earned a BA (honours) in history from Government College, Lahore in 1930. An MA in history from Punjab University, Lahore followed in 1932. He then went to England where he earned a second BA (honours) in history from Christ's College, Cambridge University, in 1935, and an LLB in 1936, also from Christ's College. He was awarded first prize in law by Christ's College in 1936 and was elected honorary scholar in the same year. Also in 1936, he was called to the bar from Middle Temple. He was the first in his family to become a lawyer.

Upon returning to India, Grover, then aged twenty-five, began practising as an advocate at the Lahore High Court in 1937. When Independence and Partition came a decade later, he shifted his practice to the East Punjab

[15] I interviewed Grover on 23 January 1980, 24 May 1983, and 23 October 1988, all in New Delhi.

High Court at Simla and in 1955 to Chandigarh when that court, renamed the Punjab High Court, was relocated there. He served as secretary of the high court bar association from 1950 to 1952, and from 1954 to 1957 was a member of the Punjab bar council. When the Fourteenth Law Commission conducted hearings in Punjab in 1956, he was co-opted by the commission.

On 10 October 1957, at age forty-five, he was sworn in as an additional judge of the Punjab High Court and was confirmed as a permanent judge on 21 November 1959. After just over a decade on the high court, by which time he was third in seniority, he was sworn in as an SCI judge on 12 February 1968,[16] three days before his fifty-sixth birthday. Had the seniority convention not been violated in 1973, he would have served as CJI for thirty-two months, from Hegde's scheduled retirement on 10 June 1974 until he reached retirement age on 15 February 1977. But the chief justiceship was not to be his. On 26 April 1973, the day after the supersession occurred, Grover announced his resignation, effective 31 May and went on paid leave immediately.[17]

He remained in New Delhi after his resignation, engaging in chamber practice and occasionally serving as an arbitrator. Shortly after the Janata government came to power, Grover, in May of 1977, accepted the chairmanship of an inquiry commission which was assigned the task of investigating charges of corruption, nepotism, and misuse of power levelled against Karnataka Chief Minister Devraj Urs and several of his ministerial colleagues. His 1979 report[18] found Urs guilty of several of the charges but the Urs government was re-elected while he was conducting the investigation, and nothing resulted from his report.

That assignment completed, Grover, on 3 April 1979, was named chairman of the Press Council which had been revived by the Janata

---

[16] A month after joining the court, Grover, sitting on a bench with CJI Hidayatullah and C.A. Vaidialingam, was stabbed on the head by an apparently deranged former sailor who had been punished for desertion by a lower court. Which of the three judges was the primary target was unclear but Grover was the only one injured. The wound was not serious and Grover was back on the bench after a few days. An account of this incident is found in M. Hidayatullah, *My Own Boswell* (New Delhi: Arnold-Heinemann Publishers, 1980), pp. 218–23.

[17] Had Grover become CJI, there would have been no Ray Court, for Ray reached age sixty-five on 29 January 1977. His letter of resignation to President V.V. Giri is reprinted in full in Nayar, *Supersession of Judges*, p. 54. See also Grover's, 'Questions That Must Be Answered', pp. 55–68.

[18] *Grover Commission of Inquiry* (Delhi: Controller of Publications, 1979).

government. In 1982, Mrs Gandhi's Congress (I), by then back in power, reappointed him for a second three-year term, which ended on 9 October 1985.

He then returned to chamber practice and arbitrations. He also served as vice-chairman of the Delhi Public School Society, as chairman of the governing body of Kamala Nehru College in Delhi, as chairman of the finance committee of the Indian branch of the International Law Association, and as a member of both the World Peace through Law Centre and the International Bar Association. His *Press and the Law* was published in 1990 (New Delhi: Vikas Publishing House).

Grover died on 13 July 1993, at age eighty-one.

XI

The Hidayatullah Court (1968–70)

It was fitting that M. Hidayatullah, a highly energetic and strong personality whose intellect and leadership qualities inspired respect and awe from colleagues, and a man who looked like he was born to be CJI, would reach the pinnacle of judicial heights. However, as K.N. Wanchoo's tenure was drawing to a close, '... speculation became strong whether I would be accepted as Chief Justice or whether some other judge would be chosen.'[1] But six weeks before Wanchoo retired, it was announced that he would become the eleventh CJI on 25 February 1968. His nearly three years at the helm was exceeded only by Sinha and S.R. Das among his predecessors. His tenure embraced important political events, including the 1969 split in the Congress party and the battle over the presidency, and controversy over decisions of the court which rejected major policy initiatives of Mrs Gandhi's government, particularly the *Bank Nationalization* and *Privy Purses* decisions in 1970. When his tenure began, the majority of his colleagues and he as well probably reflected views that were more conservative than during any earlier period.

Hidayatullah inherited an SCI at the 1960s *de facto* full strength of eleven judges, himself included. During his tenure, the SCI's composition changed very little. There were just two retirements—R.S. Bachawat in August 1969, and Vaidyanathier Ramaswami in October of the same year. Despite his

[1] Hidayatullah, *My Own Boswell* (New Delhi: Arnold-Heinemann Publishers, 1980), p. 217.

relatively long tenure, he did not have an opportunity to select many new judges who would be part of his legacy.

Three new judges joined the SCI during his reign and all three were sworn in on 1 August 1969. These were A.N. Ray of the Calcutta High Court, P. Jaganmohan Reddy of the Andhra Pradesh High Court, and I.D. Dua of the Delhi and Himachal Pradesh High Court. Because 1 August was also the sixty-fifth birthday of Bachawat these fresh appointments brought the SCI's strength up to thirteen for the first time since the early 1960s.

Ray was not Hidayatullah's first choice to fill the Calcutta seat being vacated by Bachawat. He first invited P.N. Mookerjee but he declined.[2] He had earlier met Ray, age fifty-seven and fourth in seniority, but did not know him well. He sought Bachawat's counsel, who of course knew Ray from Calcutta days, and Bachawat endorsed him.[3]

Jaganmohan Reddy, age fifty-nine and the chief justice at Andhra Pradesh was visiting relatives in the United States when he received Hidayatullah's invitation. These men had met earlier at official functions but were not well acquainted. Being from Andhra Pradesh was probably a factor in his selection, for P.S. Raju's death in 1966 and Subba Rao's resignation in 1967 had left that state without representation. Although senior to Ray in both rank and years of high court service, Ray was sworn in first. This was the first departure from the customary practice of the swearing in order being determined by seniority. Why Hidayatullah did this was puzzling to the other judges. When the author brought up this matter, he said that Ray was sworn in first because he was from the higher status Calcutta High Court.[4] Only status was involved for neither was in line to become CJI.

The choice of Dua, then the chief justice at Delhi, was the most perplexing one. Sikri and Grover were on the SCI, so there was no need for a third Punjabi, and the Delhi High Court had gained representation just two years earlier. Moreover, Dua, at nearly sixty-two, was the eldest appointed since N. Chandrasekhara Aiyar in 1950. Perhaps the fact that Dua and Hidayatullah were friends and neighbours in Delhi had something to do with Dua's promotion. Dua was the only one of this trio whom Hidayatullah knew well.

[2] Interview, 4 November 1988 in Bombay.

[3] Interview with Bachawat on 30 June 1983 in Calcutta.

[4] Interview, 4 November 1988. Hidayatullah said nothing about any of his appointees in his autobiography.

After he sent the names over, Home Minister Y.B. Chavan visited Hidayatullah and asked what he knew about their 'political ideology'. Hidayatullah's reply was that 'I didn't know yours until four days ago when you said you were a socialist.'[5] Apart from that query the three nominees met with no resistance and were quickly approved. Hidayatullah had not consulted with any of his colleagues about the appointments of Jaganmohan Reddy and Dua. Hegde said that these appointments 'took all of us by surprise.'[6] Grover said that Hidayatullah enjoyed so much respect from his colleagues that none of them inquired why he chose them.[7]

Just before retiring on 16 December 1970, Hidayatullah sent over the names of two more nominees, again without consulting any of his colleagues, including Shah who would succeed him. These were S.P. Kotval, who was then the chief justice at Bombay, and M.S. Menon, who had retired in mid-1969 after a lengthy stint as chief justice of the Kerala High Court.[8] Both were long time friends of Hidayatullah. Kotval and Hidayatullah had grown up together in Nagpur, both had practised there, and when he was the chief justice at Nagpur, it was upon his recommendation that Kotval was appointed to the Nagpur bench. Menon and Hidayatullah had become acquainted in England four decades earlier. Both were Lincoln's Inn barristers, Hidayatullah being called to the bar in 1930, and Menon in 1931. The day before he retired, Hidayatullah had written the lead judgment in the *Privy Purses* case, and termed the president's order a 'midnight order'.[9] There was no response from the executive to these nominations.

Although Hidayatullah was the youngest person appointed to the SCI during the first two decades, evidently he did not place any premium on recommending men who would have long tenures. Only Ray was close to the average age of fifty-eight, while Jaganmohan Reddy and Dua were fifty-nine and sixty-one, respectively, for an average age of 59.6. And the two he tried unsuccessfully to get on the SCI were then fifty-nine and sixty-three. They averaged 12.1 years of high court experience, more than the norm.

[5] 4 November 1988 interview. Chavan was the Home Minister until 27 June 1970. During the remainder of his tenure, Mrs Gandhi was holding temporary charge of that portfolio.

[6] 14–15 November 1988 interview.

[7] 23 October 1988 interview.

[8] 4 November 1988 interview. In *My Own Boswell* at p. 275 Hidayatullah writes: 'I lost the friendship of chief justices and judges for whom I could not find berths in the Supreme Court.'

[9] Hidayatullah, *My Own Boswell*, pp. 258–9.

Ramaswami's and Hidayatullah's retirements returned the SCI's strength to eleven. Hidayatullah was among the few CJIs who failed to appoint a judge who would be in the queue for the chief justiceship. If either Kotwal or Menon was meant to be his own replacement, his efforts were unsuccessful.

In caste terms, the Hidayatullah appointees changed little. Ramaswami (brahmin) and Bachawat (non-brahmin/Marwari) were replaced by the brahmin Ray, and two non-brahmins. The only significant change in regional diversity was the addition of a third Punjabi, but each region was left with at least two representatives. That two of the three were barristers was not surprising, for Hidayatullah was himself very much an Anglophile. In terms of religion, it is noteworthy that Hidayatullah, the nation's first Muslim CJI and the only Muslim on the SCI, did not recommend a Muslim replacement, leaving the SCI without Muslim representation. But Hidayatullah did not consider himself as the occupant of the SCI's Muslim seat. He felt strongly that he was appointed because of his merits, not because he was a Muslim.

Hidayatullah was the last of the strong CJIs. He initiated the three appointed during his tenure and, if others were pressed upon him by the government, he refused to accept them.

38. Ajit Nath Ray (1969–77)

A.N. Ray was born on 29 January 1912 in Calcutta, West Bengal, into a prominent and wealthy Bengali family. His father, Sati Nath Ray, was an advocate and civic leader in Calcutta and was one of the founders of what is now the National Medical College. He also served as president of the Indian Association, an organization of political moderates founded by Sir Surendra Nath Banerjee. Ray's physician grandfather, Dr Debendra Nath Ray, was also a prominent figure in Calcutta. He was the first Indian dean of the faculty of medicine at Calcutta University and, for some time, was honorary surgeon to the Viceroy of India.[10]

Ray was privileged to attend premier institutions of higher education. He earned his BA with first class honours in history from Calcutta University's

[10] I interviewed Ray on 29 June 1983, in Calcutta. In correspondence dated 15 November 2006 he wrote that this was the only interview he ever granted. Ray's son, Ajoy Nath Ray was appointed to the Calcutta High Court in 1990, and was transferred to the Allahabad High Court in 2005 as its chief justice.

Presidency College in 1931. While pursuing an MA in history, received in 1933 and again with first class honours, he was named a Hindu College Foundation Scholar. In 1931–2, he was editor of the Presidency College magazine. He spent the remainder of the 1930s in England, where he earned another BA in modern history from Oriel College's Honour School of Modern History, Oxford University, in 1936. He was called to the bar at Gray's Inn in 1939.

Upon returning from England, he was twenty-eight when he enrolled as an advocate of the Calcutta High Court on 26 February 1940. Seventeen years later, when he was forty-five, he was appointed an additional judge on 23 December 1957, and was confirmed as a permanent judge on 23 October 1959.

During his Calcutta years, he was active in several educational, cultural, and social institutions. From 1959 to 1969, he served as president of the governing body of Presidency College. He was honorary treasurer (1961–3) and then vice-president (1963–5) of the Asiatic Society. He was active in the affairs of Visva Bharati University, serving as a member of its *karma samiti* (executive committee) from 1963 to 1967 and 1969 to 1972, and as a life member of the *samsad* (court) from 1967. He was president of the Society for the Welfare of the Blind in Narendrapur from its inception in 1959 until 1980.

After nearly twelve years on the Calcutta bench, by which time he was fourth in seniority, Ray received an invitation from CJI Hidayatullah to become a judge of the SCI. He was fifty-seven when he was sworn in on 1 August 1969.

Less than four years later, on 26 April 1973, Ray, then fourth in seniority, became the fourteenth CJI. This was the first time the seniormost associate judge was bypassed. He was asked by Law Minister H.R. Gokhale on 24 April, the day the *Kesavananda* decision was announced, if he would accept the post. 'If I didn't accept, someone else would have been offered it. I did not hanker for it. I was asked on 24 April if I would take the job and was given two hours to decide.'[11] He served as CJI until he retired on 28 January 1977, a tenure longer than all but one of his predecessors. Had there been

[11] Interview. Some believe that S. Mohan Kumaramangalam, the face of the supersession, and Ray were related—that the mothers of Ray and Kumaramangalam were sisters. Ray told me that this was not true but that both he and his wife knew the Kumaramangalams and got together occasionally.

no supersession, Ray would not have served as CJI, for he was older than A.N. Grover and would have preceded him into retirement.

Ray's career on the high court had been that of an archetypal judge—never was he a party to any controversy. After arriving on the SCI, his opinions in the landmark decisions of the day set him apart from the three superseded judges and brought him to the attention of the government. In the *Bank Nationalization*, *Privy Purses*, and *Kesavananda* decisions, Ray supported the government's position—no other judge did so. In the *Bank Nationalization* decision, his solo dissent stood in stark contrast to the votes of his colleagues. In *Privy Purses*, a nine to two ruling, he was joined in the minority only by Mitter, and the latter's dissent was on technical grounds. In *Kesavananda*, decided by a seven–six vote, he was the most senior judge in the minority.

A few weeks after he reached retirement age, the Janata coalition was victorious at the polls. Ray had returned to his home in Calcutta and never returned to New Delhi. Mrs Gandhi was returned to power in 1980 but no one from her government ever contacted him.[12] He was one of a small number of former SCI judges who retired completely after leaving the Court. Partly this was self-imposed, a consequence of how he defined the role of a retired CJI: 'An Indian chief justice, like the Lord Chief Justice in England, should not take up any post-retirement positions. It is beneath the dignity of a retired chief justice of India to accept post-retirement positions'.[13] But there were never commission or other official requests to decline. From 1976 to 1982, he was a member of the International Permanent Court of Arbitration but accepted no arbitration requests, nor did he engage in chamber practice.

In 1973, he was elected an honorary fellow of Oriel College, and in the same year was awarded an LLD (*honoris causa*) from Punjabi University in Patiala. From 1974 to 1976 he was president of the Indian branch of the International Law Association. In the early 1980s, he served as vice-president of the Ramakrishna Mission Institute of Culture, which published his *Common Law, Its Reception in India* (Calcutta, 1988). Apart from that activity, he remained isolated and aloof. Many questions surrounding the supersession and his tenure as CJI remain unanswered. He could have

[12] Interview.
[13] Interview. Nor did he attend social functions or address groups or organizations while on the Court. His definition of the role of a judge prohibited doing so.

answered many of them but he chose not to tell his side of the story. A deeply religious man, for more than three decades he devoted much of his time to reading and engaging in spiritual pursuits. One month before his ninety-ninth birthday, Ray died on 25 December 2010. No retired judge lived longer, and with his passing away, the last link with the court's first generation was snapped.

39. Pingle Jaganmohan Reddy (1969–75)

P. Jaganmohan Reddy,[14] was born into an aristocratic, wealthy, and prominent family in the former princely state of Hyderabad on 23 January 1910, at Waddepally, Warangal district, Andhra Pradesh. His family history in Hyderabad dated back for more than five centuries. He was the son of Pingle Venkatrama Reddy who was a landlord with extensive holdings,[15] a businessman, an industrialist, a philanthropist, and a major presence in Hyderabad politics. By inheritance, he was also a *deshmukh* (revenue collector) in the days when revenue collection was farmed out to selected individuals. Among the political offices he held were president of the Hyderabad Municipal Corporation and minister of supply and deputy prime minister in the government of the Nizam of Hyderabad. Jaganmohan Reddy's father had passed the judicial examination conducted in Urdu by the Hyderabad High Court but never practised law. He took this examination to have the credentials for holding various honorary posts, including first class magistrate and honorary sessions judge. Although an uncle of Jaganmohan Reddy's was a Lincoln's Inn barrister, he never practised law, so Jaganmohan Reddy was the first member of his family to practise law as a profession.

He had the benefits of a full decade of education in England. After completing his secondary education in Leeds, he entered the University of Leeds where he received a bachelor of commerce degree in 1933. He had wanted to become a surgeon but his mother did not want him to stay away from India for the years it would take to complete medical education, so he decided to become a lawyer. He wrote that the inspiration to become a

[14] His surname is often rendered as Reddy but he said that Jaganmohan Reddy is more correct. Interviews by the author in Hyderabad on 23 June 1983 and 8 November 1988, and correspondence with his daughter, Urmila Pingle, in August 2009.

[15] During the agitation in the Telengana region, he was one of the few landlords who voluntarily gave land to his cultivating peasants.

lawyer came from Mohammed Ali Jinnah, whom he met in England.[16] In 1935, he earned a BA (Law Tripos) at Trinity Hall, Cambridge University. In 1936, he received the LLB, also from Cambridge and in 1937, was called to the bar from Gray's Inn. While at Leeds, he was president of the Indian Association and, in 1935, was elected a fellow of the Royal Society of Arts, London. He registered in the Supreme Court of England, became a member of the English bar, and practised law briefly there before returning home.

He was twenty-seven when he enrolled as an advocate of both the Bombay and Hyderabad High Courts in October 1937. After a year in Bombay he moved to Madras and spent the next three years in practice before the Madras High Court. In 1941, he shifted his practice to Hyderabad, where he would remain.

In 1942 and 1943, he was a member of the committee for Hyderabad Company Law and Insurance Law,[17] and during these same years, was a part-time lecturer in law at Osmania University. From 1941 to 1947, he served as legal advisor to the State Bank of Hyderabad, Deccan Airways, and the Hyderabad Commercial Corporation.

After some nine years of law practice and at age thirty-six, he joined the Hyderabad state judicial service. His first posting, from 9 September 1946 to 16 November 1950, was as deputy secretary and chief draftsman in the legal department. During 1946–7, he also served as a nominated expert member of the Hyderabad legislative assembly, where he prepared the drafts of the Hyderabad Income-Tax and Hyderabad Companies Acts. From April to June 1947, he officiated as secretary of the legal department. For most of 1948 (25 February– 16 November), he officiated as a judge of the Hyderabad High Court. From February 1950 to February 1952, he was divisional and sessions judge in Secunderabad. During these years, he was also a judge of the industrial court, a judge for Parsi divorce and matrimonial cases, and a member of the review board for preventive detention cases.

On 18 February 1952, at age forty-two, Jaganmohan Reddy was sworn in as a permanent judge of the then Part B High Court of Hyderabad. Shortly thereafter, he served as chairman of the commission of inquiry into the 1952 riots in Hyderabad city (the non-Mulki) Riots Commission. Also in 1952, he became a member of the syndicate and dean of the faculty of law

[16] *Down Memory Lane: The Revolutions I Have Lived Through*, second edn (Hyderabad: Book Links, 2000), pp. 112–13.

[17] His first publication, *The Hyderabad Excess Profits Tax Act* (Hyderabad, 1944), was an outcome of this assignment.

at Osmania University, Hyderabad, and held these positions until 1959. For a brief period, he was the acting vice-chancellor of the university. The Andhra High Court came into being in 1954 and functioned at Guntur but he continued on the Hyderabad High Court. On 1 November 1956, pursuant to the States Reorganization Act, the state of Andhra Pradesh came into being. At this time, the Hyderabad High Court was merged with the Andhra High Court, and the new Andhra Pradesh High Court commenced its life in Hyderabad. Jaganmohan Reddy continued as a judge of this new high court from its inception.[18] About a decade later, on 19 July 1966, he became chief justice and served in that capacity for three years until his elevation to the SCI.

He was fifty-nine when he took the oath of office as an SCI judge on 1 August 1969. Shortly after his arrival on the SCI, CJI Hidayatullah asked him to accept the assignment as chairman of the Gujarat (Ahmedabad) communal disturbances inquiry commission.[19] That assignment meant that he was away from the SCI from January through October 1970, with the result that he did not participate in the *Privy Purses* case. He was on the *Bank Nationalization* and *Kesavananda* benches and was in the majority in both. On 23 January 1975, he reached retirement age.

The next day he became the vice-chancellor of Osmania University, re- newing the close association he had with that university earlier in his career. In 1976, he headed the committee on the implementation of University Grants Commission scales of pay to the college and university teachers in Andhra Pradesh.[20] His service as vice-chancellor ended on 31 July 1977, when he resigned to head two politically delicate national commissions of inquiry established shortly after the Janata coalition replaced the Congress (I). As was true of all of his colleagues in the *Kesavananda* majority, he was

[18] When the new high court was created, all but three of the Hyderabad High Court judges became members but they were made junior to those who had served on the Andhra High Court at Guntur from 1954 to 1956. In determining seniority, Jaganmohan Reddy's four and a half years as a judge of the Hyderabad High Court were not counted, for it was a Part B one, that is, of lesser status than Part A high courts. Technically, therefore, he became a high court judge only in 1956, at age forty-six. Part B states were abolished by the Constitution (Seventh Amendment) Act, 1956.

[19] *Report of the Inquiry into the Communal Disturbances at Ahmedabad and Other Places in Gujarat on and after 18th September 1969*, 2 vols (Ahmedabad, Home Department, 1971). Often referred to as the Gujarat Riots Commission.

[20] *Report of the Committee on the Implementation of U.G.C. Pay Scales to Pay to the College and University Teachers in Andhra Pradesh* (Hyderabad: The Committee, 1976).

not approached concerning such post-retirement employment during the remainder of Mrs Gandhi's first regime.

Both these commissions functioned during 1977-8. The first, usually referred to as the Bansi Lal commission, investigated allegedly illegal acts of that former Haryana chief minister and union defence minister. Jaganmohan Reddy's report found Bansi Lal guilty on several counts.[21] The other, the Nagarwala commission, sought answers to questions that neither Jaganmohan Reddy nor anyone else has ever resolved.[22]

Those assignments completed, he returned to his home in Hyderabad and spent much of the remainder of his life writing and lecturing on contemporary issues of law, politics and education. Educational administration was a passion throughout his life. He did not engage in chamber practice, but provided free legal advice from what he humorously termed his 'troubled mind clinic'. He also served as an arbitrator when requested to do so by the SCI, also *pro bono*. In 1983, he was appointed to the board of studies of the law department of Sri Venkateswara University. From 1986 to 1994, he was a member of the board of governors of the Administrative Staff College and, after serving as president of the board of governors of the Institute of Public Enterprise for a full seventeen years, stepped down in 1995 because of failing health. He also served as a member of the jury for the Jawaharlal Nehru Award for International Understanding.

He was the author of a large number of books. These include *Quest of Justice: A Select Anthology of Articles, Essays, and Speeches* (Madras: Madras Journal Office, 1969); *Perspectives on Education and Culture* (Hyderabad: Osmania Graduates' Association, 1976); *Social Justice and the Constitution* (Waltair: Andhra University Press, 1976); *Minorities and the Constitution* (Bombay: University of Bombay, 1981); *Liberty, Equality, Property, and the Constitution* (Calcutta: University of Calcutta, 1982); *A Constitution: What it is and What it Signifies* (Visakhapatnam: Andhra University Press, 1983); *We Have a Republic: Can We Keep It?* (Tirupati: Sri Venkateswara University, 1984); *The University I Served* (Hyderabad: P. Jaganmohan Reddy, 1985); *Governors Under the Constitution* (Nagarjuna Nagar: Nagarjuna University, 1986); *Law and Society: Lectures and Writings of Justice P. Jaganmohan Reddy* (edited by M.V.K. Sivamohan, Delhi: Ajanta Publications, 1986); *The*

---

[21] *P. Jaganmohan Reddy Commission of Inquiry Regarding Shri Bansi Lal* (Delhi: Controller of Publications, 1978).

[22] *Report of the P. Jaganmohan Reddy Commission of Inquiry Regarding Nagarwala Case* (Delhi: Controller of Publications, 1978).

Judiciary from 1724 Onwards & After the Constitution (1950) (Gulbarga: Gulbarga University, 1989); *In Search of Unity and Secularism* (Aligarh: Sir Syed Academy, Aligarh Muslim University, 1989); and *Law in India: Restructuring and Reforming* (Jaipur: Printwell and Rupa Books, 1992).

His autobiography was published in two volumes: *Down Memory Lane: The Revolutions I Have Lived Through* (Jaipur: Printwell and Rupa Books, 1993 and revised edition, Hyderabad: Booklinks Corporation, 2000); and *The Judiciary I Served* (Hyderabad: Orient Longman, 1999). His writings were often provocative and some provide a view from inside the SCI, revealing information not found elsewhere in print. This is particularly true of *We Have a Republic–Can We Keep It?*, in which he wrote of the patrons of the judges appointed during the 1971–3 years when the process of selecting SCI judges changed dramatically.

He received LLD (*honoris causa*) degrees from Andhra University in 1975, Kakatiya University in 1976, and Osmania University in 1988. In 1976, he was conferred the DLitt (*honoris causa*) from Sri Venkateswara University. In 1994, he was awarded, by the Asiatic Society of Kolkata, the N.C. Sengupta Gold Medal for 'Outstanding Contributions to Society and Law: Ancient and Medieval Law'.

Jaganmohan Reddy died on 9 March 1999, at age eighty-nine.

40. Inder Dev Dua (1969–72, 1972–3)

I.D. Dua was born on 4 October 1907 at Mardan in the North-West Frontier Province of Pakistan. He was the son of Amir Chand Dua who was a wealthy moneylender.[23] Dua received a BA (honours) in English and history in 1927 from Forman Christian College, Lahore, and won the Gordon Young gold medal for finishing first in his class. When he earned the LLB from Punjab University's Law College in 1929, he became the first in his family to become a lawyer.

He began practising law in the district courts of the North-West Frontier Province in 1930. On 11 August 1933, he enrolled as an advocate of the Lahore High Court and practised there, and occasionally before the Federal Court in Delhi, until the subcontinent was partitioned in 1947. In 1943–4, he was first a member and then secretary of the Punjab state bar council.

---

[23] Interview on 6 July 1983, in New Delhi.

From his early years in Lahore he was an active member of the Indian National Congress and often represented Congress activists in habeas corpus and criminal cases. In 1945, he was a member of the defence team in the historic Indian National Army trial. Earlier he had defended the accused in the Second Lahore Conspiracy case. From 1944 to 1947 he was a representative of the non-barrister advocates on the rule-making committee of the high court.

In 1947, Dua moved his practice to the East Punjab High Court at Simla, and in 1955 to the Punjab High Court when it moved to Chandigarh. From 1956 to 1958 he served as the central government counsel for the Delhi circuit bench of the Punjab High Court. In 1958, he was elected chairman of the Punjab state bar council. Earlier he served as vice-president of the Punjab High Court bar association.

On 11 August 1958, when he was fifty, he was appointed to the Punjab High Court as an additional judge. This appointment was made permanent on 5 May 1960. When the Delhi and Himachal Pradesh High Court was established in 1966, Dua was persuaded by Subba Rao, the then CJI, to be transferred to Delhi as the seniormost associate judge. Although comfortably settled in Chandigarh and not eager to leave, Subba Rao's entreaties were successful, and Dua was sworn in at Delhi on 31 October 1966, at age fifty-nine. He became chief justice on 17 July 1967.

Two years later, after eleven years of high court experience and just two months before he would have had to retire, he was sworn in as an SCI judge on 1 August 1969. Although retirement came on 4 October 1972, he was back on the SCI the next morning, for CJI S.M. Sikri had asked him to remain as an Article 128 judge. Thirteen judges would be occupied with the *Kesavananda* hearings and Sikri needed a few other judges to deal with other cases. Dua remained on the SCI until the summer vacation commenced on 6 May 1973.

Almost immediately after leaving the SCI he moved to Jaipur where he would serve from 1973 to 1978 as the Lok Ayukta (ombudsman) for the state of Rajasthan. Upon the completion of that assignment he settled in Delhi, where he handled arbitration matters and developed a substantial chamber practice. Long an active Arya Samajist, he also served as a member of the managing committee of the post graduate D.A.V. College in Delhi and as a member of the senate of Gurukul Kangri University in Hardwar.

Dua died in New Delhi on 12 June 1987, at age seventy-nine.

XII

The Shah Court (1970–1)

J.C. Shah, the sixth and last of the CJI S.R. Das appointees to serve as CJI had a stewardship of only thirty-five days, the shortest to date, from 17 December 1970 to 21 January 1971. Prior to the official announcement that he would succeed Hidayatullah, there were rumours that he would be bypassed and that an outsider would be brought in. According to Hegde[1] and others, the outsider was Mohan Kumaramangalam, earlier a prominent member of the Communist Party and then a close confidant of Mrs Gandhi. The substance of the rumour was that Shah was to be superseded not because his tenure would be so brief but because he had written the lead judgment in the *Bank Nationalization* case earlier in 1970.[2] This rumour was discussed in Parliament by supporters of the seniority convention. The government denied that an outsider was being considered and, in late November, the Supreme Court bar association, in what was a rehearsal of its reaction to the 1973 supersession, passed a resolution in support of the convention and the promotion of Shah.[3] The rumour provoked CJI Hidayatullah to call a meeting of all the SCI judges. According to

[1] K.S. Hegde, 'A Dangerous Doctrine', in Kuldip Nayar (ed.), *Supersession of Judges* (New Delhi: India Book Company, 1973), p. 47.

[2] The nationalization of banks was the main issue over which the Congress party had split in 1969. Shah had also ruled against the government in the *Golaknath* and *Privy Purses* decisions.

[3] Hegde, 'A Dangerous Doctrine', pp. 47–8, and *Calcutta Weekly Notes* (1969–71), p. xxvi.

Hidayatullah, if Shah was superseded, 'They said, with one exception, "we will all put our resignations in your hands".'[4] The exception was A.N. Ray.[5] Hidayatullah also went to see the prime minister and reminded her that within a few days India was hosting an international convention of lawyers from around the world. If Shah was superseded, 'the whole world would know what happened'.[6] The government announced on 30 November that Shah would succeed Hidayatullah on 17 December. No earlier presumptive CJI had such short notice about his promotion.

Shah inherited a Court of ten associate justices. There were no retirements or appointments, so there was no Shah Court as that label is being used here. But his brief stewardship was important because of the failure of his nomination—'I sent his name over'[7]—of fellow Gujarati P.N. Bhagwati to fill his imminent vacancy.

By this time, both Bhagwati, the chief justice of the Gujarat High Court, and Y.V. Chandrachud, the most senior associate judge of the Bombay High Court, were viewed by members of the SCI and interested others as rising stars deserving of appointment to the Court. Both were very young by SCI standards—Bhagwati was forty-nine and Chandrachud fifty. No one younger than fifty-two had ever been appointed. Most importantly, which of the two was appointed first would have a very long tenure as CJI. Had Bhagwati been appointed at this time, the arithmetic of the seniority convention would have had him CJI from February 1977 until his own retirement in December 1986. And because he was younger than Chandrachud, there would never have been a Chandrachud Court.

Why Shah's recommendation was unsuccessful is uncertain. Bhagwati had Hegde's support, but neither Shelat's—the latter Bhagwati's former colleague at Ahmedabad—nor incoming CJI Sikri's.[8] The timing of the nomination was not opportune, for three days after Shah became CJI, Parliament

---

[4] M. Hidayatullah, 'Unjustified Departure from Settled Convention', in Palkhivala, *A Judiciary Made to Measure* (Bombay: M.R. Pai, pp. 9–15), especially p. 10. Jaganmohan Reddy confirmed this account in his *We Have a Republic: Can We Keep It?*, Tirupati: Sri Venkateswara University, , p. 92.

[5] Interview with Hidayatullah, 17 June 1983.

[6] Ibid.

[7] Interview with Shah in Bombay on 4 November 1988.

[8] Interview with Hegde, 14–15 November 1988, and with Sikri on 17 October 1988.

was dissolved and preparations for the new elections were underway. Shah received no response from the government to his nomination.[9]

Shah was not certain why the nomination failed, saying only that 'ultimately the government has the appointing power'.[10] He recalled that after it became apparent that Bhagwati would not win approval, he withdrew his nomination shortly before his retirement. Chandrachud would ultimately get to the SCI ahead of Bhagwati and the latter would have only eighteen months as CJI. One can only speculate the extent to which this result changed the history of the SCI.

Shah retired on 21 January 1971. Unsuccessful in filling his own vacancy, Sikri's tenure began with nine associate judges and Bombay was left without any representation on the Court.

[9] The nomination went straight to Mrs Gandhi who was holding temporary charge as home minister at this time.
[10] Interview with Shah.

XIII

The Sikri Court (1971–3)

When S.M. Sikri became CJI on 22 January 1971, a great deal of tension between the SCI and the government had accumulated during the previous four years. Less than a month earlier, Prime Minister Indira Gandhi announced that Parliament would be dissolved and mid-term elections held in March—the first time such an action had been taken. Earlier in December, the SCI had handed her a major defeat with its *Privy Purses* decision, a ruling many believe provoked her to call the fresh elections. In early 1970, the SCI had rebuffed her effort to nationalize the nation's largest banks, which was the issue which caused the split in the Congress party in 1969. The 1967 elections had reduced the Congress party's strength in Parliament and in the states. After the split, Mrs Gandhi's Congress had become a minority government, reduced to limping along with the support of parties to the left. This meant that constitutional amendments, often the means used to overturn, or otherwise circumvent, SCI decisions with which it disagreed, were almost impossible because the Congress could not muster the necessary two-thirds majority in Parliament. Also, in 1967, in the landmark *Golaknath* decision, the SCI had severely restricted the power of the political branches to amend the Constitution.

During these years, the SCI judges were probably the most conservative ever and serving at the same time. The government had made no secret of its frustration with them. Prior to Sikri being named the replacement for the retiring J.C. Shah, there were rumours that he would not be appointed. It had been customary to announce the name of the new CJI a month or more before the incumbent retired, but this time the official announcement came only three days before Shah retired.[1] That consideration was given to superseding Sikri was confirmed in 1973 when Mohan Kumaramangalam was reported to have said: 'We did not want to appoint even Sikri but at that time our plate was too full because of the dispute over the crisis within the Congress Party'.[2]

Six weeks after Sikri became CJI, Mrs Gandhi's Congress (I) won a massive public endorsement, capturing 352 of the 518 seats in the Lok Sabha, defeating the old guard of the Congress which, after the 1969 split, was her major opposition. This was the first national election in which the judiciary was an issue and the new government interpreted the results as endorsing a stronger Parliament–Executive and, if not a weaker judiciary, one more supportive of its policies. Around this time, the ominous phrase 'committed judges', meaning committed to the economic and social goals of the ruling party had entered the nation's political vocabulary.[3]

The new cabinet included three fresh faces that would play important roles in the attempt to change the direction of the SCI's rulings, particularly

[1] Interview with Sikri on 6 May 1983, in New Delhi. See also Hegde, 'A Dangerous Doctrine', in Kuldip Nayar (ed.), *Supersession of Judges* (New Delhi: India Book Company, 1973), pp. 46–53, especially, p. 48.

[2] Nayar, 'The 13th Chief Justice', *Supersession of Judges*, p. 36. Nayar was referring to A.N. Ray, who was, in fact, the fourteenth. Commenting on the same supersession rumours, P. Jaganmohan Reddy, who was serving on the SCI in 1971, wrote that because Mrs Gandhi had just dissolved Parliament, 'She seems to have been advised that, by and large, the people of India have great confidence in the judiciary and as she was going for elections, if she were to supersede him, it will have an adverse reaction and she might suffer at the elections'. Jaganmohan Reddy, *We Have a Republic: Can We Keep It?* (Tirupati: Sri Venkateswara University, 1984), p. 93.

[3] Nayar wrote that Sikri, in early 1971, told the Punjab and Haryana bar conference that 'There is talk of "committed judges" being brought in. I personally do not understand the meaning of the expression. If the idea is to appoint a person who will interpret the law in the light of the ideology of the ruling party, this would only be a short step from asking him to decide cases according to the wishes of the political party'. *Supersession of Judges*, p. 38. A tamer definition is committed to the goals of the Constitution. The phrase is usually attributed, probably incorrectly, to Kumaramangalam. 'Committed judges' was used by C.K. Daphtary in 'Editorial', *The Indian Advocate*, IX, nos 1 and 2 (January–June 1969). Despite that date the editorial carries the date of 18 February 1970. The 'commitment' term was used also in an article by 'Honorary editor', entitled 'The Re-Shaping of the Supreme Court', in (1) *SCC Journal Section* [1970], pp. 79–83. Either he or Daphtary implied that the term came up during, or just after, the Bank Nationalization litigation. Kumaramangalam, in his post-supersession speech to Parliament, was emphatic in denying that the government wanted judges committed to its social and economic agenda.

to get the *Golaknath* decision overruled. These were H.R. Gokhale, a former Bombay High Court judge turned politician, as the Minister for Law and Justice,[4] Kumaramangalam, a barrister who had earlier been a prominent member of the Communist Party, as Minister of Steel and Mines, and Siddhartha Shankar Ray, another barrister and long-time Congress party member who was one of Mrs Gandhi's closest confidantes, as Minister of Education, Youth Services and Culture.[5] The latter two had known Mrs Gandhi since their student days in England. Kumaramangalam probably was the most influential of Mrs Gandhi's advisors concerning SCI matters and Gokhale was the official spokesman.

Sikri inherited an SCI composed of ten judges, plus himself. On the eve of his retirement in April 1973, there were sixteen judges—the full complement of fourteen, plus C.A. Vaidialingam and I.D. Dua who had continued beyond age sixty-five under the terms of Article 128. These figures understate the changes in the SCI's composition during Sikri's tenure. There were nine new appointments, four retirements, and the death of one sitting judge. These appointments occurred during a period of just fifteen months, from July 1971 to October 1972. There had never been such a rash of appointments during such a brief period.[6] The reason for this frantic appointment activity was that the *Kesavananda* case, which would reconsider the *Golaknath* restrictions on amending power, was on the anvil. Because the latter was decided by an eleven-judge bench, thirteen would be needed for the *Kesavananda* case. Conveniently for the government, which was aware that several of the sitting judges did not subscribe to its aims, these vacancies provided it with an opportunity to shift the ideological composition of the SCI.

During Sikri's stewardship, both the process of selecting judges and the selection criteria that had prevailed during the first two decades, changed. The days of the CJI surveying the high court landscape, deciding who to

[4] Gokhale was the first law minister to be responsible for judicial appointments. For the first two decades, they were among the home minister's responsibilities. Stating publicly that he could not maintain his position and status on a high court judge's salary, Gokhale had resigned from the high court in 1966. See V.D. Tulzapurkar, 'Threats to the independence of the judiciary', *AIR 1984 Journal*, pp. 49–53, especially p. 49.

[5] Ray held this post from March 1971 to March 1972 and then returned to West Bengal as chief minister.

[6] After Hegde's appointment in July 1967, there were only four appointments during the next four years.

bring to Delhi, and seeing the government announce their appointments, ended in 1971. No longer would the CJI have virtually unfettered patronage power to promote whomever he wished to the SCI. The SCI would never again look like a private club whose head determined who would be invited as new members.

The first full published account of the changes did not appear until more than a decade later. The author was P. Jaganmohan Reddy who was on the Court throughout the Sikri years. After saying that Mrs Gandhi and Kumaramangalam wanted from the SCI a decision holding that the amending power of Parliament was unlimited, he wrote:

The selection of persons for appointment of [sic] Judges and subsequently their appointments to the Supreme Court was in furtherance of this design. Sikri, C.J., seems to have had hardly much of a say though it was made to appear he was in it. ... Eight Judges were appointed before Kesavananda Bharati's case was heard. Of the eight Judges it was said two were nominees of H.R. Gokhale; two were of Mohan Kumaramangalam of whom only one got through during Kumaramangalam's lifetime; two were of Siddhartha Shankar Ray; and two were from those Judges who were first appointed to the Allahabad High Court. It was said these were the Prime Minister's nominees. Only one was Sikri's nominee. One died before the case was heard. Of the seven out of the eight who were thus appointed and who heard the case, five upheld the Government's point of view.[7]

Although Jaganmohan Reddy did not name the eight judges,[8] this is easily done. Gokhale's choices were former Bombay High Court colleagues D.G. Palekar and Y.V. Chandrachud. Kumaramangalam was responsible for K.K Mathew of Kerala but was unsuccessful in his efforts to get V.R. Krishna Iyer appointed. S.S. Ray initiated the appointments of fellow Bengalis S.C. Roy and A.K. Mukherjea.[9] The two with Allahabad connections

---

[7] Jaganmohan Reddy, We Have a Republic, pp. 93–4. Earlier, A.N. Grover, also a member of the SCI at this time, had said that Gokhale '... started following a procedure which was hitherto unknown in the matter of appointment of Judges. He took upon himself the task of discussing with the Chief Justice or even trying to persuade him to recommend such Judges who were the nominees of the Government'. 'Questions That Must Be Answered', in Nayar, Supersession of Judges, pp. 55–68, especially, p. 64.

[8] He did name them when interviewed in Hyderabad, on 23 June 1983.

[9] In an interview with Ray at the University of Kentucky, Lexington, Kentucky, USA on 21 November 1994, when he was India's Ambassador to the United States, he agreed that he initiated and strongly pressed for the appointments of Roy and Mukherjea. He also claimed to have been influential after Kumaramangalam's death in the Krishna Iyer appointment shortly after Sikri retired, and to have been the patron of B.C. Ray of Calcutta, K.N. Saikia of Assam, and Kuldip Singh of Punjab, all appointed in the 1980s. The fingerprints of no other patron were found on as many who were appointed.

whom Jaganmohan Reddy attributes to Mrs Gandhi were M.H. Beg and S.N. Dwivedi. This accounts for all the eight judges appointed before the *Kesavananda* hearings began except H.R. Khanna, who was, according to Jaganmohan Reddy's lineup, the only Sikri nominee. The ninth appointee was A.N. Alagiriswami; he was not mentioned because he arrived as the *Kesavananda* hearings were getting underway and was not on that bench.

The judges who served during this period agreed that all or most of the 1971-2 appointees were initiated by the government and almost all agreed entirely with Jaganmohan Reddy's patron-client linkages. All agreed that Gokhale played an important role in the Palekar and Chandrachud appointments, but some believed that Chandrachud's most influential patron was former CJI Gajendragadkar who was still in Delhi as chairman of the law commission. All agreed that Kumaramangalam championed the Mathew and Krishna Iyer nominations. Other Calcutta judges, both sitting and retired, agreed that S.S. Ray initiated the S.C. Roy and A.K. Mukherjea appointments. Beg was emphatic in saying that he was chosen by Mrs Gandhi, not by Sikri.[10] Those who claimed knowledge of Dwivedi's patron agreed that he was Mrs Gandhi's choice, but some also saw the hand of H.N. Bahuguna in his selection. The latter is plausible, for Dwivedi's daughter was married to Bahuguna's son, and Bahuguna was then the Minister of Communications and general secretary of the Congress (I). They agreed that Khanna was Sikri's choice, but Sikri said that even his name was advanced first by Gokhale.[11] Finally, all evidence, including the views of five of his colleagues, points to C. Subramaniam, then the Union Minister of Industrial Development, Science and Technology and close to Mrs Gandhi, being the patron of Alagiriswami. Subramaniam had known Alagiriswami since the 1930s when they were classmates at Madras's Presidency College and he had lobbied Hegde for Alagiriswami's appointment.[12]

When I called Sikri's attention to Jaganmohan Reddy's patron-client linkages, he agreed with all of them. Whereas CJIs of the first two decades usually selected men they knew, the only one Sikri had met earlier was Khanna. This does not mean that the other eight were entirely foreign to him, for he would have known most by reputation. He consulted regularly

[10] Interview on 2 May 1983, in New Delhi. There is no evidence that G.S. Pathak, then the vice-president of India, and in whose chambers Beg had once worked as a junior, played any role in the selection of Beg.

[11] Interview on 17 October 1988.

[12] Interview with Hegde on 14-15 November 1988 in Nitte, Karnataka.

with both J.M. Shelat and K.S. Hegde, his most senior colleagues, and with other bench mates who earlier had been high court colleagues of the nominees, or otherwise knew them. These included G.K. Mitter about Roy and Mukherjea, V. Bhargava about Dwivedi, and Jaganmohan Reddy about Beg—the latter two had known each other since their England and Hyderabad days. It was Sikri's habit to read the previous three years of high court judgments of each nominee. Sikri said that his criteria included being no older than sixty, preferably younger, among the top four in seniority, and the specializations of the nominees. He was not concerned about whether the nominee was a high court chief justice and said he was not particularly concerned about regional balance considerations.[13]

None of these government nominees was literally forced upon him. He stood firm in saying that if a nominee was unacceptable to him, that person should not be appointed. Soon after he became CJI, the government pressed very hard for the appointment of Nagendra Singh, a senior ICS officer who at the time was the president of India's secretary. Sikri objected to Singh because his expertise was in international law and the SCI needed judges more familiar with municipal law. When Gokhale kept pressing Singh on Sikri, he threatened to resign.[14] At that point, Singh's name was withdrawn. Without mentioning Nagendra Singh's name, Kuldip Nayar wrote that Hegde told him that 'when this name was pressed by the law minister at a meeting of the Political Affairs Committee, Mrs Gandhi inquired whether Sikri had approved it. After learning that he had not, she said the person would not be appointed.'[15] In late 1971 or early 1972, after Mathew was appointed, the government, at the urging of Kumaramangalam and Gajendragadkar, wanted V.R. Krishna Iyer on the SCI. Sikri initially was ambivalent but was persuaded by Hegde and Shelat that Kumaramangalam was a communist.[16] There was no threat to resign and, after learning of Sikri's objection, the government withdrew his name. So, although the CJI's role changed from being the initiator to the gatekeeper, this veto power was

[13] Interview on 6 May 1983.

[14] Interview on 17 October 1988.

[15] Nayar, 'The 13th Chief Justice', *Supersession of Judges*, p. 31. Shortly thereafter, Singh was elected to the International Court of Justice and served as its president in the 1980s. Had he become an SCI judge, he would have been the only 'distinguished jurist' as defined in Article 124 of the Constitution ever appointed, for he had been neither a high court judge for five years, nor an advocate for ten years.

[16] 17 October 1988 interview. Hegde told me that during their morning walks together, Gajendragadkar pressed him to support the Krishna Iyer nomination.

significant. Sikri said that he ultimately concurred with every appointment made and that he could be held accountable for all nine appointees.[17]

Sikri recommended few names. He said he tried to recruit two or three leading advocates directly from the bar, one of which was Lal Narayan Sinha, but they were not interested. In 1972, he recommended the appointment of N.L. Untwalia, then the chief justice of the Patna High Court. Gokhale was supportive but because there were problems on the Patna bench, he wanted Untwalia to remain there for the time being. Sikri was pressed, in mid-1972, to agree to accept S.P. Mitra when the latter was on the threshold of becoming the chief justice at Calcutta. Mitra was fifty-four at this time, would have been in line to become CJI after Beg's retirement in February 1978, and would have held that post until December 1982. Mitra wanted to delay his arrival in Delhi and continue as the Calcutta chief justice for two years. A few weeks later, Chandrachud's appointment was announced and the chief justiceship was locked up until 1985. Mitra then declined to come to the SCI.[18]

The first personnel decision of the Sikri regime was the extension of V. Bhargava. He had reached retirement age on 4 February 1971, but at the request of Sikri and without interruption remained on the bench under the terms of Article 128 until the SCI's summer vacation began on 6 May 1971. Had Bhargava left in February, the SCI would have been left with only eight associate judges.

How S.C. Roy was chosen illustrates the extent to which the selection process had changed. According to his widow, Mrs Archana Roy,[19] he was approached first by his close friend, S.S. Ray, about accepting an appointment to the SCI. Again, according to Mrs Roy, Ray told him that Mrs Gandhi, whom Roy had known since their childhoods, asked him to convey her message that 'you must come to Delhi to help me'. Roy's health was not good and he was reluctant to leave Calcutta. Roy was soon invited to come to Delhi to be interviewed by Gokhale, Kumaramangalam and Ray, the purpose of which, according to Jaganmohan Reddy, an old friend from London days, 'was to ascertain his views'.[20] In May, Roy accepted the

[17] 6 May 1983 interview.

[18] A.K. Mukherjea, Mitra's junior colleague on the Calcutta bench, also came to the SCI in August 1972, and this may have been another reason why he withdrew.

[19] Interview at the Roy home in Calcutta on 29 June 1983.

[20] Interview on 17 October 1988. A similar account is found in Jaganmohan Reddy's *The Judiciary I Served* (Hyderabad: Orient Longman, 1999), pp. 218–20. S.S. Ray agreed

offer. Sikri, who had been unaware of these discussions, was then informed by Gokhale that the government would like his consent. Sikri had not met Roy, but was aware of his good reputation in Calcutta and Roy had also received a strong endorsement from Mitter. Sikri did not know that Roy, who had secured the required medical certificate, had serious health problems. Roy was fifty-nine when he was sworn-in on 19 July 1971. His appointment briefly increased the Calcutta representation to three but Mitter would reach retirement age a few weeks later.

Sworn in the same day was D.G. Palekar, sixty-one and just a few weeks before reaching retirement age. Sixth in seniority on the Bombay High Court, his first indication that he may be invited to the SCI came from S.P. Kotwal, then the Bombay chief justice, who had received a letter from Sikri asking Kotwal to inform Palekar that he should get a medical certificate. Sikri did not know Palekar and played no role in selecting him, but later said that Palekar's expertise in civil appeals was something the SCI needed. Palekar agreed that his selection was initiated by Gokhale, his former Bombay colleague and close friend.[21] Palekar was close to Gajendragadkar too and believed he had strong support from him as well. He was certain that he was the replacement for Shah ('someone had to be appointed from Bombay'), for Bombay was unrepresented after Shah retired six months earlier. Palekar was seven months junior to Y.V. Chandrachud but this was of little significance for Chandrachud, who had just turned fifty-one, was probably considered too young.

On 21 September 1971, H.R. Khanna, at age fifty-nine, was sworn in. Khanna and Sikri had long been friends and Khanna was certain that he was selected by Sikri.[22] Sikri agreed that he wanted Khanna but said that Gokhale actually mooted his name first. He was the third Delhi High Court chief justice to come to the SCI within a four-year period. K. Subba Rao had initiated Khanna's transfer from the Punjab and Haryana High Court to Delhi, which raised him to the plateau for promotion to the SCI. Khanna wrote in his autobiography that he first learned of his promotion from Gokhale and next day he received the same news from Sikri.[23] If Khanna

that Mrs Roy's account is accurate, as did A.C. Gupta. Interview with Gupta on 13 May 1983 in New Delhi.

[21] Interview with Palekar at Lonavala, Maharashtra, on 4 November 1988.

[22] Interview with Khanna in New Delhi on 17 June 1983.

[23] Hans Raj Khanna, *Neither Roses Nor Thorns* (Lucknow: Eastern Book Company, 1985), p. 61.

can be considered Sikri's choice he was the only one of Sikri's nominees who reached the SCI. Sikri's only reservation was that there were already three other Punjabis on the Court.

Less than a month later, on 4 October, K.K. Mathew took his seat on the SCI. He was sixty and third in seniority on the Kerala High Court. Mathew acknowledged that he owed his appointment to Kumaramangalam.[24] Although the two had never met, Mathew was aware that Kumaramangalam was attracted to him both by some of his dissents, particularly in the much-publicized E.M.S. Namboodiripad contempt case,[25] and by his reputation in Kerala as left-leaning, particularly concerning property rights. Mathew believed that strong support for his appointment also came from V.K. Krishna Menon, the former union defence minister. Menon had represented Namboodiripad in the Kerala High Court and was impressed by Mathew's dissent. He learned of his promotion from the Kerala chief justice, who had been informed by Sikri. But that was the extent of Sikri's involvement; he had not known Mathew and played no role in his selection. Sikri would later say that Mathew being a Christian was also a plus factor. Perhaps Mathew can also be considered a Kerala replacement for C.A. Vaidialingam, who would reach retirement the next year.

The fifth and last 1971 appointee was M.H. Beg who, earlier that year, was transferred from the Allahabad High Court to the new Himachal Pradesh High Court as its first chief justice. Beg was too junior, about fifteenth in seniority at Allahabad, to be appointed to the SCI without a quantum leap in seniority. He was fifty-eight when he was sworn in on 10 December 1971. The SCI needed a Muslim judge to replace Hidayatullah who had retired in 1970. According to Sikri, S.M. Fazal Ali, then the chief justice at Jammu and Kashmir, was also considered for this Muslim seat but he was only fifty at the time. Sikri preferred M.M. Ismail, also only fifty and a relatively junior judge of the Madras High Court. According to both Jaganmohan

---

[24] Interview with Mathew in 17 November 1988 in Ernakulam, Kerala.

[25] In *Narayanan Nambiar* v. *E.M.S. Namboodiripad*, 1968 *Kerala Law Times*, p. 299. E. M.S., again the Kerala Chief Minister, was found guilty of contempt of court for calling the judiciary 'an instrument of oppression', and saying that the judges were 'guided and dominated by class hatred, class interests and class prejudices, instinctively favouring the rich against the poor'. Mathew did not share these views but in dissent said that Namboodiripad had the right to express them and had not committed contempt.

Reddy and Mitter, Sikri didn't want Beg.[26] But Mrs Gandhi wanted him on the SCI and Sikri felt compelled to accept him. Beg was certain that he was, in fact, the choice of the prime minister.[27]

S.N. Dwivedi was fourth[28] in seniority on the Allahabad High Court and fifty-eight when he was sworn in on 14 August 1972. When his name was mooted by Gokhale, Sikri consulted Bhargava, who had served with Dwivedi at Allahabad and learned that Dwivedi was a 'leftist'. According to Hegde, Dua, and Jaganmohan Reddy, Sikri didn't want Dwivedi, for he had become aware that Dwivedi was close to Mrs Gandhi.[29] Sikri also believed that Dwivedi earlier had been a member of the Communist Party.[30] Another concern of Sikri's was the fact that Dwivedi and H.N. Bahuguna were related. Whether Bahuguna played a primary or secondary role in Dwivedi's appointment is unknown but there was no mistaking that the government wanted Dwivedi on the SCI, and Sikri ultimately acquiesced.[31] Perhaps Dwivedi can be considered the replacement for Bhargava, who had recently left the bench.

Sworn in the same day as Dwivedi was A.K. Mukherjea, fifty-seven, and fourth in seniority on the Calcutta bench. His appointment restored the Calcutta representation to its customary two following the death of S.C. Roy in late 1971. In the early 1970s, Delhi was not congenial for Bengalis; for Mukherjea died just fourteen months after his arrival. Sikri was aware that Mukherjea owed his appointment to S.S. Ray. Mukherjea's reputation was superb and Sikri was pleased to support his nomination.

[26] Jaganmohan Reddy, The Judiciary I Served, p. 220, and interview on 8 November 1988, and the Mitter interview in Calcutta on 6 June 1983. Sikri asked Jaganmohan Reddy about Beg, and his response was equivocal.

[27] 2 May 1983 interview in New Delhi. According to Austin, Beg was a longtime friend of the Nehru family. Working a Democratic Constitution: A History of the India Experience, London: Oxford University Press, p. 269.

[28] Fourth in seniority on the large Allahabad High Court does not mean that he had relatively little high court experience, for he had been an Allahabad judge for more than thirteen years.

[29] Hegde was of the view that this was not important and supported Dwivedi's appointment. Hegde interview, 14–15 November in Nitte, Karnataka.

[30] Jaganmohan Reddy, The Judiciary I Served, pp. 22–78.

[31] Jaganmohan Reddy wrote of Dwivedi saying at the farewell function before leaving Allahabad that he was going to Delhi to participate in the overruling of Golaknath. The Judiciary I Served, p. 228. Although other judges, including Hidayatullah, told this same story, there is no hard evidence that this is true.

Two weeks later, on 28 August,[32] Y.V. Chandrachud took his seat on the bench. This was the most significant appointment of Sikri's tenure largely because he was only fifty-two, younger by five years than the other eight Sikri era appointees, and would have a long tenure as CJI.[33] Chandrachud had an impeccable reputation and it was not a question of whether but when he would be appointed. P.N. Bhagwati was also regarded as deserving of appointment and the one who arrived first would have a long tenure as CJI. Chandrachud was a year and a half older and slightly senior at the Bombay bar. After the Gujarat High Court was created in 1960, Bhagwati, a Gujarati, left Bombay to become a judge there. Eight months later, Chandrachud received his Bombay High Court appointment. Bhagwati became the chief justice at Gujarat in 1967 and Chandrachud in mid-1972 was third in seniority on the larger Bombay High Court. So, in terms of both years of high court experience and seniority, Bhagwati had the edge. But Chandrachud won the race because he had something Bhagwati did not—influential patrons. These were Gokhale and Gajendragadkar. Gokhale and Chandrachud had served together on the Bombay High Court, and Gajendragadkar had been close to the Chandrachud family for decades and had long been an admirer of Chandrachud. He acknowledged that Gajendragadkar was responsible for his Bombay High Court appointment.[34] Bhagwati had strong support from Hegde,[35] but there was opposition from Shelat who earlier was Bhagwati's colleague on the Gujarat bench. Shelat warned that Bhagwati was given to pleasing the government and was too ambitious.[36] Sikri preferred Chandrachud.[37] The fact that Gokhale, Gajendragadkar, and Chandrachud were all Maharashtrian brahmins may be coincidental. Chandrachud replaced no one and raised the Bombay representation to two. With his arrival, the strength of the SCI reached the thirteen required before the *Kesavananda* hearings could begin.

[32] The warrants of appointment of Dwivedi, Mukherjea, and Chandrachud were issued on the same day, but Chandrachud's arrival in Delhi was delayed.

[33] Had A.K. Mukherjea not died, he would have retired as CJI in January 1980, and Chandrachud would have been CJI for five and a half years.

[34] Interview with Chandrachud, 3 May 1983. P.B. Gajendragadkar said the same thing in his *To the Best of My Memory* (Bombay: Bharatiya Vidya Bhavan 1983), pp. 154–5. In the same interview, Chandrachud referred to Gajendragadkar as his 'godfather'.

[35] Interviews with Hegde in November 1988 and with Bhagwati on 20 April 1983.

[36] 14–15 November 1988, interview with Hegde.

[37] Interview with Sikri on 17 November 1988.

The ninth and final appointee during Sikri's stewardship was A.N. Alagiriswami, who was sworn in on 17 October 1972, his sixty-second birthday.[38] After only four years on the Madras bench,[39] at which time he was ninth in seniority, he had come to Delhi as the first chairman on the Monopolies and Restrictive Trade Practices Commission, a move which put him in a different queue for appointment to the SCI. He filled the long vacant Madras seat. Indeed, the Madras High Court had been unrepresented for an inexplicably long eight years, since N. Rajagopala Ayyangar retired in 1964. He was the oldest appointee since N. Chandrasekhar Aiyar in 1950. Both because of his advanced age and the fact that in 1972, he was no higher than seventh in seniority on the Madras bench,[40] his appointment was unusual. On the Madras High Court, he was six years junior to P.S. Kailasam but the latter did not arrive on the SCI until five years later. Sikri had never met Alagiriswami and didn't initiate his appointment. Prior to the announcement of Alagiriswami's SCI appointment, as mentioned earlier, Subramaniam had lobbied Hegde.[41] His arrival, two weeks after the *Kesavananda* hearings had begun, brought the strength of the SCI up to the sanctioned fourteen, for the first time since 1961.

Actually there were sixteen judges on the SCI on the eve of Sikri's retirement on 25 April 1973, for Vaidialingam, who reached retirement age

---

[38] In order to avoid a break in continuity and an interruption in pension increments, it was essential that he be sworn in not later than his sixty-second birthday.

[39] Prior to becoming a Madras High Court judge, his appointment as government pleader, then a post of considerable prestige and a stepping-stone to the high court, became a matter of intense controversy because he was less senior than other judicial officers. According to the account of Vasantha Pai, a member of the Madras bar, '... Kumaramangalam [then a senior member of the Madras bar], introduced a resolution in the Madras Advocates Association condemning such appointment as one intended to erode the independence of the Judiciary and give a go-by to the long established conventions'. Pai made these remarks in a speech he delivered at the All India Lawyers Convention on the Independence of the Judiciary convened by the Supreme Court Bar Association on 11–12 August 1973, found in the *Journal of the Bar Council of India*, vol. 2, no.2, 1973, p. 326.

[40] The seniority clock keeps ticking when one is appointed to a commission of this nature. Alagiriswami was the first to have his seniority shortcoming resolved this way. Krishna Iyer's appointment to the Law Commission, after just three years on the Kerala High Court, served the same purpose.

[41] 14–15 November interview. Hegde said also that he was boosted by G. Parthasarati, at the time an advisor to Mrs Gandhi. Hegde also was a Madras Law College classmate of Alagiriswami. He, among others, said that Subramaniam and Alagiriswami were related but the latter's daughter said this was not true.

in 1972, and Dua, who turned sixty-five in October 1972, had returned to the bench under the terms of Article 128. Vaidialingam and Dua joined Alagiriswami on a bench which handled other matters during the six months of the *Kesavananda* case arguments. Thus, every judge who reached sixty-five during Sikri's tenure was extended.[42]

During the first two decades, the executive had permitted the CJIs and their colleagues to initiate the appointments of most of the new judges. As Sikri arrived, there was a reversal of roles. The executive asserted the powers clearly bestowed upon it by the Constitution and initiated the names of those it wanted on the SCI. The fact that it was the government that now dominated the selection process raises the question of whether these were men noticeably different than their predecessors and was this court-packing in the way that term is usually employed.

The answer to the first question is no. There were no changes in the backgrounds and prior careers of the new judges. They continued to be selected from the ranks of senior high court judges and brought as much experience to the SCI as earlier appointees.

Concerning the court-packing query, which suggests the government trying to populate the SCI with judges believed to be likely to support its socio-economic policies, most would agree that this was the goal of at least Kumaramangalam, although it was not until 1973 that he publicly spelled out his criteria.[43] Some judges of this era believed that the executive had started to look at the high court opinions and antecedents of potential nominees. If this is true, it is unlikely this was done very carefully and thoroughly. The fact that most of those appointed were boosted and their appointments attributed to influential benefactors with close ties to the prime minister points to the conclusion that friendships and patronage considerations trumped ideology. Indeed, the most compelling factor in most of these appointments was having patrons who were close to the prime minister. So, this was not court-packing in the conventional sense. But, no matter by whom chosen, few would argue that a Khanna, a Mathew, a Mukherjea, or a Chandrachud were not excellent appointees.

If getting *Golaknath* overruled was the executive's primary objective, and most would agree it was, the government's victory was a hollow one,

[42] Mitter had retired in September 1971 and he was extended until 7 May 1972, the date when Bhargava's extension also ended.

[43] 'Chief Justice of India: Criteria of Choice', in Nayar, *Supersession of Judges*, pp. 78–92.

for although the *Kesavananda* decision restored Parliament's authority to amend any part of the Constitution, the majority ruled that Parliament could not alter the 'basic structure' or 'essential features' of the *Constitution*. Seven of the nine Sikri era appointees (S.C. Roy had died and Alagiriswami was not a participant) were members of the *Kesavananda* bench, and five of these did support what can be considered the government's wishes. But they were in the minority with A.N. Ray. Khanna, who cast the deciding vote, and Mukherjea joined the five pre-Sikri court appointees in the majority.

The attentive public was unaware of the executive's taking charge of selecting judges. None of the sitting judges protested publicly. The observations of two of the judges during these years are very significant. When asked why he and his senior colleagues did not resist losing their selection powers, Sikri simply said, 'They have as much right as we do to select appointees. I paid no attention to who recommended them. I had the right to veto government nominees, and they had the right to veto mine'.[44] Perhaps more revealing than Sikri's comments were those of Hegde, the most outspoken of the sitting judges. Hegde had known Kumaramangalam for decades, believed he was still a Communist and didn't like him. Yet, Hegde said that although the nominees of the 1971–2 years were advanced by the government, reversing the earlier conventions, 'We didn't veto them for just that reason. If they were good, competent choices, there was no reason to reject them'.[45] In any event, Sikri and his colleagues believed there was little they could do about the government's new role. And the CJI was not entirely shut out, for the executive did permit Sikri the power to veto nominees to which he objected.

Applying the usual measures to these nine, only two of them were high court chief justices, a change from the nearly half of the pre-1971 appointees being chief justices. As for Beg, his seniority was contrived by his transfer from Allahabad to Simla. Although associate judges are usually younger at the time of appointment than those already in line to be presumptive chief justices, these appointees were not young men. Ignoring Chandrachud for a moment, the average age of the others was 59.8 years. Including

----

[44] Interview on 17 October 1988. Sikri said that the only representative of the government he dealt with was Gokhale. He never talked about appointments with Kumaramangalam or Ray.

[45] Interview on 14–15 November 1988.

Chandrachud, at age fifty-two and the youngest ever appointed up to that time, the number dips to a still above average 58.9 years. If the government was trying to pack the SCI, one would have expected younger men who would be around longer. The government's strategy seems to have been very short term—to get *Golaknath* overruled. By early 1978, the only one of the nine remaining was Chandrachud. But despite their advanced age at the time of appointment, had there been no deaths and had the convention of the seniormost associate judge becoming CJI, no less than six—all except Palekar, Mathew, and Alagiriswami—would have served as CJI. Moreover, although fewer than customary had been high court chief justices, they averaged 9.8 years of high court experience, only slightly less than the norm.

In terms of religion and caste, there were no striking departures from the past. Of the seven Hindus, five were brahmins. Beg filled the Muslim seat, vacant since Hidayatullah's retirement a year earlier, and the ninth, Mathew, was a Christian, the first since V. Bose in the 1950s. Three of the nine were barristers, as was Sikri.

In regional terms, it was business as usual—two were from the east, two from the west, three from the north, and two from the south. Five were from the old presidency high courts, two were from Allahabad, and two were from the newer high courts. Because Sikri started with nine colleagues and by the time this appointment blizzard was over there were thirteen, it is not as clear as it was earlier to determine who was replacing whom. Roy may have been perceived in part as the replacement for Mitter who retired two months later but that wasn't the main reason for his appointment. Palekar was definitely the replacement for Shah. Khanna and Mathew replaced no one in particular but served to maintain some representation of the newer high courts. Dwivedi might be considered as an Allahabad replacement for Bhargava but he, too, likely was appointed for other reasons. Mukherjea replaced either the deceased Roy or Mitter who was on the threshold of retirement. Chandrachud replaced no one and his appointment returned the Bombay contingent to two. Finally, Alagiriswami filled the long vacant Madras seat.

On the morning of 25 April 1973, sixteen judges were on the SCI. By the end of that day twelve remained. Sikri had retired and three resigned. On 6 May, Vaidialingam's and Dua's terms as Article 128 judges ended. Within two weeks, the strength of the SCI had plummeted to ten.

41. Subimal Chandra Roy (1971)

S.C. Roy, a cultured and, by all accounts, a brilliant intellectual, was born on 29 May 1912 in Calcutta into one of West Bengal's most prominent families. He was the son of Subodh Chandra Roy, a barrister who practised at the Calcutta High Court. The most well-known member of this family was his uncle, Dr B.C. Roy, who served as chief minister of West Bengal.

In 1928, Roy enrolled as a student at Presidency College but transferred to Scottish Church College, Calcutta, where he received his BA in 1932. Intent upon becoming a barrister despite his parents wishes that he compete for the ICS, he spent the next five years in England. He earned an LLB in 1935 from University College, London and was called to the bar from Lincoln's Inn in 1937. Roy won high honours throughout his academic career. He secured first class honours in the LLB examinations, first class first in the bar finals in 1937, and won the Buchanon Prize and the Langdon Medal.

Upon returning to Calcutta in 1937, he was twenty-five when he enrolled as an advocate of the Calcutta High Court, where he would spend the next thirty-four years. In addition to his private practice he served for about a dozen years as senior counsel for the union government. During these years he was also a trustee of various organizations, including the Deshbandhu Memorial Trust. A voracious reader, his personal library contained one of the best privately-owned book collections in the city.[46]

He was offered a judgeship of the Calcutta High Court in 1957 but declined because accepting it might look like nepotism and cause embarrassment to his uncle, who was then the chief minister. For the same reason he refused any brief or office that had any connection with the state government.[47]

Roy was approached about being appointed to the SCI soon after Mrs Gandhi's re-election in March 1971 but he was reluctant to leave Calcutta. The second time the offer came he was amenable and was sworn in on 19 July 1971, at age fifty-nine. He could anticipate becoming CJI on 15 February 1977 and would have served until his own sixty-fifth birthday on 29 May 1977.

[46] Interview with his widow, Mrs Archana Roy on 29 June 1983 in Calcutta. One of Roy's daughters published a tribute to her father, *Our Bapi* (privately published, 1972). Mrs Roy kindly gave me a copy.

[47] Interview and *Calcutta Weekly Notes*, LXXV (1970–1), p. cxiv.

Fate ruled otherwise. Roy suffered three heart attacks on 12 November and died later that day, less than four months after arriving in Delhi. The tenure of no earlier judge was shorter. He was in fragile health when he left Calcutta. At age thirteen he contracted spondylitis, a progressive spinal disease which affected his eyesight and caused a lifetime of pain. He walked with a stoop, could not walk very far, and could not exercise. When he joined the SCI, he also suffered from high blood pressure, failing kidneys, and heart disease.[48] His poor health notwithstanding, there were two reasons why he agreed to come to Delhi. He hoped that being an SCI judge would be easier on his health and he had become bored practising law at Calcutta and thought the SCI would bring new challenges.[49]

42. Devidas Ganpat Palekar (1971–4)

D.G. Palekar was the first other than ICS officers to reach the SCI after starting at the lowest rung of the judicial ladder, a journey that took thirty-two years. He was born on 4 September 1909 at Todur, a village in North Kanara district of what was then the Bombay Presidency, and today Karnataka. His father, Ganpat Palekar, was a landlord of substantial means and a collector of revenue from the cultivators of agricultural land.[50]

Palekar earned a BA in Sanskrit and English from Elphinstone College in Bombay in 1930 and the LLB from Government Law College, Bombay, in 1933. He was not the first lawyer in his family, for earlier there was an uncle, Shivrao Palekar, who practised in Bombay.

He enrolled as an advocate of the Bombay High Court on 2 February 1934 and for the next five years practised there and in other Bombay city courts. On 9 June 1939, at age twenty-nine, he joined the Bombay Judicial Service. He did this because, after the depression, there was more competition at the bar and judicial service was more attractive financially. His first posting was as a civil judge, junior division, and began on 10 June 1939. In September 1949, he was promoted to assistant district and assistant sessions judge. From 1954 to 1956, he served as deputy secretary

---

[48] Interview. See also *Our Bapi*, pp. 1–15, especially, pp. 4–5.

[49] Interview and *Our Bapi* ('He was getting tired of being a barrister, of being at the top. He wanted fresh pastures to feed his brain on.'), p. 11.

[50] Interview with Palekar on 4 November 1988, at Lonavala, Maharashtra.

in the Bombay legal department. From August 1956 to September 1958, he was posted as a district and sessions judge. He was appointed additional registrar of the Bombay High Court in October 1958 and was promoted to registrar on 15 January 1959. Appointment as an additional judge of the Bombay High Court came on 14 October 1961 when he was fifty-two. He was confirmed as a permanent judge on 27 August 1962.

After nearly a decade on the Bombay bench, by which time he was sixth in seniority, Palekar was elevated to the SCI. Just six weeks before his sixty-second birthday he was sworn in on 19 July 1971.

Palekar settled in Lonavala, Maharashtra, after he retired on 4 September 1974. The following year the union government appointed him chairman of the Wage Boards for Working Journalists and Non-Journalist Employees of Newspaper Establishments, the task of which was to recommend levels of salary. After the legislation which provided for this position was amended in 1979, the Janata government selected him to be the one-man tribunal charged with performing the work of the then defunct wage boards. The results of this assignment were submitted to the government as a set of recommendations in 1980.[51] Popularly known as the Palekar Award, he is better known for this than for his brief tenure on the SCI.

After completing that assignment, which took five years, he resumed his retirement at Lonavala. In 1984, the Gujarat government asked him to serve as a one-man commission to examine the demands that separate benches of the Gujarat High Court be created at Rajkot, Surat, and Baroda. Shortly after completing this task in 1985, a new government came to power in Gujarat and his recommendations[52] were never acted upon.

Palekar refused to accept remuneration for either of these positions. It was his view that retired SCI judges should not accept payment for official assignments that are in the interests of the general public. He also considered chamber practice an inappropriate activity for a retired judge.

He died on 9 December 2004, at age ninety-five.

---

[51] *Recommendations of the Tribunal for Working Journalists and Non-Journalist Newspaper Employees* (Delhi: Controller of Publications, 1980).

[52] *Report of the Commission for High Court Benches in Gujarat* (Gandhinagar: Government Central Press, 1985).

43. Hans Raj Khanna (1971–7)

H.R. Khanna was described by Khushwant Singh, the eminent novelist, journalist, and historian, as 'so clean a man that he makes angels look disheveled and dirty'.[53] Khanna had been on the receiving end of praise from many quarters ever since he wrote the courageous solo dissent in the infamous *Habeas Corpus*[54] decision during the 1975–7 Emergency, a dissent which cost him the chief justiceship in 1977.

He was born into a financially comfortable family on 3 July 1912 at Amritsar, Punjab. His father, Sarb Dayal Khanna, was an Amritsar lawyer and a prominent figure in Indian National Congress politics in that city, and served for thirty years on the municipal committee. The first lawyer in his family, his father was also very active in the Arya Samaj.

Khanna earned the BA degree in mathematics from Khalsa College, Amritsar, in 1932, and his LLB in 1934 from the Government Law College, Lahore. At Khalsa College, though shy and a self-described loner,[55] he won the election as president of the student's union and was a prize-winning debater.

In 1934, he joined the bar at Amritsar and began practising in the district courts with his father. He enrolled as an advocate of the Lahore High Court on 20 December 1940, but remained in Amritsar. Khanna was not an immediate success as a lawyer. He wrote that during the first five years he never earned as much as Rs 100 per month.[56] By the mid-1940s, however, his standing, measured by fees earned was at the front rank.

Upon learning in 1951 that the East Punjab High Court was planning to appoint some lawyers directly as district and sessions judges, he applied, was successful and, after eighteen years of private practice at Amritsar, he joined the Punjab Judicial Service on 1 February 1952. Then at age thirty-nine, he was posted first at Ferozepore as an additional district and sessions judge. In May 1956, he was transferred to Ambala with the rank of district

---

[53] 'Good Man dee Laltain: H.R. Khanna', *The Overseas Hindustan Times*, 22 March 1986. See also N.A. Palkhivala, 'Salute to Justice Khanna', *The Indian Express*, 30 January 1977, reprinted in Palkhivala, *We the People: India: The Largest Democracy*, pp. 296–300.

[54] *Additional District Magistrate, Jabalpur* v. *S.S. Shukla Etc.* [1976] *Supp. SCR* 172.

[55] Hans Raj Khanna, *Neither Roses Nor Thorns* (Lucknow: Eastern Book Company, 1985), pp. 143–4, 148. This autobiography has been very useful in preparing this biographical essay. I interviewed Khanna in New Delhi on 17 June 1983 and 3 October 1988.

[56] Khanna, *Neither Roses Nor Thorns*, pp. 10–11.

and sessions judge. Shortly after his arrival, there was an incident at the Kalka railway station where the police fired, killing four railway employees who were among a large number of such workers demanding improvements in their working conditions. Khanna was tapped to serve as the one-man commission of inquiry to investigate this matter.[57] In 1958, while still in Ambala, he was selected by the Punjab chief justice to be the special judge to try the Ram Krishna Dalmia case. Dalmia was one of the nation's most prominent businessmen and he and several others were accused of misappropriating a large amount of money from Dalmia's Bharat Insurance Company. Khanna found Dalmia guilty and sentenced him to two years in prison.[58] Both the Kalka and Dalmia investigations and reports attracted national interest and Khanna became rather well known. During the course of the Dalmia trial, he was posted as a district and sessions judge in Delhi.

On 7 May 1962, Khanna, then forty-nine, was promoted to the high court of Punjab at Chandigarh. Initially serving as an additional judge, he was confirmed as a permanent judge on 30 April 1964. Of the four and a half years as a member of this court, about two were spent in Chandigarh, and the remainder in Delhi as a member of what was then the Delhi circuit bench of the Punjab High Court. One of his Delhi neighbours, with whom he often took morning walks, was K. Subba Rao, the then CJI. When the decision was made to establish the separate Delhi and Himachal Pradesh High Court, Subba Rao tapped Khanna to be one of its foundation judges. Khanna was sworn in as the third most senior judge of this court on 31 October 1966.

In 1967, Subba Rao persuaded Khanna to conduct a politically sensitive inquiry into charges of corruption and misconduct made by the Orissa Government against more than a dozen former ministers, including three former chief ministers, most notably Biju Patnaik. Khanna's 1969 report[59] found evidence in support of some of the charges but a new government came to power in Orissa and the report was shelved.

When his Delhi High Court colleague I.D. Dua was appointed to the SCI, Khanna took his place as chief justice, effective 1 August 1969. On 22 September 1971, after some nine and a half years of high court service,

---

[57] An account of this inquiry is found in *Neither Roses Nor Thorns*, pp. 35–8.

[58] Khanna, *Neither Roses Nor Thorns*, pp. 39–42.

[59] *Report of the Commission of Inquiry* (Bhubaneshwar: Home Department, 1969). Later, Patnaik and Khanna became friends, as did Dalmia and Khanna. *Neither Roses Nor Thorns*, pp. 42, 132.

Khanna, then fifty-nine, became the third consecutive Delhi chief justice to be elevated to the SCI.

He was in line to become CJI. Had there been neither deaths nor resignations of more senior colleagues and assuming the continued operation of the seniority convention, Khanna would have succeeded S.C. Roy as CJI on 29 May 1977 and hold that post for just over a month until his own sixty-fifth birthday on 3 July 1977. Roy's death meant that Khanna was to have served as chief for four and a half months. Recalculating after A.N. Ray became CJI and Grover's resignation following the 1973 supersession, Khanna was to have become CJI following Ray's retirement on 29 January 1977, giving him five months as CJI.

But the chief justiceship was not to be his. By 1975, he was the only judge remaining on the SCI who had decided against the government's position in *Kesavananda*, which prohibited Parliament from abrogating the 'basic structure' of the Constitution. He cast the deciding vote in that landmark seven–six decision. But all agree that it was his dissent in *Habeas Corpus* in 1976 during the darkest days of the Emergency that cost him the chief justiceship. Khanna knew when he penned that dissent that this would happen.[60] His four colleagues in that epic decision had accepted the government's argument that, during a declared emergency, the right to move any court for the protection of Fundamental Rights was suspended, meaning that there could be no judicial scrutiny of the detention of the tens of thousands languishing in jails. Khanna's dissent said that the main issue in this case was not just the curtailment of personal liberty but the rule of law, and he was unwilling to accept the argument that courts could be rendered mute during a national emergency. This fearless dissent received high praise, both within and outside the country. In an unprecedented lead editorial, the *New York Times* said, 'If India ever finds its way back to the freedom and democracy that were proud hallmarks of its first eighteen [*sic*] years as an independent nation, someone will surely erect a monument to Justice H.R. Khanna of the Supreme Court'.[61]

Mrs Gandhi's Government's response to Khanna's dissent was to censor its publication, no longer invite him to official dinners, and finally, to deny him the chief justiceship. He knew that this dissent would cost him

[60] Khanna, *Neither Roses Nor Thorns*, pp. 79–80.
[61] 'Fading Hope in India', *New York Times*, 30 April 1976, p. A26.

that office.[62] After it was announced on 28 January 1977 that M.H. Beg,[63] who had decided in favour of the government in both *Kesavananda* and *Habeas Corpus*, would succeed Ray as chief, Khanna immediately submitted his resignation—news of his resignation was blocked out by the censor— with effect from 12 March, after utilizing accrued leave time due him. 28 January was almost exactly twenty-five years after his first day as a judge in Ferozepore. As he left the Court that day, he recalled that his quarter century on the bench

... flashed through my mind. ... [T]here arose a feeling of some satisfaction for having not swerved or faltered at the crucial time from what I believed was the correct course. The fact that it resulted in foregoing and losing the office of Chief Justice of India did not hurt very much for such consequence was expected from the moment I prepared my judgment in the habeas corpus case and also because many others have paid much greater price for following the voice of their conscience. Undoubtedly those moments were not without a tinge of sadness, which invariably is there at the time of parting whether from a career of life or from a dear one. It also happens that in such moments of crisis, in moments when the curtain is falling on a major part of one's life, if one has the consciousness of having done what one believed to be the right thing, one gets sustenance and support from inner and hitherto unknown reserves of strength.[64]

Khanna's resignation was followed by another wave of affection and esteem, particularly from members of the bar throughout the country. The monument that the *New York Times* thought he deserved did not materialize but the Supreme Court bar association raised the funds for a life-sized portrait of him which now hangs in courtroom number two of the SCI.[65]

A few days after his resignation, leaders of the Janata Party, who were gearing up for the March national elections, urged Khanna to stand as a candidate for Parliament. He declined, choosing chamber practice instead. This was very lucrative and leading commercial and industrial concerns sought his advice. Following its election victory, the Janata government asked Khanna to head what came to be called the Maruti Commission of

[62] Khanna, *Neither Roses Nor Thorns*, pp. 79–80. Gokhale, still the law minister at this time, later told Kuldip Nayar that he had tried unsuccessfully to persuade Mrs Gandhi not to supersede Khanna, *The Judgement: Inside Story of the Emergency in India* (New Delhi: Vikas Publishing House Pvt. Ltd., 1977), p. 169.

[63] In his autobiography, Khanna revealed his disdain for Ray and Beg by never mentioning their names. He referred to Beg as 'the judge next junior to me', and as 'the gentleman who had superseded me'. *Neither Roses Nor Thorns*, pp. 84, 91.

[64] *Neither Roses Nor Thorns*, pp. 88–9.

[65] Ibid., pp. 84, 147.

Inquiry. He declined on the ground that the inquiry would of necessity deal with Mrs Gandhi and her son Sanjay, and that because he had been superseded by Mrs Gandhi, some sections of the public might not have confidence in his objectivity.[66] In May 1977, he also declined the offer to become chairman of the Seventh Finance Commission. But he did accept the offer tendered by Prime Minister Desai to become chairman of the Eighth Law Commission, and succeeded Gajendragadkar in December 1977.[67] He served in this capacity without salary so as to underline his independence from the government.

When the Janata government unravelled in mid-1979 and Chaudhary Charan Singh became prime minister, the latter pressed Khanna to become minister of law, justice, and company affairs. Although Khanna was of two minds about this offer and asked for time to think it over, the swearing in of the new ministry was just two hours away. He was swept along with the other ministers, resigned from the Law Commission, and took the oath of office on 30 July. But his second thoughts about the correctness of holding this office increased and three days later he resigned.

Khanna then returned to his chamber practice and arbitration work and devoted considerable time to delivering lectures and to writing. In 1980, he chaired a committee appointed by the Indian Council of Medical Research which produced a 'Policy Statement on Ethical Considerations Involved in Research on Human Subjects'. Not long after Mrs Gandhi returned to power in 1980, two of her ministers inquired whether he would accept the chairmanship of the Press Commission. He declined on the grounds that the purely formal resignation of his former colleague, P.K. Goswami, from that post after Mrs Gandhi returned to power should not have been accepted.[68]

Although he had found himself unsuited in 1979 for the rough and tumble of active political life, by the summer of 1982 he was more amenable when he was invited by all nine opposition parties to be their candidate for the 1982 presidential election. The Congress (I) had put up his friend Giani Zail Singh, so the contest was between two Punjabis. Khanna knew that he

[66] Ibid., p. 95. This commission was established to inquire into the alleged misuse of state power for personal ends by Sanjay Gandhi.

[67] The commission's eightieth report, entitled *The Method of Appointment of Judges* (Government of India Press, 1980) and prepared by Khanna, was the first comprehensive study of the appointment process.

[68] Khanna, *Neither Roses Nor Thorns*, p. 135.

had no chance of winning and was soundly defeated, receiving but 27 per cent of the vote.[69]

Once again he returned to his chamber practice, arbitrations, delivering lectures, and writing. He became president of the Bharat Vikas Parishad in 1985 and became chairman of the Press Trust of India in 1988. In the late 1990s, he headed the Railway Safety Review Committee, usually referred to simply as the 'Khanna Committee', the report of which was a scathing indictment of the state of affairs in the Indian Railways which received wide publicity.[70]

Khanna left a substantial legacy in the form of published writings. These include *Judicial Review or Confrontation?* (Delhi: Macmillan Company of India, 1977); *Constitution and Civil Liberties* (New Delhi: Radha Krishna Prakashan, 1978); *Liberty, Democracy and Ethics* (New Delhi: Radha Krishna Prakashan, 1979); *Constitution and Socio-Economic Changes: Two Lectures Broadcast from All-India Radio* (New Delhi: Publications Division, Ministry of Information and Broadcasting, Government of India, 1979); *The Judicial System* (New Delhi: Indian Institute of Public Administration, 1980); *Society and the Law* (Gauhati: Ashok Publishing House, 1981); *Law, Men of Law, and Education* (Bombay: N.M. Tripathi Pvt. Ltd., 1981); *Making of India's Constitution* (Lucknow: Eastern Book Company, 1981); *Judiciary in India and Judicial Process* (Calcutta: Ajoy Law House, 1985); *Mulla on the Transfer of Property Act, 1882*, with P.M. Bakshi, seventh edition (Bombay: N.M. Tripathi Pvt. Ltd., 1985); *Neither Roses Nor Thorns* (Lucknow: Eastern Book Company, 1985); *Federal Element in the Indian Constitution* (Pune: University of Poona, 1985); *Terrorism in Punjab: Cause and Cure* (Chandigarh: Panchad Research Institute, 1987); and *Issues Before the Nation* (New Delhi: B.R. Publishing Corp., 1988).

In 1999, he was honoured by the nation when he received a Padma Vibhushan award, the second highest civilian award. Earlier, in 1979, he received an LLD (*honoris causa*) from Punjabi University, Patiala. In 2003, he was conferred an honorary life membership of the Bar Association of India.

Khanna remained active in his nineties. He often contributed articles to newspapers and his participation in the Akhil Bharatiya Adhivakta Parishad

---

[69] Ibid., pp. 136–42.
[70] For a useful summary of this report, see V. Sridhar, 'Railway Safety: A Poor Record', *Frontline*, vol. 18, issue 15, 21 July–3 August 2001.

continued. In 2003, he was appointed to represent the public interest on the board of directors of the Press Trust of India.

An authentic hero who earned iconic status, he died on 25 February 2008, at age ninety-five.[71]

44. Kuttyil Kurien Mathew (1971–6)

The second member of the Christian community to serve on the SCI, K.K. Mathew was born on 3 January 1911 at Athirampuzha, Kottayam district, Kerala. His father, Auseph Kurien, was a businessman who prospered in tobacco and other businesses.

Mathew received his BA degree in politics and economics from Maharaja College, Trivandrum, Kerala in 1932. His BL was earned from the Trivandrum Law College in 1934. He won the Harvey Memorial Prize at the BA level and the Victoria Memorial Scholarship during his BL studies. He was both the first graduate and the first lawyer in his family.[72]

He began practising law in 1935 in the district courts in Kottayam and shortly thereafter in Trivandrum. On 24 January 1939, he enrolled as an advocate of the former High Court of Travancore. Following the reorganization of states and the integration of Travancore and Cochin, the new High Court of Kerala began functioning in 1956 at Ernakulam and Mathew shifted his practice there. After twenty-five years of private practice, the Congress government, back in power in Kerala, appointed him Advocate General on 1 November 1960. He held that post only briefly, for on 5 June 1962, at age fifty-one, he was appointed an additional judge of the Kerala High Court. After two extensions, he was confirmed as a permanent judge on 27 October 1966.

After nearly a decade on the Kerala bench, by which time he was third in seniority, Mathew was brought up to the SCI. When he was sworn in on 4 October 1971, he was sixty. On the eve of the April 1973 supersession, Mathew, then seventh in seniority, was 'sounded' about accepting the chief

[71] An outpouring of tributes followed. See especially Rajinder Sachar, 'Justice H.R. Khanna: When others crawled, he stood tall', *The Tribune* (Chandigarh), 3 March 2008; Anil Diwan, 'A Profile in Judicial Courage', *The Hindu*, 7 March 2008; and V.R. Krishna Iyer, 'A Courageous Voice of Dissent', *The Hindu*, 19 March 2008.

[72] I interviewed Mathew on 17 November 1988 at Ernakulam, Kerala. His son, K.M. Joseph, was appointed to the Kerala High Court in 2004.

justiceship if it was offered to him. This was before A.N. Ray was offered that post. Mathew felt that it would not be proper to accept it, and expressed his refusal.[73]

On 10 January 1975, a year before he left the SCI, he was appointed chairman of the Mishra Death Inquiry Commission which investigated the murder of Union Railway Minister L.N. Mishra.

Mathew reached retirement age on 3 January 1976, when the Emergency was in full throttle. During his relatively brief SCI career he acquired a reputation as one of the most scholarly and brilliant judges of his era and was held in high esteem even by colleagues with different judicial philosophies.[74] He also dissented more frequently, eleven times, than any other judge during the 1967–81 years.[75]

After completing the Mishra commission work, Mathew returned to Ernakulam where he spent much of his time reading and writing. As was his habit throughout his career, he was not active in educational, cultural, social, or political activities. He did not engage in chamber practice and only once agreed to arbitrate a dispute. Not unexpectedly, he was not offered any official assignments by the Janata or Lok Dal governments during 1977–9.

After the return of Mrs Gandhi and the Congress (I) in 1980, Mathew accepted, on 21 April 1980, the chairmanship of the Second Press Commission. Although he held that post until 1983, he also took on the chairmanship of the Tenth Law Commission on 14 December 1981. His term was to be three years but extensions meant that he served until August 1985. In this capacity, he prepared and distributed a questionnaire that provoked a good deal of controversy, particularly in raising the question of

---

[73] Mathew told me that the sounding did not come from Kumaramangalam or Gokhale, but from a lesser official he declined to identify ('someone in the government'). Mathew did not tell his colleagues about this sounding, but Hegde, after he became Speaker of the Lok Sabha in 1977, learned that Mathew was, in fact, offered the chief justiceship before Ray. Interview with Hegde, 14–15 November 1988. Granville Austin wrote much the same thing: 'that Mrs Gandhi gave her assent to sounding out Justice Mathew, who was philosophically in tune with Kumaramangalam, about becoming Chief Justice before Ray was approached. She was said to be willing to supersede all judges senior to Mathew should Ray decline the appointment'. *Working a Democratic Constitution* (London: Oxford University Press, 1966), p. 280.

[74] P.K. Goswami, a colleague of Mathew's, who shared few of his economic and political views, described him as 'a real scholar, the Harlan of the SCI'. Interview in New Delhi, 8 July 1983.

[75] Gadbois, 'The Decline of Dissent on the Supreme Court, 1950–1981', in Ram Avtar Sharma (ed.), *Justice and Social Order in India* (New Delhi: Intellectual Publishing House, 1984), pp. 235–59.

whether the SCI should become a constitutional court dealing exclusively with constitutional matters, and a separate court of appeal established to deal with all other matters.[76] The results of this questionnaire were never published because there were not enough responses.

In August 1985, he left the law commission and accepted appointment as head of a commission constituted by the central government, following the June Rajiv–Longowal Accord, to determine which Hindi-speaking areas of Punjab should go to Haryana in lieu of the planned transfer of Chandigarh to Punjab. Often referred to as the 'Mathew Commission', his report was submitted in January 1986. It failed to resolve the differences between the two states but it was not expected to. That assignment completed, he returned to Ernakulam where he spent his remaining years in full retirement.

Some of Mathew's SCI colleagues believed that he was, or earlier had been, a communist. Mathew told me that this was not true. He described himself as a leftist and as less supportive of private property rights than most of his colleagues in Kerala and Delhi. He said the communist label gained currency particularly after his dissent in the *E.M S. Namboodiripad* contempt case.[77] K.S. Hegde, as conservative as Mathew was liberal, and whose anti-communist views ran deep, said there was no truth to this charge, for communism was incompatible with his Christian faith. The two remained close friends for the remainder of their lives.[78]

During the early 1980s, Mathew authored two books which revealed the wide range of his learning and legal scholarship: *The Right to Equality and Property under the Indian Constitution* (New Delhi: National, 1980); and *Three Lectures* (Lucknow: Eastern Book Company, 1983). His *K.K. Mathew on Democracy, Equality and Freedom* (Lucknow: Eastern Book Company), a collection of his addresses, essays, and excerpts from some of his judicial opinions, edited by Upendra Baxi, was published in 1978.

Mathew died on 2 May 1992, at age eighty-one.[79]

[76] The questionnaire in its entirety is found in *Reforms in Higher Judiciary and Law Commission Questionnaire* (New Delhi: Bar Council of India Trust, 1982), pp. 15–26.

[77] *Narayanan Nambiar* v. *E.M.S. Namboodiripad*, 1968 *Kerala Law Times* 299. The majority found Namboodiripad, the first communist chief minister of Kerala, guilty of contempt of court for some very critical words about judges. Mathew didn't agree with Namboodiripad's language but said he had the right to express them. For a more complete account of Mathew's dissent, see Upendra Baxi's introduction to *Democracy, Equality and Freedom* (Lucknow: Eastern Book Company, 1978), p. xvi.

[78] Interview with Hegde on 14–15 November 1988.

[79] An affectionate tribute, 'Late Mr Justice K.K. Mathew' is found in [1992] 3 SCC (*Journal*), pp. 1–2.

45. Mirza Hameedullah Beg (1971–8)

M.H. Beg was born into a prominent and wealthy Muslim family which traced its descent from ancestors who had migrated from Tashkent in Russia to the subcontinent five generations earlier.[80] Beg's lawyer father, Nawab Mirza Yar Samiullah Beg, practised first in Lucknow at the Oudh chief court, where he was active in the Indian National Congress, and served for some time as the party's joint secretary. His father became well known as the chief justice of the old Hyderabad State from 1917 to 1937, and later as law minister and president of that state's Judicial Reforms Committee. There were other relatives who were lawyers and judges as well, including an uncle who was a judge in the former Jaipur state. Beg also married into a judicial family. His wife was Kaniz Imam, the daughter of former SCI judge S.J. Imam. Her grandfather was Hasan Imam, a judge of the Calcutta High Court who resigned to become active in nationalist politics. M.H. Beg was not the only member of his generation to attain high judicial office. An elder brother, Nasirullah Beg, was for many years a judge of the Allahabad High Court and was that court's chief justice when he retired in 1967.

Beg was born on 22 February 1913 at Lucknow, Uttar Pradesh. At age three, his family moved to Hyderabad. In 1930, at age seventeen, he went to England where he completed his secondary education and then enrolled at Trinity College, Cambridge University, where he earned the BA (honours) degree in archeology, anthropology, and history in 1934. He received an MA degree in political economy from the same university in 1936. During these Cambridge days he was active in the Indian Majlis and was a member of the Shakespearean Dramatic Society. He also attended advanced classes in economics, public finance, political theory, and constitutional and international law at the London School of Economics and Political Science.

He returned to India in 1936 with plans to enter government service in Hyderabad state. But soon he decided that he wanted to become a lawyer and returned to England. Because of the war in Europe he was back in India in 1940. He took the Council of Legal Education examinations in New Delhi and obtained first class firsts in Hindu and Mohammedan Laws. In 1941, he was called to the bar from Lincoln's Inn.

The Nizam of Hyderabad offered him a post in the higher judicial service, waiving the minimum period of law practice normally required. His

[80] Interview with Beg on 2 May 1983, in New Delhi.

father objected to his son beginning his career with special treatment and advised him to commence practising law instead. His father's tenure as the Hyderabad chief justice had ended in 1937 but he continued holding high offices in the Nizam's government and believed it would not be appropriate for his son to practise in Hyderabad.

He moved to Uttar Pradesh, where he was a stranger, and enrolled as an advocate of the Allahabad High Court on 30 April 1942, at age twenty-nine. Although he settled in Allahabad, his early practice was mainly at the Meerut district courts. He also taught law part-time at Meerut College from 1943 to 1946. In the latter year he moved his practice to Allahabad where his elder brother Nasirullah was practising. Beg was to remain in Allahabad for the next twenty-five years. During most of this period (1946–63), Beg, a scholarly man and voracious reader, taught law part-time at Allahabad University. He also served as Standing Counsel to Allahabad University, and for about twelve years as Standing Counsel to the UP Sunni Central Waqf Board. Early in his career he had gained the reputation of being an expert in Mohammedan Law.

On 11 June 1963, at age fifty, he was appointed as an additional judge of the Allahabad High Court. His appointment, he believed, was delayed because his brother was serving on that court. He was confirmed as a permanent judge on 13 March 1966.

After M. Hidayatullah's retirement in December 1970, the SCI was without a Muslim judge. According to Beg, Mrs Gandhi wanted him appointed to the Muslim seat. But he had served only seven and one-half years on the Allahabad bench, and was about fifteenth in seniority. A solution to his seniority shortcoming was found when Himachal Pradesh gained statehood in 1971 and a new high court was created at Simla. Beg was transferred to this high court as its first chief justice on 25 January 1971. His sojourn at Simla was brief for he was sworn in as a member of the SCI in the same year, on 10 December, at age fifty-eight.

Beg could look forward to becoming chief justice in July 1977, following H.R. Khanna's retirement, and holding that post until his own sixty-fifth birthday on 22 February 1978. But two weeks before A.N. Ray's retirement Law Minister Gokhale told Beg, who had supported the government's side in both the *Kesavananda* and *Habeas Corpus* decisions, that the government was going to supersede Khanna and name him, the next-in-line, as CJI. He became the fifteenth CJI on 29 January 1977 and held that post for just over one year until his own retirement on 22 February 1978.

After leaving the SCI, he remained in Delhi and engaged in chamber practice and conducted arbitrations. In 1979, he was appointed a member of the executive council of Banaras Hindu University. He was also active in the International Law Association and the World Association of Judges. For some time he was a director of the board of the *National Herald* group of newspapers.

When Mrs Gandhi returned to power in 1980, he was appointed a member of a UNESCO commission set up by the union government and served as chairman of its sub-committee on the social sciences. His most important and well known post-retirement position was that of chairman of the Minorities Commission to which he was appointed on 4 March 1981. A devout Muslim, he was secular in outlook and respectful of all religions and thus a good fit for that commission. In 1988, Prime Minister Rajiv Gandhi's Government awarded him the Padma Vibhushan, the nation's second highest civilian award, for his contributions to law and jurisprudence.

He was the author of *Impact of Secularism on Life and Law* (New Delhi: People's Publishing House, 1985). He and S.K. Verma edited the sixth edition of *B.R. Verma's Islamic Law: Being Commentaries on Mohammedan Law in India, Pakistan and Bangladesh* (Allahabad: Law Publishers, 1986), and again with S.K. Verma, edited the ninth edition of *Sir Hari Singh Gour's Law of Transfer: Being Commentaries on the Transfer of Property Act, 1882* (Allahabad: Law Publishers, 1987). He and Gyanendra Kumar edited volume I of the third revised edition of *Woodroffe & Ameer Ali's Code of Civil Procedure: A Commentary on Act V of 1908, as amended up-to-date along with state amendments* (Allahabad: Law Publishers, 1987).

Not long after his term with the Minorities Commission ended, Beg died on 19 November 1988, at age seventy-five.

46. Surendra Narayan Dwivedi (1972–4)

On 1 October 1913, S.N. Dwivedi was born into a family of modest means in the village of Amauli, Fatehpur district, Uttar Pradesh. He was the son of Rajeshwari Prasad Dwivedi who was a tehsildar. After earning a BA from Ewing Christian College, Allahabad, in about 1934, he received the LLB from Lucknow University probably in 1936,[81] becoming the first in his family to be a lawyer.

[81] A letter dated 29 March 1984 from his son, Rakesh Dwivedi, was helpful in providing information about his father.

Dwivedi began his law practice in 1937 at the Hamirpur district courts. In his early years he often appeared free of charge for the poor.[82] He was active in the nationalist struggle and his participation in the 1942 Quit India Movement resulted in him being arrested twice and imprisoned for more than a year. In October 1943, he enrolled as an advocate of the Allahabad High Court, beginning a twenty-nine year association with that court. From November 1954 until his resignation in December 1955, he served as a Junior Standing Counsel for the State.

At age forty-five, on 12 May 1959, Dwivedi was appointed to the Allahabad bench as an additional judge, and confirmation as a permanent judge came on 19 September 1960. Thirteen years later, by which time he was fourth in seniority, he was promoted to the SCI. He was fifty-eight when he was sworn in on 14 August 1972 and was in the queue to serve as CJI for seven months in 1978, following Beg's retirement. It was Dwivedi who in the *Kesavananda* decision wrote: 'The Constitution is not intended to be the arena of legal quibbling for men with long purses. It is made for the common people'.[83]

He was a scholarly man whose wide-ranging intellectual interests included literature, political philosophy, European political and constitutional history, music, and metaphysics. He was the editor of the third edition of the two-volume S. *Row's Transfer of Property Act of 1882* (Allahabad: Allahabad Book Company, 1971–2). He is remembered also as a strong proponent of the Hindi language. For some time, he held the post of Pradhan Mantri of the Hindi Sahitya Sammelan and was President of the Hindustani Academy.

He learned in 1973 that he was suffering from cancer and by mid-1974 had to go on leave. Just twenty-eight months after he arrived in Delhi, he died on 8 December 1974, at age sixty-one.

47. Arun Kumar Mukherjea (1972–3)

A.K. Mukherjea was born into an upper middle-class family on 20 January 1915, in Calcutta, West Bengal. Both his father and his grandfather were lawyers. Kalipada Mukherjee, his father, a law graduate of Calcutta University, practised law in the district courts, first at Jamalpur and later

[82] Interview with V. Bhargava, earlier Dwivedi's colleague on the Allahabad High Court, on 31 May 1983, in New Delhi.
[83] [1973] *Supp. SCR* 1, 922.

at Mymensingh in today's Bangladesh. He served also as government pleader in the latter city. In 1936, he shifted to Calcutta and served as the government pleader at the Alipore district court. Mukherjea's grandfather was Bepin Bihari Mukherjee, a lawyer who practised at Jamalpur.[84]

He received a BA in philosophy from Presidency College, Calcutta University, in 1934, earning firsts in the university examinations. He then went to England where he studied at the London School of Oriental Studies. Although tempted by law, he was successful in the ICS examinations and on 29 September 1937 became an ICS officer and began his career in Bengal.

During the next thirteen years, he served in various capacities in Bengal and also spent one assignment with the Union Ministry of Transport. He acquired a reputation for having a thorough knowledge of Bengal's topography and river systems and would play a major role with three important boundary disputes. In 1946, he was appointed secretary of the Bengal Boundary Commission (the Radcliffe Commission), helping to prepare the Indian case for the partition of Bengal. He was responsible for preparing and presenting India's position before the Bagge Tribunal, where the boundary disputes between West Bengal and East Pakistan, and between Assam and East Pakistan, were adjudicated. Finally, in the 1950s, after he had left the ICS and at the request of the then Bengal Chief Minister, Dr B.C. Roy, he prepared the briefs for the state of West Bengal for presentation before the States Reorganization Commission.

By the late 1940s, Mukherjea's interest in the ICS waned and he was increasingly attracted by the legal profession. He returned to England and was called to the bar from Gray's Inn in 1950 and the following year he retired prematurely from the ICS. Then age thirty-six, he enrolled as an advocate of the Calcutta High Court in April 1951. Despite this late start, success came quickly and he served also as senior government counsel for the union government for several years. Only eleven years after joining the bar he was appointed an additional judge of the Calcutta High Court on 26 February 1962 at age forty-seven, and was confirmed as a permanent judge on 12 December 1963.

He was fourth in seniority at Calcutta and aged fifty-seven when he was sworn in at the SCI on 14 August 1972. He was to have served for nearly seven and one-half years and was to have been CJI from October 1978 until

[84] Correspondence dated 3 July 1983 with his son, Kalyan Mukherjee. Justice Mukherjea chose to spell his surname differently than his father and son.

January 1980. Death from a heart attack, however, removed him from the bench on 23 October 1974, at age fifty-nine.

Not only had Mukherjea brought a rich and varied professional background to the SCI, but he was, by even the highest standards, a brilliant intellectual and a true Renaissance man. He was a student of the humanities, particularly philosophy, history, and logic at Presidency College, and claimed Bertrand Russell as his intellectual idol. He was well versed in the mathematical sciences and statistics, having studied under Professor P.C. Mahalanobis, the internationally acclaimed statistician and founder of the Indian Statistical Institute in Calcutta. Mukherjea was also an accomplished scholar of Sanskrit literature and grammar. His greatest love was music.[85]

He was a prominent figure in the cultural, educational, and public life of Calcutta, and unselfishly gave of his time to promote a variety of interests, particularly university administration. From 1968 to 1971, he served as acting chancellor of Jadavpur University. During the same years (1970–1), he was vice-chairman of the Indian Statistical Institute. He was a member of the senate of Calcutta University and from 1971 to 1973 he chaired the University Grants Commission Committee for the development and reorganization of that university. He was also a member of the committee which made recommendations concerning the reorganization of Visva Bharati University, and a member of the governing body of the Government College of Arts and Crafts, Calcutta. For some time he was also chairman of the Indian Academy of Philosophy, a member of the Council of the Asiatic Society, and a member of the Sangeet Natak Academi in both Calcutta and New Delhi.

48. Yeshwant Vishnu Chandrachud (1972–85)

Y.V. Chandrachud was born into a family of lawyers[86] on 12 July 1920 at Pune, Maharashtra. He was the son of Vishnu Balkrishna Chandrachud who, in 1912, earned one of the first LLM degrees from Bombay University.

[85] Justice Sisir Kumar Mukherjea's, 'In Memoriam: The Late Justice Arun K. Mukherjea', *Calcutta Weekly Notes*, LXXVIII (26 November 1973), pp. xv–xvi.

[86] Interviews with Chandrachud in New Delhi on 23 January 1980, 3 May 1983, and 8 December 1988. His son, Dr Dhananjaya Y. Chandrachud, followed his father's footsteps, and became a Bombay High Court judge in 2000.

The latter practised law in Pune from 1912 to 1927 but his heart was more in teaching, and he was one of the founders of the Pune Law College and a professor of law there. He was also for some time the chief justice of Sawantwadi State and later the *dewan* of that small princely state. Better known as a lawyer was his father's elder brother, N.B. Chandrachud, who also practised in Pune. The Chandrachud family was well off by the standards of the day. In addition to the earnings of his father and uncle, they were *jagirdars*[87] of several villages.

He earned his BA degree in history and economics from Elphinstone College, Bombay, in 1940. He then returned to Pune, where he earned an LLB in 1942 from the Pune Law College. He compiled an outstanding record as a student, passing both law examinations in the first class and earning a first class first—the only one in the entire Bombay presidency that year—in the second LLB examination. His academic achievements won the prestigious Sir Mangaldas Nathubhai Legal Scholarship, the Judge Spencer Prize, and the Gussie K. Kanga Prize.

In November 1943, at age twenty-three, he enrolled as an advocate of the Bombay High Court. After two years of practice at the Pune district courts, he shifted to the Bombay High Court where he was to remain for nearly three decades. In the early 1950s, he served as secretary of the Advocates Association of Western India. In December 1952, he began to represent the Bombay government in the high court as an additional assistant government pleader. In May 1956, he was promoted to assistant government pleader and in June 1958, became government pleader. He attracted national attention as the prosecutor in the sensational Nanavati trial in the late 1950s. At the age of forty, young especially by Bombay standards, he was appointed an additional judge of the Bombay High Court on 19 March 1961. That judgeship was made permanent on 21 December of the same year.

Earlier in his career, from 1949 to 1953, he was a part-time professor of law at the Government Law College, Bombay, earning Rs 285 per month for teaching five classes per week.[88] During his years on the bench, he headed the pay commission which fixed the pay scales of Bombay Municipal Corporation officers. He also served as the arbitrator in a dispute

[87] They owned land in several villages.

[88] Part-time professors, at that time, were selected by a committee composed of chief justice M.C. Chagla, and associate judges Gajendragadkar and S.R. Tendolkar. Chandrachud's students included Fali S. Nariman and Soli J. Sorabjee, both of whom would rise to the top tier of the nation's legal profession.

between the Bombay Electricity Supply and Transport Undertaking and its employees' union. In 1969, he was selected by the union government to conduct the delicate investigation into the circumstances relating to the death of Deen Dayal Upadhyaya, who was president of the Bharatiya Jana Sangh at the time of his death.[89]

After more than eleven years on the Bombay bench, by which time he was third in seniority, Chandrachud was invited to become a member of the SCI. He was fifty-two, younger than any previous appointee[90] when he was sworn in on 28 August 1972. Chandrachud was one of a small number of judges who, relatively early in their careers, were viewed as SCI material.[91] The only question was when, not if, he would reach Delhi. If overall merit was the major criterion, it would have been hard to explain the denial of an SCI judgeship to one with Chandrachud's credentials.

Chandrachud was, however, hesitant about accepting the SCI invitation.[92] His two seniors on the Bombay bench were to retire soon and he could look forward to serving as chief justice of that premier high court for a decade. Although he gave up that glamorous post to become the juniormost judge of the SCI, he could, according to the calculus of the seniority convention, look forward to holding the topmost judicial post in the nation for five and a half years, following A.K. Mukherjea's scheduled retirement in January 1980. The premature death of Mukherjea meant that Chandrachud was the seniormost judge on the eve of CJI M.H. Beg's retirement in early 1978.

When he was sworn in as CJI on 22 February 1978, he was just fifty-seven, an age when most future SCI judges are still serving on their high courts. Seven and a half years later, on 12 July 1985, he retired, closing out a quarter of a century of distinguished service as a high court and SCI judge.

[89] Y.V. Chandrachud Commission of Inquiry, *Report Regarding the Facts and Circumstances Relating to the Death of Shri Deen Dayal Upadhyaya* (New Delhi: Ministry of Home Affairs, 1970).

[90] Hidayatullah was also fifty-two when he became an SCI judge, but was ten months older than Chandrachud.

[91] According to Hidayatullah, during his own years on the SCI, both Chandrachud and P.N. Bhagwati were viewed as destined for promotion. Interview with Hidayatullah, 4 November 1988.

[92] See his reply to the Bombay Bar Association's farewell to him in *The Bombay Law Reporter* (*Journal Section*), LXXIV (1972), p. 713.

Chandrachud's retirement years were very active ones. For the first few years, he remained in Delhi and engaged in chamber practice and conducted arbitrations. From 1985 to 1987, at the behest of the union government, he served as chairman of the Assam–Meghalaya Boundary Commission. In 1986, he began serving as chairman of Sakal Papers Pvt. Ltd., publishers of a Marathi newspaper. In 1989, he returned to Bombay, where he continued his chamber practice and arbitration work. At the request of the SCI he determined the compensation for the dependents of the victims of a fire that took sixty lives. He headed a committee appointed by the Maharashtra government to deal with another chapter of the long-festering dispute between Maharashtra and Karnataka over Belgaum. His most remembered post-retirement activity was his 1997 report on allegations of bribery, betting, and match-fixing by cricket players which attracted national and international attention.

He lent his talents, administrative skills, and stature to a wide variety of institutions and other activities. He devoted considerable time to educational matters, including being a visiting professor at several universities and law colleges. The founding president of the India International Rural Cultural Centre in 1979, he remained active in this organization for the remainder of his life. He served as chairman of the Social Security Foundation and was a member of the National Council for Older Persons. He was president or chairman of the International Law Association (Indian branch); the Asiatic Society of Bombay; the Indian Law Society Law College (formerly Pune Law College); a trustee of the S.P. Mandali Trust; the Centre for Policy Research of the Social Science Research Council; and the Shikshana Prasaraka Mandali of Pune which operates forty-one educational institutions in Maharashtra. He was also chairman of the International Review Board of the Bombay City Eye Institute and Research Centre and editor-in-chief of the Government Law College *Law Review*.

He was the author or editor of several publications, including *The Basics of the Indian Constitution: Its Search for Social Justice and the Role of Judges* (New Delhi: Publications Division, Ministry of Information and Broadcasting, Government of India, 1989); *Laws of India, 1836 to Date with Commentary and State Amendments*, 6 vols (New Delhi: Bharat Law House, 1999–2001); *Ratanlal & Dhirajlal's The Code of Criminal Procedure Act II of 1974: With Exhaustive Notes, Comments, Case-law References, and State Amendments*, in collaboration with V.R. Manohar and Avtar Singh, seventeenth edition (Nagpur: Wadhwa and Company, 2007); *P. Ramanath Aiyar's The Law*

Lexicon, second edition (Nagpur: Wadhwa and Company, 2000); *Durga Das Basu's Shorter Constitution of India*, thirteenth edition, with V.R. Manohar and Bhagabati Prasad Banerjee (Nagpur: Wadhwa and Company, 2001); *Ratanlal & Dhirajlal's The Indian Penal Code*, twenty-ninth edition with V.R. Manohar (Nagpur: Wadhwa and Company, 2002); *Ramaiya's Guide to the Companies Act*, with S.M. Dugar, sixteenth edition, 3 vols (Nagpur: Wadhwa and Company, 2004); *Ratanlal & Dhirajlal's Law of Evidence*, twenty-first edition with V.R. Manohar (Nagpur: Wadhwa and Company, 2004); with S.S. Subramani and B.P. Banerjee, *Durga Das Basu's Commentary on the Constitution of India*, eighth edition, 8 vols (Nagpur: Wadhwa and Company, 2007); and *P. Ramanatha Aiyar Concise Law Dictionary*, third edition (Nagpur: Wadhwa and Company, 2007).

Paying homage to him is *A Chandrachud Reader: Collection of Judgments with Annotations* (New Delhi: Documentation Centre for Corporate & Business Policy Research 1985), edited by V.S. Deshpande. Particularly valuable in this book is Upendra Baxi's, '"The Fair Name of Justice": The Memorable Voyage of Chief Justice Chandrachud', pp. 72–99. The Justice Y.V. Chandrachud Memorial Lecture is sponsored annually by the KIIT Law School.

His tenure as CJI was by far the longest in the SCI's history and spanned years of momentous changes in the country, including two presidents and four prime ministers. As his tenure progressed relations among the brethren became increasingly fractious. Chandrachud was a man of the middle and struggled to maintain some collegiality among strong personalities to his left and right. It could not have been much fun being CJI during those years.

A cultured gentleman with impeccable manners, a man of unquestioned integrity and fairness, and unpretentious despite his great learning, he died at age eighty-eight, on 14 July 2008.

49. Alwar Naicker Alagiriswami (1972–5)

On 17 October 1910, A.N. Alagiriswami was born into a Telugu-speaking family at Nagampatti, Tiruneveli District, in Tamil Nadu. His father, Alwar Naicker, a moneylender and an agriculturist with large landholdings, was a man of substantial means.[93]

---

[93] I met with Dr Hamsapriya Srinivasan, Alagiriswami's daughter, on 26 June 1983 in Madras.

Alagiriswami was the first university graduate and the first lawyer in his family. He received a BA (honours) degree in history, economics, and politics in 1932, followed by an MA from Presidency College, Madras. He had wanted to become a physician, but his test scores were not high enough. He turned to law, and received the BL from Madras Law College in 1934. During these student years he was active in the Indian National Congress, attended the Karachi Congress meeting in 1931, and wore khadi throughout his life.

He enrolled as an advocate of the Madras High Court on 16 March 1936 and practised for the next five years at the district courts in Madurai. Because he had a difficult time earning a living during these post-depression years, he applied for the Madras judicial service, was selected, and on 3 December 1941, at age thirty-one, he was posted as a district munsif at Gurzala. From April 1947 to September 1948 he served as the private secretary to the Madras chief minister. In 1948-9, he held the post of additional deputy secretary of the department of law. From 18 October 1949 to 14 April 1950, he was attached to the ministry of law in Delhi for additional legal training. During the period of October 1951–November 1953, he was back in Madras as joint secretary in the department of law. In this capacity, he was appointed secretary of the Expert Committee on Trade Marks, which meant being in Bombay from 13 November 1953 to 1 August 1954. He was promoted to secretary of the Madras department of law on 2 August 1954 and held that post until 17 May 1959, when he was appointed principal judge of the Madras city civil court.

His career took a different turn when, effective 1 July 1960, he retired from judicial service and accepted the post of government pleader. This was then a position of considerable prestige and was a stepping-stone to a high court judgeship. He held that position until 11 August 1966 when, at age fifty-five, he was appointed an additional judge of the high court. He was confirmed as a permanent judge on 18 November 1967.

In August 1970, four years after joining the high court and then nearly sixty, he went to Delhi to become the first chairman of the Monopolies and Restrictive Practices Trade Commission. He was serving in that capacity when he was sworn in as an SCI judge on 17 October 1972, his sixty-second birthday.

After retiring on 17 October 1975, he returned to Madras. He served as an arbitrator in several disputes, including one at the invitation of the International Chamber of Commerce dealing with a dispute between

Finland and North Korea. He declined to head any commissions of inquiry, including one concerned with the question of prohibition in Tamil Nadu, because he knew the findings would not be implemented. He served as chairman of the advisory board of Grindlays Bank from 1976 to 1982. He often provided free legal advice but never engaged in remunerative chamber practice.

He died on 15 February 1983, at age seventy-two.

XIV

The Ray Court (1973–7)

The announcement that A.N. Ray would be the next CJI came late in the afternoon of 25 April 1973, Sikri's last day as CJI. Fourth in seniority, Ray was vaulted over the heads of J.M. Shelat, K.S. Hegde, and A.N. Grover, all of whom immediately submitted their resignations. All CJIs appointed since 1950 have been on the basis of the most senior associate judge. Promotion by the sole criterion of seniority was just a convention, but after being the means of 'selecting' the previous thirteen CJIs, it had achieved the status of a settled constitutional convention.[1]

This supersession provoked an immediate and nationwide expression of outrage. When the announcement was made, the government offered no justification but it was perceived by all its critics who included, among many others, former CJIs, the nation's most eminent lawyers, leaders of the opposition, and the press, as an attack on the independence of the judiciary. After twenty-three years of the attentive public paying little attention to who the judges were and how they were selected, the supersession ignited a national seminar on the value of a robustly independent judiciary, the proper criteria for selecting judges, and the role of the executive in the selection process.

[1] This Ray Court material draws heavily upon my interviews. I met nine of the ten judges appointed during Ray's tenure. More than two dozen earlier and subsequent judges had things they wanted to say about Ray. All these interviews are cited elsewhere in this book and, in order to avoid the clutter of multiple footnotes, only a few are cited here. My three-hour interview with Ray is the only one he ever granted. Letter from Ray dated 15 November 2006.

On 2 May, the government sought to justify its appointment of Ray. Its main spokesman was not Law Minister H.R. Gokhale, but S. Mohan Kumaramangalam, the Minister of Steel and Mines whom most suspected was the architect of this decision. A friend of Mrs Gandhi from their student days in London, he was an influential figure in shaping her policies at that time. His presence in her cabinet was a matter of alarm to many, for before joining the Congress (I) he had been a prominent spokesman for the Communist Party.

Addressing Parliament, he began by saying that the appointment of Ray had to be considered within the context of the 'confrontation' between the government and the SCI since the *Golaknath* decision in 1967. He proceeded to criticize that decision, *Bank Nationalization*, *Privy Purses* and, handed down the day before the supersession, *Kesavananda*. He condemned the SCI's overall record of thwarting the government's economic reform initiatives. He said the government expected that Ray 'will be able to help put an end to this period of confrontation'.[2]

He began discussing the matter of a judge's attitudes and values. In choosing a CJI he said:

We have to take into consideration ... his basic outlook, his attitude to life, his politics—not the party to which he belongs but what it is that makes the man—through which spectacles he looks at the problems of India. To look upon a Judge as something above the crowd, far away—to think that he is not like us...has no relationship to reality.[3]

He warned members of Parliament that 'you cannot run away from the fact that the way in which judges look at a matter, their philosophy and outlook, do determine the decisions that they take. He quoted Abraham Lincoln's

[2] The quoted materials here are from the *Lok Sabha Debates* (New Delhi: Lok Sabha Secretariat, 2 May 1973) cols. 368–93. Kumaramangalam's speech is reprinted in Nayar, *Supersession of Judges*, pp. 78–92, under the title 'Chief Justice of India: Criteria of Choice'. An expanded and somewhat different version is found in S. Mohan Kumaramangalam, *Judicial Appointments: An Analysis of the Recent Controversy over the Appointment of the Chief Justice of India* (New Delhi: Oxford and IBH Publishing Company, 1973). An important, but overlooked, book which supports the supersession is A.R. Antulay, *Appointment of a Chief Justice: Perspectives in Judicial Independence, Rule of Law and Political Philosophy underlying the Constitution* (Bombay: Popular Prakashan, 1973). Kumaramangalam told Nayar that Hegde was the target of the supersession: '... he was a brilliant Judge but of a different philosophy. We could not simply have him'. Kuldip Nayar, *Supersession of Judges* (New Delhi: India Book Company, 1973), p. 15.

[3] CJI P. Sastri, in *State of Madras* v. *V.G. Row*, said very much the same thing: 'it is inevitable that the social philosophy and the scale of values of the judges ... should play an important part ...' [1952] SCR 597 and 607.

observation that, in choosing judges, 'we must take a man whose opinions are known'.[4]

The core of Kumaramangalam's rationale for the supersession is found in these words:

Certainly, we as a Government have a duty to take the philosophy and outlook of the Judge in coming to the conclusion whether he should or he should not lead the Supreme Court at this time. It is our duty in the Government honestly and fairly to come to the conclusion whether a particular person is fit to be appointed the Chief Justice of the Court because of his outlook, because of his philosophy as expressed in his ... opinions, whether he is more suitable or a more competent Judge. ... We do not want any committed judges. No judge has to commit himself. But we do want judges who are able to understand what is happening in our country; the wind of change that is going across our country; who is able to recognize that Parliament is sovereign. ... We are entitled surely to look at the philosophy of a Judge. We are entitled to look into his outlook. We are entitled to come to the conclusion that the philosophy of this Judge is forward-looking or backward-looking and to decide that we will take the forward-looking Judge and not the backward-looking Judge.

The Kumaramangalam doctrine is unexceptionable to Americans, accustomed as they are to a Supreme Court staffed by judges chosen largely on these grounds. But this was not the Indian way. Political considerations had never before been explicitly endorsed by any government spokesman. Kumaramangalam's rationale was presented so bluntly that it made the supersession seem immensely more ominous to those who valued an independent judiciary comprised of judges manifestly free from executive patronage.[5]

It was clear that Kumaramangalam believed that Ray met these criteria. Ray had a record of supporting Mrs Gandhi's policies said to be reformist and progressive. In the ten-to-one *Bank Nationalization* decision, he was the

---

[4] There are many instances where the appointing president was disappointed. As he was leaving office, American President Dwight Eisenhower was asked if he had made any mistakes as president. He replied 'yes, two, and they are both sitting on the Supreme Court'. Lawrence Baum, *The Supreme Court*, sixth edn (Washington, DC: CQ Press, 1998), p. 45.

[5] The supersession spawned a vast literature, most critical of it. In addition to Nayar's *Supersession of Judges*, see N.A. Palkhivala (ed.), *A Judiciary Made to Measure* (Bombay: M.R. Pai, 1973); and K.S. Hegde, *Crisis in Indian Judiciary* (Bombay: Sindhu Publications). Nayar's book contains chapters by, among others, Shelat, Hegde, Grover, Chagla, and Palkhivala, each of whom condemned the supersession. Palkhivala's book contains essays critical of both the supersession and Ray by a galaxy of prominent lawyers and retired judges, including Setalvad, Daphtary, Subba Rao, Hidayatullah, and Shah. Not all judges disagreed with the supersession.

sole dissenter. In the nine-to-two *Privy Purses* decision, he was effectively the lone dissenter, for Mitter's dissent was on narrow technical grounds. In the seven-to-six *Kesavananda* decision, he was the senior judge in the minority, supporting the government's arguments. In these same decisions, the superseded trio was in the majority upholding the right to property. Thus, there was sufficient evidence for Kumaramangalam to believe that Ray was likely to be supportive of Mrs Gandhi's social and economic reform policies.

Although it was the Kumaramangalam rationale that was at the centre of the controversy, the fact that Ray was given the chief justiceship stamped him as the government's man. There was concern that he would feel beholden to Mrs Gandhi and act accordingly.[6] At the top of the list of the government's objectives was to get *Kesavananda* overruled and it hoped that Ray could, and would, lead the SCI to accomplish that goal. According to Ray, he was offered the post by Gokhale on the 24th and given just two hours to decide,[7] the obvious implication being that he too would be superseded if he declined. Accepting the post cost him the respect of many earlier and present judges, particularly of M. Hidayatullah, who was responsible for his 1969 appointment. He refused Ray's personal invitation to attend the swearing-in ceremony.

Ray would not have become CJI had the seniority convention been followed—he would have retired before Grover's tenure as CJI had ended. He held that post for forty-five months, a tenure exceeded earlier only by Sinha. Because of the concern that Ray would be compliant with efforts by the government to implement the Kumaramangalam doctrine—to help populate the Court with judges believed to be supportive of the government's policies—the judges appointed during his tenure are of particular interest.

He took over a decimated SCI. Within just a few days, six senior judges were gone—Sikri by retirement, Shelat, Hegde, and Grover by resignation, and Vaidialingam and Dua by virtue of their Article 128-extended terms expiring on 6 May. So, from sixteen judges on 25 April, the strength of

[6] Fari Nariman, *Before Memory Fades*, p. 169.

[7] Jaganmohan Reddy provided a different account. He wrote that Ray knew at least a week earlier that he was to become the CJI. See *The Judiciary I Served* (Hyderabad: Orient Longman, 1999), pp. 242–6. Hegde and Hidayatullah believed he knew even earlier. Mathew, seventh in seniority at this time, said that before Ray was offered the post he was 'sounded' about accepting the chief justiceship if it was offered to him. Mathew felt it would be improper to accept it and this matter was dropped.

the Court fell to ten. This meltdown provided an ideal opportunity for appointing judges who met Kumaramangalam's criteria.

Ten new judges were sworn in during Ray's tenure. Two appointed during Sikri's reign died (A.K. Mukherjea in October 1973 and S.N. Dwivedi in December 1974). There were four routine retirements (D.G. Palekar in September 1974, P. Jaganmohan Reddy in January 1975, A.N. Alagiriswami in October 1975, K.K. Mathew in January 1976), and H.R. Khanna resigned in January 1977 on the eve of Ray's retirement. Of the sixteen judges on the Court on 25 April, only Beg and Chandrachud were still on board when Ray retired.

Ray claimed to have initiated the appointments of all ten. He said that after he made the decision as to whom to appoint, he sent a letter to Law Minister Gokhale. He and Gokhale would meet and then the name would be passed on to the prime minister. He said that every name he proposed was appointed, and that 'all appointments were made purely on merit as I defined it'.

Sworn on 17 July 1973, three months after the controversy that followed the supersession, were P.N. Bhagwati and V.R. Krishna Iyer, two of the most significant appointments in the SCI's history. These two brilliant men with megawatt energy represented a new breed. In time, they would achieve iconic status and leave an indelible mark on the SCI, Indian jurisprudence, the nation, and put the SCI on the world map. Their combined efforts, though not in lockstep, moved Indian jurisprudence in new directions.

According to Ray, 'I brought Bhagwati to the SCI'. The fifty-one-year-old Bhagwati had been the chief justice of the Gujarat High Court since 1967 and had been considered for appointment on two earlier occasions. He had been recommended by fellow Gujarati CJI Shah in late 1970. The government did not say no. It simply did not respond. It is plausible that the fact that he was Shah's nominee hurt Bhagwati's chances, for the government had not been happy with Shah's rejection of its positions in the *Golaknath*, *Bank Nationalization*, and *Privy Purses* decisions. Several serving judges at the time, and Bhagwati himself, believed that it was J.C. Shelat, Bhagwati's former Gujarat High Court colleague, with whom he had long and poor relations, who was most influential in Bhagwati's failure to be appointed. Aware of the resistance to Bhagwati, Shah withdrew his nomination so as not to stain Bhagwati's record. Even if Shelat had not opposed him, Bhagwati's age would likely have been a hurdle, for he was only forty-nine at that time.

When Bhagwati's name was brought up again in 1972, CJI Sikri was supportive and Hegde strongly endorsed him. He wanted Bhagwati appointed before Chandrachud so that he would have the long tenure as CJI. But Shelat's strong opposition persuaded Sikri to resist his appointment. Others, and Bhagwati himself, believe that the main reason for his failure to get appointed was resistance from Gokhale and P.B. Gajendragadkar, still in Delhi as chairman of the Law Commission, friends of Chandrachud and fellow Maharashtrians who wanted Chandrachud on the SCI first so that he would have a long tenure as CJI.[8] Bhagwati did not have such influential patrons, thus tipping the decision in Chandrachud's favour. Rivals, and not friendly ones, dating back to their years at the Bombay bar, Bhagwati never got over his second place finish and relations between these two men were strained throughout their years on the SCI.

Though he had been twice rejected, it was not unexpected that he was ultimately appointed. He had become a high court chief justice at an unusually young age and had a reputation of being brilliant. Also by then, he had acquired a reputation of being a man with 'progressive' views, especially in the area of promoting free legal aid for the poor. Bhagwati believed that Gokhale, in 1973, pressed for his elevation and Ray offered no resistance. He believed that Gokhale supported him all along but wanted Chandrachud on board first. And when Ray became CJI, Shelat was gone. Bhagwati filled the Gujarat seat vacant since Shelat's resignation three months earlier.

Krishna Iyer had been recommended a year earlier when Sikri was the CJI. The initiator was Kumaramangalam, a long-time friend of his. At that time Krishna Iyer was a member of the Law Commission, having been appointed in September 1971 after Kumaramangalam persuaded Gajendragadkar to accept him. The purpose of this move was to overcome his seniority shortcomings, for he had been on the Kerala bench for only three years and was about ninth in seniority. No high court judge that junior had ever been appointed to the SCI.

In late 1972, Gokhale informed Sikri that the government wanted Krishna Iyer appointed to the SCI. He had Gajendragadkar's support as well. The latter and Hegde took their morning walks together and Hegde said that Gajendragadkar lobbied him to support the appointment of Krishna Iyer. Gokhale was ambivalent, as was Sikri, but the latter leaned

[8] Interview with Bhagwati, 3 October 1988.

towards accepting him. Shelat, Grover, and Hegde, Sikri's three most senior colleagues, particularly the vehemently anti-communist Hegde, strongly opposed Krishna Iyer and persuaded Sikri to reject him. They painted him with the same brush as Kumaramangalam whom Hegde had known since their days together in Madras. Krishna Iyer had never been a member of the Communist Party but had many communist friends, had defended jailed communists, had been a cabinet minister in the first communist-led government in Kerala, and had a reputation as a leftist.

He was fifty-seven when he was sworn in on 17 July 1973. By this time, Shelat,[9] Hegde, and Grover were gone. Had they not resigned after the supersession, each would have become CJI and it is unlikely that he would have been appointed until 1977 at the earliest. Kumaramangalam was gone also, having died in a plane crash in May. Gajendragadkar was still Law Commission chairman and presumably continued to support his appointment. S.S. Ray, by then back in West Bengal as chief minister, claimed that he should get most credit for Krishna Iyer's appointment because he took up cudgels for him after Kumaramangalam's death.[10]

The Bhagwati and Krishna Iyer appointments were transformative ones. Though quite different and having arrived with different baggage and reputations, both broke the mould of previous appointees and represented the first of a new generation of judges. Both came with an agenda and a mission which can be described as reformist and pro-weaker sections. Both sought to move the SCI in new directions which they described as progressive, and both found the label 'judicial activist' an appropriate description of themselves.

According to P.K. Goswami, who at age sixty was sworn in on 10 September 1973, his appointment was initiated by the government. But Ray told me that Goswami was his choice—'there had never been anyone from Assam, and Goswami was chief justice there'. He stressed that Assam was the main consideration, not Goswami himself. Gokhale knew Goswami from the occasions when they appeared against each other in litigation before the SCI, and Goswami said it was Gokhale who informed Ray that the government wanted him on the court. Goswami, who described

[9] Shelat would later write forewords to Krishna Iyer's, *Some Half-Hidden Aspects of Indian Social Justice* (Lucknow: Eastern Book Company, 1980); and *Social Justice: Sunset or Dawn*, second edn (Lucknow: Eastern Book Company, 1987).

[10] Interview with S.S. Ray, then India's Ambassador to the United States, in Lexington, Kentucky, USA, on 21 November 1994.

himself as conservative, said that the government had been criticized in some circles for appointing the 'leftist' Krishna Iyer, and decided it was prudent to appoint a 'centrist' one.

Seven days later, the fifty-seven-year-old R.S. Sarkaria was sworn in. Ray said that he chose Sarkaria because 'no Sikh had been appointed and I felt one should'. Sarkaria's own account is very different. In 1973, he said that two prominent Sikh leaders, Zail Singh, then the Punjab Chief Minister, and Gurdial Singh Dhillon, then the Lok Sabha Speaker, persuaded Mrs Gandhi that the time had come for a Sikh to be appointed. Gokhale was put in charge of the search committee and he worked closely with Zail Singh. In September, Gokhale travelled to Chandigarh where the Punjab and Haryana chief ministers hosted a dinner attended by high court judges. It was no secret that Gokhale was shopping for what Sarkaria termed 'a suitable Sikh'. Within a few days, and after gaining Mrs Gandhi's approval, Zail Singh extended the invitation to Sarkaria, who at this time was fifth in seniority on the Punjab and Haryana High Court. The chief justice at the time was another Sikh and next three in seniority were Hindus. Gokhale soon informed Ray, who had earlier not met Sarkaria, that the government wanted Sarkaria on the bench.

A full year passed before the appointment of the fifty-five-year-old A.C. Gupta of the Calcutta High Court on 2 September 1974. According to Ray, 'I felt we needed from Calcutta a representative of the *Indian* Bar [Ray's emphasis]', implying that Indian-educated judges were a lesser breed. The previous eight Calcutta High Court judges promoted to the SCI had been barristers.[11] Ray said that Gupta, then fourth in seniority, was the replacement for A.K. Mukherjea—'the vacancy was from Calcutta'—who had died a year earlier. Ray, of course, knew Gupta well. Gupta had never met Gokhale and was certain that he was selected by Ray. An invitation to Gupta was not extended—his appointment was simply announced. After agreeing to the first four government-initiated nominees, Ray became more of a player in the selection process.

N.L. Untwalia, the fifty-nine-year-old chief justice of the Patna High Court, was sworn in on 3 October 1974. After nearly seventeen years on the Patna bench, he was among the most senior among high court judges in the nation. According to both Ray and Untwalia, his appointment was initiated

---

[11] B.K. Mukherjea was not a barrister, but his appointment was to the Federal Court in 1948.

by Ray. Two years earlier, CJI Sikri spoke to Gokhale about extending an invitation to Untwalia. Gokhale was agreeable but because of problems in Patna he wanted Untwalia to remain there for a while longer. Ray had earlier met Untwalia only briefly to discuss filling Patna vacancies. Before his recommendation of Untwalia, Ray sought the views of Jaganmohan Reddy, Palekar, Mathew, and Khanna, all of whom endorsed him. A judge from Patna was needed, for that high court had been unrepresented since Ramaswami's retirement in 1969.

Ray said he chose S.M. Fazal Ali because he was very senior, had been chief justice of the Jammu and Kashmir High Court for seven years, and he 'was the first from the Jammu and Kashmir High Court and represented Patna as well'. Ray had become acquainted with him during a visit to Srinagar in 1975. Fazal Ali was quite certain that his appointment was initiated by Ray. He was a veteran of nearly seventeen years of high court service and was the most senior chief justice in the country. Yet he was only fifty-four when he was sworn in on 2 April 1975. It cannot be said that he was appointed to fill the Muslim seat, for Beg was still there.

Ray's last three appointees came during the Emergency. The first was P.N. Shinghal, sworn in on 11 June 1975, at age sixty. According to Ray, 'he was very senior and was the Rajasthan chief justice. I had met him in Rajasthan, was very impressed by him, and submitted his name to Gokhale. The court needed a Rajasthan representative'.[12] Shinghal, one of a very few with administrative as well as judicial experience, was the first native son of Rajasthan to reach the SCI. His appointment brought the strength of the court to its sanctioned fourteen judges.

Ray had met Jaswant Singh also during his visit to Srinagar and although 'I took Fazal Ali first, I formed an excellent opinion of Jaswant Singh. He was a good advocate-general, had handled the Sheikh Abdullah case very well and he came from a good family—the family background is very important'.[13] Ray claimed credit for Singh's appointment and Singh said this was his understanding as well. Singh was to have retired from the Jammu and Kashmir High Court just two days before he was sworn in at Delhi on 23 January 1976. He learned of his appointment from Governor

[12] Because I did not meet Shinghal, I was unable to ascertain whether he believed he was selected by Ray.

[13] An outsider would consider this an unusual consideration, but this is not so in India. Two other CJIs said very much the same thing.

L.K. Jha. He had no direct communication with Ray and was not asked if he would accept.

Singh's and Ray's accounts notwithstanding, others believe that the fingerprints of Om Mehta, a close friend and distant relative—Singh's son-in-law was Om Mehta's nephew—were on the Singh appointment. Mehta was a fellow Kashmiri and was then the Minister of State in the Ministry of Home Affairs. He was close to Mrs Gandhi, and wielded much influence.[14] One of the judges recalled that most of them were attending a wedding in Delhi at which Jaswant Singh was present. During a conversation with Singh, he mentioned that Singh would be retiring in a few days. At this point, a senior home ministry official in attendance said, 'Oh no, he will be your colleague on the SCI within a few days'. The judge said he was embarrassed by this, described the appointment process as 'ridiculously secret', and said that only Ray would have known that Singh was about to be sworn-in. The date of his swearing in was 23 January 1976.

The final appointee of Ray's stewardship and the last during Mrs Gandhi's first regime, P.S. Kailasam, came a full year after Singh's. Ray explained that Kailasam was very senior, was the chief justice of Madras, and 'I needed someone to replace Alagiriswami'. Kailasam was in fact the most senior high court judge in the nation in terms of years of service and was sixty-one when he was sworn in on 3 January 1977. Although he was a cousin of Kumaramangalam, that relationship did not help him get to Delhi before his Madras colleague Alagiriswami, who was nearly six years his junior. 'I was let down by my friends', said Kailasam. He had met neither Ray nor Gokhale and said that he learned later from Ray that Gokhale had opposed his appointment and that Ray went to Mrs Gandhi to secure approval for his appointment. So Kailasam agreed that he was selected by Ray and for the reasons Ray gave.

There are several striking characteristics about the Ray Court appointees. Seven of the ten were high court chief justices, including the last five, a higher percentage than any previous CJI. Seniority has always been an important selection consideration. Someone, more likely Ray than the executive, was placing more emphasis on selecting chief justices than was customary.

---

[14] Kuldip Nayar wrote: 'Gokhale told me that Mehta started meddling with the judges when he came to Home. Since the home secretary was also secretary of the Department of Justice—transferred to Ministry of Law—Om Mehta could easily influence some decisions'. *The Judgement: Inside Story of the Emergency in India* (New Delhi: Vikas Publishing House Pvt. Ltd., 1977), p. 151.

Moreover, when such a premium is placed on seniority, particularly in this instance where there was some apprehension that Ray would be agreeable to government-initiated appointees, the most unexceptionable appointee would be a high court chief justice. If the government was looking for judges likely to endorse its policies, it would be a remarkable coincidence if seven of those selected happened to be chief justices. Being a high court chief justice during the Ray years was a valuable credential to have.

Often seniority correlates with advanced age, with the most senior appointees being older than the norm. But this is not the case with the Ray appointees. The average age of these men, 58.2, was virtually identical to that of earlier appointees. The average age of the six high court chief justices was about the same—58.4 years. Four of the ten were in their sixties. The appointment of judges sixty or older was not unknown before Ray's time—twelve of the preceding forty-nine were sixty or older. Friendly or 'convenient' judges could be found in any age group, making the appointment of men in the twilight of their careers unexpected, unless the government and/or Ray had very short-term goals, particularly to get *Kesavananda* overturned. And most of these men had above-average (11.4 years) high court experience.

Another striking characteristic of the Ray Court appointees is the regional diversity they reflected. In terms of geography, he left the most representative court ever. The ten appointees came from nine high courts— two were from Jammu and Kashmir. Two of the nine—Gauhati and Jammu and Kashmir—had never before been represented, and Rajasthan saw its first native son appointed. Ray said repeatedly that 'I wanted the Supreme Court as representative as possible; I made sure that each state was represented. If there was a Madras vacancy, I tried to appoint a Madras judge'. Surely it was Ray, not Gokhale or someone else in the government, who can be credited with such emphasis on regional diversity. Striking also is that half of his appointees came from among the youngest high courts. Only two were drawn from the usually overrepresented presidency high courts. The dozen sitting judges when Ray retired were from eleven different high courts.

The Ray years also saw the appointment of the first Sikh, and the Muslim representation, which had been one since 1964, became two again. Of the eight Hindus appointed, two were brahmins. Noteworthy also is that although Ray himself was a classic barrister with a very English definition of a judge's role and behaviour, there was not a barrister among his appointees.

The Ray years were good for high court chief justices, the newer high courts, minorities, non-brahmins, and home-grown advocates.

In terms of their backgrounds and career histories, because all of them were recruited from high courts, there is little to distinguish them from earlier judges. Krishna Iyer, who carried controversial political baggage, was the major exception. There was nothing to prevent the government or Ray from shopping among the fraternity of senior advocates with pro-government reputations. There is no evidence that this was done. Ray said he made only one effort to recruit from the bar but that unnamed senior advocate from the Calcutta bar wanted too much time to think over the offer. The government, as per Kumaramangalam's criteria, was looking not for men with different backgrounds but for ones believed to be inclined to support its agenda.

If the government's main goal was to get *Kesavananda* overruled, or at least the boundaries of the 'basic structure' doctrine defined, and Ray expected to be the means, he failed. In November 1975, when seven of his appointees were on board, Ray convened a thirteen-judge bench to review *Kesavananda*. N.A. Palkhivala argued that the case Ray had chosen did not raise any questions concerning the basic structure doctrine. Even judges inclined to reverse *Kesavananda* agreed with Palkhivala and Ray had no choice but to dissolve that bench three days later.[15]

Largely because the Ray appointees came from so many different high courts, the matter of who was replacing whom was not as apparent as in earlier years. The Gujarati Bhagwati can be considered Shelat's replacement, though this cannot be considered very salient to his appointment. Gupta, from Calcutta and the first appointee after Mukherjea's death, filled the vacant Calcutta seat. Following Palekar's retirement in September 1974, another Bombay judge was not appointed, leaving Chandrachud as the sole Bombay representative. The next appointee was Untwalia, who restored Patna's representation. Following the death of Dwivedi in December 1974, there was no replacement for him from Allahabad; the next appointee was Fazal Ali. After Jaganmohan Reddy retired in January 1975, Andhra Pradesh would remain unrepresented for the remainder of Ray's tenure.

---

[15] H.R. Khanna provides a useful account of this event in *Neither Roses nor Thorns*, (Lucknow: Eastern Book Company, 1985), pp. 73–5. Excerpts from the submissions of Palkhivala and V.M. Tarkunde, and the responses of judges during oral argument in this case, are found in Prashant Bhushan, *The Case That Shook India* (New Delhi: Vikas Publishing House Pvt. Ltd., 1978), pp. 256–67.

His vacant seat was filled by Shinghal of Rajasthan. After Alagiriswami retired in October 1975, Madras went unrepresented until Kailasam was appointed in January 1977. So the Ray appointees, with some exceptions, reflected a diminished concern for state fill-ups and a greater concern for nationwide diversity. Three came from the east, three from the north, and two each from the south and west.

Although Ray claimed to have initiated the appointments of all of them, his appointees were almost unanimous in saying that the first four were the executive's choices and that Ray initiated the appointments of the remaining six. Only concerning the Untwalia appointment did he seek the advice of a colleague. According to his definition of the CJI's role, the selection of judges was entirely his responsibility. He claimed that none of his nominees was rejected by the executive.

All evidence points to the conclusion that Ray played a much greater role in selecting judges than Sikri did. The selection criteria he employed seems to differ little from past practice. It would be incorrect to conclude that the Ray judges were political appointees in terms of the conventional definition of that label. If the executive pressed Ray to locate or accept high court judges believed to be pro-government, evidence to support this is lacking. One incident, though, requires mention. In October 1975, Ray telephoned R.S. Pathak, the chief justice of the Himachal Pradesh High Court, to inquire about his interest in being appointed to the SCI. According to Pathak, Ray wanted to know his views on the basic structure doctrine. Pathak refused to answer the question and the conversation ended.[16]

Ray was not close to his brethren. He was described as aloof from his colleagues, imperious, and an enigma. Some of the judges, including some of his appointees, said that Ray was 'completely' or 'entirely' with the government, but some gave him credit for being open and honest about his belief that Mrs Gandhi was the nation's saviour and for not hiding his support for the Emergency. The gist of this charge is that it was his fealty to Mrs Gandhi rather than ideology that motivated him.[17] Ray has been subjected to a great deal of criticism,[18] much of it beyond the scope of this

[16] Interview with Pathak in New Delhi on 1 October 1988. This story is not a secret. Dr L.M. Singhvi said the same thing in a 12 July 1983 interview.

[17] One of his colleagues described Ray as 'a very elegant man, wore expensive suits, had fourteen pairs of expensive shoes, yet the government believed he was a socialist'.

[18] Granville Austin wrote that Ray

... developed an adulatory attitude toward the Prime Minister, which was remarked upon by many observers and associates. He made himself amenable to her influence by telephoning frequently,

book, but he chose not to tell his side of the story or to respond to any of the criticism.

A day before he retired on 28 January 1977, it was announced that M.H. Beg had been selected to be the new CJI, superseding H.R. Khanna, who resigned immediately. Thus, Ray left an SCI comprised of eight of his ten appointees, plus Beg and Chandrachud. Unlike most retiring CJIs, Ray did not fill his own vacancy. Only Bhagwati, among his appointees, would later become CJI.

Ray departed from the court without ceremony and returned immediately to his Calcutta home where he lived in virtual seclusion until his death nearly thirty-four years later. He never heard from Mrs Gandhi again and he never returned to Delhi.[19]

50. Prafullachandra Natvarlal Bhagwati (1973–86)

Born on 21 December 1921 at Ahmedabad, Gujarat, P.N. Bhagwati was the youngest ever appointed to the SCI. The son of N.H. Bhagwati, an SCI judge in the 1950s, his was a family of modest means but grand ambitions.[20] His father was a hard taskmaster who instilled a strong work ethic and expected his children to excel at all levels of their schooling. Each of his seven sons earned first class honours in all their university examinations and most were very successful in their chosen fields.[21]

The eldest of the seven, P.N. Bhagwati received a BA (honours) degree in mathematics from Elphinstone College, Bombay, in 1941, finishing in

---

using the 'RAX' telephone system directly connecting the most senior officials of government. He would also ask her personal secretary's advice on simple matters, conveying the impression that the Prime Minister's views might be heard concerning an ongoing case.

Austin's source was N.K. Seshan, Mrs Gandhi's personal secretary. Before Austin's book was published, he sent this information to Ray and asked for his comments. Ray did not reply. *Working a Democratic Constitution: A History of the Indian Experience* (New Delhi: Oxford University Press, 1966), p. 290, fn. 42.

[19] Letter from Ray to the author dated 15 November 2006.

[20] Interviews with Bhagwati on 24 January 1980, 20 April 1983, and in 1988 on 31 March, 20 August, 3 October, and 30 October, all in New Delhi, and correspondence dated 26 September 2009 and 28 February 2010.

[21] Sumit Mitra, 'Chief Justice P.N. Bhagwati: Age of Activism', *India Today*, 15 August 1985, pp. 56–61, especially, pp. 60–1. Among them is Dr Jagdish Bhagwati, an internationally acclaimed economist who holds a prestigious chair at Columbia University, New York, USA.

the first class and being selected a Dakshina Fellow. He then began work on an MA in economics but was swept into active participation in the Independence struggle. He was caught distributing the banned journal, *Congress Patrika*, and spent a month in jail. After being released he worked underground with the Congress Socialist Party during the 1942 Quit India Movement. He never completed the MA but earned an LLB from the Government Law College, Bombay, in 1945, finishing in the first class in the law examinations.

On 8 October 1946, when his father was a Bombay High Court judge, he enrolled as an advocate of that high court. In 1960, Bombay state was bifurcated and the state of Gujarat and the high court of Gujarat came into existence. He was invited to become a foundation member but turned down the offer because although he was born in Ahmedabad, Bombay was his home. The Gujarat chief justice-designate talked with his father and he was persuaded to accept the judgeship. When only thirty-eight, he was sworn in as an additional judge on 21 July 1960 and was confirmed as a permanent judge on 6 April 1961. On 16 September 1967, at age forty-five, when many practising lawyers who would later become high court judges were still at the bar, he became chief justice.

Bhagwati is among the pioneers of legal aid initiatives. In 1970, he was appointed chairman of the Legal Aid Committee[22] established by the Gujarat government, and directed the first Pilot Project for Free Legal Aid. Later he served as chairman of the Gujarat Judicial Reforms Committee.[23] Before leaving for the SCI, he served as a member of the boards of studies of Bombay University and the M.S. University at Baroda, and the senate of Gujarat University. For many years he was closely associated with the activities of the Bharatiya Vidya Bhavan in Ahmedabad, including being chairman of its Bhagwati Institute of Journalism. During his tenure as chief justice, he served briefly as Gujarat's acting governor in 1967 and 1973.

After nearly fourteen years on the Gujarat bench, six of these as chief justice, and at age fifty-one, he was sworn in as a judge of the SCI on 17 July 1973. Twelve years later, after being the seniormost judge longer than anyone in the SCI's history, he became the nation's seventeenth CJI on 12 July 1985. He served in that capacity for eighteen months, until his sixty-fifth birthday on 21 December 1986.

[22] *Report of the Legal Aid Committee* (Gandhinagar: Government Central Press, 1971).
[23] *Report of the Judicial Reforms Committee* (Gandhinagar: Government of Gujarat, 1976).

Bhagwati was one of the best-known judges in the SCI's history. He has been described as brilliant, charming, gregarious, witty, scholarly, ambitious, outspoken, a humanist, a populist, a man of enormous energy, a human rights activist driven by a reformer's zeal, and a crusader for India's large downtrodden population. His most enduring legacies will be his successful efforts to open the doors of the SCI to India's poor and his pioneering work in promoting human rights. During his SCI tenure he was the most prominent advocate for expanding legal aid programmes, and served as chairman of the National Committee on Judicare (1976–7)[24] and, after 1980, as chairman of the National Committee for the Implementation of Legal Aid Schemes.

A liberal judicial activist who welcomed this label,[25] he sought to circumvent what he considered barriers of the inherited Anglo-Saxon jurisprudence. His name and Public Interest Litigation (PIL) became synonymous. He made human rights meaningful for the disadvantaged and gave the SCI a pro-people image, creating new rights in this process. He was a champion of the causes of workers and labourers, especially bonded and child labourers. Through creative interpretation of the *Constitution* and laws, particularly by liberalizing the doctrine of *locus standi* which meant setting aside the customary procedural norms, he facilitated access to the SCI by the poor.

He was also dogged by controversy: 'controversy has always chased me ....'[26] He wrote an adulatory letter to Mrs Gandhi following her return to power in 1980 which was leaked to the press and greatly embarrassed him and provided grist for his critics. He was also accused of being a publicity-seeker, hawking his judgments, and playing to the gallery. But, even his

---

[24] *Report on National Judicare: Equal Justice and Social Justice* (New Delhi: Ministry of Law, Justice, and Company Affairs, Controller of Publications, 1978).

[25] 'I believe that a judge should be goal-oriented, result oriented.' Mitra, 'Chief Justice P.N. Bhagwati: Age of Activism', *India Today*, 15 August 1985, p. 59. In his case the apple did fall far from the tree. His quite conservative father felt that judges should not use the term 'social justice'. He once wrote that

The considerations of social justice imported by the Labour Appellate Tribunal in arriving at the decisions in favour of the respondent [workmen] were not only irrelevant but untenable. Social justice is a very vague and indeterminate expression and no clear-cut definition can be laid down which will cover all situations. ... [T]he concept of social justice does not emanate from the fanciful notions of any particular adjudicator but must be founded on a more solid foundation.

Muir Mills Co., Ltd. v. Suti Mills Mazdoor Union, Kanpur [1955] 1 SCR, 991, 1001–2.

[26] Mitra, 'Chief Justice P.N. Bhagwati: Age of Activism', p. 58.

detractors would concede that he was of great value to the nation in many important ways.

After his retirement, he remained in New Delhi and commenced chamber practice and arbitration work but found time to do little of either. His name was considered in 1987 as the Congress (I) candidate for vice-president of India but the nomination went to Shankar Dayal Sharma.

An intrepid traveller and man of boundless energy, he travelled the globe promoting human rights. He was elected as a Member, Vice-Chairman, and finally Chairman of the UN Human Rights Committee. He was appointed regional advisor for Asia and the Pacific to the UN High Commissioner for Human Rights,[27] as a member of the committee appointed by the Organization of African Unity which looked into events that led to the 1994 genocide in Rwanda, as a member of the Goldstone Commission of Inquiry which investigated police involvement in political killings in South Africa, and as a member of the International Mediation Team appointed to mediate between the Inkatha and the African National Congress before elections in South Africa. He carried out several missions for the United Nations Center for Human Rights, the Commonwealth Secretariat, and the International Commission of Jurists. As early as 1978, he was a member of the International Labor Organization's Committee of Experts and served in that capacity for twenty-seven years.

He held the post of chairman of the advisory board of the Geneva-based Center for the Independence of Judges and Lawyers, served as a member of the executive council of the South Asia Association for Regional Cooperation in Law, as chairman of the South Asia Task Force on the Judiciary, as chairman of the World Congress on Human Rights, and as vice-chairman of the permanent standing committee of Lawasia. He was a member of the International Advisory Council of the World Bank for Legal and Judicial Reforms. He was especially active in the area of women's rights and presided over the People's Tribunal for Violence against Women at the Vienna Human Rights Congress, and promoted human rights among tribals, particularly tribal women, in several Asian countries. He served as vice-chairman of El Taller (an international human rights development organization located in Algeria), a member of the international jury for the

[27] Report of Justice P.N. Bhagwati, Regional Advisor for Asia and the Pacific of the United Nations Commissioner for Human Rights, *Human Rights and Immigration Detention in Australia: Report of the Mission to Australia 24 May to 2 June 2002* (Geneva: United Nations High Commissioner for Human Rights, 2002).

Templeton Prize for Progress in Religion, and chairman of the jury which selected World Environment Foundation awards. He was a member of the Permanent Court of Arbitration at The Hague. His expertise has been utilized by a number of countries, including Cambodia, Nepal, Ethiopia, Mongolia, and South Africa, when framing their constitutions, particularly their chapters on human rights. He organized judicial colloquia for judges on the subject of human rights in several Commonwealth countries. His travels also included lectures and addresses, mainly on human rights, in dozens of countries.

Within India, as he left the SCI, he was a member of the legal aid committee established by the union government to provide legal aid to the victims of the Bhopal gas tragedy. Among his many other activities, he served as chancellor of both the Shri Lal Bahadur Shastri Sanskrit Vidyapeety and the University of Hyderabad, and as chairman of the search committee for a new vice-chancellor of Delhi University. He was a member of the law faculties of both Delhi University and the M.S. University of Baroda. He was president of the managing council of Somaiya Vidyavihar and headed the advisory council of the Centre for Media Studies. He was vice-chairman of the project advisory panel of the Green Rating Project. He served as chairman of a task force constituted by the Ministry of Welfare to reconsider guidelines relating to adoption. He was a one-man committee which conducted the inquiry into panic withdrawals by ICICI Bank customers in Gujarat, and served as chairman of the takeover committee of the Securities and Exchange Board of India which recommended a greater role for shareholders in company takeovers. He was chairman of a committee which examined proposals for competitive versus negotiated bids for electrical power generation and development, and chairman of a ministry of communication panel dealing with cross-media ownership issues. He was head of the jury which selected the Federation of the India Chambers of Commerce and Industry award for environmental conservation and pollution control. He also chaired a ministry of finance panel that selected the first national recipient of the award for excellence in corporate governance. He served on the board of directors of the *The Times of India* and as its external ombudsman. He has served as chairman of the Indian Council of Jurists, of the jury which selected the 2002 Law Day award recipients, of the Global Convention on Climate Change, and of the SM Charitable Trust.

Among the honours bestowed upon him was the Padma Vibhushan, the nation's second highest civilian award in 2007. In 1985, he received the International Bar Association's highest award for his promotion of legal aid. He received LLDs (*honoris causa*) from Andhra University in 1986, the University of Malaya on 2007, and Columbia University (New York, USA) in 2009. In 1988, he received the Bharat Gaurav ('Pride of India') award from the Bharatiya Sathi Sangthan in recognition of his judgments which helped women, children, and the exploited. He was made a Fellow of the American Academy of Arts and Sciences. In 2003, he was elected an honorary member of the International Commission of Jurists. In 2010, at a ceremony in Abuja, he was inducted into the Hall of Fame of the Nigerian Institute of Advanced Legal Studies. The Moot Court Competition at the National Law School of India University bears his name. A tribal community which benefited from one of his judgments renamed its village Bhagwati Puram.

Bhagwati is the author of *Law, Freedom and Social Change* (Bangalore: Bangalore University, 1979); *Toward a Brighter India* (Hyderabad: AWARE Publications, 1984); *Legal Aid as a Fundamental Human Right* (Dharwad: Jagrut Bharat, 1985); *Law as an Instrument for Social Change* (Madurai: Society for Community Organization Trust, 1985); and *Dimensions of Human Rights* (Madurai: Society for Community Organization Trust, 1987). He edited, with the assistance of M.C. Bajawat, the *Casebook on Income Tax Law* (Bombay: N.M. Tripathi Pvt. Ltd., and New Delhi: Bar Council of India Trust, 1987). He is also the author of *Democracy and Human Rights* (New Delhi: Indian Institute of Foreign Trade, 1997). He is a co-author of *Judicial Independence in Sri Lanka: Report of a Mission, 14–23 September 1997* (Geneva: Center for the Independence of Judges and Lawyers, 1998).

His contributions to modern Indian law, particularly his human rights jurisprudence, have attracted attention and praise in India and abroad. Mool Chand Sharma is the author of *Justice P.N. Bhagwati: Court, Constitution, and Human Rights* (New Delhi: Universal Book Traders, 1995); Sheeraz Latif A. Khan wrote *Justice Bhagwati on Fundamental Rights and Directive Principles* (New Delhi: Deep & Deep Publications, 1996); and Ram Kishore Choudhury and Tapash Gan Choudhury edited *Judicial Reflections of Justice Bhagwati* (Kolkata: Academic Foundation & Publication Pvt. Ltd., 2008). Praise for his contributions is also found in Upendra Baxi's 'Au Revoir, Justice Bhagwati', *Lex Et Juris*, vol. I, no. 9, pp. 34–5 (January 1987); and N.R. Madhava Menon's, 'The Dawn of Human Rights Jurisprudence: A

Tribute to the Judicial Statesmanship and Activism of Chief Justice P.N. Bhagwati' (1987) 1 *Supreme Court Cases (Journal)*, pp. 1–12. Michael Kirby, a fellow judicial activist and judge of the high court of Australia, paid rich tributes to Bhagwati in *Collected Writings and Speeches of Justice P.N. Bhagwati: An Australian Appreciation* (Law and Justice Foundation of New South Wales, 1998).[28]

In 2006, he was re-elected as member for a fourth term on the United Nations Human Rights Committee and in 2007, he was appointed chairman of the Independent Group of Eminent Persons appointed by the President of Sri Lanka to conduct an investigation. In his ninetieth year, the high octane Bhagwati remains active—he delivered a lecture on India's human rights law at the Columbia University Law School in New York in 2009.

51. Vaidyanathapuram Rama Ayyar Krishna Iyer (1973–80)

On 15 November 1915, V.R. Krishna Iyer was born at Palghat, Palakkad district, located in the then Madras presidency and now in the state of Kerala. A brahmin 'by accident of birth' and a spiritual and thoroughly secular man, he described himself as an agnostic and both he and his wife were associated with the rationalist movement.[29] The son of V.V. Rama Iyer, a prominent and well-to-do lawyer who practised in Tellicherry and elsewhere in Malabar, he grew up in comfortable economic circumstances.

He received his BA degree in English and economics from Annamalai University, Annamalai Nagar, Tamil Nadu in 1935. He was elected editor of

---

[28] www.lawfoundation.net. Last visited 3 October 2010.

[29] I had the opportunity to interview him in New Delhi on three occasions—22 January 1980, 25 June 1983, and 30 December 1988. He also prepared seven pages of biographical materials for me in 1983. He asked that his name be rendered as I have at the top of this essay—he wanted 'Ayyar' included, even though he always rendered it as V.R. Krishna Iyer, as I have done throughout. The quotations are from these sources unless indicated otherwise. Useful also in preparing this biographical essay was his memoirs, *Leaves from My Personal Life* (New Delhi: Gyan Publishing House, 2004) and his *Wandering in Many Worlds: An Autobiography* (Noida, Uttar Pradesh: Dorling Kindersley (India) Pvt. Ltd., 2009). After the death of his wife Sarada in 1974, who shared his passion for improving the lives of the socially and economically downtrodden, and who was a constant source of support and an integral part of his personality—his soul mate in the deepest sense of that term—he sought to find a communicable link between the living and the dead, and wrote about this journey in *Death and After* (Delhi: Konark Publishers, 2003).

the English section of *Annamalai Miscellany* and was awarded the Srinivasa Sastry prize for proficiency in English. He aspired to be a journalist and writer but there were few employment opportunities as a journalist and his father urged him to become a lawyer. He attended the Madras Law College, earning the BL degree in 1937.

He enrolled as an advocate of the Madras High Court on 19 September 1938 and, during the next decade, practised with his father in the Malabar district courts. His clientele was varied and included both rich industrialists and landlords and poor peasants and labourers. The large fees he obtained from the former enabled him to represent the latter at little or no cost. In these early years, he protested against police torture, the harassment of workers, and exploitation of the peasantry by feudal landlords. He also represented some prominent political figures, particularly from the left of the political spectrum, but including Congressmen. Rather quickly, he acquired a reputation as an outspoken leftist and became what he termed 'a legal public figure'. Because he represented communists and the oppressed classes, he was soon surrounded by controversy. During the 1946 violence in which the communists participated, he often represented them in preventive detention cases, and continued to do so after the communists' 1948 'Calcutta Thesis' which advocated an increased use of violence. Although he was opposed to violence, because he represented many of the arrested leaders, he acquired the label of being a dangerous leftist.

Accused of actively helping communists in their violent activities and providing hideouts for them, he was arrested in May 1948. The grounds—'concocted lies and outrageous distortions'[30]—for his arrest could not be supported by the Madras government and he was released, but only after spending a month in jail. He is the only SCI judge to have been jailed by his own countrymen. This first-hand experience with jail conditions and the inhuman treatment of prisoners began a lifetime passion for prison reform and the treatment of prisoners as human beings.[31]

In 1952, with his strongest support coming from the Communist Party of India-Kisan Mazdoor Praja Party alliance and the Muslim League, he was

---

[30] Krishna Iyer, *Wandering in Many Worlds*, p. 63.

[31] 'The Sunil Batra jurisprudence, though delivered in the seventies in the Supreme Court as judgments, was inscribed in my soul in 1948 in Cannanore Central Jail.' *Wandering in Many Worlds*, p. 66. *Sunil Batra* v. *Delhi Administration and Ors* [1979] 1 SCR 392, has been described by Upendra Baxi as '...the most significant decision on prison justice since the inception of the Supreme Court of India and the independence of India.' *The Supreme Court and Politics*. Lucknow: Eastern Book Company, p. 238.

elected to the Madras Legislative Assembly from Malabar (Tellicherry) as a left-leaning independent, defeating other socialist rivals and the Congress party candidate. During these years as a legislator he gained recognition as a leading member of the opposition and as a committed socialist.

After the state of Kerala was carved out of the Madras presidency, he was elected in 1957 to the Kerala legislative assembly, again as an independent with strong support from the left, particularly the Communist Party. This election resulted in the first communist-led government to gain power in an Indian state. During its two-year existence, he served as Chief Minister E.M.S. Namboodiripad's home minister, minister for law,[32] justice, irrigation, inland navigation, power, prisons, social welfare, agriculture, and cooperatives. Among his initiatives were reforms in prisons not found in other states, innovative irrigation and hydroelectric projects, and the nation's first master plan for water resources.

He did not always agree with his communist colleagues. When Namboodiripad rejected his recommendation for an inquiry into a police firing, and Krishna Iyer refused to use the preventive detention statute, he was relieved of the home portfolio. Krishna Iyer has been labelled as a communist himself. In his words, 'I was *never* [his emphasis] a member of the Communist Party—I am too individualistic, but I had many communist friends.'

After that government was dismissed in 1959 he returned to the bar, but practising mainly at the Kerala High Court. In 1960, he again stood for election to the Kerala legislative assembly, and again as an independent. He was defeated by the CPI (Marxist) candidate by seven votes, but filed an election appeal challenging this outcome, and 'I was elected by the court.'

He contested the 1965 assembly election 'as a radical in the cause of social justice' and at first was backed by CPI (M). But he refused to use that party's election symbol, stood as an independent, and lost to the CPI (M) candidate. Again he returned to the high court bar.

Three years later, on 12 July 1968 and at age fifty-two, when another CPI (M)-dominated government was in power, he was appointed a permanent judge of the Kerala High Court.[33] At the swearing in ceremony, he made clear what he planned to do on the bench:

---

[32] When holding the law minister portfolio, he initiated the appointment of Anna Chandy, the first female high court judge in India's history.

[33] M. Hidayatullah, then the CJI, approved his appointment.

The forensic institutions and the legal system itself need a new orientation, a modern grammar and vocabulary and simpler techniques of social engineering, if they are not to be accused of exotic, expensive, obsolescent and tardy features. I shall endeavour, in a humble measure, to be a judicial activist and treat my career ahead as a fresh call to service in the cause of the Rule of Law, which not merely keeps the executive in leash but insists upon the basic and equal right of every individual to a really free and good life.[14]

On the bench, first in Ernakulam and later in Delhi, he was a crusading maverick. In his words, '... a sharply different social philosophy marked me out as an unorthodox socialistic, people-oriented jurisprudent, unbound by obsolete precedents and fossil forensic praxis, innovating pragmatic processes and sensitising legal justice with substantive values'.[35]

After only three years on the Kerala bench, at which time he was about ninth in seniority, he was appointed a member of the Law Commission of India in September 1971. He recalled:

One day, my good friend Mohan Kumaramangalam [then Union Minister for Steel and Mines, earlier a prominent member of the Communist Party] called me demanding that I go to Delhi as a member of the Central Law Commission. I was unwilling, but had to yield to his unrelenting pressure. He later disclosed his objective. Dr Gajendragadkar, former Chief Justice, was to be the Chairman of the Law Commission and I would be holding a high place under him, he argued. The Prime Minister and the Supreme Court would be able to perceive my progressive capability and consider the prospect of sending me to the Supreme Court, which, in his view, needed a departure from archaic principles, jurisdic orthodoxy, and colonial-cum-capitalist jurisprudence. I consented to shift my venue of juristic activity to Delhi.[36]

During his two years on the Law Commission, his most noteworthy contribution concerned legal aid for the poor. This was not a new interest of his, for during his tenure as law minister in Kerala he initiated the nation's first comprehensive legal aid programme. His Law Commission report, *Processual Justice to the People: Report of the Expert Committee on Legal Aid, 1973*,[37] laid the foundation for poverty jurisprudence and is regarded a classic on the topic.

[14] Krishna Iyer, *Wandering in Many Worlds*, p. 161.
[35] V.R. Krishna Iyer, *Legally Speaking* (New Delhi: Universal Law Publishing Company Pvt. Ltd., 2003), p. 317.
[36] Krishna Iyer, *Wandering in Many Worlds*, p. 166. The next year he was offered the chairmanship of the Monopolies and Restrictive Practises Trade Commission. He turned that down—'I was too dangerous for it.'
[37] New Delhi: Department of Legal Affairs, Ministry of Law, Justice, and Company Affairs, Government of India, 1974.

He was fifty-seven when he was sworn in as an SCI judge on 17 July 1973. His appointment was greeted by mainstream lawyers and many others with a chorus of boos, mainly because of his reputation as a leftist and because many believed that S. Mohan Kumaramangalam was his patron. Led by prominent advocate Soli J. Sorabjee, 150 lawyers gathered to protest his appointment on the ground that he was a Marxist.[38]

His tenure on the SCI, at first, was marked by considerable controversy. He came with an agenda which seemed to violate the norms of judicial detachment. He was unabashedly pro-poor, pro-downtrodden, and pro-weaker sections. He was the SCI's first judge to depart emphatically from the hoary inherited common law and seek to adapt it to Indian conditions. He pushed the boundaries of legitimate debate to the left and moved the centre in the process. Later he wrote that 'If you ask me which trend of jurisprudence I inaugurated happily I would say it was Public Interest Litigation and Epistolary Process and the *Ratlam Municipality* case'.[39] He was the SCI's first openly socialist judge and he sought to employ the Constitution and the law as tools to achieve social and economic justice for all Indians. He also departed from the tradition of the aloof judge who cloistered himself, and often ventured outside the SCI to express his views on public platforms, often on the left of the political spectrum.

As the single vacation judge in June 1975, it fell to Krishna Iyer to rule on Prime Minister Indira Gandhi's request for an absolute stay order after the Allahabad High Court had set aside her election on the grounds that she had violated the election law. He gave her less than she wanted, ruling that she had lost her status and privileges as a member of Parliament but could retain her position as prime minister.[40] The infamous Emergency was declared a few days later.

---

[38] Upendra Baxi, *Courage, Craft, and Contention: The Indian Supreme Court in the Eighties* (Bombay: N.M. Tripathi Pvt. Ltd., 1985), p. 27.

[39] Krishna Iyer, *Legally Speaking*, p. 320. In *Municipal Council, Ratlam v. Vardhichand & Ors [1981] SCR 97*, he and O. Chinnappa Reddy ruled that financial constraints did not absolve the municipality to provide sanitation facilities to its residents, the slum dwellers in this instance. For more on this landmark decision, see his *Wandering in Many Worlds*, pp. 173–7. On pages 238–9, he wrote that 'Public Interest Litigation and liberal expansion of *locus standi* and access to justice were my creation, although, brother Bhagwati also claims justly that he too has to be considered a founder of these creative revolutions in the administration of justice. I am too close to brother Bhagwati to deny anything credible he claims.'

[40] He discusses this matter in *Wandering in Many Worlds*, pp. 179–81.

A brilliant intellectual, he was intimidating to many of his brethren and cast a large shadow over the SCI. The language he used, variously described as strange, poetic, florid, colourful, quaint, funny, bewildering, and incomprehensible, resulted in opinions such as the readers of the law reports had never before seen, and compelled them to expand their own vocabularies. He later wrote that he was criticized for his 'unjudicial unenglish (the love of the long word or odd mintage—I confess my guilt)'.[41] But his main message was clear to all—that the mistreatment of any human being was unacceptable to him, and that the SCI must strive to provide justice to all, particularly the disadvantaged. Although he often shocked his colleagues and the bar, he pricked their consciences and none could openly disagree with his assessment of the ills of Indian society. And none questioned his compassionate humanism and honesty of conviction. His creed was: 'I am a human being and nothing that affects or afflicts anyone's life is alien to me'.[42]

His record on the Court ranks him among its leading workhorses. The SCR reveal that he participated in 510 reported decisions during his seven and a half years tenure and wrote opinions in 291 (56.4 per cent) of these.[43] No earlier judge had written as high a percentage of opinions to participations. Some will be surprised to learn, given the perception of him as having expressed points of view that set him apart from his colleagues, that he never wrote a dissenting opinion nor was he ever in the minority in a non-unanimous decision. It was his view that divided decisions were not as good as unanimous ones and that writing dissenting opinions served little purpose. He tried to draw his colleagues towards his views, sometimes successfully, but often had to make concessions to achieve unanimity. He did write twenty-four separate concurring opinions published in SCR, and many of these, he acknowledged, were thinly disguised dissents.

---

[41] Iyer, *Legally Speaking*, pp. 318–19.

[42] Ibid., p. 318.

[43] Vijay K. Gupta, *Decision Making in the Supreme Court of India* (Delhi: Kaveri Books, 1995) wrote on page 151 that Krishna Iyer participated in 740 decisions, wrote the decision of the Court in 393 (53.1 per cent) of these, and wrote twenty-seven (3.7 per cent) concurring opinions, for a total participation of 56.8 per cent. Gupta used the *All India Reporter*, and I used the *Supreme Court Reports*. There is no reporter which carries all judgments of the SCI. Judges have some discretion to decide which of their decisions are to be reported, and the editors of the *Supreme Court Reports*, *All India Reporter*, and *Supreme Court Cases* have discretion over which and how many cases they publish.

By the time he left the SCI on 15 November 1980,[44] he had become a towering judicial figure. His people-oriented jurisprudence, particularly in the field of criminal jurisprudence and jail reforms, has left a mark that will unlikely ever be erased. His early critics came to believe that his missionary zeal for human rights was genuine. Upon his retirement, he was feted by the bar in an unprecedented show of respect and affection. The then president of the SCI bar association, Dr L.M. Singhvi, whom no one ever accused of being a leftist, presided over a well-attended retirement dinner in his honour. Singhvi's affectionate farewell speech lamented his departure and recalled that it was 'in stormy weather that you first took your seat on the Supreme Court Bench. Some members of the Bar were apprehensive that your appointment may not contribute to the traditions of judicial detachment. But those who came to scoff stayed on to respect and to admire'. He went on to praise Krishna Iyer as a 'great intellectual and a great gentleman', a man who opened the Court's doors wider to the poor, the needy and the indigent, and 'helped humanize our legal system'.[45]

An intense, driven man of great restless energy, he did not go quietly into the night after leaving the SCI. Unlike many retired judges who engaged in lucrative chamber practice and conducted arbitrations for large fees, he eschewed such money-making pursuits.[46] He served as an SCI judge for only seven-plus years, a small portion of his long life, and those few years were sandwiched between many decades of activism in the cause of human rights. But those years made him a national figure and provided him a larger constituency to spread his human rights and social justice exhortations throughout India and abroad.

During his first thirty years after leaving the bench, few denials of justice escaped his attention and he was always ready to take action against the next violation of human rights. In the best sense of this term he was an agitator, repeatedly reminding all that there is a large downtrodden population—his definition included women—that needed help. He was critical, but nearly

[44] Had Y.V. Chandrachud and P.N. Bhagwati been superseded in 1978, as some prominent public figures demanded, Krishna Iyer was next in line for the chief justiceship.

[45] 'Address Presented to Hon'ble Shri Justice V.R. Krishna Iyer on his Retirement from the Supreme Court of India' (1981) 1 SCC (Journal), pp. 1–2.

[46] Shortly after leaving the SCI, he acknowledged doing one arbitration for compensation 'by mistake'. One of his former SCI colleagues, defensive about his own lucrative chamber practice, said, 'I am not Krishna Iyer'.

always constructively so, of the behaviour and policies of all branches of the government, including the courts. His often flame-throwing rhetoric notwithstanding, his unpretentiousness and charm and his inability to hold grudges disarmed his critics, most of whom came to realize that he was a valuable colleague in the human experience.

He accepted few requests to head official investigatory commissions, committees, or tribunals, and when he did he refused to accept a salary. In 1984, he accepted Andhra Pradesh Chief Minister N.T. Rama Rao's request to chair the Bhaskara Rao inquiry commission; his charge there was to inquire into various allegations of misdeeds during the brief life of that ministry. In 1986, the union government appointed him as chairman of an expert committee dealing with women in custody. This resulted in the *Report of the National Expert Committee on Women Prisoners*.[47] In 2000, he accepted the chairmanship of the Advisory Panel on Enlargement of the Fundamental Rights for the National Commission to Review the Working of the Constitution. In 2002, at the request of the Kerala chief minister, he served as chairman of a committee regarding the formation of guidelines governing parole and remissions of sentences of prisoners. In 2007, he accepted the chairmanship of the Kerala Law Reforms Commission. There was likely some hesitation on the part of national and state governments about asking him to head official bodies, for they might not be pleased with his candour in the reports they received.

His most high-profile activity after retirement occurred in 1987 when he stood for the presidency of India as the combined opposition's candidate.[48] He accepted the nomination reluctantly, agreeing to do so because 'there were principles to be fought for'. The opposition's agreement on his candidacy was not as complete as in most other presidential elections. The Bharatiya Janata Party was less than enthusiastic about him, both because of his left orientations and because his nomination was spearheaded by the CPI(M) and the CPI. L.K. Advani, a BJP leader, in a letter to him, wrote that: 'You are a handmaiden of the Soviet Union and, therefore, we are not in a position to support you.'[49] Given the way the president is elected—by an electoral college comprised of members of Parliament and

---

[47] Delhi: Government of India, Ministry of Human Resources Development, 1987, 2 vols.

[48] His candidacy for the presidency is discussed in *Wandering in Many Worlds*, pp. 244–55.

[49] Krishna Iyer, *Wandering in Many Worlds*, p. 253.

the state legislatures, with voting reflecting party strength—the outcome was a foregone conclusion. He polled just 27.5 per cent of the votes, losing to his friend Ramaswamy Venkataraman, the Congress (I) Party's candidate.

When he left the SCI he retired only in the sense that the Constitution compelled his departure. His post-court years have been filled with a wide variety of activities, most relating to the cause of human rights. Writing and incessant lecturing, sometimes two in one day, engaged much of his time. He was constantly on the move, both within India and abroad, sharing with others his passion for human rights. An incomplete list of his activities during the past seventy years of his life is long and varied.[50]

He held the post of president of the following organizations, located throughout the country and abroad: Kerala Hockey Association; Kerala Fine Arts Society; International Center for Kathakali; Kerala Club; Malayalee Association; Sri Narayana Kendra; Institute of Socialist Legal Studies; Indian Society of Criminology; Indian Institute of Natural Law; Organization for Protection of Human Rights in Sri Lanka; Krishna Menon Memorial Society; Kerala Law Academy and Center for Advanced Legal Studies; K.P.S. Menon Memorial Society; Indian Council of Social Welfare (Kerala Branch); Indian Association of Lawyers; Indian Society of International Law; Committee for Protection of Democratic Rights and Secularism; Forum of People's Voice; World Council of Deontology, Citizen's Action Committee for Clean Politics; Center for Industrial Safety and Environment Concerns; All India Save Education Committee; Advisory Board of the Public Interest Legal Support and Research Center; International Association of Democratic Lawyers; and founder-president of the Independent Initiative. He was the vice-president of the Foundation for the Establishment of an International Court of Criminal Justice, Institute of Constitutional and Parliamentary Studies, and the Indian Society of International Law.

He served as chairman of the National Centre for Quality of Life and Work, Indian People's Human Rights Tribunal; Institute of Asian Studies; National Expert Committee on Woman Prisoners; National Campaign Committee for Central Legislation on Construction Labour; Steering

---

[50] Most of his activities through 2000 have been chronicled by Vinod Sethi, his long-time close associate and secretary-general of the Capital Foundation Society. See his 'Participation in Social Organizations and Professional Bodies', www.vrkrishnaiyer. org/achievements.htm, and 'Life's Long Voyage of Justice V.R. Krishna Iyer', www. vrkrishnaiyer.org/article1.htm. Both were last visited on 3 October 2010.

Committee in Decentralized Planning for the Eighth Five Year Plan; Sub-Committee for Establishment of a School of Indian Legal Thought in the Mahatma Gandhi University; Lok Raj Sangathan; Forum for Democracy and Communal Amity; Board of Governors of the Institute of Asian Studies, Gujarat Concerned Citizens Tribunal; Indian Peoples' Human Rights Commission Tribunal; and the First World Assembly on Law, Justice, and Rehabilitation.

He served as patron of the Indian Council of Legal Aid and Advice; Indian National Section of the International Association of Penal Law, Punjab Prisoners Welfare and Human Rights Association; All India Lawyers' Union; Indian Council of Legal Aid and Advice; People's Council for Social Justice; Madras Institute of Magneto Biology; All India Dalit Development Research Institute; and the Indo-Socialist States Friendship Organization.

He was a member of the executive committee of the Indian Council of Social Science Research; Presidium of the National Council of the Indo-Soviet Cultural Society; Central Animal Welfare Board; Kerala State Sports Council; Central Prohibition Committee; Board of Trustees of the Ved Vignan Maha Vidya Peeth; Governing Council of the Brahma Vidyalaya Society; Sponsorship Committee of the International Center for Trade Union Rights; Planning Commission's Steering Group on Social Welfare; Advisory Committee of the State Institute of Encyclopedic Publications; Democratic Lawyers Association; and the Sri Narayana Guru Center.

Other activities include being the founder-secretary of the Society for the Prevention of Cruelty to Animals; vice-chairman of the Animal Welfare Board of India; founder-director of the Kerala Law Academy; trustee of the S. Mohan Kumaramangalam Charitable Trust; founding patron of the Capital Foundation Society; secretary of the Indo-German Democratic Republic Friendship Society; secretary of the North Malabar Football Association; member of the World Society of Victimology; treasurer of the World Association of Judges; fellow of the Indian Society of Criminology; and visiting professor at the National Law School of India and Aligarh; Kerala, and Calicut Universities.

His awards and honours[51] include the Padma Vibhushan—the nation's second highest civilian award—, the LLD (*honoris causa*) from Annamalai

---

[51] The source for most of these, again through 2000 and apparently compiled by Vinod Sethi, is www.vrkrishnaiyer.org/awards.htm. Last visited on 3 October 2010. See also, 'The Living Legend' at www.vrkrishnaiyer.org/. Last visited on 3 October 2010.

University, the National Law School of India University, Bhagatpur University, and the National University of Advanced Legal Studies, the DLitt (*honoris causa*) from the University of North Bengal and Dakshina Bharat Hindi Prachar Sabha; Soviet Land Nehru Award; Order of Friendship from the Government of Russia; Shri Jehangir Gandhi Medal and Award for Industrial Peace; Distinguished Fellow of the Indian Law Institute, Baba Saheb B.R. Ambedkar National Award from the Bharatiya Dalit Sahithya Academy; MA Thomas National Human Rights Award; title of 'Living Legend of Law' awarded by the International Bar Association; Cardinal Padiyara Award from the Qatar Syro-Malabar Cultural Association; Manavasamanvaya Award from the Kerala Sanskrit Academy; V.K. Rajan Memorial Award; Subramania Bharati Award; Archbishop Benedict Mar Gregorios Award; Dr C.K. Kareem Foundation Award; Sankaranarayanan Thampi Award; Niyaem Ratna Award; C.H. Mohammed Koya Foundation Award; R.V. Thomas Award; Yashwantrao Chavan National Award for National Integration; Democratic Values, and Social and Economic Development; C. Kesavan Memorial Keerthi Mundra Award from the Kerala Freedom Fighters Association; Gold Medal for delivering the XIV World Federation of the Catholic Medical Associations World Congress Oration; Fellow of the Indian Society of Criminology; Kumarappa-Reckless Award from the Indian Society of Criminology; Vyloppilli Award from the Sahrudaya Vedi; Honorary Fellow of the Indian Association for Environmental Management; Manavasamanvaya Award from the Kerala Sanskrit Academy; Manava Seva Award by Rotary International from the Asiatic Society, Calcutta; Naresh Chandran Sen Gupta Medal; Ramasraman Award; Honorary Member of the Rotary Clubs of Cochin and Trivandrum South; For the Sake of Honour Award from the Rotary Clubs of Coimbatore and Cannanore; Shri Dasharathmal Singhvi Citation and Award from Banaras Hindu University; Naresh Chandra Sen Gupta Gold Medal from the Asiatic Society, Calcutta; National Assembly for Guidance and Service Award; Capital Foundation Award; State Award from the Indian Medical Association; Honorary Life Membership of the Bar Association of India; Vagbhadanana Award; Human Rights Lifetime Achievement Award from the Krishna Menon Memorial Society; Manava Seva Award from Rotary International; and Honorary Member of the American Association of Judges. There is a V.R. Krishna Iyer Chair on Public Law and Policy Choice at the National Law School of India University.

Over the past five decades, he has produced a prodigious outpouring of writings which often reveal familiarity with the world's classic literature. A wordsmith of the highest order, he may have published more than the combined total of the fifty judges who preceded him. The vast majority deal with the topics of law, human rights, and social justice. The following list of ninety books, an astonishing number, is the most complete ever compiled, but some may have been overlooked:[52]

Police in a Welfare State (New Delhi: Asia Book Centre, 1959); *Cuban Panorama* (Trivandrum: Prabath Book House, 1967); *Law and the People: A Collection of Essays* (New Delhi: People's Publishing House, 1972); *Law, Freedom, and Change* (New Delhi: Affiliated East-West Press Pvt. Ltd., 1975); *Law India: Some Contemporary Challenges* (Nagpur: Nagpur University College of Law, 1976); *Jurisprudence and Jurisconscience a la Gandhi* (New Delhi: Gandhi Peace Foundation, 1976); *Social Mission of Law* (Bombay: Orient Longman Ltd., 1976); *The Pathology and Prognosis of Criminology in India* (Bombay: Tata Institute of Social Sciences, 1976); *Ambedkar Memorial Lectures, 1976*, (New Delhi: Jawaharlal Nehru University, 1976); *India's Wobbling Voyage to Secularism: The Nehru Facet Plus a New Gloss* (Ahmedabad: Gujarat University, 1976); *Law and Social Change: An Indian Overview* (Chandigarh: Publication Bureau, Punjab University, 1978); *Social Justice and the Handicapped Humans* (Trivandrum: Academy of Legal Publications, 1978); *The Integral Yoga of Public Law and Development in the Context of India* (New Delhi: Institute of Constitutional and Parliamentary Studies, 1979); *Of Law and Life* (New Delhi: Vikas Publications House Pvt. Ltd., 1979); *The Social Dimensions of Law and Justice in Contemporary India: The Dynamics of a New Jurisprudence: Problems, Perspectives, and Prospects* (Nagpur: All India Reporter, 1979); *Some Half-Hidden Aspects of Indian Social Justice* (Lucknow: Eastern Book Company, 1980); *Perspectives in Criminology, Law, and Social Change* (New Delhi: Allied Publishers Pvt. Ltd., 1980); *Justice & Beyond* (New Delhi: Deep & Deep Publications, 1980); *Minorities, Civil Liberties, and Criminal Justice* (New Delhi: People's Publishing House, 1980); *Law Versus Justice: Problems and Solutions* (New Delhi: Deep & Deep Publications, 1981);

[52] This list omits books in Malayalam and Tamil and has been compiled from several sources, including Vinod Sethi at www.vrkrishnaiyer.org/books.htm. Last visited on 3 October 2010. In 2010, the (United States) Library of Congress online catalog at http://www.loc.gov/ lists eighty-four of his publications. Last visited on 3 October 2010. The National Law School of India University library in 2010 held twenty-six. http://www.nls.ac.in/lib/opac/opac.php. Last visited on 3 October 2010. Krishna Iyer could locate only fifty-seven of his books when he wrote his autobiography in 2009.

Parliament, Planning and the Law (Ahmedabad: Harold Laski Institute of Political Science, 1981); *A National Prison Policy: Constitutional Perspective and Pragmatic Parameters* (Waltair: Andhra University Press, 1981); *Law, Society, and Collective Consciousness* (New Delhi: Allied Publishers Pvt. Ltd., 1982); *Law, Justice, and the Disabled* (New Delhi: Deep & Deep Publications, 1982); *Indian Social Justice in Crisis* (Madras: Affiliated East-West Press Pvt. Ltd., 1983); *Indian Socialism: Perspectives & Problems* (Bangalore: Raghothaman Smaraka Pratishthana, 1983); *The Court and the Common Man* (Madras: University of Madras, 1983); *Justice in Words and Injustice in Deeds for the Depressed Classes* (New Delhi: Indian Social Institute, 1984); *Woman Unbound: A Plea for Gender Justice* (Madurai: Society of Community Organization Trust, 1984); *Indian Justice: Perspectives and Problems* (Indore: Vedpal Law House, 1984); *Human Rights and the Law* (Indore: Vedpal Law House, 1984); *A Random Miscellany, Legal and Other* (New Delhi: People's Publishing House, 1984); *Law and Religion* (New Delhi: Deep & Deep Publications, 1984); *Environmental Pollution and the Law* (Indore: Vedpal Law House, 1984); *Judicial Justice: A New Focus Towards Social Justice* (Bombay: N.M. Tripathi Pvt. Ltd., 1985); *Constitutional Challenges and Democratic Response* (Dharwad: Jagrut Bharat, 1985); *In Search of Social Justice* (Dharwad: Jagrut Bharat, 1986); *A Constitutional Miscellany* (Lucknow: Eastern Book Company, 1986); *Equal Justice and Forensic Process: Truth and Myth* (Lucknow: Eastern Book Company, 1986); *Justice V.R. Krishna Iyer on the Muslim Women (Protection of Rights on Divorce) Act, 1986* (Lucknow: Eastern Book Company, 1987); *Our Courts on Trial* (Delhi: B.R. Publishing Corporation, 1987); *The Indian Judiciary: To Be or Not To Be* (Gulbarga: Prasaranga, Gulbarga University, 1987); *Social Justice: Sunset or Dawn*, second ed. (Lucknow: Eastern Book Company, 1987); *Law and the Urban Poor in India* (Delhi: B.R. Publishing Corporation, 1988); *The Indo-Sri Lankan Accord: An Appraisal* (Madurai: Indo-Sri Lankan Friendship Society, 1988); *Legal Services Authorities Act: A Critique* (Madurai: Society for Community Education Trust, 1988); *The Indian Presidency: Nascent Challenges and Novel Responses* (New Delhi: Deep & Deep Publications, 1988); *The New Afghan Dawn* (with Vinod Sethi) (New Delhi: Indo-Afghan Friendship Society and Capital Foundation Society, 1988); *The Indo-Sri Lanka Accord: A Social Audit* (Bombay: Lawyers Collective, 1988); *Law, Lawyers, and Justice* (Delhi: B.R. Publishing Corporation, 1989); *Social Democracy and Dalit Egalite* (Madras: University of Madras, 1989); *Salvaging Democracy: Some Reflections* (Delhi: Konark Publishers Pvt. Ltd., 1990); *Human Rights and Inhuman Wrongs* (New Delhi:

B.R. Publishing Corporation, 1990); *Freedom of Information* (Lucknow: Eastern Book Company, 1990); *Dr Ambedkar and the Dalit Future* (New Delhi: B.R. Publishing Corporation, 1990); *Ambedkar Centenary: Social Justice and the Undone Vast* (New Delhi: B.R. Publishing Corporation, 1991); *Religion and Politics* (Delhi: Konark Publishers Pvt. Ltd., 1991); *Justice at Crossroads* (New Delhi: Deep & Deep Publications, 1991); *Environmental Protection and Legal Defense* (Delhi: Sterling Publishers Pvt. Ltd., 1992); *Access to Justice: A Case for Basic Change* (Delhi: B.R. Publishing Corporation, 1993); *Current Pathological Problems of India: Some Reflections* (New Delhi: Capital Foundation Society, 1993); *Healing the Broken Palmyra: Towards a Just Peace in Sri Lanka* (Madurai: Indo-Sri Lankan Friendship Society, 1993); *Indian Federalism: Dialectics & Dynamics* (Guwahati: Ashok Publishing House, 1993); *Nehru and Krishna Menon* (Delhi: Konark Publishers Pvt. Ltd., 1993); *Declining Judicial Culture & Other Essays* (Madurai: Society for Community Organization Trust, 1994); *Democracy and Federalism: Presentations* (Secunderabad: Andhra Pradesh Judicial Academy, 1995); *Parliamentary Privileges: An Indian Odyssey* (with Vinod Sethi) (New Delhi: Capital Foundation Society, 1995); *Human Rights: A Judge's Miscellany* (New Delhi: B.R. Publishing Corporation, 1995); *Peoples' Commission on GATT: Report on the Constitutional Implications of the Final Act Embodying the Results of the Uruguay Round of Multinational Trade Negotiations* (New Delhi: Centre for Study of Global Trade Systems and Development, 1996); *Essays on Press Freedom* (with Vinod Sethi) (New Delhi: Capital Foundation Society, 1996); *Report of Peoples' Commission on Intellectual Property Rights: A Quick First Report on Moves to Amend the Indian Patents Act, 1970, and Impending Review of TRIPS Agreement* (New Delhi: National Working Group on Patent Laws, 1998); *The Dialectics & Dynamics of Human Rights in India: Yesterday, Today, and Tomorrow* (Calcutta: Eastern Law House, 1999); *Human Rights in India: Yesterday, Today, Tomorrow* (Calcutta: Eastern Law House, 1999); *Some Thoughts on Human Rights in India* (Pune: Department of Law, University of Pune, 2000); *A Judge's Extra-Judicial Miscellany* (New Delhi: B.R. Publishing Corporation, 2001); *Death and After* (Delhi: Konark Publishers, 2003); *Judicial Justice in Action: A Fundamental Audit* (Chandigarh: Publication Bureau, Punjab University, 2003); *Legally Speaking* (New Delhi: Universal Law Publishing Company Pvt. Ltd., 2003); *A Constitutional Miscellany* (Lucknow: Eastern Book Company, 2003); *Towards a Natural World: The Rights of Nature, Animal Citizens, and Other Essays* (Gurgaon: Hope India, 2004); *Leaves From My Personal Life* (New Delhi: Gyan Publishing House, 2004); *Off the Bench* (New

Delhi: Universal Law Publishing Company Pvt. Ltd., 2004); *Rhetoric Versus Reality: Essays on Human Rights, Justice, Democratic Values* (Gurgoan: Hope India, 2004); *A Judge's Miscellany on Superannuation* (Delhi: B.R. Publishing Corporation, 2004 reprint); *Random Reflections* (New Delhi: Universal Law Publishing Company Pvt. Ltd., 2005); *Sublime Footprints* (New Delhi: Gyan Publishing House, 2007); *The Majesty of the Judiciary* (New Delhi: Universal Law Publishing Company Pvt. Ltd., 2007); *Judge's Potpourri* (New Delhi: Universal Law Publishing Company Pvt. Ltd., 2007); *Law and Life* (New Delhi: Universal Law Publishing Pvt. Ltd., 2008); *Dynamic Lawyering* (New Delhi: Universal Law Publishing Company Pvt. Ltd., 2009); *The Indian Law: Dynamic Dimensions of the Abstract* (New Delhi: Universal Law Publishing Company Pvt. Ltd., 2009); *Wandering in Many Worlds: An Autobiography* (Noida, Uttar Pradesh: Dorling Kindersley (India) Pvt. Ltd., 2009); and *Wake up Call for Indian Republic* (New Delhi: Gyan Publishing House, 2010).

No other judge, before or after him, has received as much attention from scholars and other writers. Books about or celebrating the life of Krishna Iyer include O.N. Gupta, *A Gandhi in the Supreme Court* (Delhi: Legal Literacy Society, 1980); Hari Swarup, *For Whom the Law is Made: Mind and Faith of Justice V.R. Krishna Iyer* (New Delhi: Veena Publications, 1981); Rajeev Dhavan, R. Sudarshan and Salman Khurshid (eds), *Judges and the Judicial Power: Essays in Honour of Justice V.R. Krishna Iyer* (London: Sweet & Maxwell and Bombay: N.M. Tripathi Pvt. Ltd., 1985); Shailja Chander, *Justice V.R. Krishna Iyer on Fundamental Rights and Directive Principles* (New Delhi: Deep & Deep Publications, 1992); Mool Singh, *Justice Iyer's Jurisconscience* (Jaipur: RBSA Publishers, 1993); P. Krishnaswamy, *Justice V.R. Krishna Iyer: A Living Legend* (New Delhi: Universal Law Publishing Company Pvt. Ltd., 2000); M.P.R. Nair (ed.) and Vinod Sethi (associate editor), *Justice Krishna Iyer at 90* (New Delhi: Universal Law Publishing Company Ltd., 2005); Swamy Krishna, *V.R. Krishna Iyer* (New Delhi: Universal Law Publishing Company Pvt. Ltd., 2005); E.X. Joseph, *V.R. Krishna Iyer: Splendour of Humanism and Justice* (Delhi: Konark Publishers Pvt. Ltd., 2005); Sebastian Champappilly, *Muslim Law: An Analysis of Judgments Rendered by Justice V.R. Krishna Iyer* (Cochin: Southern Law Publishers, 2006); C. Raj Kumar and K. Chockalingam (eds), *Human Rights, Justice, and Constitutional Empowerment: Essays in Honour of Justice V.R. Krishna Iyer* (New Delhi: Oxford University Press, 2007); and I. Sharath Babu and Rashmi Shetty, *Social Justice and Labour Jurisprudence: Justice V.R. Krishna Iyer's Contributions* (New Delhi: Sage Publications Pvt. Ltd., 2007).

Despite failing eyesight and other infirmities of old age, his passion for human rights and social and economic justice for the disadvantaged is undiminished. He has tackled new issues, including changes resulting from post-1991 economic liberalization in India. He believes strongly that there have been too many departures from constitutionally mandated socialism, that the already well-off have benefited most, that the level of honesty in public life has plummeted, and that the lot of the poor remains unimproved. The SCI has not been spared from his biting criticism. He has been very citicial of the behaviour of some of the judges and of the process of selecting the 'robed brethren.'[53] At age ninety-five in 2010, he continues to be a frequent contributor to *The Hindu* and *Frontline*. A larger than life and truly iconic figure, shall we ever see his likes again?

52. Parbati Kumar Goswami (1973–8)

P.K. Goswami was the first Gauhati High Court judge to be appointed to the SCI.[54] Born on 1 January 1913 at Sivasagar, Sivasagar district, Assam, he was the son of Bamdev Goswami who, at the time of his death at age thirty-five, was the head clerk in the deputy commissioner's office at Sibsagar. His family had been wealthy but with the death of his father and uncle and other financial setbacks, the family was reduced to difficult financial circumstances. Orphaned at the age of two, he needed scholarship assistance to go to college.[55]

Goswami earned his BA (honours) in economics from Cotton College in 1933, and his BL from Earle Law College, both in Guwahati, in 1936. He

---

[53] Iyer, *Wandering in Many Worlds*, pp. 210–28.

[54] When established in 1948, in what is now Guwahati, it was designated the Assam High Court. Until then Assam had been served by the Calcutta High Court. When Nagaland gained statehood in 1963 its name was changed to the Assam and Nagaland High Court. It was renamed the Gauhati High Court in 1971 after its geographical jurisdiction was extended to include the new states of Meghalaya, Manipur, and Tripura, and the Union Territories of Mizoram and Arunachal Pradesh. The latter two became states in 1987 and came within the ambit of the Gauhati High Court, meaning that this court serves all seven states of the North East region. There are benches of the Gauhati High Court in each of the newer six states. *The Gauhati High Court, 1948–1973* (Gauhati: Souvenir Committee, Gauhati High Court, 1974).

[55] I interviewed Goswami in New Delhi on 4 June and 8 July 1983, and 30 September 1988.

earned a first class first in the BL examinations, and was the recipient of the Gunabhiram Barooah Silver Medal. He was the first lawyer in his family.

He began practising law at age twenty-five in 1938 in the magistrate's court at Dibrugarh. After completing the required five years of experience as a pleader, he enrolled as an advocate of the Calcutta High Court on 1 September 1943. He continued to practise in the district courts at Dibrugarh where, in 1947, he was appointed government pleader and public prosecutor. He resigned from that post in 1949 and returned to private practice. Only in 1958, ten years after the Assam High Court was created did he shift his practice to Guwahati. In that year he was appointed a member of the Assam law commission, and served until 1967. From 1962 to 1967, he was also a member of the bar council.

During the 1950s and 1960s, he developed an increasingly successful practice, representing in particular the European tea planters and their India Tea Association. This litigation brought him to Delhi frequently. He was first offered a high court judgeship in 1961 but declined because of financial considerations. Thereafter, during the course of his trips to Delhi, first CJI K. Subba Rao and then CJI K.N. Wanchoo urged him to accept an appointment to the Gauhati bench. He ultimately agreed and was sworn in as a member of the Assam and Nagaland High Court on 12 May 1967, at age fifty-four. He was the first Assamese to be appointed directly from the bar—earlier Assamese appointees had been service judges. In 1968, he served as a one-man tribunal under the terms of the Unlawful Activities (Prevention) Act which investigated various aspects of the Mizo rebellion. On 31 January 1970, just thirty-two months after joining this small high court, he became its chief justice. He was the acting governor of Assam and Nagaland from December 1970 to January 1971. During his high court years he was also the founder of the All-Assam lawn tennis association.

Before he was asked if he would accept an appointment to the SCI, the president signed the warrant of appointment. He had been reluctant to go to Delhi, for he liked being the high court chief justice and wasn't eager to become the most junior SCI judge. After just over six years of high court experience, he was sworn in on 10 September 1973. Aged sixty at this time, mandatory retirement came on 1 January 1978. He is remembered by many for his criticism of CJI M.H. Beg for meeting with acting president B.D. Jatti during the pendency of the *Rajasthan Dissolution* decision.[56]

---

[56] *State of Rajasthan v. Union of India* [1978] 1 SCR 1.

In May 1978, not long after his retirement, the Janata government—and this is a tribute to his reputation as an independent judge—appointed him as chairman of the Second Press Commission. Goswami accepted this post as an honorary assignment, without accepting the customary salary. After Mrs Gandhi returned to power in January 1980, Goswami, as a matter of formality, submitted his resignation, just as he had done six months earlier when the Charan Singh-led Lok Dal replaced the fallen Morarji Desai government. But whereas the Charan Singh government had not accepted his resignation, Mrs Gandhi did. The reason probably was, as H.R. Khanna wrote in his autobiography, that Mrs Gandhi's government was aware that Goswami's report was nearly complete and that it contained criticism of her treatment of the press during the 1975–7 Emergency.[57]

After this abrupt departure from the Press Commission in January 1980, Goswami remained in Delhi and engaged in chamber practice. He also served as an arbitrator when requested to do so by the SCI and high courts. In 1985, Chief Minister N.T. Rama Rao of Andhra Pradesh announced that Goswami would head a commission of inquiry to investigate the so-called Karamched incident in which five tribals had been killed. This appointment was made without Goswami's prior approval. He declined because it was a state-level assignment and he believed that retired SCI judges should accept only national commissions appointed by the central government. For the same reason he declined Karnataka Chief Minister Ramakrishna Hegde's request that he accept the post of Lok Ayukta in that state.

In the 1980s, Goswami was a contributor to Hidayatullah's *Constitutional Law of India*, and later endowed the Justice P.K. Goswami Memorial Lecture, delivered from time to time in Guwahati.

Goswami died on 13 December 1992, at age seventy-nine.

---

[57] Khanna, *Neither Roses Nor Thorns*, pp. 134–5. Goswami's appointment as Press Commission chairman had been strongly supported by H.R. Khanna, his friend and former colleague. After Goswami's ouster, Khanna was offered the same post. Khanna wrote that 'As Goswami had not been appointed ... at my recommendation I felt in all conscience not proper on my part to take over his place when he was virtually shunted out'. When the *Report of the Second Press Commission* was published (Delhi: Controller of Publications, 2 vols, 1982), Goswami was nonetheless listed as chairman.

53. Ranjit Singh Sarkaria (1973–81)

The first member of the Sikh community to reach the SCI, R.S. Sarkaria was born into a family of Jat Sikh farmers on 16 January 1916, at Patiala, Patiala district, Punjab. He was the son of Atma Singh Sarkaria, a civil engineer who spent his professional career in government service in the former Patiala state, retiring as chief engineer for irrigation. This elder Sarkaria was the first university graduate in the family, having received his BA degree from Punjab University. The ruler of Patiala financed his travel to England where he received a BSc (honours) in engineering from London Engineering University.[58]

One of ten children, R.S. Sarkaria was the only one to enter the legal profession. He received his BA from Government College, Lahore in 1936, and his LLB from University Law College, Lahore in 1939, where he was the Gold Medalist in the Law Moots.

After practising briefly as a pleader in his hometown, Sarkaria enrolled as an advocate of the Patiala High Court on 22 February 1940. His career in private practice was short and, on 14 April 1943, at the age of twenty-seven, he joined the Patiala state judicial service. His first post was that of subordinate judge-cum-magistrate and he served in that capacity for the next eight years. In 1948, Patiala became part of the new Patiala and East Punjab States Union (PEPSU). In 1951, he was promoted to district and sessions judge in the PEPSU superior judicial service and continued in that capacity after the merger of PEPSU into the reorganized state of Punjab in 1956. In mid-1962, by then a super-selection grade district and sessions judge, he became the registrar of the Punjab High Court. One of his responsibilities was to assist in translating the Constitution into Punjabi.

During his tenure as registrar he played a significant role in drafting the Punjab Judicial and Executive Functions Separation Act of 1964, much of which was adopted by Parliament when it enacted the 1973 Criminal Procedure Code. He also drafted the 1963 Punjab Superior Judicial Service Rules and played a major role in the drafting of the revisions of the rules relating to the recruitment and conditions of service of subordinate judges. He served as a representative of the Punjab High Court in 1966

---

[58] Interview on 15 July 1983 in New Delhi. He also provided the author with a prepared account of his life and career, dated 2 May 1983. See also Dhavan and Jacob, *Selection and Appointment of Supreme Court Judges*, pp. 79–80.

when, following the boundary changes of that year, the personnel of the subordinate judiciary had to be allocated to the reorganized states and territories of Punjab, Haryana, Himachal Pradesh, and Delhi.

Sarkaria's tenure as registrar ended when, at age fifty-one, he was sworn in as an additional judge of the Punjab and Haryana High Court on 13 June 1967. He was confirmed as a permanent judge on 27 September 1967. Six years later and when fifth in seniority, he was invited to become a member of the SCI. At first he declined the invitation, for he was comfortably settled in Chandigarh, happy with his work as a high court judge, not ambitious, and was reluctant to give up the enjoyment of spending weekends at his Patiala farm. But after further consideration he accepted the offer, and was sworn in on 17 September 1973, at age fifty-seven.

In February 1976, Mrs Gandhi's government asked him to conduct an investigation into charges of corruption, favouritism, and other alleged improprieties made against former Tamil Nadu chief minister M. Karunanidhi and several of his Dravida Munnetra Kazhagam cabinet colleagues. His May 1978 report provided evidence to support many of the allegations. By then, Mrs Gandhi's government had been defeated at the polls, his report was suppressed by the Janata government, and no action was taken on it. But it was published by M.G. Ramachandran's AIADMK government.[59] This investigation was controversial and received national attention, a result of which was that Sarkaria became rather well known.

After seven years on the SCI, he reached retirement age on 16 January 1981, closing out thirty-eight years of judicial service. He returned to his Chandigarh home and resumed his lifelong interests in gardening, reading English and Punjabi literature, and studying comparative religions, particularly the Sikh scriptures. Unlike many retired SCI judges, he did not engage in chamber practice, but did provide free legal advice occasionally. He also resumed his ties with Punjabi University, Patiala, and was a member of its academic council in 1983–4. In the early 1970s, he had served that university as a member of the law faculty and its senate and syndicate. In 1980, the university conferred upon him an honorary LLD. In 1981 and

---

[59] *Sarkaria Commission of Inquiry, Tamilnadu,* 4 vols (Madras: Director of Stationary and Printing, Government of Tamil Nadu, 1978). Many believe that this investigation was an effort to punish Karunanidhi for not toeing the government's line during the Emergency. See Kuldip Nayar's discussion in *The Judgement: Inside Story of the Emergency in India* (New Delhi: Viksas Publishing Pvt. Ltd.), p. 121. The complainant was Karunanidhi's successor and rival, M.G. Ramachandran.

1982, he declined the requests of CJI Chandrachud to return to the court as an Article 128 judge. He also declined requests of the union government to head several commissions of inquiry.

Sarkaria's life of quiet retirement ended in 1983 when he agreed to chair the Commission on Centre-State Relations, popularly known as the Sarkaria Commission. This commission, established because of increasing controversy, particularly complaints from the states over the working of Indian federalism, was asked to review the relationships between the centre and the states, and to recommend changes within the framework of the Constitution. As chairman, Sarkaria was given the status of a cabinet minister. This work took more than four years, and his nearly 1,600 page report was submitted in late 1987 and released in January 1988.[60] Two decades later, this Sarkaria Commission report is still often discussed.

Immediately after the report was submitted, he agreed to head another controversial and politically delicate central government panel,[61] this one to suggest a new administrative set-up for the union territory of Delhi and to recommend whether or not Delhi should receive statehood. But after more than a year of work, and the report nearly completed, the government, apparently to forestall an expected recommendation that Delhi's status be raised to statehood, announced that Sarkaria had accepted the chairmanship of the Press Council of India. This work began on 19 January 1989. He was reappointed for a second term and served until 23 July 1995.

Again he returned to Chandigarh to commence a second retirement. Long interested in translating various works from English to Punjabi, earlier in his career he published the *English-Hindi-Punjabi Dictionary of Legal and Administrative Terms* (1950); *Ik Lapp Husan Di* ('Handful of Beauty'), an anthology of English poems rendered into Punjabi verse (1969); and a Punjabi translation of *Shakespeare's King Lear*, published by Punjabi University in 1973. Later, he was the author of *Freedom of Information and Official Secrecy* (Bhopal: Makhanlal Chaturvedi Rashtriya Patrakarita Vishwavidyalaya, 1991), and *A Guide to Journalistic Ethics* (New Delhi: Press Council of India, 1995).

---

[60] *Report of the Commission on Centre-State Relations*, 2 vols (Delhi: Government of India Press, 1988).

[61] Committee on the Reorganization of the Delhi Set-Up.

In 2000, at age eighty-four, Sarkaria answered another call to serve his nation when he agreed to head the advisory panel on union–state relations for the National Commission to Review the Working of the Constitution.

Sarkaria was ninety-one when died on 12 October 2007.

54. Alak Chandra Gupta (1974–82)

The first advocate from the Calcutta High Court to be appointed to the SCI,[62] A.C. Gupta was born into an upper class family in Calcutta on 5 December 1918.[63] His father, Atul Chandra Gupta, was a prominent member of the Calcutta High Court bar, and was one of the two Calcutta lawyers co-opted by the Law Commission to assist the commission's inquiries in West Bengal. His grandfather, Umesh Chandra Gupta, was also a lawyer. A.C. Gupta grew up in a rich intellectual and cultural atmosphere. His brother, Praful Chandra Gupta, was a noted historian who became vice-chancellor of Vishwa Bharati University.

Gupta received his BA in English from Presidency College, Calcutta, in 1938, and an MA in English from the same institution in 1940. He received the Shakespeare Gold Medal for proficiency in English at the BA level and another gold medal for his performance in the law examinations. He had considered a career as a professor of English, but turned to law, and earned a BL from University Law College, Calcutta, in 1943.

After apprenticing for a year with his father, Gupta enrolled as an advocate of the Calcutta High Court on 31 August 1945. Nineteen years later, on 24 February 1964, at age forty-five, he was appointed as an additional judge of the Calcutta High Court. This appointment was made permanent on 24 February 1966. In 1967, he served as a one-man commission of inquiry, usually referred to as the Bagmari Commission of Inquiry, which investigated a riot between the Sikh and Hindu communities.

---

[62] The eight earlier appointees from the Calcutta High Court were barristers. B.K. Mukherjea was a not a barrister but he was appointed to the Federal Court in 1948.

[63] The SCI and Calcutta High Court records list Gupta's official birth date as 1 January 1917. But he was, in fact, born on 5 December 1918. Interview with Gupta on 13 May 1983 in New Delhi. His correct birth date was not a secret. See, *India Who's Who 1979–1980* (New Delhi: INFA Publications, 1980). I met Gupta for a second time on 22 October 1988 and again in New Delhi.

After ten years on the Calcutta bench and fourth in seniority, he was promoted to the SCI. When he was sworn in on 2 September 1974, he was fifty-five (fifty-seven according to the official records).

In July 1977, shortly after the Janata government came to power, Gupta accepted the chairmanship of the Commission of Inquiry on Maruti Affairs. This was a politically delicate assignment, for the major target of this investigation was Mrs Gandhi's son Sanjay. The fact that the Janata government chose Gupta, who was appointed to the SCI when Mrs Gandhi was prime minister, was an acknowledgement of Gupta's reputation for impartiality and integrity. His report, completed in May 1979, documented the misuse of state power by Sanjay.[64] Shortly after it was published, Mrs Gandhi was returned to power and the report was then withdrawn and no action taken on it.

After retiring on 1 January 1982, he remained in Delhi where he engaged in chamber practice. Most of his time, however, was devoted to serving as an arbitrator when asked to do so by the SCI and private parties. In 1985, at the SCI's request, he agreed to be the mediator in the much publicized Kamani case, where a family dispute had led to the closing of a large company, resulting in 700 employees losing their jobs. Three years into this protracted dispute, and after one of the Kamani family members expressed no faith in him, he announced his resignation, but the CJI persuaded him to continue. In 1988, he and a retired Calcutta High Court judge agreed to conduct an investigation into the role of the Uttar Pradesh government, the police, and the Provincial Armed Constabulary into the communal riots that had occurred in May 1987 in Meerut. This inquiry was initiated by the Indian Peoples' Human Rights Commission (IPHRC), a citizen's group chaired by Gupta's former SCI colleague, V.R. Krishna Iyer.[65] From 1991 to 2000, he headed the board of directors of The Statesman, a leading national newspaper published in Calcutta.

Gupta was a genuine intellectual and a connoisseur of the arts. He was a voracious reader, particularly of English and Bengali literature.

He died in Calcutta on 7 November 2002, at age eighty-three.

---

[64] Report on the Commission of Inquiry on Maruti Affairs, 2 vols (New Delhi: Controller of Publications, 1979).

[65] 'Tribunal to Investigate Meerut Riots', The Indian Express, 29 February 1988.

55. Nand Lall Untwalia (1974–80)

The second member of the Marwari community to serve on the SCI, N.L. Untwalia was born into a middle-class family on 1 August 1915 at Sitamarhi, Sitamarhi district, Bihar. His father, Govind Bux Untwalia, was a tradesman who ran the ancestral wholesale and retail businesses dealing with salt, kerosene, cement, and lime.[66]

The first university graduate and the first lawyer in his family, he received his BA in economics and mathematics from Greer Bhumihar Brahmin (G.B.B.) College[67] in Muzaffarpur, Bihar, in 1937. He then proceeded to Calcutta, where he received his BL from the University Law College in 1940.[68]

He returned to Muzaffarpur and, at age twenty-five, began practising in the district courts as a pleader in November 1940. He enrolled as an advocate of the Patna High Court on 6 March 1944 but remained at Muzaffarpur until 1947 when he moved his practice to the Patna High Court. Eleven years later, and at age forty-two, he was appointed an additional judge of the Patna High Court on 2 January 1958. He was confirmed as a permanent judge on 4 November 1958. After nearly fifteen years as an associate judge, he became chief justice on 29 September 1972.

Promotion to the SCI came two years later. He was fifty-nine and brought to the SCI nearly seventeen years of high court experience when he was sworn in on 3 October 1974. He retired on 1 August 1980.

Although some members of the Marwari community urged him to remain in Delhi so that he would be available to serve as an arbitrator, he had no interest in doing so. He had suffered a heart attack in 1976 and had not been in good health during his remaining tenure on the SCI. He had been a widower since 1957, was alone in Delhi, and chose to return to Patna to be close to his daughter and son.[69]

After Charan Singh became prime minister in 1979, he was offered the chairmanship of the Law Commission but did not want to leave Patna.

[66] Interview on 3 December 1988 at Patna, Bihar.

[67] Now known as Langat Singh College.

[68] He went to Calcutta for his legal education because his was a very orthodox, strict vegetarian family. Patna did not have a purely vegetarian hostel but there was one in Calcutta where all the boarders were Marwaris.

[69] Untwalia's adopted son, Bishwa Nath Agrawal, served as a Patna High Court judge from 1986 to 1999 and, in October 2000, after a brief detour as chief justice of the Orissa High Court, became an SCI judge.

He was one of the very few SCI judges who went into full retirement after leaving the SCI. He was offered other post-retirement assignments but was not interested. In Patna, he became active in a several cultural, religious, and educational activities. He served as president of the managing committee of the local Ramakrishna Mission and for some time was the executive chairman of the Patna chapter of Bharatiya Vidya Bhavan.

Untwalia died at age seventy-seven on 7 December 1992.

56. Syed Murtaza Fazal Ali (1975–85)

The first to come to the SCI from the Jammu and Kashmir High Court, S.M. Fazal Ali[70] was born on 20 December 1920 in Moradabad, Moradabad district, in Uttar Pradesh. The scion of a prominent and wealthy Muslim judicial family he represented the eighth consecutive generation of lawyers. He was the son of Sir S. Fazl Ali who was one of the members of the SCI's first bench. This father and son combination served a total of more than fifty years as high court, federal court, and supreme court judges.

Although born in Uttar Pradesh, his family moved to Bihar when Fazal Ali was very young. He earned his BA (honours) in English from Patna College in 1940, and the BL (first class) from Patna Law College in 1943. As was the case with many of the brightest young men of his generation, he aspired to be chosen for the ICS. In 1942–3, he attended the ICS coaching classes at Aligarh Muslim University but his hopes were not realized.

On 7 November 1944, at age twenty-three, he enrolled as an advocate of the Patna High Court and commenced his practice there. At this time, his father was that court's chief justice. In 1949, he became an advocate of the Federal Court and during the next few years appeared before the SCI as well. In Patna, he was a member of the panel of lawyers which handled Bihar government litigation. During these years he authored several study guides on the topics of Hindu Law, Torts, Criminal Law, Mohammedan Law, and Law of Contracts for a series entitled *Questions and Answers of Patna University Law Examinations*.

---

[70] He chose to spell his surname differently than his father's to avoid confusion. Interview with Fazal Ali on 23 April 1983 in New Delhi.

At the uncommonly young age of thirty-seven, younger at the time of high court appointment than any other who would reach the SCI,[71] he became a permanent judge of the Jammu and Kashmir High Court on 8 April 1958. He was the first judge appointed under the terms of the Constitution of Jammu and Kashmir which had recently come into effect. Prime Minister Nehru felt it necessary, given the circumstances at the time in that state, to have an outsider who was a Muslim. His appointment meant that all the high courts in the nation, except the tiny Sikkim one, had gained representation on the SCI.

Nearly a decade later, on 3 December 1967, when he was just forty-six, he became that court's chief justice. While serving in that capacity, he was appointed as chairman of the Unlawful Activities (Prevention) Tribunal in 1971. He was chairman of the Maintenance of Internal Security Act advisory board from 1972 to 1975 during these years he was also a member of the Nehru Award Jury. He also played a major role in completing the separation of the judiciary from the executive in the state. It was at his initiative in September 1972 that a Judicial Officers Training Institute, the first of its kind in the country, was established to provide practical judicial training for new subordinate judiciary recruits, and refresher courses for more senior judicial judges.

Promotion to the SCI came on 2 April 1975. Although he had been a high court judge for nearly seventeen years, including more than seven as chief justice, he was only fifty-four when he arrived in Delhi. But he could not look forward to the chief justiceship, for P.N. Bhagwati was already on the Court, and he would reach retirement age during Bhagwati's tenure as CJI. Fazal Ali was the youngest ever appointed who was not in line to become CJI. Although he was a Muslim, he was not appointed to fill the Muslim seat, for M.H. Beg was already on board.

During the course of his decade on the SCI, Fazal Ali was active with the Institute of Criminology and Forensic Sciences and was closely associated with Jamia Millia University, the premier Muslim university in Delhi. He also served as chairman of the selection committee for recruitment of judicial and technical members of the recently created Customs, Excise and Gold Control Appellate Tribunal.

Just a few months before reaching retirement age, Fazal Ali died of a heart attack on 20 August 1985, at age sixty-four.

---

[71] R.S. Pathak was also thirty-seven when appointed to the Allahabad High Court, but he was a few months older than Fazal Ali.

57. Prakash Narayan Shinghal (1975–80)

The first native son[72] of Rajasthan to reach the SCI, P.N. Shinghal was born into a middle-class family on 15 October 1915 in Bharatpur, Bharatpur district. He was the son of Babu Prasad Shinghal who was a district and sessions judge in the former Bharatpur state. One of his uncles held the same post in Alwar state and another served as chief justice of that state.[73]

Shinghal earned his BA in French from Allahabad University in 1935. He then went to Lucknow where he completed a two-year combined course for the MA and LLB, receiving both these degrees from Lucknow University in 1937. In 1976, he would receive an LLD (*honoris causa*) from Jodhpur University.

From 1937 to 1941, he practised law in the district courts at Aligarh. In the latter year, at age twenty-five, he joined the Alwar state judicial service. During the 1940s, he served as law secretary and legal remembrancer in Alwar state and as cabinet secretary of the Matsya union government, after which he was awarded the certificate of merit, the highest service award in the state. On 25 June 1950, he was appointed a district and sessions judge in Rajasthan,[74] and was posted first at Alwar and next at Kota. From February 1951 to July 1952, he served as chief electoral officer and secretary to the Rajasthan government. He spent the July 1952 to March 1955 period in Delhi as secretary to the Election Commission of India.

In December 1955, by special selection and at age forty, he was appointed to the Indian Administrative Service. Shinghal was the only SCI judge who had experience as an IAS officer. In that capacity he served as special officer in the Rajasthan government secretariat in charge of the integration of services preceding and following the 1956 reorganization of states. From September 1956 to June 1958, he was back in Delhi serving as deputy secretary, Ministry of Home Affairs, and working on matters pertaining to the States Reorganization Act. In 1958, after three years in the IAS, he decided to resign and revert to the Rajasthan higher judicial service. For the next three years he was posted at Jodhpur as a district and sessions judge.

---

[72] K.N. Wanchoo was the chief justice of the Rajasthan High Court when he was appointed to the SCI in 1958 but he was born in Madhya Pradesh and had come to Rajasthan by way of the Allahabad High Court.

[73] I was unable to meet Shinghal but received correspondence from him dated 27 April and 3 June 1983, and 13 March and 25 June 1984.

[74] The state of Rajasthan and its high court came into being in 1949.

On 21 June 1961, at age forty-five, he was appointed an additional judge of the Rajasthan High Court, and this appointment became permanent on 28 November 1963. During his fourteenth year on the Rajasthan bench, he became chief justice on 17 February 1975.

Promotion to the SCI came later the same year, on 6 November 1975 when he was sixty. His retirement on 14 October 1980 brought to a close a nearly forty-year career as a judge and administrator.

After leaving the SCI, Shinghal settled in Lucknow to a life of quiet retirement, with no plans for other private or official work. He was strongly of the view that chamber practice was an improper activity for a retired SCI judge. During his first three retirement years, his only noteworthy activity was to serve as an honorary and non-official member of the law panel of the University Grants Commission which brought him back to Delhi for brief periods. The leisurely pace of retirement ended in September 1983 when he accepted the chairmanship of the Fourth Central Pay Commission. This was a major responsibility for these commissions make recommendations, usually accepted by the government, affecting the salaries, allowances, and retirement benefits of millions of central government employees. In 1985, the work of this commission was expanded to include the pension structure of some seven million existing pensioners as well.

Shortly before his report[75] was completed, Shinghal died on 17 October 1986, at age seventy-one.

58. Jaswant Singh (1976–9)

On 25 January 1914, Jaswant Singh[76] was born at Mirpur, which was then a district headquarters of the princely state of Kashmir and which is now located in Pakistan-occupied portion of the state of Jammu and Kashmir. He was a descendant of the old aristocracy for his ancestors, several generations

---

[75] *Report of the Fourth Central Pay Commission* (Delhi: Controller of Publications, 1986).

[76] His name is almost invariably rendered as simply Jaswant Singh but he said that Singh is his surname. Interviews in New Delhi on 5 July 1983 and 12 December 1988, and correspondence dated 6 May 1983 and 6 December 1988. His widow, Mrs Lajja Rani, provided additional information via correspondence dated 24 September 2009. Jaswant Singh was related to former CJI M.C. Mahajan, who was his mother's sister's husband.

earlier, were rulers of Kashmir. He was the son of Raja Raghubir Singh, a prosperous banker and philanthropist in Mirpur. Although he had passed the law examination administered by the state government he was not trained as a lawyer and never practised law, so Jaswant Singh can be considered the first lawyer in the family.[77] No family of an SCI judge was more tragically affected by the 1947 Partition. His parents, two sisters, and a brother were killed near Mirpur during the 1947 raids.

Singh received his BA in economics, history, Sanskrit, and Hindi from Forman Christian College, Lahore in 1933, and his LLB from Government Law College, Lahore in 1935. He ranked at the top in the first examination in law, winning the certificate of honour.

In March 1936, at the age of twenty-two, he joined the bar as a pleader in Jammu. Earlier he had applied for both the judicial service and the civil service but, for 'extraneous reasons' he believed, was not accepted. He also finished at the top in the examination for the post of customs and excise inspector but nothing came of this. On 6 May 1938, he enrolled as a vakil of what was then known as the High Court of Judicature of Jammu and Kashmir state and, in March 1942, he enrolled as an advocate of that court.[78] In August 1944, he was appointed public prosecutor at Jammu, the first of several state law officer positions he would hold over the next twenty-three years. During 1945–7, he served as acting public prosecutor at Srinagar and Mirpur. In May 1947, he became an assistant to the state's advocate general and, on 8 August 1948, he was promoted to assistant Advocate General. Although he held that title until 1956, he had functioned since 1949 as acting Advocate General. In 1956, he became the state's advocate general, a post he held for the next eleven years until his appointment to the high court. Among the important cases he participated in were the Sheikh Abdullah Sedition and the Sheikh Abdullah Conspiracy cases. In the latter it was Singh, then the senior prosecution counsel, who withdrew the case against the accused. In 1966–7, he served a term as president of the Jammu bar association and from 1973 to 1976 he was a member of the university council and law faculty at Jammu University.

---

[77] His son, Anil Dev Singh, was appointed to the Delhi High Court in 1990 and became chief justice of the Rajasthan High Court in 2002.

[78] After the Constitution of Jammu and Kashmir was enacted in 1956, it became the High Court of Jammu and Kashmir. The convention is that the Jammu region of the state is represented by a Hindu.

From 16 March to 15 May 1967, when Chief Justice M. Fazal Ali was serving as acting governor, Singh was an acting judge of the Jammu and Kashmir High Court and became a permanent judge on 3 December 1967 at age fifty-three. Seven years later, on 2 April 1975, he became the chief justice.

Less than a year later, and just two days before reaching retirement age, Singh was sworn in as a judge of the SCI on 23 January 1976 He was the first native son of Jammu and Kashmir to be appointed to the SCI.[79]

Singh's brief tenure on the SCI ended with his retirement on 25 January 1979. He remained in Delhi and engaged in chamber practice and arbitration work. But this was not to last long, for in 27 August 1979 the union government appointed him chairman of the board of arbitration, Ministry of Labour, for joint consultative machinery and compulsory arbitration for central government employees. He worked in that capacity until December 1981. Concurrently, in September 1981, he was appointed as chairman of what is invariably referred to simply as the Jaswant Singh Commission. The initial charge of this commission was to examine all aspects of the demand for the establishment of a separate bench of the Allahabad High Court for the twenty-five districts in the western region of Uttar Pradesh. Later the scope of this commission was expanded to include addressing the same questions of the need and feasibility of circuit benches of the high courts of Tamil Nadu, Karnataka, Madhya Pradesh, and the states of the Northeast. Completing this work in 1985, his reports[80] generated considerable controversy, and little action was taken on them.

He then resumed his New Delhi chamber practice and arbitration work but, in August 1985, this was interrupted again when he accepted still another central government assignment, this one to make a preliminary inquiry into allegations of corruption, nepotism, and misuse of power by the then Haryana Chief Minister Bhajan Lal and his son-in-law. After a month-long inquiry, he concluded that there was insufficient evidence to support the charges.

[79] Fazal Ali had come to the state from Bihar and was perceived as an outsider.

[80] *Report on the General Question of Having Benches of the High Courts at Places Away from Their Principal Seats and Broad Principles and Criteria to be Followed in Regard Thereto; Report on the Demand for Additional Benches of the Madhya Pradesh High Court in Certain Regions of the State; Report on the Need for a Bench of the Madras High Court in Southern Region of Tamil Nadu;* and the four-volume *Report of the Jaswant Singh Commission.* These four reports were published in New Delhi by the Government of India, Department of Justice, in 1986.

In 1996, his *Jammu and Kashmir: Political and Constitutional Development* was published in New Delhi by Har-Anand Publications.

Jaswant Singh died on 29 December 2002, at age eighty-eight.

59. Palapatti Sadaya Goundar Kailasam (1977–80)

P.S. Kailasam was born at Palapatti, Salem district, Tamil Nadu on 12 September 1915. His father, Sadaya Goundar, was a member of the landed aristocracy—a zamindar with substantial landholdings. Among Kailasam's relatives were some well known political figures. Dr P. Subbarayan, his father's cousin, had been both a Tamil Nadu and central government minister. S. Mohan Kumaramangalam, the architect of the 1973 supersession, was his cousin.[81]

He earned a BSc in Botany from Presidency College, Madras in 1935. He aspired to be a botanist but finding employment opportunities in that field limited he turned to law and received his BL from Madras Law College in 1937.

He was twenty-two when he enrolled as an advocate of the Madras High Court on 18 August 1938, commencing a thirty-nine year association with that court. He was appointed to the post of public prosecutor on 1 January 1956 and from 15 August to 13 September 1960, he was acting Advocate General.

A few weeks later, on 20 October 1960, and at age forty-five, he was appointed as a permanent judge of the Madras High Court. Nearly sixteen years later he was named acting chief justice on 11 March 1976, and was confirmed as chief justice on 8 April 1976. During his tenure as chief justice, he was instrumental in the establishment of the Tamil Nadu Legal Aid and Advice Board.

He was sixty-one when he was sworn in as a judge of the SCI on 3 January 1977. At that time, in terms of length of service as a high court judge, he was the most senior one in the nation and was also the first Madras chief justice to accept appointment to the SCI.

Kailasam's forty-four month tenure on the SCI ended with his retirement on 12 September 1980, after which he returned to his home in Madras. His only post-retirement employment was aborted before it began. In

---

[81] I interviewed Kailasam in Madras on 24 June 1983. P. Chidambaram, who would become a prominent national political figure and union cabinet minister, is his son-in-law. Kailasam's wife, Soundara Kailasam was an eminent Tamil poet and writer.

March 1981, he agreed to chair a commission of inquiry established by the central government to investigate allegations against the Tamil Nadu and Kerala governments concerning the sale of alcohol. But before this inquiry commenced he was accused by one of the parties of being biased towards the other and he resigned.

Awarded annually by the Tamil Nadu Tennis Association is the Justice P.S. Kailasam Memorial Award for performance in the junior nationals. Another legacy is the Justice P.S. Kailasam Medical and Educational Foundation.

On 10 August 1986, Kailasam died in Madras at age seventy.

XV

The Beg Court (1977–8)

The next-in-line to follow Ray as CJI was H.R. Khanna but it came as little surprise when, just hours before Ray's retirement on 28 January 1977, the government announced that M.H. Beg, the second most senior associate judge, was to be the fifteenth CJI. Two weeks earlier Beg had been informed that Khanna would be superseded and he would get the chief justiceship.[1]

Khanna resigned immediately in protest, and the public and press reaction was overwhelmingly critical, particularly because the victim was Khanna. All knew that he was being penalized for his courageous solo dissent in the *Habeas Corpus* decision of a year earlier. Speaking for the government, Law Minister Gokhale lamely attempted to justify the supersession by saying that Khanna would have reached retirement age just five months later, and that 'It is the view of the government that appointments to the high office of chief justice should not be for such a short duration. Mr Justice Beg ... will have a longer period of about thirteen months'.[2] This time there was no mention of a judge's views on economic and social change being a consideration in the selection of a CJI. Kuldip Nayar later wrote that 'Gokhale told me that he had tried to persuade Mrs Gandhi not to supersede Khanna but she didn't listen to him'.[3] The supersession of Khanna was one of Mrs Gandhi's last major acts during her first regime, for a few days earlier she

[1] Interview with Beg on 2 May 1983, in New Delhi.
[2] 'Beg is named chief justice; Khanna quits', *The Times of India*, 29 January 1977.
[3] Kuldip Nayar, *The Judgement: Inside Story of the Emergency in India* (New Delhi: Vikas Publishing House Pvt. Ltd., 1977), p. 169.

had announced that the postponed national and state elections would be held in March.

Beg had been a loyal soldier as an associate judge and had supported the government in *Kesavananda* and *Habeas Corpus*. He was perceived by the attentive public and most of his colleagues, as was Ray before him, as a trespasser sitting in a chair that was not rightfully his. One difference, however, was that Beg, unlike Ray, would have become CJI even if Khanna had been permitted to hold that post. Khanna would have reached retirement age on 3 July 1977 and Beg would have followed him until his own sixty-fifth birthday on 22 February 1978. So the supersession gave Beg thirteen months as CJI instead of eight.

In the second month of Beg's stewardship, Mrs Gandhi's government was routed and the Janata coalition took over. There was some support in high Janata circles for asking Beg to step down and replacing him with Khanna. But Khanna himself told Prime Minister Morarji Desai that this would be improper and counselled against such a move.[4]

Beg inherited a Court of twelve judges, including himself. There was one retirement (P.K. Goswami in December 1977) during his tenure and three judges were appointed. There was little reason to expect that the new government would allow Beg much of a voice in selecting judges. However, according to K.S. Hegde and all other sitting and retired judges who spoke on this matter, the Janata government did not press names on Beg. Hegde, by then back in Parliament and Speaker of the Lok Sabha, was not consulted about any of the Beg appointments. The Janata had pledged in the election campaign to restore the independence and prestige of the judiciary but said nothing about restoring the pre-1971 primacy of the CJI in the selection process. The most noteworthy change during the Janata regime concerning SCI appointments was the requirement that the CJI consult his two seniormost colleagues about nominees and apprise the government of their views. Beg's seniormost colleagues were Chandrachud and Bhagwati. He consulted them and passed on their views.[5]

Appointed first was V.D. Tulzapurkar; he was sworn in on 30 September 1977 at age fifty-six. He was a veteran of fourteen years as a Bombay High Court judge and was second in seniority. Beg advanced Tulzapurkar's

---

[4] H.R. Khanna, *Neither Roses Nor Thorns* (Lucknow: Eastern Book Company, 1985), pp. 90–1. Hegde was of the same view. Interview, 14–15 November 1988.

[5] Interview with Chandrachud on 8 December 1988 and Bhagwati on 3 October 1988.

name after seeking and receiving Chandrachud's endorsement. He travelled to Bombay to become acquainted with him and shortly thereafter his appointment was announced. Since the retirement of D.G. Palekar, three years earlier, the Bombay High Court had been represented only by Chandrachud. Bombay usually had two, sometimes three, representatives.

Also sworn in on 30 September was fifty-seven-year-old D.A. Desai, fourth in seniority on the Gujarat High Court. According to Beg, and both Desai and Bhagwati agreed,[6] most responsible for Desai's appointment was Bhagwati, his former colleague at Gujarat, long-time friend, and comrade-in-arms committed to improving the lot of the disadvantaged. Beg also consulted Chandrachud, and he too supported Desai's appointment. Beg had not met Desai earlier. He invited him to come to Delhi for discussions and the appointment was announced a few days later.

The official announcement of Desai's appointment on 26 September precipitated an unprecedented controversy at Ahmedabad which quickly spread to Delhi.[7] The Gujarat bar association argued that this was another supersession because the seniority convention had been violated. The association argued that B.J. Diwan, who was very popular with the bar, should have been appointed because he was the chief justice. In fact, about half of judges appointed since 1950 had not been high court chief justices, more than a half dozen were fourth or lower in seniority when appointed, and no public controversy had followed those appointments. The association alleged also that this was a 'clear case of nepotism' because Desai was related to Prime Minister Morarji Desai—the two were distantly related. The Ahmedabad lawyers also disagreed strongly with CJI Beg's description of Desai as 'the ablest judge of the Gujarat High Court'. Another component of the controversy was that both Diwan and S.H. Sheth, the latter the most senior associate judge, had been punitively transferred during the Emergency while Desai was not.

[6] Interviews with Beg on 2 May 1983, Desai on 29 September 1988, and Bhagwati ('I am responsible for Desai's appointment') on 3 October 1988.

[7] For a complete and well-documented account of this controversy, see Rajeev Dhavan and Alice Jacob, *Selection and Appointment of Supreme Court Judges: A Case Study* (Bombay: N.M. Tripathi Pvt. Ltd., 1978), pp. 13–33. My account borrows from this book. They wrote that the first salvo was fired by M.C. Chagla, who implied that Gujarat Chief Justice B.J. Diwan was the superior choice and said that the appointment of Desai was wrong, and faulted the Janata for ignoring its campaign pledge to restore the independence of the judiciary, pp. 21–2.

Bhagwati, a former Gujarat chief justice, was drawn into this controversy. A resolution of the Gujarat High Court Advocates Association that passed by 125 votes to 4 said that it '... shrewdly suspects that the recommendation was largely, if not solely, influenced by Mr Justice Bhagwati ...'. Implicit also was that the bar did not like Desai either. Desai agreed: 'I was not regarded as a courteous judge; I was not well-liked'.[8]

Soon the SCI bar association joined the fray and passed the following resolution:

The Supreme Court Bar Association strongly disapproves the appointment of Mr Justice D.A. Desai as a Judge of the Supreme Court disregarding the superior claims of more senior High Court Judges including the present Chief Justice of the Gujarat High Court. The Association therefore resolves not to attend the Swearing-in-Ceremony of Mr Justice D.A. Desai. The Association wishes to put on record its complete satisfaction at the appointment of Mr Justice V.D. Tulzapurkar to the Supreme Court.[9]

The final appointee of Beg's tenure was R.S. Pathak, the most senior high court judge in the country. Beg claimed to have initiated this one, and Pathak was certain that this was true. Then only fifty-three, Pathak was sworn in on 20 February 1978, just a day before Beg retired. Although he was the chief justice of the Himachal Pradesh High Court at this time, most of his fifteen years of high court grooming was spent on the Allahabad High Court. Beg knew Pathak very well, for earlier these two practised at the Allahabad bar and during the 1960s were colleagues on the Allahabad High Court. Beg's ties with the Pathak family dated back to his earliest days in Allahabad when he apprenticed under Pathak's father. Although there is an appearance of cronyism, it must be stressed that Pathak was viewed by many, much earlier, as solidly on track to the SCI. Pathak had been sounded by CJI Ray three years earlier, but after Ray asked for his views on the basic structure doctrine, Pathak had refused to answer and the conversation had ended.

All these three were significant appointments. Each of them made a mark on the SCI, and Pathak, if the seniority convention was later restored, would be in line for nearly three years as CJI. The most striking thing about these three is their relative youth—an average age of 55.3 when appointed. Though young, all had substantial high court experience, averaging 12.9 years. In religion and caste terms, all three were brahmins. Beg himself was

---

[8] Interview with Desai on 29 September 1988.
[9] Dhavan and Jacob, *Selection and Appointment of Supreme Court Judges*, p. 30.

a barrister, but the three were Indian-educated advocates. None of them was a regional or state fill-up, or a replacement. The vacancies were those of H.R. Khanna (Punjab and Haryana/Delhi), A.N. Ray (Calcutta), and P.K. Goswami (Gauhati), while the Beg appointees came from Bombay, Gujarat, and Allahabad/Himachal Pradesh. The judges serving when Beg departed continued to be representative of the geographic diversity of the country—four from the north and west, three from the east, and two from the south. They represented ten high courts.

The similarities not withstanding, their years on the SCI would reveal that the three could hardly have been more different in terms of their philosophies and styles. Tulzapurkar was an old school judge faithful to the common law traditions, very much a British-style legalist. Desai was nearly a polar opposite—a liberal-left judicial activist, impatient for change. He was critical of the common law heritage and machinery and wanted much of it scrapped for its failure to deliver speedy and inexpensive justice to the downtrodden. Pathak hovered over the middle ground, sensitive to the winds of change and the need for some reform, but wishing to remain within the confines of the Constitution and conscious of the limitations of judicial power.

The strength of the SCI was increased by four judges during Beg's tenure.[10] None of these new seats were filled until several months after he retired. O. Chinnappa Reddy said that Beg, during a December 1977 visit to the Andhra Pradesh High Court, offered him a judgeship, but nothing came of this.[11] In the same month Beg paid a visit to the Rajasthan High Court. A.P. Sen said that Beg tried to persuade him to remain in Rajasthan as chief justice but said nothing about being promoted to the SCI.[12] According to A.D. Koshal, Beg, by then retired, told him that he had recommended his appointment without first seeking his consent.[13] Each of these had been transferred during the Emergency and reached Delhi in July 1978. Whether Beg took the initiative in setting in motion these appointments, or whether these names were advanced by the government and Beg was merely the messenger is not known, but all three believed that Beg's role was significant. Because their appointments were not announced until six months after Beg was gone, they must be considered appointees of

[10] The Supreme Court (Number of Judges) Act, 1977.
[11] Interview with Chinnappa Reddy on 9 November 1988 in Hyderabad.
[12] Interview with Sen on 11 May 1983, in New Delhi.
[13] Interview with Koshal on 27 November 1988, in New Delhi.

the Chandrachud years. The Law Minister during Beg's tenure was Shanti Bhushan, but the three who were appointed, and Chinnappa Reddy, Sen, and Koshal believed that his role was more passive than active.

Beg had a difficult time as CJI. Upendra Baxi has written: 'There were clear indications that brother justices did not accept the leadership of Chief Justice Beg. The Court almost ceased to be an institution and became an assembly of individual justices'.[14] His colleague P.K. Goswami, in a separate opinion in the *Rajasthan Dissolution*[15] decision, criticized Beg for meeting with acting president B.D. Jatti before that decision was announced.[16] Near the end of his tenure, he suffered the humiliation of failing to gain the support of his brethren when he started criminal proceedings against two national newspapers.[17]

When Beg retired on 21 February 1978, he bequeathed to Chandrachud an SCI comprised of thirteen judges, one more than he had inherited.

60. Vidyaranya Dattatraya Tulzapurkar (1977–86)

V.D. Tulzapurkar was born into a middle-class family on 9 March 1921 in Bombay, Maharashtra. He was the son of D.A. Tulzapurkar who practised as an advocate of the Bombay High Court for nearly half a century.[18]

He was the only SCI judge to have received his law degree before completing his BA. He received an LLB from Government Law College, Bombay in 1941, and his BA from Bombay's Elphinstone College followed in 1943.

On 1 December 1942, at age twenty-one, he enrolled as an advocate of the Bombay High Court. In 1947, he also qualified as an attorney-at-law. This meant that he passed the demanding examination to be a solicitor

---

[14] Upendra Baxi, *The Indian Supreme Court and Politics*, Lucknow: Eastern Book Company, p. 189.

[15] *State of Rajasthan v. Union of India* [1978] 1 SCR 1.

[16] Beg felt it necessary to issue a press statement saying that the acting president met him only to extend an invitation to him to attend a wedding reception. This incident is discussed in Upendra Baxi (ed.), *K.K. Mathew on Democracy, Equality and Freedom* (Lucknow: Eastern Book Company, 1978), p. x.

[17] In *Re Sham Lal* (1978) 2 SCC 479. See Rajeev Dhavan and Balbir Singh, 'Publish and Be Damned—the Contempt Power and the Press at the Bar of the Supreme Court', *Journal of the Indian Law Institute*, vol. 21, no. 1 (January–March 1979), pp. 1–30.

[18] Interview with Tulzapurkar in New Delhi on 14 July 1983.

and worked in that capacity for a few years. No other SCI judge had that experience.

On 16 July 1956 at age thirty-five, and at the urging of M.C. Chagla, the Bombay chief justice, he accepted appointment as a judge of the city civil court and additional sessions judge. On 19 April 1962 he was promoted to principal judge.

At age forty-two he was appointed an additional judge of the Bombay High Court on 21 December 1963, and was confirmed as a permanent judge on 22 September 1966. Nearly fourteen years later, and on the eve of his promotion to the SCI, he was the most senior associate judge and had served briefly as acting chief justice. Both at the bar and during his years as a judge, Tulzapurkar's life was the law and he was involved in few off-the-bench activities though he once served as the chairman of a committee which dealt with the affiliation of colleges with Bombay University.

During the 1975–7 Emergency, Tulzapurkar was one of the few high court judges who spoke out loudly against measures the government had taken to stifle dissent. His bold decision in *N.P. Nathwani* v. *Commissioner of Police*,[19] handed down in December 1976, struck down a police order banning a public gathering of lawyers who were to meet to criticize the Emergency. He minced no words in condemning this invasion of civil rights. On 16 January 1977, just a few days before Mrs Gandhi announced that national elections would be held in March, but Tulzapurkar could not have known that, he delivered a speech at Nagpur that attracted national attention. The essence of his remarks, which revealed no fear of retribution, was very critical of the denigration of judges and the censorship of court proceedings during the Emergency. It was one of the most trenchant criticisms of the Emergency by a sitting judge. This speech was censored for about three weeks before it was reported in the national newspapers.[20] Had Mrs Gandhi not been defeated at the polls, it is unlikely that Tulzapurkar would have been appointed to the SCI.

Tulzapurkar was fifty-six when he was sworn in at the SCI on 30 September 1977. On the bench it was evident that he was a judge of the old school attached to the inherited Anglo-Saxon model and the traditions associated with it, particularly how judges should behave. Blunt and

[19] [1976] 78 *Bombay Law Reporter* 1.
[20] The full text of this speech is found in 'Inaugural Address', *AIR* 1977 *Journal*, pp. 33–8, and was also published in *Bombay Law Review Journal*, LXXIX (1977), pp. 6–14.

outspoken, he did not hesitate to criticize colleagues whose behaviour he found unacceptable.[21]

After eight and a half years on the SCI and thirty-five years as a judge, he retired on 9 March 1986. He returned to Bombay where he engaged in chamber practice and often served as an arbitrator.

Tulzapurkar died on 1 October 2004, at age eighty-three.

61. Dhirajlal Ambelal Desai (1977–85)

Born on 8 May 1920 at Surat, Surat district, Gujarat into a middle-class family, D.A. Desai was the son of A.J. Desai who was a revenue officer in the Bombay Presidency subordinate provincial civil service. He was very distantly related to Morarji Desai who was India's Prime Minister when he was promoted to the SCI.[22]

Desai received his BA degree in history and economics from M.T.B.[23] College in Surat in 1942 and his LLB two years later from the Sarvajanik Law College, also in Surat. The first lawyer in his family, he aspired to become a college teacher but fell short of earning a first class degree which at that time was a requisite for a teaching position. His father then persuaded him to become a lawyer. During his student days he was active in the freedom struggle. He was not arrested but was beaten with lathis by the police.

After enrolling as an advocate of the Bombay High Court in October 1945 he began practising at the district courts in Surat where he was to spend the next fifteen years. Although his practice was a general one, he handled a large number of criminal cases,[24] and often represented employees and tenants. He was also active in politics during these years and from 1949 to 1957 was closely associated with the Congress Socialist Party.

When the state of Gujarat came into existence in 1960, he enrolled as an advocate of the Gujarat High Court but never practised there. On 11

[21] See his, 'Judiciary: Attacks and Survival', *AIR 1983 Journal*, pp. 9–18, and 'Threats to the Independence of the Judiciary', *AIR 1984 Journal*, pp. 49–53.

[22] Interviews with Desai on 30 April 1983 and 29 September 1988 in New Delhi. Although most render his first name as Dhirubhai, he said that Dhirajal is correct and is his preferred usage.

[23] Maganlal Thakordas Balmukundas.

[24] His mother objected to him representing alleged dacoits (robbers) and murderers and said that because the fees he earned defending such people was tainted, she would not eat the food he provided.

May 1960, at age forty, he accepted appointment as an assistant judge and assistant sessions judge and was posted in Ahmedabad. On 4 November 1961, he was promoted to district and sessions judge. He served in that capacity first at Baroda and later in Bhavnagar and Nadiad.

On 19 February 1968, at age forty-seven, he was sworn in as an additional judge of the high court. The first service judge to be appointed, he was selected by long-time friend, P.N. Bhagwati, who was then the Gujarat High Court chief justice. He was confirmed as a permanent judge on 25 February 1970.

In 1971, he became a member of the Gujarat Judicial Reforms Committee and, in 1972, he was named chairman of the Gujarat Labour Laws Review Committee.[25] The next year he headed a pay commission for restructuring and modifying the pay scales and conditions of service of employees of Gujarat primary and secondary school teachers and university non-teaching staff.[26] A strong proponent of legal aid, from 1973 until he left for the SCI, in 1977, he was chairman of the Gujarat High Court legal aid committee. In 1974, he was appointed vice-chairman of the Gujarat state legal aid committee.

Although he was unable to become a teacher as a young man, throughout his life he was very active in the field of education. He was an honorary professor of law at his alma mater from 1949 to 1960. He was also a member of the Surat Sarvajanik Educational Society for many years. Later he served as vice-chancellor of the Brihad Gujarat Sanskrit Parishad and as a member of the senate of the Maharaja Sayagirao University in Baroda.

Promotion to the SCI came on 30 September 1977 when he was fifty-seven and fourth in seniority at Ahmedabad.

Desai served seven and a half years on the SCI, reaching retirement age on 9 May 1985. In 1978, he created and served as chairman of the Free Legal Aid Society, renamed the Supreme Court Legal Aid committee in 1981. In 1980, he led the Indian delegation to the Eleventh Congress of the International Democratic Lawyers Association at Malta.

On the SCI, he gained a reputation for being passionate about improving the conditions of labourers and tenants. Although often described as a

---

[25] *Report of the Labour Laws Review Committee*, 3 vols (Gandhinagar: Government of Gujarat, 1974).

[26] *Report of the Gujarat State Second Pay Commission*, 3 vols (Ahmedabad: Government of Gujarat, 1975).

socialist, he believed the label 'activist' to be a more accurate one. A man who could be outspoken and blunt, he once described the inherited Anglo-Saxon legal system as '... utterly alien to the genius of the country. This is a smuggled system from across the shores imposed upon us by the empire-builders for their own political motives and during the foreign rule a class came into existence which has enormously benefited by the justice delivery system to the detriment of the teeming millions'.[27]

On 1 September 1985, Desai began a three-year term as chairman of the Eleventh Law Commission. He also was chairman of a judicial reforms commission in 1986. When his law commission term ended on 31 August 1988 and after the unsuccessful efforts of first K.K. Mathew and then E.S. Venkataramiah, his efforts to resolve the Punjab–Haryana boundary dispute also failed. In 1993, he was a member of the Citizens' Tribunal which investigated the events at Ayodhya in 1992.[28] He also served as a member of the Presidential Commission of Inquiry into Crimes Committed by Israel in Lebanon. In 1993, he headed an inquiry which investigated alleged breaches of confidentiality and related matters concerning examinations at Delhi University.

Desai was the recipient of the National Citizens Award for his contribution to jurisprudence and the Gujarat Vikas Sangh recognized his services to Gujarat when it conferred upon him the Gujarat Ratna Award.

He was the editor of *Role of Law and Judiciary in Transformation of Society: India-German Democratic Republic Experiments* (New Delhi: Kalamkar

[27] Though frequently cited, the primary source could not be located. This quote is taken from V.D. Tulzapurkar, 'Judiciary: Attacks and Survival', pp. 9–18, especially p. 11. It has also been written that Desai described the Indian judicial system as 'cancer-ridden' and said: 'I propose to remain in the system, corrode it and refill it with new elements so that the system can effectively render justice.' Govind Das, *Supreme Court in Quest of Destiny* (Lucknow: Eastern Book Company, 1987), pp. 193–4; and A.G. Noorani, 'Extra-judicial activity of judges', *The Indian Express*, 15 February 1983. M.C. Setalvad, not known for views critical of the inherited legal system, once expressed, though in less colourful language, views similar to Desai's. In the course of an address at the Poona Law College in 1940, he said: 'The result ... has been ... the imposition on this country of a legal system, which, in many respects, is entirely unsuitable to the habits and minds of the people and to the economic conditions of this country.' M.C. Setalvad, *My Life: Law and Other Things* (Bombay: N.M. Tripathi Pvt. Ltd., 1970), p. 72. Nearly two decades later, when serving as chairman of the Law Commission and preparing its landmark *Fourteenth Report*, Setalvad recanted and said that what he told those Poona law students was mistaken. Ibid., p. 72.

[28] This tribunal issued two reports—the *Report on the Enquiry Commission*, and the *Judgement and Recommendations* (New Delhi: Tribunal, 1993).

Prakashan, 1984), and was the chief editor (with M.L. Jain and N.R. Madhava Menon) of the twenty-third revised edition of *Ratanlal & Dhirajlal's Law of Crimes*, 2 vols (New Delhi: Bharat Law House, 1987–8). He was the author of *Sardar Patel's Contribution to the Framing of India's Constitution* (Vallabh Vidyanagar: Sardar Patel University, 1989); and *Law Reforms in India* (Guwahati: Ashok Publishing House, 1990).

Two books honouring him have been published: B.M. Shukla (ed.), *Law and Social Justice: A Critical Review of Justice D.A. Desai's Important Judgments* (Jaipur: Rawat Publications, 1998), and Ghanshyam Shah (ed.), *D.A. Desai: Social Justice, a Dialogue* (Jaipur: Rawat Publications, 1998).

Desai died on 13 May 2004, at age eighty-four.

62. Raghunandan Swarup Pathak (1978–89)

R.S. Pathak was born on 25 November 1924, at Bareilly, Bareilly district, Uttar Pradesh, into a prominent and well-to-do family.[29] He was the son of Gopal Swarup Pathak, a distinguished lawyer and politician with close ties to the Nehru family. The elder Pathak accepted appointment as an additional judge of the Allahabad High Court in 1945, but after about six months resigned and returned to the bar and political life. In the 1950s, he was a member of the Law Commission, was elected to the Rajya Sabha in 1960, and served as the Union Law Minister in 1966–7, Governor of Karnataka from 1967 to 1969, and Vice-President of India from 1969 to 1974.

He received the BSc degree from Ewing Christian College, Allahabad in 1945, the LLB from Allahabad University in 1947, and an MA in political science in 1948. He obtained a diploma in French and German during these years and was awarded the Sastri Medal in International Law.

Pathak enrolled as an advocate of the Allahabad High Court on 8 November 1948 and was twenty-four when he began his law practice in January 1949. During his years at the bar he declined offers to be Standing Counsel for Income Tax and government advocate because these posts would limit his private practice. At the unusually young age of thirty-seven,

---

[29] I had the opportunity to interview Pathak in New Delhi on three occasions—on 17 April 1983 and 1 October and 22 December 1988. On 9 September 2009, his widow, Mrs Asha Pathak, provided information about his post-retirement activities via correspondence.

he was appointed an additional judge at Allahabad on 1 October 1962 and was confirmed as a permanent judge on 23 July 1963. Nearly a decade later, by which time he was twelfth in seniority on this largest of the high courts, he agreed to be transferred to Himachal Pradesh as its chief justice. He was sworn in at Simla on 18 March 1972. Forty-seven at this time, he was hesitant about accepting this post because, had he remained at Allahabad, he was in line to serve as chief justice of that prestigious high court for nine years.

Promotion to the SCI came on 20 February 1978 when he was fifty-three, and on 21 December 1986 he became the eighteenth CJI. He was to reach retirement age on 24 November 1989. But after the death in 1988 of Nagendra Singh, India's representative on the International Court of Justice at The Hague, the government proposed that Pathak fill the remainder of his term. He won the election in April 1989 and resigned from the chief justiceship on 18 June 1989, closing out a distinguished career of nearly twenty-seven years as a high court and SCI judge. His two-year term on the World Court ended in 1991.

Dating back to his student years, he evinced what would be a lifelong interest in international law. He was a founder member, and later the honorary president of the Indian Society of International Law. He was a member and later president of the Indian branch of the International Law Association. In 1969, he was appointed chairman of the All India University Teachers' International Law Research Group. He also participated in several Indo-Soviet international law conferences (in Delhi in 1978, Moscow in 1983, and again in Delhi in 1985) and in two Indo-West German International Law colloquia (in Delhi in 1983 and in Heidelberg in 1984). He was a member of the advisory board of the international law, common patrimony, and international equity project of the United Nations University project which held meetings at The Hague in 1984, Rio de Janeiro in 1985, and Strasbourg in 1986. In 1985, he served as chairman of the World Congress on Law and Medicine. When CJI, he served as president of the Indian Council of Legal Aid and Advice and the Indian Law Institute, as pro-chancellor of Delhi University and as patron-in-chief of the committee for implementing legal aid schemes. In 1998, he headed the committee for the selection of the next vice-chancellor of the Banaras Hindu University.

After his term on the world court ended he remained active in a variety of ways. He often served as an arbitrator at the request of the SCI and private parties and was a member of the permanent court of arbitration in The Hague. He was closely associated with the Olympics, and served as co-president of the Switzerland-based court of arbitration for sport (the final court of appeal for disputes arising at Olympic games) for the Olympics in Atlanta in 1996, in Nagano in 1998, in Sydney in 2000, and in Salt Lake City in 2002. He was president of the court of arbitration for the 1998 Commonwealth Games in Kuala Lumpur.

He served as a member of the International Union for Conservation of Nature Commission on Environmental Law. After serving as a member of The Tribune Trust since 1994, he became its president in 2002. In 1997, he was appointed chairman of the Sarvodaya International Trust at the National Gandhi Museum. He also held the posts of chairman of the National Committee for the Promotion of Economic and Social Welfare, president of the Centre for Research on Environment, Ecology and Development, member of the board of advisors of the Foundation for International Environment Law and Development, London, and chairman of the Nehru Trust of India Collections in the Victoria and Albert Museum. He was elected chairman of the World Congress on Law and Medicine in 1985, and was a member of the International Panel of Chief Justices on Genetic Technology (Seoul, 1987).

He received an LLD (*honoris causa*) from Punjab University, and was named Honorary Master of the Bench of Gray's Inn. In 1993, he became a fellow of the Institute for Advanced Studies in the Humanities of the University of Edinburgh.

Pathak was the editor (with R.P. Dhokalia) of *International Law in Transition: Essays in Memory of Judge Nagendra Singh* (New Delhi: Lancer Books in collaboration with Martinus Nijhoff Publishers, Boston, 1992); and editor of *Human Rights in the Changing World* (New Delhi: International Law Association, 1988)

He was eighty-one when he accepted appointment, in 2005, as the one-man commission to investigate allegations made in the Volker report that External Affairs Minister Natwar Singh and his son had misused their positions and benefited financially from lucrative contracts from the United Nations Oil-for-Food Program. Known as the Justice R.S. Pathak Inquiry Authority, the charges and his investigation attracted nationwide attention. His report in 2006 resulted in the resignation of Natwar Singh.

Pathak enjoyed a reputation as a self-effacing gentleman judge and as a cultured man of impeccable manners. He died on 18 November 2007, at age eighty-two.

XVI

The Chandrachud Court (1978–85)

Within a year after coming to power, the Janata government had to make a decision about the next CJI, for M.H. Beg would reach retirement age on 22 February 1978. The Janata was pledged to restore the independence of the judiciary but had not committed itself to restoring the convention of promoting the seniormost associate judge to the chief justiceship. But until January, the best guess was that Y.V. Chandrachud, the next-in-line, would follow Beg.

At that time, however, *The Times of India* published, on the front page, the texts of two statements expressing the view that Chandrachud was unfit to be CJI. The first, the product of prominent Bombay lawyers, retired judges, journalists, and intellectuals, argued that both Chandrachud and next-in-line P.N. Bhagwati had disqualified themselves because of their opinions supporting the executive in the 1976 *Habeas Corpus* decision. Using the most critical language ever published in a newspaper about named judges, the group argued that both judges having

... so let down Indian citizens as to arrive at a result in total disregard to precedent, by reasoning manifestly unsound, and to dress it up by expressions that will testify only to a marked inclination to rule in favour of the State, are unworthy of holding the office of chief justice of India. They were put to a test and found wanting ...[1]

---

[1] 'Chief Justice: govt move queried', *The Times of India*, 7 January 1978. In that decision (*A.D.M. Jabalpur v. Shiv Kant Shukla* [1976] *Supp. SCR* 172), both expressed the view that the right to move any court for the protection of the Fundamental Rights was suspended during a declared emergency. The result was that tens of thousands

They also accused both men of being 'committed judges' whose SCI appointments at a relatively young age were the work of Law Minister H.R. Gokhale 'with an eye to guaranteeing the succession of committed judges' to the chief justiceship. They argued that 'to restore the convention of seniority now would be to perpetuate a hierarchy built upon commitment'.

The second statement was issued by the elder judicial statesman M.C. Chagla. He said that although he had known and admired Chandrachud for decades, the latter's opinion in the *Habeas Corpus* decision was 'a grave misdeed' of such magnitude that Chandrachud was undeserving of being CJI. Recalling the *New York Times* praise for Khanna's brave dissent and its criticism of the majority judgment, Chagla said that it would be a 'national disgrace' if Chandrachud was made CJI, and that 'we would be making ourselves the laughing stock of the whole judicial world'.[2]

If the Janata leaders, many of whom had spent the Emergency period in jails under the legislation upheld by the *Habeas Corpus* majority, were of a mind to retaliate, these attacks provided a rationale for another supersession. But in the government's first official comment, Prime Minister Morarji Desai added no heat when he said: 'It is not the lawyers who are going to make the appointment'.[3] He did not, at this juncture, commit his government to a restoration of the seniority convention. A month after the controversy began, Law Minister Shanti Bhushan told the press that the government had decided to seek the advice of all SCI judges and all the high court chief justices.

The controversy ended on 19 February when the newspapers carried the headline that Chandrachud had been appointed the new CJI. Accompanying stories said that Chandrachud's promotion was certain until the Bombay protests, that what weighed most with the government was the fact that supersession was a policy of the discredited Congress (I) government, and that it was wisest at this juncture to return to the seniority convention. Two days later, Desai said that Chandrachud was made CJI because of all the present and former SCI and high court judges consulted, all except

---

remained languishing in jails. Had both men been superseded, V.R. Krishna Iyer was next in seniority.

[2] Ibid. These charges have been assessed by Upendra Baxi, *The Indian Supreme Court and Politics* (Lucknow: Eastern Book Company, 1978), pp. 188–98; and Rajeev Dhavan and Alice Jacob, *Selection and Appointment of Supreme Court Judges: A Case Study* (Bombay: N.M. Tripathi Pvt. Ltd., 1978), pp. 119–25. Both are appalled by the charges and find no merit in them. I agree.

[3] 'New CJ according to statute', *The Hindustan Times*, 12 January 1978.

two high court chief justices expressed the view that Chandrachud should be appointed.[4] Elsewhere it was reported that Khanna, the victim of the second supersession, had 'strongly pleaded for following the principle of seniority'.[5] But the last word was that of Desai, who introduced the only note of forgiveness in the entire controversy. Asked his reaction to Chagla's condemnation, he said simply that the Emergency 'was a time when everyone functioned in a state of fear and that cannot be forgotten'.[6]

Chandrachud was CJI for seven and a half years, by far the longest tenure before or since,[7] and spanned years of momentous change in the nation. Although it had always been the CJI's leadership that lacked continuity, Chandrachud was the only survivor at the helm of a major institution during these years. During his tenure there were two presidents, four prime ministers, and five law ministers.[8] The turnover among the latter was especially significant for the law minister was the government's point man concerning the selection of judges. Some were passive concerning Chandrachud's nominations, while others were active in the sense that they found some of his nominees unacceptable and pressed Chandrachud to accept their own choices.

---

[4] 'CJ's appointment by consensus, says PM', *The Indian Express*, 21 February 1978.

[5] 'Chandrachud to have longest spell as C.J.', *The Times of India*, 19 February 1978. K.S. Hegde, a victim of the 1973 supersession and now the Lok Sabha Speaker, told Desai that if the Janata superseded Chandrachud, they would be doing what Mrs Gandhi did. Interview with the author, 14–15 November 1988.

[6] 'CJ's appointment by consensus, says PM.'

[7] A distant second was Sinha's fifty-two months. Chandrachud's tenure was actually two years longer than was anticipated when he joined the Court. Chandrachud, S.N. Dwivedi, and A.K. Mukherjea were appointed by the same notification in 1972. The executive determined that the swearing-in order would be Dwivedi, Mukherjea, and Chandrachud. This meant that Dwivedi would follow Beg as CJI until 1 October 1978, Mukherjea would follow and serve as CJI until his own retirement on 20 January 1980, at which time Chandrachud's turn would come. But the deaths of Dwivedi and Mukherjea not long after their arrival resulted in Chandrachud being the next-in-line in 1978.

[8] The Law Ministers were Shanti Bhushan (1977–9), S.N. Kacker (1979–80), P. Shiv Shankar (1980–2), J. Kaushal (1982–4), and A.K. Sen (1984–7). There was a sixth, Chandrachud's former colleague H.R. Khanna (1979), but he resigned three days after being sworn in. Appointed when Bhushan was Law Minister were Koshal, Chinnappa Reddy, A.P. Sen, and Venkataramiah; when Shiv Shankar was Law Minister were Islam, Varadarajan, A.N. Sen, Balakrishna Eradi, and R.B. Misra; and when Kaushal was Law Minister were Madon, S. Mukharji, Thakkar, R.N. Misra, and Khalid. Though Shiv Shankar was not the law minister when the final five of the Chandrachud era were sworn in, his presence was still felt.

He inherited a Court of thirteen judges. This included him and the Court was five short of the full strength of eighteen. Nine of these would retire during his tenure: Jaswant Singh (January 1979), N.L. Untwalia (August 1980), P.S. Kailasam (September 1980), P.N. Shinghal (October 1980), V.R. Krishna Iyer (November 1980), R.S. Sarkaria (January 1981), A.C. Gupta (January 1982), A.D. Koshal (March 1982), and D.A. Desai (May 1985), ten if we include Chandrachud's own retirement in July 1985. There were fourteen fresh appointments, two of whom were gone before Chandrachud retired (Koshal retired in 1982, and Baharul Islam resigned in 1983 to return to active politics).

The first three, A.D. Koshal, O. Chinnappa Reddy, and A.P. Sen were sworn in on 17 July 1978. Koshal and Chinnappa Reddy had learned earlier from CJI Beg that he had recommended them for promotion to the SCI,[9] but nothing came of these recommendations before his retirement. In April, Chandrachud, who had concurred with Beg's recommendations, resubmitted their names. Each had been punitively transferred during the Emergency—Koshal to Madras, Chinnappa Reddy to Chandigarh, and Sen to Rajasthan. Although the popular view is that their appointments were a reward for their freedom-fighting from the bench, Chandrachud said this was not the compelling reason for their appointments and the three judges agreed. Each of them had enjoyed their sojourns away from home, had earned high marks from their hosts, and believed that the latter in particular put them on a firm footing for promotion to the SCI. Indeed, all three had excellent reputation and credentials, and Chinnappa Reddy and Sen in particular were rising stars before their transfers. So while standing up to the executive during the Emergency must have been a selection criterion, it was not the only one.

These men were not pressed on Chandrachud by anyone in the Janata government. Law Minister Bhushan simply accepted Chandrachud's recommendations. Chandrachud said, as had Beg earlier, that the Janata government was not particularly interested in SCI appointments and never suggested that pro-Janata judges be promoted. Chandrachud had not met any of these earlier.

Koshal, at sixty-one and the eldest of the three, was serving as the chief justice of the Punjab and Haryana High Court. Chandrachud said that the primary consideration in selecting Koshal was that the court needed

[9] Pathak confirmed this and said that Beg sought his views about each of them. Interview with the author on 1 October 1988.

a Punjabi, for the Punjab representation had fallen from four a few years earlier to only Sarkaria.

Chinnappa Reddy was fifty-five and fourth in seniority on the Andhra Pradesh High Court. Chandrachud said that he thought that he was a Christian, and the SCI needed a Christian to replace Mathew who had retired two years earlier. Only after Chinnappa Reddy arrived in Delhi did Chandrachud learn that although he was born into a Christian family, he earlier had embraced agnosticism. The fact that Andhra Pradesh had been unrepresented since Jaganmohan Reddy's retirement more than three years earlier may have been a consideration as well.

Sen was fifty-four and serving as the chief justice of the Madhya Pradesh High Court. Madhya Pradesh had been unrepresented since Hidayatullah's retirement in 1970, so this was likely among the considerations in his appointment. Although senior in rank to Chinnappa Reddy, his swearing in followed the latter's. Only status was involved for, assuming the continuance of the seniority convention, Bhagwati would have been CJI when the two reached retirement age.

The last of the Janata regime appointees, sworn in on 8 March 1979 was the fifty-four-year-old E.S. Venkataramiah. Fifth in seniority on the Karnataka High Court, the chief justice and the next most senior were on the threshold of retirement, K. Bhimiah had already turned down an invitation and the fourth in seniority was not asked. Chandrachud had become acquainted with him earlier in Bangalore. Venkataramiah believed that a consideration in his selection was the fact that he was the first direct appointment from Karnataka. K.S. Hegde had reached the SCI via the Delhi and Himachal Pradesh High Court, and since Hegde's resignation six years earlier Karnataka had not been represented.

In July 1979, the Janata government, which had been unravelling almost from its inception, collapsed. Its successor, the Charan Singh-led Lok Dal government, lasted only a month but continued as a caretaker government until the national elections at the end of the year. In December, Chandrachud went directly to President Sanjiva Reddy with the recommendation that V.S. Deshpande,[10] the chief justice of the Delhi High Court, and Yasoda Nandan, the seniormost associate judge at Allahabad, be appointed. Because the government was a caretaker one, Chandrachud did not first talk to

---

[10] Deshpande, a fellow Maharashtrian brahmin, and Chandrachud were long-time friends. He would later edit A Chandrachud Reader: Collection of Judgments with Annotations (New Delhi: Documentation Centre for Corporate & Business Policy Research, 1985).

Law Minister S.N. Kacker or anyone else in the government. The President, because no government had approved these names and because the seventh national election was just a few weeks away, put these recommendations on hold. After the Congress (I) returned to power nothing further was heard of these nominations.

There were two vacancies when Mrs Gandhi's second regime began but the new government was in no hurry to fill them. Indeed, it was at this time that lengthy delays in filling vacancies started to become commonplace. From August through November 1980 there was a retirement each month—first Untwalia, then Kailasam, Shinghal, and Krishna Iyer. So by mid-November, the Court's strength had fallen to twelve and Sarkaria was to retire in January 1981. December 1980 and January 1981 saw five judges appointed, and all were appointed during P. Shiv Shankar's first spell as Law Minister.

The first was Baharul Islam who was sworn in on 4 December. At nearly sixty-three and a retired Gauhati High Court chief justice, he was the oldest ever appointed to date. Islam acknowledged that he owed his appointment to Shiv Shankar.[11] Chandrachud resisted this appointment but Shiv Shankar was insistent, telling Chandrachud that 'there was no harm in taking him', and ultimately he had to compromise. Although it was not the Muslim seat that Islam filled (S.M. Fazal Ali was on the bench), another Muslim, Syed Sarwar Ali of the Patna High Court, had declined an invitation prior to Islam's appointment. Islam restored representation of the Northeast region, for Goswami had retired three years earlier.

A few days later, on 19 December, A. Varadarajan, sixth in seniority on the Madras High Court, became the first member of the Scheduled Caste community to reach the SCI. Caste played a role in his selection. He was sixty and had served nearly eight years on the Madras bench. This breakthrough appointment was initiated by Shiv Shankar but had Chandrachud's support as well. Both the government and Chandrachud were in agreement that the Scheduled Castes needed to be represented. No more than a half dozen Scheduled Caste judges were serving on the high courts at this time.[12] K. Bhimiah of the Karnataka High Court, the most senior one, had earlier declined an invitation. Chandrachud had not

[11] Interview with the author on 4 October 1988, in New Delhi.

[12] According to Varadarajan, in mid-1983 there were six Scheduled Caste high court judges in the country—two in Andhra Pradesh, and one each in Tamil Nadu, Kerala, Maharashtra, and West Bengal. Interview with the author on 13 May 1983.

met Varadarajan, and the first word the latter received of his impending appointment came from the law ministry. The government's handling of this appointment was embarrassing to Varadarajan. Law Minister Shiv Shankar, himself of the OBC community, trumpeted in Parliament that Mrs Gandhi's government '... could take credit for Mr Varadarajan's appointment [which] gave tremendous satisfaction to the teeming downtrodden in the country',[13] implying that merit was not an important consideration. His appointment restored representation for Madras High Court. It had been unrepresented since Kailasam's retirement two years earlier.

Sworn in next was sixty-year-old A.N. Sen, the chief justice of the Calcutta High Court, on 28 January 1981. Calcutta usually had two representatives on the SCI but since A.N. Ray's retirement four years earlier only A.C. Gupta was there, and he was just a year away from retirement. Sen was the first barrister appointed since A.K. Mukherjea in 1972. With fifteen years of High Court grooming, he was among the most senior high court judges in the nation and was an obvious choice. Shiv Shankar, however, opposed his nomination but ultimately Chandrachud prevailed.

Two days later, the arrivals of Chief Justice V. Balakrishna Eradi of the Kerala High Court, and R.B. Misra, third in seniority at Allahabad, completed this blizzard of appointments. Chandrachud had received Balakrishna Eradi's agreement to come to Delhi six months earlier but the formal offer did not come until January. Krishna Iyer, though by then retired, was consulted by Chandrachud. He preferred that he be replaced by his left-leaning friend, P.S. Poti, then the number two at Kerala but supported Balakrishna Eradi. He was fifty-eight and had been a high court judge for thirteen years. He had been senior to Krishna Iyer on the Kerala bench, but the latter reached Delhi eight years ahead of him and had retired before Balakrishna Eradi arrived. He was one of the few high court judges who accepted an invitation after one of his juniors had been appointed.

R.B Misra, then fifty-nine and a veteran of thirteen years of high court experience, came to the SCI by default, for he was the third choice from Allahabad. That court's Chief Justice, Satish Chandra, had been invited in 1979 but declined, probably because he expected to be chief justice for more than eight years of what is often said to be largest high court in all of Asia and, with Pathak not reaching retirement age until late 1989, he would not have become CJI. Chandrachud, in late 1979, tried to gain approval for the

---

[13] *The Hindustan Times*, 4 December 1980.

appointment of Yasoda Nandan, the seniormost associate judge. The latter was agreeable but after Mrs Gandhi returned to power, her government took no action. In late 1980, Chandrachud extended the invitation to Misra, who was next in seniority. Misra believed that he was Chandrachud's choice but didn't rule out the government being the initiator, for the latter would have been aware of his disagreement with the *Kesavananda* decision. Misra joined Pathak as representatives of Allahabad.

These five appointments brought the Court's strength back to sixteen, but more than two years would pass before others were appointed.[14] Gupta retired in January 1982, Koshal two months later, Islam resigned in January 1983, and the strength of the Court again was down to thirteen.

On 15 March 1983, after months of rumours and protracted negotiations between Chandrachud and the government (Jaganath Kaushal had replaced Shiv Shankar as law minister in January 1982), a quartet was sworn in. Each of these was very senior—both on his own high court and in all-India seniority terms. Three were chief justices and the fourth an acting chief justice.

D.P. Madon, nearly sixty-two and the Bombay chief justice, was sworn in first. He was also the first member of the Parsi community to accept a judgeship. Having spent more than fifteen years on the Bombay bench, he was the most experienced of the Chandrachud era appointees and was also the first chief justice of Bombay to agree to come to Delhi; the earlier eight had been associate judges. According to Madon he was sounded first in 1975. When the Janata coalition came to power he believed it didn't want him because of what he had said in his report about the involvement of the Jan Sangh and the Rashtriya Swamamsevak Sangh (RSS) in the 1970 communal riots.[15] Mrs Gandhi had used his report to castigate the Jan Sangh and the RSS for communalism. Whether his appointment was initiated by Chandrachud or the government was a matter of disagreement between Madon and Chandrachud. Madon believed it was Law Minister Kaushal. Chandrachud said this was not the case—that he had recommended

---

[14] According to Ramakrishna Hegde, *The Judiciary Today: A Plea for a Consortium* (Bangalore: Government of Karnataka, 1986), p. 54, the Estimates Committee of the Lok Sabha in its thirty-first report submitted to the Lok Sabha on 17 April 1986 'shows that the Chief Justice of India submitted as many as four names in 25 June 1981, *none of which were approved by the Government of India*' [italics in original]. These four must have been nominees for high court appointments.

[15] *Report of the Commission of Inquiry into the Communal Disturbances at Bhiwandi, Jalgoan, and Mahad in May 1970*, 7 vols (Bombay: Government Press, 1970).

Madon. But Chandrachud acknowledged that he had first recommended M.N. Chandurkar, a Maharashtrian brahmin who was second in seniority at Bombay. With Madon's appointment, the Bombay representation increased to three.

S. Mukharji came from the Calcutta High Court where, after fourteen years as an associate judge, two weeks earlier he had become the acting chief justice. When he was in Delhi in August 1982 as a member of the Finance Commission, Chandrachud inquired whether he would accept an SCI appointment. Mukharji was hesitant because he would have had a long tenure as the Calcutta chief justice. He asked Chandrachud who else was to be appointed, for he wanted to calculate the swearing-in order and determine whether he would become CJI. Chandrachud would not reveal the names but gave Mukharji the birthdates. With the latter information he discovered the name of Chandurkar who had been a high court judge longer and was likely to have been sworn in first. Mukharji would still have become CJI but Chandurkar would have preceded him, reducing Mukharji's tenure to one year. Chandrachud approached Mukharji again in January 1983, and told him who was on the revised list. Chandurkar's name had been dropped and Mukharji, fifty-five at this time, agreed to be appointed. Some believe that a contributing factor in his appointment was the stay order he issued in the convoluted West Bengal Poll case where his ruling supported the Congress (I) position.[16] His appointment restored Calcutta's representation to two for Gupta had retired in 1982.

The appointment of M.P. Thakkar, fifty-nine and the Gujarat chief justice, was somewhat of a surprise, if only because with Bhagwati and Desai already on the SCI, Gujarat seemed well-represented. Although many credit Thakkar's appointment to behind the scenes lobbying by Bhagwati who had chosen Thakkar for the Gujarat High Court fourteen years earlier, Chandrachud said this was not the case and Bhagwati agreed. Chandrachud said that it was Shiv Shankar, no longer the law minister but still an influential judge-maker, who pressed Thakkar on him. Thakkar said that the government was aware that he had supported the two supersessions, the Emergency, and was of the view that the *Kesavananda* decision should be overruled. Neither Chandrachud nor Bhagwati supported the appointment of Thakkar but Chandrachud in the end relented.

[16] For an account of this matter, see Upendra Baxi, *Courage, Craft and Contention: The Indian Supreme Court in the Eighties* (Bombay: N.M. Tripathi Pvt. Ltd., 1985), p. 31.

The final member of this foursome was fifty-six-year-old R.N. Misra, the chief justice of the Orissa High Court. Who initiated his appointment is uncertain, but the consensus view is that his name was advanced by the executive. Representing Orissa may have been a consideration, for Orissa had long been perceived from Delhi as a relatively unimportant state and had not been represented since B. Jagannadhadas from 1953 to 1958. Misra believed that he should have been sworn in before Mukharji because he was chief justice of his court and Mukharji was the acting chief justice at Calcutta. When multiple appointments are made on the same day, high court seniority almost always determines the swearing-in order. An acting chief justice is still an associate judge, meaning that Misra was the senior of the two. Chandrachud, however, because Mukharji had been a high court judge for fourteen years and Misra thirteen, recommended that Mukharji be listed first and the government agreed. In this instance, the order had important consequences. Had Misra been sworn in before Mukharji, he would have followed Venkataramiah and served as CJI for nearly two years, leaving Mukharji only six months as CJI. Because Mukharji was sworn in before him, Misra would have reached retirement age before the end of Mukharji's tenure. But Mukharji's premature death in 1990 resulted in Misra becoming CJI for nearly two years.

Fifteen months would pass before the fourteenth and final appointment of the Chandrachud regime came on 25 June 1984. This was V. Khalid who, after more than a decade as a Kerala High Court judge and a brief detour to the Jammu and Kashmir as its chief justice, was sworn in just a week before his sixty-second birthday. His name was put on the table by Kaushal but Chandrachud wanted him too. There may have been an element of reward, for Khalid had agreed to go to Srinagar where there were problems on the high court. Chandrachud had met Khalid in Ernakulam and was impressed with him. Again Chandrachud sought Krishna Iyer's assessment of his fellow Keralite and he was supportive. Only Syed Sarwar Ali of Patna, who had earlier declined an invitation, had more seniority among Muslim high court judges. Khalid was the first Muslim from South India to serve on the SCI and his arrival raised the Kerala representation to two.

The Khalid appointment brought the SCI to its full strength for the first time since it was raised to eighteen in 1977. A few weeks before Chandrachud retired in July of 1985, Desai retired. He then made another effort to gain government approval for Chandurkar but for a second time was unsuccessful. For the first and only time, the government gave reasons why a Chandrachud nominee was unacceptable. Mrs Gandhi personally told Chandrachud that 'my party people think he is unlikely to be helpful to us'. In all other instances, the government gave no reasons and said simply 'please suggest another name'.[17]

There were others, in addition to those already mentioned, whom Chandrachud wanted on the Court but who failed to win government approval. More than once he urged the promotion of G.P. Singh, Chief Justice of the Madhya Pradesh High Court. Singh had an excellent reputation but he had run afoul of the Congress (I) government in Madhya Pradesh, particularly by refusing to accept certain government nominees for judgeships.

Finally, those who declined offers, in addition to Satish Chandra, Sarwar Ali, and Bhimiah, included M.M. Ismail in 1980 when he was chief justice of the Madras High Court. Chandrachud, without naming them, told me that half a dozen high court judges declined offers to come to the SCI during his tenure. Four prominent senior advocates also declined invitations extended by Chandrachud in 1979. These were Fali Nariman, K. Parasaran, S.N. Kacker, and K.K. Venugopal.

Before the end of his tenure, Chandrachud began expressing publicly his frustrations with the selection process. In 1983, he said that the present procedure is 'outmoded' and should be 'given a decent burial'.[18] On the same occasion, he said that appointments were 'not purely based on merit'.[19] After retiring, he spoke frequently about his experiences: 'Appointments which I opposed were not made. Names were recommended, names were strongly pressed. When I did not agree, those names were dropped';[20] 'Mrs Gandhi never overruled me, but the government has got every weapon in its hands, so the vacancies are kept unfilled'; 'The government tries artful persuasion, drops hints, and keeps egging you'. Speaking at the India International Centre on 6 February 1988, he said: 'No one is interested in having a good judiciary. No one is interested in having good judges'. He

---

[17] Interview with Chandrachud, 8 December 1988.

[18] Quoted in Law Commission of India, *New Forum for Judicial Appointments*, One Hundred Twenty-First Report (New Delhi: Ministry of Law, Justice, and Company Affairs, July 1986), p. 93.

[19] *The Hindustan Times*, 27 February 1983.

[20] Interview with the author, 8 December 1988. Similar versions of the quoted materials that follow are found in many sources, including A.G. Noorani, 'Crisis in Judiciary', *The Indian Express*, 30 April 1986; Law Commission, *One Hundred Twenty-First Report*, p. 67; and Hegde, *The Judiciary Today*, pp. 50–2.

discussed his nominees and the government's often with Mrs Gandhi and acknowledged that there were instances where he had to 'give in' and accept government nominees, and other instances where 'some of those I wanted to appoint were not acceptable to the government'. No one was literally forced upon him. Both Chandrachud and the government had a veto but both were hesitant to use it. The government only once expressly used its veto power and Chandrachud only once used his; but the distinction between a veto and a refusal by either side to agree to a nominee is hardly significant. Chandrachud was emphatic in denying that there was ever any horse trading—that I'll take one of yours if you'll approve this one of mine. The often difficult negotiations were the main reason why it was common for vacancies to remain unfilled for lengthy periods. It appears that the executive at times wore him down to the point where he became so concerned about the Court being short-handed, and so wearied by the drawn-out negotiations, that he grudgingly accepted some names pressed upon him. As one of his bench mates said: 'if he hadn't compromised there wouldn't have been any appointments at all'. Chandrachud, nonetheless said, as all of his predecessors had, 'I have to take responsibility for everyone appointed while I was CJI'.[21]

Before he made a recommendation, he read ten judgments of the high court judge being considered. Until Mrs Gandhi returned to power in 1980, Chandrachud, as required by the Janata government, did consult his two most senior colleagues (Bhagwati and Krishna Iyer) and included, with his own recommendations, their views. On some occasions the executive, as it was entitled to, sought the views of some of his colleagues about names under consideration. Thereafter, Chandrachud sought his brethren's counsel infrequently, partly because the government no longer insisted upon it but more because of the poor interpersonal relations among his colleagues. Bhagwati had different views about who should be appointed and made these views known to the law ministers. Chandrachud learned to be careful about whom he consulted and, not infrequently, consulted with none of his fellow judges before passing on nominees to the government. During his tenure, he had to battle on two fronts—with the executive and with some of his colleagues.

In late 1981, the most important SCI decision to date concerning judicial appointments was handed down. *S.P. Gupta* v. *Union of India*[22] dealt

[21] Interviews with Chandrachud, 3 May 1983 and 8 December 1988.
[22] [1982] 2 SCR 365.

with the constitutional validity of the non-consensual transfer of high court judges and, as such, is beyond our scope here. But it weakened the role of the CJI in SCI appointments. During the course of the lengthy hearings, Chandrachud suffered the humiliation of having to file an affidavit.[23]

By the early 1980s, the organized bar, divided into warring camps, was also claiming a role in the selection process. Its role was not constructive. The names of some believed to be under consideration for SCI judgeships were often the targets of furtive smear campaigns characterized by ugly rumours and outright lies, or 'motivated' stories spread by 'lobbies', to use the Indian labels. Fuelled by the clandestine selection process, such behaviour made the selection process not just untidy but occasionally very ugly and was an added burden to Chandrachud.

He was a gentleman and was unaccustomed to the rough and tumble that characterized the selection process and the atmosphere on the Court after Mrs Gandhi returned to power. Turning to a collective look at the Chandrachud judges, two things are most striking—their geographic diversity, and their lengthy high court experience and seniority. The fact that the fourteen judges came from thirteen high courts (only Calcutta gained two seats) was not coincidental, for regional diversity was among Chandrachud's main criteria. Five were from the south, four from the east, three from the west, and two from the north. The five high courts which failed to gain a representative were Patna, Delhi, Himachal Pradesh, Rajasthan, and Sikkim. But Fazal Ali from Patna was there throughout Chandrachud's tenure and Sarwar Ali of Patna had been invited. The Delhi High Court is an anomaly because of its location and the fact that its bench contains judges from several different states. Rajasthan never had more than occasional representation, and both Himachal and Sikkim were the two smallest high courts. The former had never been represented by a native son, and Sikkim, its high court then composed of just two judges, had never been represented. This blizzard of retirements and appointments means that it is not possible, in every instance, to determine who was replacing whom, but if we add the vacancies in January and February 1978 (Goswami and Beg) which fell to Chandrachud to fill, in addition to the ten who retired, of the ten high courts who lost a representative (Gauhati

---

[23] There is a large literature on the transfer policy and the *Gupta* (often referred to as the First Judges Case) decision. See especially Baxi, *Courage, Craft and Contention* (Bombay: N.M. Tripathi Pvt. Ltd, 1985).

and Punjab and Haryana lost two each), eight secured a replacement. After Untwalia of Patna and Shinghal of Rajasthan retired, those states were unrepresented. And four high courts which had not been represented for some time regained a seat: Andhra Pradesh in Chinnappa Reddy, Madhya Pradesh in A.P. Sen, Karnataka in Venkataramiah, and most noticeably Orissa, unrepresented for nearly three decades, in R.N. Misra.

A premium was also placed upon high court seniority. Eight were high court chief justices, Mukharji was an acting chief justice, and Islam was a retired Gauhati chief justice. Chandrachud told the author that 'it is difficult to overlook a high court chief justice if he is good, unless the number two or three is head and shoulders better. If there is only a marginal difference, the chief justice must be taken'. These men arrived in Delhi with an average of twelve years of high court experience.

In social and religious terms, these men reflected great diversity. The first member of the Scheduled Caste community and the first Parsi were appointed. Two were Muslims and, if Chinnappa Reddy is labelled according to his religion at birth, a Christian. The remaining nine were Hindus, and five of these, as was Chandrachud, were brahmins.

In terms of age at the time of appointment, the average was 58.8, only a fraction higher than the norm. As Chandrachud moved into retirement, fourteen of the sixteen sitting judges (all except Mukharji and R.N. Misra) were in their sixties. Only Venkataramiah and Mukharji among the Chandrachud era appointees were in line for the chief justiceship.

In sum, the Chandrachud years were good, in representational terms, for the newer high courts (only four appointees came from the old presidency high courts) and smaller states, for religious minorities, for the appointment of the first Scheduled Caste judge, for brahmins, and for high court chief justices.

When Bhagwati succeeded Chandrachud, the Court was composed of sixteen judges—carry-overs Bhagwati, Fazal Ali, Tulzapurkar, and Pathak, plus the dozen remaining Chandrachud era appointees.

63. Anand Dev Koshal (1978–82)

A.D. Koshal, who by age nineteen had completed his higher education and had begun practising law, was born on 7 March 1917 at Ahmedgarh, then part of the former Malerkotla State but today in the Sangrur district of Punjab. He was the son of Tulsi Ram Koshal who, after retiring from government service as an engineer, became active in the family business of moneylending and managed the joint family's substantial landholdings.[24]

A.D. Koshal must have been a precocious student for his early education was so accelerated that he completed high school at age thirteen. After attending Forman Christian College in Lahore for two years, he was seventeen when he completed his BA in physics and mathematics from the Government College in Ludhiana in 1934. He then returned to Lahore where he earned the LLB from the Government Law College in 1936, becoming the first lawyer in his family.

Koshal started practising law in the Ludhiana district courts in 1936. In 1939, he became an advocate of the former Malerkotla State High Court[25] and practised there until 1945, at which time he returned to Ludhiana. After the East Punjab High Court was established in post-Partition India, Koshal, in 1948, enrolled as an advocate of that court but continued to practise at Ludhiana. During his career at the bar, he never practised at the high court level.

Although he was not active in the nationalist movement, he was arrested in December 1931 and briefly detained because he was wearing a Bhagat Singh badge.[26] From 1955 to 1960, Koshal, an Arya Samajist, served on the board of management of Arya College, Ludhiana.

After more than two decades of private practice and at age forty-two, he joined the Punjab judicial service on 2 February 1960. He was first posted as an additional district and sessions judge at Ferozepore. On 13 March 1961, he was promoted to district and sessions judge and transferred to Amritsar. He remained there until 10 July 1966, when he became legal remembrancer and law secretary to the Punjab government. When Punjab was bifurcated and the state of Haryana created later that year, he held the same post in Haryana from 1 November 1966 to 18 June 1967. On the latter date, he was appointed registrar of the High Court of Punjab and Haryana.

Less than a year later, Koshal, then fifty-one, was sworn in as an additional judge of the Punjab and Haryana High Court on 28 May 1968 and was confirmed as a permanent judge on 5 January 1970. On 27 June 1976, he learned that he was being summarily and for punitive reasons

---

[24] Interview with Koshal on 27 November 1988, in Bangalore.

[25] Malerkotla was then a Muslim princely state located near Ludhiana.

[26] Bhagat Singh, who headed the revolutionary Indian Socialist Republican Army, had been hung by the British earlier that year.

transferred to the Madras High Court. The Emergency was on, and Mrs Gandhi's government was interfering with administrative matters at his court, particularly in trying to get its own people appointed as district and sessions judges. Koshal objected to this and as a result he was uprooted and moved from one end of the country to the other. With effect from 5 July, he served as a judge of the Madras High Court until 31 July 1977, an experience he found very enjoyable. When the Janata government offered him the opportunity to return to Chandigarh, he did, resuming his Punjab and Haryana High Court judgeship on 8 August 1977. He became chief justice on 1 November 1977.

Promotion to the SCI came less than a year later. He was sixty-one when he was sworn in on 17 July 1978. He reached retirement age on 7 March 1982, bringing to a close a forty-six year career as a lawyer and judge. He returned to his home in Ludhiana and began a chamber practice. That continued until January 1986 when, at age sixty-nine and at the request of then Chief Minister Ramakrishna Hegde, he returned to South India to become the first Lok Ayukta in Karnataka.[27]

64. Onteddu Chinnappa Reddy (1978–87)

The first self-described Marxist[28] to serve on the SCI, O. Chinnappa Reddy was born into an upper middle-class family at Jambuladinne, Kurnool district, in Andhra Pradesh on 25 September 1922. His grandfather was a lawyer as was his father, Sauri Reddy who practised at the Gooty district courts.

His father was a fifth generation Roman Catholic. But his son adamantly rejected any religious label: 'I profess and practise no religion; my wife does not and my children do not .... I refuse to be classified as belonging to any religion or any community. I prefer to be a human being and an Indian. I

[27] By 1988, about ten states had Lok Ayuktas ('people's commissions') to investigate allegations against state ministers and other high officials. About six of these, including Karnataka, included the chief minister within the Lok Ayukta's ambit, and had laws which compelled the government to table Lok Ayukta reports in the legislative assembly. A. Surya Prakash, 'Ombudsman or Bogeyman', *Indian Express*, 18 December 1988.

[28] Interviews on 10 May 1983 in New Delhi, and 9 November 1988 in Hyderabad. His first name is usually rendered as Ontethupalli but he told me that Onteddu is correct.

will certainly be offended if you call me a Hindu or a Christian or a member of any caste'.[29]

After receiving his primary and secondary education at mission schools in Gooty, he attended Loyola College in Madras, where he received an MA in mathematics in 1941. His BL was earned at the Madras Law College in 1943.

He was twenty-one when he enrolled as an advocate of the Madras High Court on 21 August 1944 and would practise there for the next decade. When the state of Andhra was created in 1954, he shifted his practice to Guntur where the new Andhra High Court was located. After the 1956 reorganization of states resulted in a redefined state of Andhra Pradesh, and the high court moved to Hyderabad, he moved with it. A modern-day Robin Hood, the fees he earned from wealthy clients were used to defend the poor. On 21 June 1960, he was appointed public prosecutor[30] for Andhra Pradesh and served in that capacity until his appointment to the Andhra Pradesh High Court.

It was on 21 August 1967, at age forty-four, when he was sworn in as an additional judge; confirmation as a permanent judge came on 27 November 1967. He was among the high court judges punitively transferred during the Emergency. He was moved from the south to the north and became a judge of the Punjab and Haryana High Court on 28 June 1976. While on the Chandigarh bench, he served as acting chief justice from 28 June to 13 August and from 4–23 October 1976. After the Janata government offered each transferred judge the opportunity to return home, CJI Beg urged him to remain at Chandigarh, where by then he had earned a good reputation[31] and would have a long tenure as chief justice. He considered staying, for his experience at Chandigarh had been happy one but his family, largely because

---

[29] Letter to the author dated 9 March 1984. His views on religion were expressed in his separate opinion in *S.P. Mittal v. Union of India* [1983] 1 SCR 729.

[30] Public prosecutor would seem to be an unlikely post for a Marxist, but 'I had been a leading criminal lawyer, knew the tricks of the police, and tended to be more pro-defendant than pro-prosecution'. This quote is from Chinnappa Reddy during the 10 May 1983 interview.

[31] He believed that his chances for appointment to the SCI improved while in Chandigarh. There was an instance where the president of the bar association had died in custody, and he wanted to present a court reference on his behalf. His fellow judges, fearing the wrath of the Union Defence Minister Bansi Lal, refused to associate themselves with the reference. Chinnappa Reddy went ahead and delivered it and became a hero of the bar.

of the difficulties with an unfamiliar language and social environment, wanted to return to Hyderabad. He resumed his Andhra Pradesh judgeship on 9 September 1977.

It was on 17 July 1978 that Chinnappa Reddy, then age fifty-five and fourth in seniority at Hyderabad was sworn in as an SCI judge. Earlier, S. Mohan Kumaramangalam had wanted to get him on the SCI. These two had been friends dating from their days together in Madras in the 1940s and 1950s. But he was then too junior on the Hyderabad court. Kumaramangalam was a party to the invitation he received in March 1973 to become chairman of the Monopolies and Restrictive Practices Commission, the purpose being that this post would overcome his seniority deficiencies and serve as a launching pad for an SCI appointment. He declined this offer because there was talk at this time of bifurcating that commission, making it a less important post.

After more than nine years of service and by then the seniormost associate judge, he retired on 25 September 1987.

During the course of his career at the bar and on the bench, he was active in educational affairs in Andhra Pradesh. He served as a member of the board of studies of Osmania, Andhra, and Kakatiya Universities, and of the senate and syndicate of Sri Venkateswara University. A voracious reader, he was also a connoisseur of Western classical music.

He returned to his Hyderabad home after leaving Delhi. He did not believe that chamber practice was an appropriate activity for a retired judge. In December 1987 he agreed to serve as a one-man commission for the state of Kerala. Known as the Chinnappa Reddy Commission, his task was to examine charges of corruption against a former Congress (I) minister. In March 1988, he became chairman of the Third Backward Classes commission in Karnataka. Utilizing both status and means criteria, his report entitled *The Justice-Journey of the Karnataka Backward Classes: The Report of the Third Karnataka Backward Classes Commission*[32] recommended eliminating, from the benefits of reservation, the more affluent and powerful segments of Karnataka's backward classes. This report became a widely quoted classic on the subject.

In 1991, he was appointed to the three-judge committee which investigated and found proof of allegations of corruption against SCI judge

---

[32] *The Justice-Journey of the Karnataka Backward Classes: The Report of the Third Karnataka Backward Classes Commission*, 2 vols (Bangalore: Government of Karnataka, 1990).

Veeraswami Ramaswami. In 1992, he headed a panel which inquired into alleged negligence that lead to the death of CJI Mukharji in London a year earlier. In the same year, he was a member of the unofficial citizen's tribunal that investigated the events surrounding the destruction of the Babri Masjid at Ayodhya. In 1999, he began serving as a member of the Andhra Pradesh Lok Satta Election Watch committee, a non-partisan group promoting better governance and particularly fighting against the illegal use of money in elections. In 2000, he accepted the chairmanship of the National Commission to Review the Working of the Constitution's Special Group on the Directive Principles of State Policy.

A brilliant, well-read, and articulate intellectual, Chinnappa Reddy wore his socialism on his shirt sleeve and during his years on the SCI often expressed these beliefs in decisions and off-the-bench speeches.[33] His publications include *From a Man's World to a Human World* (New Delhi: Centre for Women's Development Studies, 1990); *Religion, Caste, and the Threat to Secularism* (Thiruvananthapuram: Department of Publications, University of Kerala, 1993); and *In the Wonderland of Law: Real Case Stories* (New Delhi: Vikas Publishing House, 1999). He was a co-author of the *Report of the People's Commission on GATT* (New Delhi: Centre for Study of Global Trade System and Development, 1996). A selection of his contributions to Indian law and society are chronicled in R. Venkataramani, *Judgments by O. Chinnappa Reddy: A Humanist* (New Delhi: International Institute of Human Rights Society, 1989).

He was in his mid-eighties when his *The Court and the Constitution of India: Summits and Shallows*, an assessment of the first sixty years of SCI decisions, was published (New Delhi: Oxford University Press, 2008).

65. Ananda Prakash Sen (1978–88)

A.P. Sen was born on 20 September 1923 at Mamyo in Burma. His parents were living in Nagpur at the time but he was born in Burma because of the Bengali practice of the first child being born in the home of the maternal grandfather who, in Sen's case, was an advocate at the Rangoon High

---

[33] Particularly revealing in his 'Socialism under the Constitution: Promise and Performance', *Indian Bar Review*, vol. X, no. 1 (1983), pp. 82–93. Here he laments the dearth of socialism in India's socialist republic.

Court. Although his ancestors had moved from Bengal to Nagpur in 1868, his family continued to speak Bengali at home and four generations later were still considered Bengalis.[34]

The Sens were a family of lawyers. A.P. Sen was the son of Jnanaranjan Sen, who, after a stint as Advocate General of the Central Provinces and Berar, became a judge of the Nagpur High Court. Vivekranjan Sen, the brother of J. Sen, was also a judge of that court. In time, not only would A.P. Sen follow in his father's footsteps and become a high court judge himself but so would his younger brother, C.P. Sen. In just two generations this family produced four high court judges. A.P. Sen did not add to this judicial family for he never married.

Sen received a BSc in mathematics from Science College, Nagpur, in 1943. He had wanted to become a teacher of mathematics but his family's tradition was law and he was persuaded to move in that direction. He received his LLB from the Nagpur Law College in 1945.[35]

He was twenty-one when he began practising law in June 1945 in the district courts of Nagpur. In November 1947, he enrolled as an advocate of the Nagpur High Court. After the establishment of the Madhya Pradesh High Court at Jabalpur on 1 November 1956, he shifted his practice there. It was at his initiative that the Madhya Pradesh bar council was constituted in 1958.

Twenty-one years after he began his law practice, Sen was appointed Advocate General of Madhya Pradesh in June 1966. He was serving in that post when, on 7 November 1967 and at age forty-four, he was appointed an additional judge of the Madhya Pradesh High Court. He was confirmed as a permanent judge on 29 July 1968.

Because of his refusal to cower to the subtle and overt pressures on the judiciary during the Emergency[36] he was summarily transferred to the Rajasthan High Court on 20 June 1976. Prior to this transfer, his water was cut off for two months. After the Emergency ended, CJI Beg tried

---

[34] I interviewed Sen on 11 May 1983 and 10 September 1988 in New Delhi, and learned more about him via correspondence with his brother, C.P. Sen, dated 17 August 2009.

[35] A colleague of his father was Vivian Bose and it was at his father's initiative that M. Hidayatullah was appointed government pleader. The latter was one of A.P. Sen's teachers at the law college.

[36] It was Sen's judgment in 1975 in *Shiv Kant Shukla* v. *A.D.M. Jabalpur* that was among the several high court decisions overturned by the SCI in 1976 in the infamous *habeas corpus* decision of the same name.

to persuade him to remain at Jodhpur, where Sen had been acting chief justice from 1 February to 12 May 1977, and from 28 December 1977 to 28 February 1978, and would have been confirmed as the permanent chief justice. Although his twenty months in Rajasthan had been professionally and personally happy ones, he preferred to return to Jabalpur. He did that, effective 28 February 1978, and assumed the chief justiceship of the Madhya Pradesh High Court on that date.

On 17 July 1978 and at age fifty-four, he was sworn in as an SCI judge. He was hesitant to accept this promotion for he would have been chief justice of his high court for nearly eight years. Having been schooled in the old traditions of the role of a judge, he was never comfortable with the changes that were in progress during his years on the Court. When he retired on 20 September 1988, he was the SCI's most senior associate judge.

Upon retiring, he left immediately for the ancestral home in Nagpur and had no retirement plans other than reading and relaxing. During his retirement years he played a prominent role in developing the Saraswat Sabha Library, the only Bengali library in Nagpur, and endowed a wing of it in the memory of his father. He also served as president of the local Kali temple of Bengalis. He accepted no official assignments after leaving Delhi.

He was seventy-nine when he died on 26 January 2003.

66. Engalaguppe Seetharamiah Venkataramiah (1979–89)

From the humblest of beginnings, E.S. Venkataramiah's rise to the highest judicial office in the land is a compelling story. [37] He was born on 18 December 1924 into a poor family at Manikanahalli, a parched, hardscrabble village in the Mandya district of Karnataka. His father, T.V. Seetharamiah, earned nine rupees per month as a school teacher and farmed a small plot of land to supplement his modest salary.

Venkataramiah was nineteen when he received his BA in history, economics, and politics from Maharaja's College in Mysore City in 1943. He began his legal education at the Poona Law College and transferred to the Raja Lakhamangouda Law College at Belgaum, where he received his LLB in 1945. He secured two gold medals at the BA level, won a first class first in the LLB examinations, and was named a fellow of the Karnatak Law

[37] Interviews on 16 April 1983 and 2 October 1988, in New Delhi.

Society. After receiving his law degree, he remained in Belgaum for a year to teach at his alma mater. He was both the first graduate and first lawyer in his family.

He then moved to Bangalore where, at the age of twenty-one, he commenced practice as a pleader in the subordinate courts on 2 June 1946. On 5 June 1948, he enrolled as an advocate of the Mysore High Court. Eighteen years later, on 2 June 1966, he was appointed special government pleader and, on 6 June 1969, as government advocate. He was holding the latter position when, on 5 March 1970, he became the state's advocate general. On 25 June 1970, at age forty-five, he was appointed to the Mysore High Court[38] as an additional judge and was confirmed as a permanent judge on 20 November 1970.

During his thirty-three years in Bangalore, Venkataramiah was involved in a variety of activities, most relating to law and education. His own childhood gave him an understanding and appreciation of the sufferings of the poor. Long before state governments were involved in providing legal aid for the poor he served as secretary, from 1948 to 1956, of the privately-funded Legal Aid Society. From 1948 to 1952, he was in charge of law reporting for the *Mysore Law Journal*. In 1960–1, he served as secretary of the high court advocates association and was instrumental in building the association's library. He played a major role in founding the B.M.S. Law College in Bangalore and, from 1963 to 1968, served as a professor and principal. He was president of the Mysore state Commission of Jurists and, in 1968, he served as conference secretary of the International Commission of Jurists meeting held in Bangkok. He was also a member of the council of management of the Gokhale Institute of Public Affairs and was chairman of Karnataka's Legal Aid and Advice Board from 1976 to 1979.

After nearly nine years on the Karnataka bench, by which time he was fifth in seniority, he was promoted to the SCI. When he was sworn in on 8 March 1979, he was fifty-four. According to the arithmetic of the seniority convention he was in line to become CJI upon R.S. Pathak's retirement on 25 November 1989, which meant that he would serve as CJI for only twenty-three days. But when Pathak was elected to the International Court of Justice and resigned on 18 June 1989, the next day Venkataramiah became the nation's nineteenth CJI and held that post for six months.

---

[38] Renamed Karnataka High Court, in 1973.

In April 1986, he was appointed chairman of a commission to determine which Hindi-speaking areas of Punjab should be given to Haryana in lieu of the earlier decision that Punjab would keep Chandigarh. This assignment came on the heels of earlier SCI judge-led commissions which had made recommendations on the same issue. Venkataramiah's recommendations were equally unacceptable to Punjab and no action was taken on his report. While on the SCI, he was president of the Court's Legal Aid Committee. In 1988, he served as chairman of the committee to select the president of the Central Excise and Revenue Tribunal. Before leaving the SCI he also served as chairman of the Citizen Development Society (New Delhi) and as president of the Indian Law Institute.

Venkataramiah has the distinction of writing what is probably the longest opinion in the SCI's history—his 244-page concurring opinion in the *First Judge's Case* in 1981.[39] After nearly eleven years on the SCI he reached retirement age on 18 December 1989. Unlike many of the retired judges of his day who remained in Delhi, he returned to his home in Bangalore. A soft-spoken, unassuming, and scholarly man who was at heart a teacher, he was one of the very few judges who taught after leaving the bench. For some time he held the M.K. Nambiar Constitutional Law Chair at the National Law School of India University in Bangalore. His close association with the B.M.S. Law college continued when he served as a member of the senate academic council and the board of examiners. He also served as chairman of the Bangalore branch of the Bharatiya Vidya Bhavan, the Sri Aurobindo Society, and the Institute for Social and Economic Change. In 1990, he became a member of the Board of Directors of *The Pioneer*, a Lucknow-based newspaper. In 1996, he became chairman of the Sarvodaya International Trust. In 1995, he chaired a committee which recommended improvements in the Food Adulteration Act, and served as an advisor to the Karnataka government on the Cauvery River issue. In 1989, he won the election for the first president of the Indian branch of the International Institute of Human Rights.

During his SCI years and thereafter, he was the author of a number of publications. These included *Women and Law* (Varanasi: Banaras Hindu University, 1985); *A Free and Balanced Press* (New Delhi: TRF Institute for Social Sciences Research and Education, 1986); *Freedom of*

---

[39] *S.P. Gupta v. Union of India* [1982] 2 SCR 365. The seven judges, each of whom wrote separately, used no less than 1,090 pages.

the *Press: Some Recent Trends* (Delhi: B.R. Publishing Corporation, 1987); *B.N. Rao, Constitutional Adviser* (Bombay: N.M. Tripathi Pvt. Ltd., 1987); and *Citizenship: Rights and Duties* (Bangalore: B.V. Nagarathna Publishers, 1988). He was the editor of *Human Rights in the Changing World* (New Delhi: Regional Branch of the International Law Association, 1988), and, with co-author P.M. Bakshi, *Indian Federalism: A Comparative Study* (Bangalore: B.V. Nagarathna Publishers, 1992). His *Justice Imperiled: A Memoir* was published in 1992 (Bangalore: B.V. Nagarathna Publishers).

Venkataramiah was seventy-two when he died on 24 September 1997.

67. Baharul Islam (1980–3)

B. Islam,[40] at nearly sixty-three, the eldest appointed judge to the SCI to date, was born on 1 March 1918 at Udiana, Kamrup district of Assam. He was son of Tamjir Ali, a farmer and landowner of modest means.

The seventh Muslim to serve on the SCI, he received his BA (honours) in economics from Cotton College, Guwahati, Assam, in 1938. For the next six years, in order to save money for his legal education, he worked as a teacher in a government high school. In 1944, he proceeded to Aligarh Muslim University, where in 1946 he received both an MA in English language and literature and the LLB. He was the first graduate and the first lawyer in his family.

In December 1947, at the age of twenty-nine, he enrolled as a pleader of the Calcutta High Court and began his law practice at the Guwahati district courts. In 1951, he enrolled as an advocate of the Assam High Court.

For a quarter century prior to his appointment to the Gauhati High Court,[2] Islam, who described himself as a believer in democratic socialism, was very active in politics, first in the Socialist Party and later in the Congress Party. From 1948 to 1956, he was a member of the executive committee of the Assam Socialist Party and, in 1953, attended the Asian Socialist Conference in Rangoon. He joined the Congress party in 1956 and during the 1957–72 years held several party offices, including returning officer for the Assam Pradesh Congress Committee and executive member of the

---

[40] Although his surname is almost invariably listed as Baharul Islam, he said it is simply Islam, with Baharul being his given name. Interview with the author on New Delhi on 4 October 1988. He is not the Baharul Islam who is the author of *Shah Bano* (New Delhi: Rajiv, 1986).

Guwahati District Congress Committee. On 3 April 1962, he was elected to the Rajya Sabha on a Congress party ticket. In 1967, while still a member of the Rajya Sabha, and again supported by the Congress, he contested a seat for the Assam legislative assembly, but was unsuccessful. In 1968, he was re-elected for another term in the Rajya Sabha. After the Congress party split in 1969 he aligned himself with Mrs Gandhi's Congress (I).

During the 1960s he served as a member of the advisory board in Assam established under the terms of the Preventive Detention Act and, from 1961 to 1968, as a member of the advisory board created by the West Bengal Security Act for Manipur. Islam was also active in educational affairs, having served as a member of the executive council of Guwahati University for two terms and of Dibrugarh University for one term. From 1962 to 1963, he was a member of the Assam Khadi and Gramudyog.

On 20 January 1972, he resigned from the Rajya Sabha in order to accept the appointment as a judge of the Gauhati High Court.[41] The first Muslim to serve on that high court, he was sworn in on 20 January 1972, when he was fifty-three. On 11 March 1979, he became acting chief justice and was made permanent chief justice on 7 July 1979. He held that position for less than a year for he reached retirement age on 1 March 1980.

Immediately thereafter, Islam returned to active politics but his efforts in 1980 to return to the Rajya Sabha were unsuccessful. He contested as an independent—the Congress (I) promised only its second preferences.

On 4 December 1980, nine months after retiring from the Gauhati bench, Islam was sworn in as a judge of the SCI, the first retired high court judge to be appointed since N. Rajagopala Ayyangar in 1960. His appointment came as a considerable surprise, in part, because of his advanced age but more because his career had been spent largely in active politics.

His sudden departure from the SCI precipitated a great deal of controversy and criticism. On 13 January 1983, just six weeks before his sixty-fifth birthday, he announced his resignation, and the next day it was revealed that he had received the Congress (I) nomination for the Barpeta (Assam) Lok Sabha constituency for the election to be held in a few weeks.

---

[41] K.S. Hegde had done the same thing in 1957—he resigned from the Rajya Sabha to become a judge of the Mysore High Court. The Assam High Court came into being in 1948. Its name was changed to the Assam and Nagaland High Court, in 1963 and to the Gauhati High Court, in 1971. It serves the seven northeastern states of Assam, Nagaland, Meghalaya, Manipur, Mizoram, Arunachal Pradesh, and Tripura.

Although not the first SCI to resign to enter the political arena,[42] in Islam's case the criticism was heightened by the fact that, just a month earlier, he had written the controversial majority judgment which granted Bihar's Congress (I) Chief Minister Jagannath Misra a reprieve from trial for forgery and criminal misconduct.[43] That decision was widely criticized by the press, and when Islam received the Congress (I)'s endorsement for the Lok Sabha, sections of the press, not very delicately, raised the question of whether there was a quid pro quo between his opinion in that case and his nomination from Mrs Gandhi's government.[44]

Because of the turmoil in Assam, the election in the Barpeta constituency could not be conducted. In May 1983, the Congress (I) announced that Islam would be its nominee for a Rajya Sabha seat. Elected unopposed, this third term spanned from 15 June 1983 to 14 June 1989. During these years he served as chairman of the committee for social security for legal practitioners, and a non-official committee for the welfare of the handicapped. Outside of the Rajya Sabha, he served as chairman of the Society for Law and Justice.

Islam's career was spent mainly in the political arena, interrupted by short stints as a high court and SCI judge. No previous judge, except for those who died shortly after arriving in Delhi, had a shorter tenure on the SCI.

He died on 5 February 1993, at age seventy-four.

68. Appajee Varadarajan (1980–5)

The first member of the Scheduled Caste community to reach the SCI, A. Varadarajan was born on 17 August 1920, at Jolarpettai in the North Arcot district of Tamil Nadu. He was the son of B. Appajee Pillai, who owned a grocery shop and employed tenants to farm his agricultural property.[45]

---

[42] K. Subba Rao had resigned in 1967 to contest the presidential election.

[43] *Sheonandan Paswan v. State of Bihar* [1983] 2 SCR 61.

[44] See, 'A Bad Decision', *The Times of India*, 18 January 1983; Chaitanya Kalbag, 'Ends of Justice', *India Today*, 31 January 1983; and Hemendra Narayan, 'Baharul says he did not resign to become MP', *The Indian Express*, 28 February 1983.

[45] Interviews with the author on 13 May 1983 in New Delhi and 20 November 1988 in Madras.

Varadarajan received a BA degree in economics and political science from Loyola College, Madras, in 1941, and his BL degree in 1943 from Madras Law College. He was the first graduate and lawyer in his family.

After enrolling as an advocate of the Madras High Court on 4 September 1944, he practised there and at the district courts. On 7 November 1949, at age twenty-nine, he joined the Madras judicial service. Posted first as a munsif in Ariyalur, he began a thirty-one-year climb from the lowest rung of the judicial ladder to the SCI. He served as a munsif until 4 August 1957 when he was promoted to subordinate judge. From 1962 to 1964, he was a judge of the small causes court and city civil court in Madras City. He was next appointed an additional district and sessions judge and also held the title of chief rent controller. On 15 December 1966, he was promoted to district and sessions judge. During 1968–9 he was the presiding officer of the labour court in Madurai and, in 1969, served briefly as presiding officer of the industrial tribunal in Chennai. Also in 1969, he headed the inquiry into the police firing at Tenkasi in Tirunelveli district. From 11 December 1970 to 31 December 1972, he was the judicial member of the Tamil Nadu committee for the examination of the jurisdiction of civil and criminal courts.

On 15 February 1973, when serving as an additional judge on the Madras city civil court and after nearly twenty-four years in the subordinate judiciary, Varadarajan was appointed an additional judge of the Madras High Court. Age fifty-two at this time, he was the first member of the Scheduled Caste community appointed to that court which, not many years earlier, had been largely the preserve of the brahmin community. His judgeship was made permanent on 27 February 1974.

After nearly eight years on the Madras bench, by which time he was sixth in seniority, he became the first from the Scheduled Castes to reach the SCI. He was sixty when he was sworn in on 10 December 1980.

When Varadarajan's nearly five years on the SCI ended on 17 August 1985, he returned to his home in Madras. He was eighty-nine when he died on 15 October 2009.

69. Amarendra Nath Sen (1981–5)

A.N. Sen was born into a prominent Bengali family on 1 October 1920 at Calcutta, West Bengal. His grandfather was Rai Bahadur Baikuntha Nath

Sen, a self-made man born in a village who rose to become a prominent lawyer in Murshidabad district. He became a wealthy man and a zamindar with considerable landholdings. Active in the Indian National Congress, he served as the first non-official chairman of the Murshidabad district board established as part of the Montague–Chelmsford reforms. He was also chairman of the reception committee in 1917 when the Indian National Congress held its annual meeting in Calcutta.[46]

Tarak Nath Sen, A.N. Sen's father, was not a lawyer but a businessman who also looked after the family's properties in Berhampore. He was also politically active and for some time served as chairman of the Murshidabad District Board. A.N. Sen himself was also active in the nationalist movement. He was offered a Congress ticket for the 1951–2 West Bengal legislative assembly election but declined, having eschewed active politics after he began practising law.

Sen received his BA (honours) in economics from Scottish Church College, Calcutta, in 1940, followed by the BL degree from University Law College, Calcutta, in 1943. Among the awards he received was the coveted Sir Ashutosh Law Prize. Although he had passed the bar examinations in Calcutta, because he wanted to practise on the prestigious and more lucrative original side of the Calcutta High Court, which was then restricted to barristers, he wanted to go to London to become a barrister. Because of the war, he was admitted to Inner Temple in absentia and passed the first two parts of the examinations in India. He did get to London in 1946 and was called to the bar at the end of that year.

He enrolled as an advocate of the Calcutta High Court on 23 January 1947, at age twenty-six. He was appointed an additional judge on 15 November 1965 when he was forty-five. He was not eager to become a judge but accepted the invitation to satisfy his father's wishes. His judgeship was made permanent on 25 July 1966. After fourteen years on the Calcutta bench, he became chief justice on 26 December 1979 and looked forward to holding that prestigious post for nearly three years.

Just over a year later, however, he was sworn in as an SCI judge on 28 January 1981. He was then sixty and among the most senior high court judges in the country. Sen retired on 1 October 1985. P.N. Bhagwati, the then CJI, urged him to remain on the SCI under the terms of Article 128. He was not interested and planned to return to Calcutta. But soon, he

[46] Interviews with the author, in New Delhi, on 21 April 1983 and 24 October 1988.

accepted the chairmanship of the Press Council of India, and held that post from 10 October 1985 to 18 January 1989. He was eighty-nine when we died on 2 January 2010.

70. Vettath Balakrishna Eradi (1981–7)

V. Balakrishna Eradi was born into a matriarchal and aristocratic family on 19 June 1922 at Calicut, in the Malabar district of Kerala. He was the son of C. Krishnamoose who was the first member of the Namboodri community to become a judicial officer.[47] He started as a munsif and retired as the seniormost district and sessions judge in the Madras presidency. Balakrishna Eradi's uncle served as the chief justice of the former princely state of Cochin.

After receiving his BA in physics and mathematics from Madras Christian College in 1941 he earned the BL from Madras Law College in 1943. He secured the only first class in the BL examinations and stood first in the Madras presidency.

On 15 January 1945, he commenced practising law as an advocate of the Madras High Court. In addition to his private practice, during the 1950–6 years he served as junior counsel for the Madras government and as Standing Counsel for the Madras Court of Wards.

When the Kerala High Court was created in 1956, he shifted his practice to Ernakulam. In January 1961, he was appointed senior government pleader. He was holding that position when, at age forty-four, he was appointed an additional judge of the Kerala High Court on 5 April 1967. Confirmation as a permanent judge came on 16 October 1967. In becoming a high court judge, he was, in a sense, vindicating his father who had wanted to be a Madras High Court judge but fell victim to the prevailing anti-brahmin sentiments. After nearly thirteen years as an associate judge, he became chief justice on 19 January 1980.

While on the Kerala bench, in 1975 he was appointed by the state government as a single member commission of inquiry, usually referred to as the Eradi Commission, to investigate charges of misconduct against the

---

[47] Interviews with the author on 7 May 1983 and 28 October 1988, in New Delhi. Biographical material is found also in 'Justice V. Balakrishna Eradi', www.supremecourtcaselaw.com/jus_vberadi.com. Last visited on 3 October 2010.

then minister of finance and forests. In 1977, he served as chairman of the high court committee to introduce reforms in legal education.

Balakrishna Eradi served only one year as the Kerala chief justice before he was sworn in as an SCI judge on 30 January 1981, at age fifty-eight. While serving on the SCI, he agreed, in early 1986, to serve as chairman of the Ravi and Beas waters tribunal, established to decide how the waters would be shared by Punjab, Haryana, and Rajasthan. He submitted his report[48] the following January but because the parties could request clarifications and Punjab wanted a complete reconsideration of the award, his work on this tribunal continued for many more years. On 19 June 1987, he retired from the SCI

Most retired SCI judges from South India return home after retirement but Balakrishna Eradi chose to remain in Delhi. In March 1988, he became the president of the National Consumer Disputes Redressal Commission, established under the terms of the 1987 Consumer Protection Act, and held this position until his seventy-fifth birthday in 1997. In 1990, he was appointed by the President of India to serve as the single-member commission to conduct a fact-finding inquiry into a disturbance which occurred at Rashtrapati Bhavan during the swearing in ceremony of the ministry of the Chandrashekar government. On 22 October 1999, he was appointed by the Ministry of Law, Justice and Company Affairs as chairman of the committee on law relating to the insolvency of companies. His report was submitted the following year and many of his recommendations were incorporated into the Companies (Second Amendment) Act, 2002.

Among the many spiritual, cultural, and social service organizations in which he was active was the International Center for Kathakali in New Delhi; he was elected its president in 1982. He served as president of Swaralaya, a music society. He became a member of the council of management of the Sri Sathya Sai Baba central trust in 1972 and was a trustee of the Sri Sathya Sai Baba Institute of Higher Medical Sciences Hospital at Puttaparthy in Andhra Pradesh. He also served as a trustee of the Delhi Bhagwati Saptah Trust. He was the author of *Consumer Protection Jurisprudence* (New Delhi: LexisNexis, Butterworths, 2005).

---

[48] *Report of the Ravi and Beas Water Tribunal* (New Delhi: Government of India, Ministry of Water Resources, 1989).

In 1992, he was the recipient of both the National Press of India Golden Jubilee award and the Rajiv Gandhi Excellence Award. In 1993, he received the Shiromani award and in 1996 the National Citizenship Award.

He was eighty-eight when he died on 20 December 2010.

71. Ram Briksha Misra (1981–6)

R.B. Misra, the son of Raj Deo Misra, a poor farmer, was born on 15 June 1921 in the village of Bagha in the impoverished district of Deoria, Uttar Pradesh.[49]

The first graduate and the first lawyer in his family, he earned his BA in Sanskrit, English literature, and philosophy from St. Andrew's College, Gorakhpur in 1941 and, with borrowed money, an LLB from Allahabad University in 1944. He aspired to join the provincial judicial service but his efforts were unsuccessful. He enrolled as an advocate of the Allahabad High Court on 26 March 1946.

Twenty-two years later, on 3 January 1968 and at age forty-six, he was sworn in as an additional judge of the Allahabad High Court. Confirmation as a permanent judge came on 23 July 1969. Thirteen years later, by then third in seniority on the Allahabad bench, he became an SCI judge on 30 January 1981. Aged fifty-nine at this juncture, he reached retirement age on 15 June 1986.

He returned to his village with plans to establish and administer a trust designed to keep educated youth in the village and district. For many years he had been funding scholarships for poor students. But later, in 1986, the union government appointed him as chairman of the Pay Committee for Public Enterprises, an assignment that brought him back to Delhi. Also in 1986, and concurrent with the latter work, he accepted the job of completing the remaining work of the Fourth Pay Commission after the death of its chairman, P.N. Shinghal. In November 1988, he accepted the post of Lok Ayukta for Himachal Pradesh. From 1 October 1992 to 11 April 1993, he served concurrently as president of the state's Consumer Disputes Redressal Commission.

---

[49] Interviewed on 1 June 1983 and 27 October 1988. A son, Ram Prakash Misra, was an Allahabad High Court judge from 1999 to 2007.

A passion throughout his life was the study of religion and philosophy. In 1987, he was selected to be chairman of the Prayag Mahila Vidyapeeth and in 1998, was the recipient of the Uttar Pradesh Ratna Award.

Misra was eighty when he died on 27 December 2001.

72. Dinshah Pirosha Madon (1983–6)

The first member of the Parsi community to serve on the SCI,[50] D.P. Madon was born on 7 April 1921 in Bombay. The first lawyer in his family, he was the son of Pirosha Madon, a prominent and wealthy stockbroker who served as director of the Bombay stock exchange.[51]

Madon received his BA (honours.) in English literature and French from Elphinstone College, Bombay, in 1941. In his youth, he aspired to be a journalist and writer but these were low-paying positions and his father preferred that he become a lawyer. He had planned to go to London to earn barrister credentials but was prevented from doing so because of World War II. He earned his LLB from Government Law College, Bombay in 1943. Among the honours he received were the Sir Narayan Chandavarkar Hindu Law Scholarship and the Sir John Heaton Prize. He also won the Sirur Inter-Collegiate Debating Trophy, was named a fellow of the Government Law College, and stood first in both LLB examinations.[52]

His thirty-nine year association with the Bombay High Court began when he enrolled as an advocate on 21 November 1944. On 2 November of the following year, he qualified as an original side advocate. He would spend the next twenty-three years in practice at the Bombay High Court, but also before other high courts, the SCI, and East African courts. Early in

[50] He was not the first Parsi invited to serve on the SCI. H.M. Seervai and N.A. Palkhivala, in the late 1950s, declined invitations, as did Fali Nariman in the late 1970s. Parsis took to law early—six of the first ten students admitted by Lincoln's Inn were Parsis. Samuel Schmitthener, 'A Sketch of the Development of the Legal Profession in India', *Law & Society Review*, vol. III, nos 2 and 3 (November 1968–February 1969), p. 365. The Parsis, practitioners of Zorastrianism, are a dwindling community—the 2001 census reported that there were less than 70,000 in the country. See Anjali Doshi, 'Fading Away', *India Today*, 27 September 2004, pp. 40–1.

[51] The author interviewed Madon on 28 April 1983 in New Delhi, 7 November 1988 in Bombay and 28 May 1990 in Lexington, Kentucky, USA.

[52] The D.P. Madon Prize in Constitutional Law is awarded annually by the law college.

his career he authored *Principles and Practice of the Sales Tax*[53] and, from 1952 to 1955, he served as a part-time professor of law at his alma mater. For decades he was very active in the Masons and served as India's grand master from 1976 to 1982. A voracious reader, at home with the world's classic literature, he was well known in intellectual circles in Bombay.

On 25 September 1967, at age forty-six, he became an additional judge of the Bombay High Court; this judgeship was made permanent on 6 August 1969. He achieved national attention when he served as a one-man commission of inquiry, usually referred to as the D.P. Madon Commission of Inquiry, to ascertain the causes of the communal rioting which took place in Maharashtra in 1970.[54] On 10 February 1976, in the teeth of the Emergency, he wrote the judgment in *Binod Rao* v. *Minocher Rustom Masani*[55] which struck down as unconstitutional the censorship of free speech. After nearly fifteen years on the Bombay bench, he was appointed acting chief justice on 11 August 1982 and permanent chief justice on 31 August 1982.

Less than a year later, and less than a month before reaching age sixty-two, Madon was sworn in as an SCI judge on 15 March 1983. His brief tenure ended on 7 April 1986.

He returned to Bombay where he had long been active in the cultural and social life of the city, and engaged in chamber practice and conducted arbitrations. He also served as a member of the senate and executive council of Bombay University. In July 1990, he accepted appointment by the V.P. Singh Government as the one-man commission of inquiry charged with looking into the election violence that occurred in the Meham constituency in May 1990, forcing the cancellation of the election. He was given a deadline of three months to submit his report but after four months had passed without being provided with an office, staff, or budget, Madon, who could be very outspoken, sent a strongly worded and widely publicized letter to the home ministry announcing his resignation.[56]

---

[53] Bombay: Progressive Corp., 1947.

[54] *Report of the Commission of Inquiry into the Communal Disturbances at Bhiwandi, Jalgaon, and Mahad in May 1970*, 7 vols (Bombay: Government Press, 1970). This report is cited often as a classic study of the causes of communal violence.

[55] (1976) 78 *Bombay Law Reporter* 125. Why Madon wasn't among the high court judges punitively transferred during the Emergency remains a mystery.

[56] Rahul Pathak, 'Judge sends in resignation, inquiry is dead: Meham probe gets official burial', *Indian Express*, 12 December 1990. See also Rahul Pathak, 'I feel like an animal in a zoo', says Meham judge', *Indian Express*, 24 November 1990.

Again he returned to Bombay and resumed chamber practice. He died on 24 June 1994, at age seventy-three.

73. Sabyasachi Mukharji (1983–90)

On 1 June 1927, S. Mukharji was born in Calcutta into a prominent Bengali legal-judicial family. He represented the fifth consecutive generation to be involved with law.[57] The first was Iswar Narahari Sivamoni, a Hindu law jurist who worked as an assessor in the Calcutta provincial appellate court in the early nineteenth century. His son, Pandit Gobinda Chandra Vidyararna, was a subordinate judge in the Bengal judicial service. His son, Rai Bahadur Bepin Behari Mukharji, was a judge of the small causes court in Calcutta. S. Mukharji's father, Rai Bahadur Bejoy Behari Mukharji, was a member of the Bengal provincial civil service who, after retiring as director of Land Records and Surveys, qualified for law and joined the profession. S. Mukharji's elder brother, Dr P.B. Mukharji, was appointed to the Calcutta High Court in 1949 and was chief justice from 1970 to 1972.

Mukharji was educated at Presidency College, Calcutta, where he earned a BA (honours) in economics in 1946. Active in politics, he was elected as general secretary of the college students union. He proceeded to England and was called to the bar from Middle Temple in 1949. He was chosen to represent Middle Temple on the Inns of Court Students Union. During these years in England, he was active in socialist politics and, in 1948–9, he was the general secretary of the Indian Socialist Group in Europe. He was associated first with the Congress Socialist Party, then the Socialist Party and finally with the Praja Socialist Party. Before returning to Calcutta he worked in the chambers of Reginald William Goff, who later became lord justice of the court of appeal.

Upon returning to India, at age twenty-two, he enrolled as advocate of the Calcutta High Court on 23 November 1949. During the next nineteen years, he practised at both that high court and the SCI. From 1958 to 1968 until his appointment to the Calcutta bench, he served as Standing Counsel for the Income Tax Department. In 1964–5, the union government appointed him a member of the study team on administrative tribunals of the administrative reforms commission. During his years at

[57] Interviews with the author on 26 April 1983 and 1 October 1988, in New Delhi.

the bar he remained active in politics. In 1967, he was nominated by the Congress party to contest a Lok Sabha seat. At his request this nomination was withdrawn.

Mukharji was first offered a high court judgeship in 1966 but turned it down because he was considering contesting the 1967 election. He accepted when the offer was renewed and at the uncommonly young age of forty-one was sworn in as a permanent judge on 31 July 1968. In addition to his work as a judge, his expertise in economics led to his appointment, in 1982, as a member of the Eighth Finance Commission. During his Calcutta years he was closely associated with the Ramakrishna Mission and the Sarat Bose Academy. Active also in the Tagore Society for Rural Development dating to the early 1960s, he served as its chairman from 1972 to 1982. At the time of his death, he was president of the Kali Bari in New Delhi.

By 1 March 1983, he was the most senior judge and was named acting chief justice. Only fifty-five at this time and anticipating being confirmed, his tenure in that glamorous post would have been seven years. But the call from the SCI came and he was sworn in as an SCI judge on 15 March.

When the Congress government fell and the National Front government took over in early December 1989, one of its first tasks was to name the next CJI. If there was any concern about the vitality of the seniority convention, it was dispelled when it was announced on 12 December that Mukharji would be the twentieth CJI, succeeding E.S. Venkataramiah upon the latter's retirement on 18 December. Sixty-two at this time, Mukharji was to serve as CJI for two and a half years. But this was not to be, for after just nine months as CJI, he died in London after a heart attack on 25 September 1990, at age sixty-three.

74. Manharlal Pranlal Thakkar (1983–8)

M.P. Thakkar was born on 4 November 1923 at Gyobingauk in Burma, where his father, Pranlal L. Thakkar, was the owner of a rice mill. Their family home was the village of Babra in the Rajkot district of the former Saurashtra state, now part of Gujarat. In 1941, after the onset of World War II, the family returned to Gujarat. Thakkar's family background can be described as upper middle-class.

After completing his elementary and secondary education in Burma and returning to India, he was able to begin his law studies without first earning a bachelor's degree. He received the LLB degree from Sir L.A. Shah Law College in Ahmedabad, Gujarat, in 1944. He was the first lawyer in his family. All his ancestors were businessmen.

At age twenty-four, he enrolled as an advocate of the former Saurashtra High Court at Rajkot on 10 August 1948. After the merger of Saurashtra into the state of Bombay in 1956, he continued to practise mainly at Rajkot, which after 1956 was a bench of the Bombay High Court. When Bombay state was bifurcated into Maharashtra and Gujarat on 1 May 1960, he shifted his practice to the new Gujarat High Court at Ahmedabad.

During his fifteen years as a practising lawyer, he was very active in the Socialist Party and the trade union movement. He devoted a great deal of time promoting the growth of trade unions and served as president of several, including the Saurashtra Bank Employees Union, the Post and Telegraph Workers Union, the Electricity Workers Union, and the Mill Workers Union. His law practice was consistent with his party and union sympathies—his clients were, for the most part, workers and tenants, not the owners of factories and landlords.[58] His passion for social justice for the poor continued throughout his life and was reflected in many of his SCI decisions.

Fifteen years after he began his law practice, Thakkar became a judge of the Ahmedabad City Civil and Sessions Court on 23 January 1963. Some six and a half years later, on 2 July 1969 and at age forty-five, he was sworn in as an additional judge of the Gujarat High Court. Confirmation as a permanent judge came on 27 November 1973 and on 20 August 1981, he became its chief justice. After assuming this office, he served as co-chairman of the Gujarat State Legal Aid and Advice Board. In 1982, he was the major force in establishing the nation's first Lok Adalats ('people's courts') for the speedy disposal of cases through mutual settlements.[59]

Thakkar was fifty-nine when he was sworn in as an SCI judge on 15 March 1983. Before this appointment he was on the record for having supported the two supersessions ('the superseded judges were guilty of supporting the status quo'), the imposition of the Emergency in 1975, and for his disagreement with the 1973 *Kesavananda* decision ('Parliament is accountable to the people; judges are not'). Although he left a legacy as a

---

[58] Interview with the author on 29 April 1983 in New Delhi, and correspondence dated 13 March 1984.

[59] *Gujarat Legal Aid Ambulance Project: Lok Adalat* (Ahmedabad: Gujarat State Legal Aid and Advice Board, 1983).

vigorous proponent of the rights of the disadvantaged, he is remembered also for his role on two controversial commissions of inquiry. On 20 November 1984, three weeks after the assassination of Prime Minister Indira Gandhi, Thakkar was appointed to head the commission to investigate the sequence of events leading to, and all the facts relating to, the assassination. This commission was also charged with determining whether there was any conspiracy behind the murder and whether there were deficiencies in the security system. Known as the Thakkar Commission, two reports were submitted, an interim report on 19 November 1985,[60] and the final report on 27 February 1986.[61] When they were made public in 1989, his findings were subjected to a great deal of criticism.

The second was the report of the Thakkar-Natarajan Commission, often referred to as the Fairfax Commission. From April through November 1987, Thakkar and fellow SCI judge S. Natarajan conducted this inquiry which dealt with the finance ministry's employment of an American detective agency to investigate alleged economic offences such as the holding of illegal foreign bank accounts. This matter was a fight between the Congress (I) government led by Rajiv Gandhi on one side, and former Finance Minister V.P. Singh on the other. The Thakkar–Natarajan Commission report[62] supported the former.

Thakkar's tenure on the SCI ended amidst another controversy. Several weeks before his retirement on 4 November 1988, the government announced his appointment to a three-year term as chairman of the Twelfth Law Commission. Some saw this as an executive favour to a sitting judge, raising concerns about the independence of the judiciary. The criticism notwithstanding, upon his retirement from the bench, he began a three-year term as Law Commission chairman.

Thakkar died on 9 February 2001, at age seventy-seven.

---

[60] *Report of Justice Thakkar Commission of Inquiry on the Assassination of Late Prime Minister Smt. Indira Gandhi: Interim Report* (New Delhi: Controller of Publications, 1986).
 [61] *Report of Justice Thakkar Commission of Inquiry on the Assassination of the Late Prime Minister Smt. Indira Gandhi: Final Report* (New Delhi: Controller of Publications, 1986). See also *Memorandum of Action Taken on the interim and Final Reports of Thakkar Commission of Inquiry for the Purpose of Making an Inquiry into the Assassination of Smt. Indira Gandhi, Late Prime Minister* (New Delhi: Ministry of Home Affairs, 1986).
 [62] *Report of Justices Thakkar-Natarajan Commission of Inquiry into Utilisation of Fairfax Group, Inc.* (New Delhi: Ministry of Finance, 1988).

75. Ranga Nath Misra (1983-91)

R.N. Misra was born on 26 November 1926 at Banpur, Puri district, Orissa. He was the son of Pandit Godavaris Misra who started out as a school teacher at Sakhigopal, became active in Congress politics and rose to become minister of education in Orissa and the founder of Utkal University.[63]

Misra earned four university degrees. He received his BA in 1947, an LLB in 1949, and an LLM from Allahabad University in 1951. In 1950, he earned an MA from Ravenshaw College in Cuttack, Orissa. He received gold medals for having stood first in the university in the LLB and LLM examinations.

On 18 September 1950 at age twenty-three, he enrolled as an advocate of the Orissa High Court, commencing a thirty-three year association with that court. From 1959 to 1961, he served as Standing Counsel for the Income Tax Department and, from 1965 to 1969, he was Standing Counsel for the Commercial Taxes Department of the Orissa Government.

Misra was first offered an Orissa High Court judgeship in 1967, but because his sons had not completed their education, he declined for financial reasons. When the offer was renewed two years later, he accepted a permanent judgeship and, on 4 July 1969, at age forty-two, he was sworn in on the Orissa bench. Eleven years later, on 5 November 1980, he was named acting chief justice, and was confirmed as permanent chief justice on 16 January 1981.

Two years later, after nearly fourteen years of high court experience, Misra, then fifty-six, was sworn in as an SCI judge on 15 March 1983. He was the first appointee from Orissa since B. Jaganadhadas thirty years earlier. On 26 April 1985, he became the chairman of a commission of inquiry to investigate allegations of organized violence in Delhi following the assassination of Prime Minister Indira Gandhi six months earlier. The anti-Sikh riots, which had engulfed Delhi in the days following the assassination, resulted in the deaths of thousands of Sikhs. His report, invariably referred to as the report of the Ranganath Misra Commission, was

---

[63] Interview with the author on 20 April 1983 in New Delhi. He preferred that his given name be rendered as Ranga Nath. Two of his brothers were active in Congress politics. Loknath Misra was elected a Member of Parliament and Raghu Nath Misra was active at the state level. His father-in-law, Hirihar Mohapatra, was a judge of the Patna High Court. Although the province of Orissa was created in 1936, until the establishment of the Orissa High Court in 1948, Orissa shared the Patna High Court.

released in February 1987.[64] The conclusions of this report were equivocal, vaguely blaming the police for the riots, stopping short of identifying the guilty parties, and absolving the ruling Congress (I) from any complicity in the riots. The report was widely criticized, particularly by leaders of the Sikh community and by civil rights organizations.

While on the SCI, he served as chairman of the National Committee for Implementation of Legal Aid Schemes. Misra did not anticipate becoming CJI, but the untimely death of CJI Mukharji on 25 September 1990 resulted in Misra, then the most senior associate judge, becoming CJI. Immediately following Mukharji's death, he was named acting chief justice and was sworn in as the twenty-first CJI on 5 October. After a fourteen-month tenure, Misra reached retirement age on 26 November 1991.

In October 1993, he was chosen to be the first chairman of the National Human Rights Commission and served in that capacity until 1996. In 1998, he was nominated by the Congress party for a seat in the Rajya Sabha from Orissa, and served in Parliament from 2 July 1998 to 1 July 2004. During his Rajya Sabha tenure, he was chairman of the ethics committee, and also chairman of the All-India Congress Committee Human Rights Committee. In 2000, he was appointed a member of the Ministry of Agriculture's National Commission on Cattle and, in 2004 was elected chairman of the Indo-Iranian Friendship Society. After leaving the Rajya Sabha he was appointed chairman of the National Commission for Religious and Linguistic Minorities. His report, submitted in 2007 but not made public until December 2009, recommended that Dalit Muslims and Christians be given the benefits of reservation accorded to the Scheduled Castes and Scheduled Tribes. He also served as chairman of the National Commission for Scheduled Castes and Scheduled Tribes. A recognized student of Sanskrit, he served as chairman of the Sanskrit Board and the Sanskrit Year Program.

Misra (with Ashok Soni) was the editor of the thirteen volume *Bharat's Digest of Supreme Court Cases, 1950 to date* (New Delhi: Bharat Law House Pvt. Ltd., 2000–8). He edited, in collaboration with Vijender Kumar, the fifteenth edition of *Mayne's Treatise on Hindu Law & Usage* (New Delhi: Bharat Law House Pvt. Ltd., 2003). His *Minorities and Human Rights* was published in 2002. On the occasion of his eightieth birthday, a festschrift entitled *Sriranganathsrih: Gems of Law & Dharmasastra: Justice Ranganath*

---

[64] *Report of Justice Ranganath Misra Commission of Inquiry*, 2 vols (New Delhi: Controller of Publications, 1987).

Misra, edited by Abha Kulshreshtra and Sushna Kulshreshtha, was published (New Delhi: Sanjay Prakashan, 2006).

76. Vazhakkulangarayil Khalid (1984–7)

The eighth Muslim to serve on the SCI, V. Khalid was born on 1 July 1922 at Kannur, Kannur district in the former Malabar state, now Kerala. He was the son of C.C. Marakkar, who was a merchant in the coffee and tea business.[65]

Khalid earned a BSc in mathematics, physics, and chemistry from Presidency College, Madras, in 1941. After teaching for a year at the Malappuram government high school to help support his parents, he decided he was better suited for law, and received his BL from Madras Law College in 1945. He was both the first member of his family to join the law profession and the family's first graduate.

He was twenty-five when he enrolled as an advocate of the Madras High Court on 8 March 1948, but chose his home town of Cannanore to begin his practice in a munsif's court. The following year he shifted his practice to the Tellicherry district court. Although the Kerala High Court was established in 1956 at Ernakulam, Khalid remained at Tellicherry until 1964, when he moved his practice to Ernakulam. While at Cannanore, he won the election in 1948 as an independent candidate to the Cannanore municipal council. Also active in various educational endeavours, he played a major role in the establishment of Sir Syed College in Cannanore and served as the president of the Muslim Education Association from 1967 to 1972.

He was appointed an additional judge of the Kerala High Court on 3 April 1972, at age forty-nine. Confirmation as a permanent judge came on 7 March 1974. After more than eleven years on the Kerala bench,[66] by which time he was the most senior associate judge and, at sixty-one, on the cusp of retirement was transferred to the Jammu and Kashmir High Court as its chief justice. He was sworn in on 24 August 1983. The matter of his transfer to Srinagar had come up in November 1980 but he declined

---

[65] Interview with the author on 21 November 1988, in Madras.

[66] It was Khalid and P.S. Poti whose decision in the Rajan case attracted national attention. Rajan had died in custody during the Emergency, and it was consequent upon their judgment (*Eachara Wariar* v. *State of Kerala*, 1977 *Kerala Law Times* 335) that the Kerala home minister resigned.

because of concerns about the harsh Kashmir winters, and because he aware of a protracted battle between Kashmir Chief Minister Farooq Abdullah and the central government over the transfer of Chief Justice M.B. Farooqi. Khalid agreed with the centre's position and consented to the transfer. From 2 February to 3 March 1984, he served as acting governor of Jammu and Kashmir.

Only ten months after moving from one end of the country to the other and just a week before his sixty-second birthday, he was sworn in as a judge of the SCI on 25 June 1984. His brief tenure ended with his retirement on 1 July 1987.

He returned to Madras where he accepted occasional arbitration requests from the SCI. In 1991, he served as a one-man commission of inquiry appointed by the state government to look into the deaths of individuals in police custody.

XVII

The Bhagwati Court (1985–6)

The government of Prime Minister Rajiv Gandhi's first opportunity to appoint a CJI came in mid-1985. P.N. Bhagwati had been in the same *Habeas Corpus* majority as Y.V. Chandrachud but if there was any question about whether the seniority convention would be observed those doubts were removed early, for on 10 May it was announced that he would succeed Chandrachud on 12 July. No presumptive CJI's appointment had been announced that much in advance since the 1960s. No one had waited in the wings for the chief justiceship longer than Bhagwati. Throughout the entire Chandrachud regime, he was the seniormost associate judge.

Bhagwati inherited a Court comprised of sixteen judges, himself included, so there were two vacancies. By the time he reached retirement age seventeen months later, the size of the Court had shrunk to fourteen. Seven months earlier, the SCI's strength had been increased by eight to twenty-six.[1] Law Minister A.K. Sen informed Bhagwati that the government wanted the eight appointed soon.[2] Bhagwati opposed increasing the number of judges and wanted the Court divided into two permanent benches—one for hearing constitutional cases and the other for appeals.[3]

---

[1] The Supreme Court (Number of Judges) Amendment Act, 1986, came into force on 9 May 1986.

[2] Interview with Sen on 27 December 1988, in New Delhi.

[3] The author interviewed Bhagwati on four occasions. Much of what follows has been drawn from these interviews. Interviewed also were all five of Bhagwati's appointees.

Including Bhagwati's own retirement, six judges retired during his watch and S. M. Fazal Ali died in August 1985. The retirements were those of A. Varadarajan (August 1985), A.N. Sen (October 1985), V.D. Tulzapurkar (March 1986), D.P. Madon (April 1986), and R.B. Misra (June 1986). Five new judges joined the Court during Bhagwati's stewardship.

In was well known that Bhagwati had arrived with a mission and wanted to locate and see appointed judges who shared his own social and economic views.[4] He wanted 'activists' with the 'right judicial philosophy'. He was a zealous crusader for improving the lot of the nation's under classes, particularly opening the court's doors to the least privileged. He wanted judges who shared his passion for public interest litigation (PIL). But it is unlikely that any earlier CJI was as unsuccessful in gaining government approval for his choices. He found Sen, the Law Minister during his entire tenure, a formidable foe. Sen was an old school patrician who did not agree with Bhagwati's crusading views. There was no love lost between them from the outset.

Two things happened early on which poisoned the appointment atmosphere of Bhagwati's entire tenure. Firstly, within two weeks after becoming CJI, Bhagwati was pressed by Sen to accept Delhi High Court Chief Justice Prakash Narain. Bhagwati refused to accept him and went so far as to threaten to resign if Narain was forced upon him.[5]

Secondly, one of the three names on Bhagwati's first list of nominees was P.B. Sawant of the Bombay High Court. Sawant was a Bhagwati-like advocate of pro-downtrodden liberal judicial activism and was a leader of the PIL movement in Maharashtra. The two had known each other for many years and Bhagwati was very eager to have him on the SCI. Sawant, though, was eighth in seniority on the Bombay bench and four senior judges and several senior advocates of the Bombay High Court, through the governor of Maharashtra, protested to President Zail Singh that if Sawant was appointed, he would be superseding seven more senior judges and some of these judges were likely to resign.[6] Anxious to quell the protest, Sen asked

[4] See, for example, Sumit Mitra, 'Chief Justice P.N. Bhagwati: Age of Activism', India Today, 15 August 1985, pp. 56–61.

[5] Sumit Mitra, 'Supreme Court: Tug of War', India Today, 15 January 1986, p. 47. Sen denied that he pressed Bhagwati to recommend Narain. Sen's and Bhagwati's accounts about other matters also differed.

[6] Letter to the author from Sawant dated 29 August 1990. See also, Ramakrishna Hegde's The Judiciary Today: A Plea for a Consortium (Bangalore: Government of Karnataka, 1986), p. 53.

Bhagwati to withdraw the Sawant nomination.[7] Bhagwati did so—Sawant was not vetoed. So, right out of the gate, there was a contentious atmosphere between Sen and Bhagwati over appointments and this unpleasantness continued throughout Bhagwati's reign.

The other two nominees went through without a hitch and were sworn in on 29 October 1985. The first of these was G.L. Oza, sixty-one years old and the Madhya Pradesh chief justice. With nearly eighteen years of high court service, he was near the top of the all-India seniority rankings. He was one of the first proponents of legal aid in Madhya Pradesh and well known for his pro-downtrodden views. Oza and Bhagwati had become acquainted nearly thirty years earlier, when both were appearing in a labour-management case being heard by the Labour Appellate Tribunal. Bhagwati was representing the company's management and Oza the workers. In 1982, Bhagwati had failed to persuade Chandrachud to recommend the appointment of Oza. He was an unabashed votary of Bhagwati-style jurisprudence and was the latter's first choice. As he was leaving Jabalpur for Delhi, Oza was quoted as saying that both Bhagwati and V.R. Krishna Iyer had inspired him to do more to help the poor.[8] This appointment filled no particular vacancy and raised the Madhya Pradesh representation to two.

Sworn in the same day was B.C. Ray, a veteran of eleven years on the Calcutta High Court. Almost fifty-nine, he was the youngest of the Bhagwati appointees. Eighth in seniority at Calcutta, he was the least senior judge ever appointed to the Court. But it was understood that Varadarajan having retired in August, Ray was appointed to continue Scheduled Caste representation. Of less than a dozen Scheduled Caste judges serving on the high courts, Ray was the most senior. Bhagwati met Ray for the first time when Ray came to Delhi to be sworn in.

Bhagwati's second list, sent over in October 1985, included four names— M.M. Dutt of Calcutta, K.N. Singh of Allahabad, S. Natarajan of Madras, and P.R. Gokulakrishnan, also from Madras but who earlier that year had been transferred to Gujarat as chief justice. The latter's nomination was withdrawn and Bhagwati replaced him with Sawant. Sawant was told by

---

[7] For an account of this matter which Bhagwati said was accurate, see Sumit Mitra, 'Supreme Court: Tug of War', *India Today*, 15 January 1986, p. 47. Though eighth in seniority, Sawant had been a high court judge for a dozen years, more than many others appointed earlier to the SCI.

[8] *Jabalpur Law Journal*, vol. 34, 1985, pp. 35–6.

Bhagwati on 6 March to get ready to come to Delhi,[9] but at the last minute his name was dropped. The remaining three met with no resistance but were not sworn in until 10 March 1986.

M.M. Dutt, sixty-one, fourth in seniority and nearly five years senior to Ray on the Calcutta bench, and with more than fifteen years of high court service, was selected, according to Bhagwati, to fill the seat recently vacated by A.N. Sen. Bhagwati had neither earlier met nor sought Dutt's consent before he learned of his promotion on the evening television broadcast on 6 March. Dutt was Bhagwati's choice—he believed that Dutt had been involved in legal aid and was likely to be 'progressive'.

K.N. Singh learned from Law Minister Sen in September 1985 that he was being considered for promotion and soon thereafter Bhagwati conveyed the same message. These two were not well-acquainted, having met briefly only a few weeks earlier. Six months would pass before Singh, fifty-nine, with more than fifteen years of service and second in seniority at Allahabad, would be sworn in. Because he was a cousin of V.P. Singh, Union Minister of Finance, some wondered whether his cousin was instrumental in his promotion. K.N. Singh did not think this was the case because relations between the two had not been close for years. Both Bhagwati, who said that V.P. Singh had nothing to do with his selection, and Sen were in favour of Singh's appointment but it is uncertain who the initiator was. His appointment raised the Allahabad representation to three, but R.B. Misra was on the threshold of retirement and Sen agreed that this was a factor in his appointment.

It was Bhagwati who advanced the name of S. Natarajan of the Madras High Court. He was sixty-one and third in seniority, with thirteen years of experience on the Madras bench. He had acquired a reputation of being a supporter of Bhagwati-style activism and the two knew each other well. He had been active in legal aid initiatives in Madras and it was in that capacity that he came to know Bhagwati, Krishna Iyer, and D.A. Desai. When they came to Madras to participate in seminars and other functions dealing with justice for the poor, Natarajan shared platforms with them.[10] Another factor in his appointment was that Madras had been unrepresented after Varadarajan's retirement. Natarajan learned of his promotion to the SCI the same way Dutt did, on television on 6 March. There had been no direct

[9] 29 August 1990 letter from Sawant.
[10] Interview with Natarajan on 24 April 1988, in New Delhi.

communication with anyone involved in the selection process. The official word of his promotion reached him the next morning and it instructed him to keep this confidential until the official announcement was made! Bhagwati had telephoned him on the 7 March, as he had with Dutt and Singh, and told him to come to Delhi immediately, for he was leaving for a conference in the Philippines on the 10th and wanted the three sworn in before he left.

Bhagwati would serve another nine months as CJI but these March appointments were his last. He did send over two more lists but nothing came of them. His nominees were not explicitly rejected—they were simply ignored, left to wither on the vine. In May, he recommended M.H. Kania, the Bombay chief justice, K. Jagannatha Shetty, number two at Karnataka, and Sawant again. Why Kania and Jagannatha Shetty were not appointed is not clear. The poor relations between Bhagwati and Sen suggests that Bhagwati's determination to get Sawant on the Court may have been at least part of the explanation but Sen said that he assented to all three and then sent the names to the prime minister's office. Bhagwati said that the government was 'waiting for me to retire', and said that he believed that by repeatedly pressing for the appointment of Sawant he had 'poisoned the process'. Sawant was the one he wanted the most and he may have hoped that by recommending Kania, Sawant would be approved too. Kania, of course, was well aware that he was not Bhagwati's first choice from Bombay. Bhagwati had known him from their days at the Bombay bar and he had met Jagannatha Shetty during his visits to Bangalore. At this time there was a need for a Bombay judge, after the retirement of Chandrachud and of Tulzapurkar in March and Madon in April, that premier high court was without representation. All three on this list would later be appointed to the SCI after Bhagwati retired—Kania and Jagannatha Shetty were Pathak's first two appointees and Sawant reached the Court in 1989 when E.S. Venkataramiah was CJI.

In October 1986, Bhagwati sent over his fourth and final list. The three nominees were P.D. Desai, formerly of the Gujarat High Court but since 1983 the chief justice of the Himachal Pradesh High Court, S.S. Sandhawalia, formerly of the Punjab and Haryana High Court, but since 1983 the chief justice of the Patna High Court, and K.N. Saikia, the seniormost associate judge of the Gauhati High Court. Again there was no response from the government to any of these. Two months later Bhagwati retired.

Only five of the dozen recommended during Bhagwati's seventeen months were accepted. For a man who wanted to redefine the Court's mission and was eager to bring to Delhi men who either shared his goals or would not stand in the way, Bhagwati's inability to gain approval for his choices appointed was very disappointing. He told the author that his experience with the government concerning the appointment of judges was 'absurd and humiliating', and on the eve of his retirement he said: 'I cannot help saying that the non-appointment of Judges of the Supreme Court for several months has operated as an act of cruelty to the existing Judges who are carrying an intolerable burden. ...'[11]

Bhagwati only occasionally consulted with his colleagues about his choices. Pathak, who would follow him as CJI, was among those not consulted. As with all other CJIs, Bhagwati said there was no bargaining or horse-trading and that he was responsible for the appointments of all five. Only Narain was pressed on him by the government and only in this instance did Bhagwati exercise a veto.

Turning to the characteristics of the five appointees one is struck by how elderly they were. Collectively, they were older than any others appointed by any of Bhagwati's sixteen predecessors. All five were older than the norm and all were gone by late 1991. Three of the five were sixty or older, and the youngest, B.C. Ray, was just a month short of his fifty-ninth birthday. Their average age was 60.3 years. Bhagwati wanted to leave a mark on the Court with his appointments and the appointment of such elders did not contribute to that goal. In fairness, both Sawant and Desai were fifty-five when Bhagwati nominated them and there may have been other high court judges whom Bhagwati wanted but who were simply too junior to be recommended. None of the five was in line to become CJI though Mukharji's premature death resulted in Singh serving as CJI for sixteen days. Had Sawant been appointed in 1985, he would have been CJI from 1992 to 1995.

Partly reflecting their advanced ages, the five had accrued an average of 14.7 years of high court experience, ranging from Ray's eleven to Oza's seventeen—a figure higher than under any earlier CJI. Only Oza was a chief justice when appointed.

[11] 'Law Day Speech Delivered by Shri P.N. Bhagwati, Chief Justice of India, on November 26, 1986' (1987) 1 SCC, pp. 46–54, especially, p. 48.

In geographic terms, half the states were left without representation, and half of the fourteen judges were from Calcutta, Uttar Pradesh, and Madhya Pradesh. No earlier CJI had left a less geographically representative SCI.

All five were Hindus and these included one brahmin (Oza) and Ray from the Scheduled Castes. No effort was made to appoint a Muslim after Fazal Ali's death but Khalid was still on the Court. All five were Indian-educated advocates.

Bhagwati may have been the least successful CJI in getting his nominees approved. By this measure, his stewardship was a failed one. For the disagreements that began shortly after he became CJI—his refusal to agree to Narain and his intransigence concerning Sawant—Bhagwati, in his words, 'paid a heavy price'. When he left the SCI on 21 December 1986, of the twenty-six sanctioned judgeships, only fourteen were on board when the gavel was passed to Pathak.

77. Goverdhan Lal Jamnalal Oza (1985–9)

G.L. Oza was born on 12 December 1924 into an upper middle-class family in Ujjain, Ujjain district, in the princely state of Gwalior, presently in Madhya Pradesh. His father, Jamnalal Oza, was an accountant for a private company.[12]

Oza was both the first graduate and the first lawyer in his family. He received the BSc degree in physics, chemistry, and mathematics in 1946, and his LLB in 1948 from Holkar Science College,[13] Indore. In 1950, he earned an MA in political science from Christian College, also located in Indore. Beginning in his teenage years, he became very active in the freedom movement and missed a year of school when he went underground. Active in campus politics, he was elected president of the Ujjain Students Congress in 1942. In 1946–7, he served as president of the Students Congress in Indore.

He enrolled as an advocate of the Madhya Bharat High Court at Indore on 11 February 1949. After the reorganization of states in 1956 this court became a bench of the new Madhya Pradesh High Court. Oza spent twenty

---

[12] Interview with the author on 22 April 1988, in New Delhi.
[13] Later split into two separate colleges, Holkar College and Government Arts and Commerce College.

years in private practice at Indore, choosing not to shift his practice to Jabalpur, the headquarters location of the new high court. His practice was a diverse one and his clients ranged from the wealthy to the poor. But, in labour-management cases, he accepted only employee briefs and gained a reputation as a foe of industrial houses. One of the first proponents of legal aid in Madhya Pradesh, he founded the Legal Aid and Education Society in 1972.

During his years at the bar, he served as a part-time lecturer in law from 1965 to 1968 at the Government Arts and Commerce College. He served two terms as secretary of the Indore bar association in the 1960s and was elected the first secretary and later vice-president of the high court bar association. In 1954, he was one of the lawyers who appeared on behalf of the public before the Indore Firing Inquiry Commission.

Oza was very active in the Socialist Party during his years at the bar, and attended the Asian Socialist Conference at Rangoon in 1952. In the same year he contested a legislative assembly seat in as a Socialist Party candidate and was defeated by the Congress party candidate. During these years, he was also active in the trade union movement, both as a labour leader and as a lawyer providing free legal services to workers and tribals.

At age forty-three, he was sworn in as an additional judge of the Madhya Pradesh High Court on 19 July 1968. This appointment was to the Indore bench and this judgeship was made permanent on 19 December 1970. He remained at Indore, except for one year at Gwalior, until 1980 when he moved to Jabalpur. The practice in Madhya Pradesh then was that, upon becoming the most senior associate judge and in line for the chief justiceship, one came to Jabalpur if not already there.

On 3 January 1984, he became acting chief justice. By this time, the practice of having an outsider as chief justice of each high court was being implemented. He was to have been transferred to the Karnataka High Court as its chief justice but the transfer of its chief justice was delayed. After nearly a year as acting chief justice, he was confirmed as the permanent chief justice on 1 December.

Oza was sworn in at the SCI on 29 October 1985 when he was nearly sixty-one. With more than seventeen years of high court service, he ranked about third in all-India seniority. His tenure on the SCI ended when he turned sixty-five on 12 December 1989.

During his retirement years, he strove to improve legal education in Madhya Pradesh and, beginning in 1998, he headed the Geeta Bhawan Trust.

He died on 28 June 2001, at age seventy-six.

78. Bankim Chandra Ray (1985–91)

The second member of the Scheduled Caste community to reach the SCI, B.C. Ray was born on 1 November 1926 at Kanthalberia in the 24 Pargannas district of West Bengal. He was the son of Bhuson Chandra Ray, a zamindar with large landholdings. Though socially disadvantaged, his family can be described as relatively wealthy.[14]

Ray was the first university graduate in his family and the first to join the legal profession. When a youngster, he chose law after being inspired by two of Bengal's most eminent lawyers, Deshbandu Chittaranjan Das and Sir Rash Behari Ghosh. He received his BA in English from Ripon College, Calcutta in 1946. Illness delayed his legal education but in 1951 he received both the LLB from University Law College, Calcutta, and an MA in political economy from Calcutta University.

On 16 June 1952, he enrolled as an advocate of the Calcutta High Court and commenced his practice not only there but in the lower courts as well. During his student years he became a member of the Congress party and remained active in the Congress during his more than two decades of private practice. In 1955, when only twenty-nine, he was the Congress candidate for a West Bengal Legislative Assembly seat but was defeated by the Communist Party candidate. From 1953 to 1969, he served as chairman of the 24 Pargannas Cooperative Land Mortgage Bank and was a director of the West Bengal Cooperative Land Mortgage Bank.[15] He also held the post of secretary of the 24 Pargannas Red Cross.

After twenty-two years of private practice, and at age forty-seven Ray was appointed an additional judge of the Calcutta High Court on 10 June

[14] Interview with the author on 22 April 1988 in New Delhi and correspondence with his daughter, Dalia Ray, on 23 September 2009. In West Bengal, the distinction between Scheduled Caste and the OBC was so blurred that fellow Bengalis were uncertain whether he belonged to the OBC or Scheduled Caste community.

[15] Both banks were created by the Congress government to help the weaker sections, especially poor agriculturalists, and its officers were chosen by the Congress party.

1974. Although this appointment was continuous and he was confirmed as a permanent judge on 9 December 1976, there was some suspense about whether the latter would happen. The Emergency was on and twice he received three-month extensions as an additional judge. He was the first member of the Scheduled Caste community to be appointed to the Calcutta High Court.

Eleven years after joining the Calcutta bench, and three days before his fifty-ninth birthday, he was sworn in as an SCI judge on 29 October 1985. He was eighth in seniority at Calcutta but was the most senior of the few Scheduled Caste judges then serving on the high courts.

After he retired from the Court on 1 November 1991, he returned to Calcutta and engaged in chamber practice and served as an arbitrator.

He died on 7 September 2001, at age seventy-four.

79. Murari Mohan Dutt (1986–9)

M.M. Dutt was born on 30 October 1924 at Howrah, Howrah district in West Bengal. He was the son of Gour Mohan Dutt, an advocate who practised at the Calcutta High Court and who, for some time, was the secretary of the high court bar association. His grandfather was also an advocate of the high court but practised mainly at the Howrah district courts. Dutt's family can be described as upper middle-class.[16]

He earned a BSc in physics, chemistry, and mathematics from Vidyasagar College, Calcutta, in 1944. He aspired not to be a lawyer but to be accepted into one of the higher governmental services. Not successful in that pursuit, he was urged by his father to earn a law degree. Dutt received his LLB from Ripon Law College,[17] Calcutta, in 1948. Still not enthusiastic about a career as a lawyer, it was not until 29 January 1952, when he was twenty-seven, that he enrolled as an advocate of the Calcutta High Court. For the first few years he practised with his father. During his years at the bar, he was among the earliest promoters of legal aid.

Despite this rather late start, only seventeen years after commencing private practice, he was sworn in as an additional judge on 18 September

[16] Interview with the author on 24 April 1988, in New Delhi.
[17] Now Surendranath Law College.

1969, at age forty-four. Confirmation as a permanent judge came on 25 May 1971.

His major non-professional interest was the Boy Scouts movement. In the 1950s and 1960s, he served first as secretary and later Howrah district commissioner of the Bharat Scouts and Guides. Later he would serve as president of the West Bengal Fellowship of Former Scouts and Guides and as vice-president of the All-India Fellowship of Former Scouts and Guides.

He was sworn in at the SCI on 10 March 1986. Age sixty-one at this time, Dutt had completed more than sixteen years of service and was fourth in seniority on the Calcutta bench. His brief tenure on the SCI ended on 30 October 1989.

When the MCKV Institute of Engineering was established in 1999, he was appointed a member of its advisory board. He was also on the advisory board of the Bimal Chandra College of Law, Murshidabad, West Bengal.

80. Kamal Narain Singh (1986–91)

On 13 December 1926, K.N. Singh was born into a wealthy zamindari family in Chakdiha, a village in Allahabad district in Uttar Pradesh. His father, Deo Raj Singh, managed the family's extensive landholdings.[18] His family belongs to the same family tree as the Raja of Manda, V.P. Singh, who served as India's prime minister from 1989 to 1990.

K.N. Singh's family had no tradition of acquiring modern education and he was the first university and law graduate of the entire Raja of Manda clan. He earned his BA in English, Hindi literature, and history from Ewing Christian College, Allahabad in 1946. He considered a career in the military and was selected for both the Indian Air Force and Army. But at the urging of his father, who was frequently involved in property litigation, he turned to law. He enrolled in a combined LLB and MA degree programme at the University of Allahabad and received the former in1948 and the latter in diplomacy and international affairs in 1949. He then began work on an LLM but his studies ended when he was nominated by the Congress party to contest the district board election in Allahabad.

---

[18] Interview with the author on 3 September 1988 in New Delhi, and correspondence dated 26 October 2009.

Although he had joined the district bar as a pleader in 1950 he did not practise law until 1957. During the 1942 Quit India Movement, he was among those who clandestinely distributed prohibited political literature and was arrested twice and jailed briefly. He continued to be politically active during his college years, mainly in the rural parts of Allahabad district. As a Congress candidate, he was elected to the Allahabad district board and served from 1951 to 1958. During these years he held the office of chairman of the Public Works, Education and Public Health departments. In 1958, the district board was replaced by an interim zilla parishad he was a member until 1962. He also served on the district planning committee for the first two Five Year plans, was a director of the cooperative bank, was an elected member of the District Congress Committee, and took an active part in the first three national elections—as a campaigner, not as a candidate.

Singh did not begin practising law until he was thirty when he enrolled as an advocate of the Allahabad High Court, on 4 September 1957. He specialized in election law and represented mainly Congress politicians whose elections were challenged, or who were challenging the election of others. Among those he represented were Lal Bahadur Shastri, Dr Ram Manohar Lohia, Raj Narain, and Charan Singh.

On 28 January 1963, when he was appointed junior Standing Counsel for the Uttar Pradesh Government, his career in active politics ended. He was promoted to Senior Standing Counsel on 26 April 1967. In that year he was sounded about an appointment to the Allahabad High Court but was not eligible because he had not completed ten years at the bar. He was appointed Advocate General on 3 March 1970 but held that post only until 3 May 1970.

Three months later, on 25 August 1970 and after only thirteen years of law practice, he became an additional judge of the Allahabad High Court. Age forty-three at this time, he was the first Rajput ever appointed to this high court. His judgeship became permanent on 25 August 1972.

After more than fifteen years on the Allahabad bench he was sworn in as an SCI judge on 10 March 1986. Aged fifty-nine, he was third in seniority on the large Allahabad bench and was among the nation's most senior high court judges. Had he not been appointed to the SCI, he was in line to become chief justice at Allahabad but knew that he would be transferred to another high court.

He was not in line to become CJI because S. Mukharji's tenure was to have continued until 31 May 1992. Mukharji's death in 1990, however, meant that Singh would be the seniormost following R.N. Misra's retirement. He became CJI on 25 November 1991 and reached retirement age on 13 December, eighteen days later. No one earlier had a shorter stint as CJI.

On 1 January 1992, a few weeks after retiring, he was appointed chairman of the Thirteenth Law Commission and held that post until 1994. His major post-retirement activity was serving as president of the managing committee of the Udai Pratap College Educational Society in Varanasi, Uttar Pradesh. He served on the board of directors of the International Asset Reconstruction Company. He presided over a number of arbitration tribunals where questions of commercial law were involved and, in 2009, was president of the Non-Olympic Games Association of India. He engaged in some chamber practice and, an avid golfer, was elected President of the Delhi Golf Club.

81. Sivasankar Natarajan (1986–9)

S. Natarajan was born on 29 October 1924 at Salem, Salem district in Tamil Nadu. His was an affluent family, having been zamindars with large landholdings for several generations. Both his father, K. Sivasankar Mudaliar, and his grandfather were college graduates but spent their lives managing their properties. His great-grandfather was a lawyer who practised in Salem. Natarajan married into a family that was prominent in Tamil Nadu's political life. His father-in-law, P.T. Rajan, was a well known barrister, a leading figure in the Justice Party, and a cabinet minister during much of the 1930s in the Madras Presidency. His wife's uncle, M. Bakthavatsalam, was a minister from 1947 to 1965 and chief minister from 1965 to 1967.[19]

His childhood dream was to be a physician but he lacked the prerequisites for medical college admission. He received a BA in economics from Loyola College, Madras, in 1943, and the BL from the Madras Law College in 1946. He enrolled as an advocate of the Madras High Court on 4 August 1947. His practice, however, was almost entirely at the Salem district court so that he could help his father manage the family's properties.

In 1959, he was appointed additional public prosecutor at Salem and held that post until 1965. In mid-career, and after eighteen years of practice

---

[19] Interview with the author on 24 April 1988 in New Delhi and correspondence dated 21 August 2009.

at Salem, he was appointed a district and sessions judge (grade II)[20] on 2 September 1965. He joined judicial service largely to fulfil his father's dream that he become a judge. Age forty at this time, he was first posted at Coimbatore. After his promotion to principal judge in 1968 he headed the Annamalai Bus Disaster Inquiry Commission in 1968–9. In September 1969, he was transferred to Madras city as chief presidency magistrate and, on 18 December 1971, was promoted to a grade I district and sessions judge.

Natarajan was appointed an additional judge of the Madras High Court on 15 February 1973 when he was forty-eight and became a permanent judge on 27 February 1974. He would spend thirteen years on the Madras bench. He became well known for his legal aid initiatives and, during his last four years on the bench, was the advisor to the Legal Aid Society.

During his years as a lawyer and a judge in Tamil Nadu, he was active in a wide variety of organizations. In 1980, he became chairman of the board of trustees of Ethiraj College for Women and served in that capacity for the next eighteen years. He was also president of the Madras Cosmopolitan Club; president of the Indian Officers Association; chairman of the board of studies for the MA in Criminology at Madras University; member of the boards of legal studies at Bharathiar University in Coimbatore and Bharati Dasan University in Tiruchirapalli; vice-president of both the Tchaikovsky Music Club and the Madras Music Academy; and president of the Tamil Nadu branch of the Indian Council for Social Welfare. He was also very active in the Masons and, in the late 1980s, was the deputy grandmaster for India.

When he was sworn in at the SCI on 10 March 1986, he was sixty-one and third in seniority on the Madras bench.

Shortly after his arrival in Delhi, he was asked by CJI Pathak to co-chair with his senior colleague M.P. Thakkar what is known as the Thakkar–Natarajan or Fairfax Commission. Their charge was to investigate the employment of an American company by the Finance Ministry, headed at the time by V.P. Singh, to look into the financial dealings of Indian nationals abroad. When their report[21] was made public in December 1987, it generated a great deal of criticism and controversy.

[20] This rank was used in Tamil Nadu and was comparable to additional district and session judge elsewhere.

[21] *Report of the Justices Thakkar-Natarajan Commission of Inquiry: Inquiry into Utilization of the Fairfax Group Inc.* (New Delhi: Ministry of Finance, 1987).

As his retirement age drew near, the then CJI, E.S. Venkataramiah, anguished over the fact that about 3,000 cases filed before 1975 had not been heard or disposed of, sought government approval for the extensions under the terms of Article 128 of Natarajan, G.L. Oza, and M.M. Dutt, the latter two being on the cusp of retirement as well. His proposal was that these three would sit as a separate bench and dispose of these old cases. The government took no action on this recommendation.

After retiring on 29 October 1989, he returned to Chennai and for years conducted arbitrations and often participated in conferences and seminars relating to law. He was also closely involved with a number of religious and charitable public trusts. He devoted a great deal of time to managing the affairs of the Ethiraj College, the results of which included increasing the stature of the college and nearly tripling its enrolment.

Following a dispute regarding an election of the president of the Indian Olympic Association, the SCI ordered fresh elections. Pending the election, Natarajan was himself appointed by the Madras High Court and confirmed by the SCI to be the interim president of the association. After holding that office for several months, he and another retired SCI judge, A.D. Koshal, supervised the holding of fresh elections and the dispute was resolved.

Another unusual activity was his appointment by the SCI as chairman of the management committee of the Tamilnadu Department of Racing. The state government had passed legislation abolishing horse racing on the ground that racing activity was a game of chance. He held that position for nearly four years, until the SCI ruled that racing was a game of skill and the race club was returned to private hands. In 2010, he was serving as chairman of the board of directors of Nippo Batteries Co. Ltd.

XVIII

The Pathak Court (1986–9)

Twenty-four years after becoming a judge of the Allahabad High Court and after nearly nine years of experience on the SCI, the government announced, on 13 November, that the sixty-two-year-old R.S. Pathak would become the nation's eighteenth CJI on 21 December 1986. A man with a regal bearing and a mild temperament, his personality and style were quite different from his predecessor. Philosophically, he was a man of the middle and several of his colleagues would later volunteer the compliment that he brought relative peace to the SCI.[1]

He inherited a Court comprised of just fourteen judges, including him. Thus, there were a dozen vacancies. If both Pathak and the government were of a mind to bring the Court up to full strength and were able to agree on the fresh appointments, his tenure could have witnessed more personnel changes than any of his predecessors. Rajiv Gandhi was the Prime Minister; and Pathak dealt with four different law ministers—A.K. Sen, P. Shiv Shankar holding dual portfolio, Bindeshwari Dubey, and B. Shankaranand.

There were five retirements during his tenure: V. Balakrishna Eradi (June 1987), V. Khalid (July 1987), O. Chinnappa Reddy (September 1987), A.P. Sen (September 1988), and M.P. Thakkar (November 1988).

---

[1] Unless otherwise indicated, most of the material has come from interviews with Pathak on 1 October and 22 December 1988 in New Delhi, and with all except Verma of the dozen appointed during his tenure.

The first two Pathak appointees, sworn in on 1 May 1987, were M.H. Kania, the chief justice of the Bombay High Court, and K. Jagannatha Shetty of Karnataka, whose path to the SCI included a brief stopover in Allahabad as chief justice. Both had been nominated by Bhagwati a year earlier. Neither was rejected—the government simply did not respond. Bhagwati had not consulted with Pathak about these men. Shortly after becoming CJI Pathak, during a visit to Bombay, secured Kania's consent to be nominated and during a visit to Allahabad, secured Jagannatha Shetty's consent. He then resubmitted both names in early 1987 and they were quickly approved. Bhagwati's failure to secure government agreement was not caused by questions about the merit of these men but probably because Bhagwati nominated them and they were part of a package that included P.B. Sawant. Because their nominations were effectively dead when Pathak became CJI, their appointments must be credited to him.

Kania was fifty-nine and with more than seventeen years on the Bombay bench, near the top of the all-India seniority list. With no one from Bombay on the SCI since the retirements of Chandrachud and Tulzapurkar, a major reason for the Kania appointment was to re-establish Bombay representation.

Jagannatha Shetty, also very senior with nearly seventeen years of high court service, was sixty when appointed. For the first time Karnataka had two representatives on the Court.

Five months later, the trio of L.M. Sharma of Patna, M.N.R. Venkatachaliah of Karnataka, and S. Ranganathan of Delhi, all choices of Pathak, was sworn in on 5 October 1987. Sharma was fifty-nine and second in seniority at Patna after fourteen years on the bench. He became aware of the possibility of promotion to the SCI in May when Pathak, who had never met him, called to seek his consent. In mid-September, he received a call from Law Minister Shiv Shankar informing him that upon Pathak's recommendation his appointment had been approved. Thus, the large Patna High Court was represented on the SCI for the first time since N.L. Untwalia's retirement in 1980 and only for the second time since Vaidyanathier Ramaswami in the 1960s.

In July, Pathak, who had earlier met Venkatachaliah in Bangalore, telephoned him to inquire about his willingness to accept a judgeship. Word that he had been approved came in September, this time from Pathak himself. Venkatachaliah was fifty-seven and after a dozen years on the Karnataka bench was third in seniority. Unusual about this appointment was that only five months earlier his Karnataka colleague Jagannatha Shetty had joined the Court, and another former colleague, E.S. Venkataramiah, was on the SCI as well.

Ranganathan was the first to reach the SCI from the Delhi High Court since Khanna in 1971. There had been efforts to promote other Delhi High Court judges during the previous decade. Chandrachud, in 1979, had tried to get V.S. Deshpande. In 1985, the government was unsuccessful in gaining Bhagwati's approval of Prakash Narain and earlier, in 1987, Pathak had failed to gain government agreement for his nomination of T.P.S. Chawla. According to both Pathak and Ranganathan, his decision in the Mrs Gandhi assassination case was not, as believed by many, a selection factor. More important was that the Court needed income tax expertise and Ranganathan had lengthy experience in that area. Pathak and Ranganathan were not well-acquainted and prior to the announcement of his appointment neither Pathak nor the law ministry had sought his consent. Official word of his appointment came from the secretary of the Department of Law, Justice and Company Affairs. When he joined the SCI he was fifty-nine, had been on the bench for a decade, and was third in seniority.

Next to arrive on the Court was N.D. Ojha, Pathak's former Allahabad colleague who had accrued sixteen years of high court experience and was then the chief justice of the Madhya Pradesh High Court. Pathak had secured Ojha's consent in October 1987 and he became an SCI judge on 18 January 1988. Ojha was sworn in at Pathak's residence, literally just two hours before his sixty-second birthday. The warrant of his appointment had been issued only earlier that day. Ojha rushed to Delhi from Jabalpur for a break in service would have reduced his pension. Ojha may not have been Pathak's first choice for earlier he had recommended H.N. Sheth, who had been the Allahabad chief justice until his transfer to the Punjab and Haryana High Court in 1986. It was after the Sheth nomination failed to win government approval that the invitation was extended to Ojha. His appointment meant that for the first time India's largest state had three representatives on the SCI.

Nominated around this same time was Chittatosh Mookerjee who, after a year as chief justice at Calcutta, had become the Bombay chief justice in late 1987. He was from a prominent Bengali family—his forebears included Sir Asutosh Mukherjea who had served on the Calcutta High Court at the beginning of the century. Pathak was eager to have him, but there were already three Bengalis on the court.

Nearly a year would pass before the next appointments.[2] Ojha's arrival had brought the Court's strength up to seventeen but it was reduced to fifteen after the retirements of A.P. Sen and Thakkar. In April, after consulting both A.P. Sen and Venkataramiah, his two most senior colleagues, as he regularly did, Pathak sent over the names of four nominees and recommended another four in July. Other names were advanced by Shankaranand who had become the law minister in June. Months of difficult discussions and negotiations followed until agreement was reached on five men. Pathak was eager to have N.P. Singh from Patna appointed as well, and sworn in first, which would have given him about two years as CJI, but the government would not have him.[3]

This quintet was sworn in on 14 December 1988, and was the largest and most demographically diverse group ever to join the Court on the same day. S.R. Pandian, the acting chief justice at Madras, and retired Gauhati Chief Justice K.N. Saikia, were the first two from Backward Classes communities to reach the SCI. The others were T.K. Thommen, a Christian and number two at Kerala; A.M. Ahmadi, a Bohra Muslim and second in seniority on the Gujarat High Court; and Kuldip Singh, the second Sikh to serve on the Court and who at this time was an additional solicitor-general of India.

Sworn in first was Pandian, fifty-nine and after nearly fifteen years on the Madras bench the most senior of the five. Most significant about his appointment was that he was the first of the OBC population to reach the SCI. Pathak had met him in Madras earlier in the year. Rumours of his appointment began circulating in July but neither Pathak nor Shankaranand contacted him to gain his consent. Only in early December was his promotion announced. According to Pathak, he was the initiator, believing that it was time for the Backward Classes to be represented. There likely was enthusiastic support from Shankaranand, a member of the Scheduled Caste community, who was known to be eager to see representatives of the weaker sections appointed. Before Pathak recommended Pandian, he

---

[2] Exasperated by appointment delays caused by the government, in November 1988, a bench of R.N. Misra and Venkatachaliah set a 7 December deadline for filling SCI and high court vacancies. They stated that if this was not done, 'the entire record about such recommendations be submitted to the court for its scrutiny'. Quoted from 'Govt told to appoint judges by Dec. 7', *The Times of India*, 18 November 1988. See also, the editorial 'Justly incensed' in the *Indian Express*, 21 November 1988.

[3] He was ultimately appointed to the SCI in 1992.

solicited the views of the then Tamil Nadu governor, P.C. Alexander, and received a favourable assessment.

Thommen first learned of the possibility of an SCI appointment fully eighteen months earlier when Pathak sought his consent. But Pathak's recommendation bore no fruit at that time. Pathak then sounded V.S. Malimath, formerly the chief justice at Karnataka but since 1985 the Kerala chief justice. Malimath, however, declined the invitation, possibly because two of his Karnataka juniors, Venkataramiah and Jagannatha Shetty, were already on the Court. In July 1988, Pathak again recommended Thommen, whose strong academic credentials appealed to him and this time the nomination cleared. This appointment served two purposes: Kerala had been unrepresented since V. Balakrishna Eradi retired a year earlier and the Christian community was now represented again. The sixty-year-old Thommen had been on the Kerala bench for nearly fourteen years.

A.M. Ahmadi's nomination was pressed strongly by Thakkar, his recently retired former Gujarat colleague who wielded a good deal of influence in government circles. The Court needed both a Muslim and a Gujarat judge. There had not been a Muslim since Khalid's retirement eighteen months earlier—the longest stretch ever without Muslim representation. And the Gujarat representation had fallen from three to none following Thakkar's retirement. Of the twenty-two Muslim judges on the high courts at this time, the fifty-six-year-old Ahmadi was second in seniority only to Syed Sarwar Ali of Patna, and he had indicated a few years earlier that he was not interested in coming to Delhi. Pathak had earlier met Ahmadi in Gujarat but no communication between these two preceded Ahmadi's swearing in. He learned of his appointment from Shankaranand. Ahmadi had served a dozen years on the Gujarat bench.

In 1986, according to K.N. Saikia, Bhagwati told him that he was being recommended but nothing came of this. In 1987, he was nominated by Pathak but was dropped by the government without explanation. In both these instances, a reason may have been that Saikia had been a Janata Party candidate in the 1977 Assam Legislative Assembly elections. In July 1988, Saikia was again nominated by Pathak and this time his nomination was cleared. Pathak was not the only one involved in Saikia's appointment. S.S. Ray, who had known Saikia from their Calcutta days, claimed some credit.[4] Also, he may have been aided by the 1988 selection milieu, particularly with

---

[4] Interview with the author on 21 November 1994 in Lexington, Kentucky, USA.

Shankaranand now the law minister. Saikia was a member of the Backward Class-designated Ahom community. Helpful also was the fact that he was from the Northeast which had been unrepresented since Islam's resignation in 1983. Saikia had been on the Gauhati court for nearly a decade and at the time he was sworn in, he was nearly sixty-three years old—the eldest ever appointed to the SCI.

Pathak secured Kuldip Singh's consent to be nominated in August. These two had known each other for nearly two decades; when Pathak was the chief justice at Himachal Pradesh, Singh appeared often in that court. Pathak and Singh acknowledged that Singh's nomination was initiated by the governor of Punjab, S.S. Ray. He also had strong support as well from Buta Singh, the then union home minister. Two salient considerations in Singh's selection were that there had not been a Sikh on the Court since R.S. Sarkaria retired in 1981 and there had not been a Punjabi since A.D. Koshal retired in 1982. Singh was only the third advocate to accept an invitation to become an SCI judge. In agreeing to accept the offer, he was concerned about the swearing-in order for he wanted to become CJI. The earlier two direct-from-the bar appointees (S.M. Sikri and S.C. Roy) were in line to become CJI. Singh and Ahmadi were both fifty-six and the one sworn in first would have nearly three years as CJI. Pathak told Singh that he would recommend that he be sworn in before of Ahmadi. The government, however, did not accept Pathak's recommendation and Singh learned shortly before the swearing-in day that Ahmadi would be listed ahead of him. He considered withdrawing because he believed his claim was stronger than Ahmadi's. Later Singh would say publicly that 'I was perturbed [but] friends like S.S. Ray persuaded me ... to join the Court anyway'.[5]

The final appointee of the Pathak era was J.S. Verma, the chief justice of the Rajasthan High Court since 1986, after having been transferred from the Madhya Pradesh High Court. Pathak had secured his consent in December 1988 and on 3 June 1989, just two weeks before Pathak resigned, Verma was sworn in. Aged fifty-six and with close to seventeen years of high court experience, he was among the most senior judges in the country.

As noted earlier, Pathak had inherited a Court composed of only fourteen judges, himself included, five of whom retired during his tenure. The twelve new appointees brought the strength up to twenty. At least five

[5] 'More Than a Green Judge', *Outlook India*, 22 January 1997, online at www.OutlookIndia.com, and interview with the author on 1 January 1989.

of his nominees failed to gain government approval and some of the names advanced by the law minister were not acceptable to him. But according to Pathak, there was no horse-trading. Shiv Shankar once suggested 'let's marry our two lists', but Pathak refused such quid pro quo proposals.

Neither side found it necessary to exercise a veto but each had to make compromises, particularly before agreement was reached over the five December 1988 appointees. No reasons were given when a Pathak nominee was not accepted by the government. He was asked simply to 'suggest another name'. But Pathak said that none appointed during his years at the helm were appointed without his approval.

Of the four law ministers during his tenure, Shiv Shankar, according to Pathak, was the most difficult with whom to negotiate. That Shiv Shankar was very unhappy with the composition of the SCI, some members of which had been appointed during his own tenure as law minister, could not have been expressed more emphatically and colourfully than when, in late 1987, he complained publicly that the SCI was 'composed of elements from the elite class [with] unconcealed sympathy for the haves, i.e., zamindars [and that the] anti-social elements, that is, Foreign Exchange Regulation Act violators, bride-burners and a whole horde of reactionaries have found their haven in the Supreme Court'.[6]

Pathak bequeathed a geographically diverse SCI to incoming CJI E.S. Venkataramiah. The twenty on the bench, as he left, represented thirteen of the eighteen high courts, the most noticeably unrepresented being the Andhra Pradesh High Court, for Chinnappa Reddy had not been replaced. In regional terms, his appointees included five from the south (this includes Ranganathan who, though he came from the Delhi High Court, was a Tamilian), three from the west, and two from both the north and the east.

The average and median age of these men was an above the norm 59.4 years. High court seniority continued to be a major selection criterion. Five had served as high court chief justices and a sixth was an acting chief justice. No one lower than third in seniority was among the other half dozen and

---

[6] 'Contempt Notice to Shiv Shankar', *The Times of India*, 11 February 1988. This outburst led to a contempt citation but he was not found guilty by the SCI. See *P.N. Duda v. P. Shiv Shankar*, AIR 1988 SC 1208. Recall that two decades earlier the chief minister of Kerala, E.M.S. Namboodiripad, was found guilty of contempt for saying something very similar. *AIR* 1970 SC 2016. See also A.G. Noorani, 'Courts and Contempt Power', *Frontline*, vol. 17, issue 8, 15–28 April 2000.

their average length of high court service was fourteen years, more than the norm.

Diversity of religious affiliation also characterized these men—the second Sikh, the ninth Muslim, and the third Christian were among them.

In caste terms, the appointment of the first two OBC representatives was significant. At the other end of the social spectrum four brahmins were appointed and these (Sharma, Venkatachaliah, Ranganathan, and Ojha) were consecutive appointments over a four-month period.

Pathak resigned on 18 June 1989, six months before his sixty-fifth birthday. After the death of International Court of Justice Judge Nagendra Singh, the government succeeded in filling the remainder of his term with another Indian. Pathak took his seat at The Hague in July.

The fact that a dozen judges were appointed during his two and a half years as CJI was a significant accomplishment. Five of them—Kania, Sharma, Venkatachaliah, Ahmadi, and Verma—would serve as CJIs during the 1991–8 years.

82. Madhukar Hiralal Kania (1987–92)

A nephew of Harilal J. Kania, India's first CJI, M.H. Kania was born on 18 November 1927 in an upper middle-class family in Bombay. His father, Hiralal J. Kania, was a lawyer who practised at both the Bombay's High Court and small causes court. Although born and raised in Bombay, Kania continued to identify himself as a Gujarati and that is the language his family considered its native tongue.[7]

Majoring in economics he earned a BA (honours) degree from Elphinstone College, Bombay, in 1947. He had considered entering an occupation where his economics training could be used but opportunities were limited and the salaries low. He became a lawyer because that was the family tradition. He received an LLB from Government Law College, Bombay in 1949. Having finished among the top four in his class, he was named a fellow of Government Law College for the 1949–50 year.

He enrolled as an advocate of the Bombay High Court on 1 November 1949 at age twenty-one. From 1956 to 1962, in part to earn extra income during the lean early years at the bar, he taught part-time at the Government

[7] Interview with the author on 23 April 1988, in New Delhi.

Law College. He practised at both the high court and the Bombay city civil court, appearing often for Maharashtra state in the latter. From 5 December 1964 to 15 January 1967, he was assistant government pleader in the city civil court and was government pleader in the same court from 16 January 1967 to 3 November 1969.

After twenty years at the bar, on 4 November 1969 and at age forty-one, Kania was sworn in as an additional judge of the Bombay High Court and was confirmed as a permanent judge on 2 November 1971. During his high court tenure, he served on an advisory board dealing with drug offenders and bootleggers constituted by the state government. From 1985 to 1987, he was chairman of the managing committee of the Ramji Girls High School. During the Emergency he participated with D.P. Madon in *Binod Rao v. Minocher Rustom Masani*,[8] which struck down as unconstitutional the censorship of free speech, remembered as one of the boldest high court decisions of that period.

After sixteen years on the Bombay bench, he was named acting chief justice on 21 October 1985 and was confirmed as chief justice on 23 June 1986. He was sworn in as an SCI judge on 1 May 1987. Age fifty-nine at this time and with more than seventeen years of high court service, he was among the most senior judges in the country. During his SCI tenure he served as chairman of the Income-Tax Tribunal Selection Committee.

He was in the queue to become CJI for six months following Mukharji's retirement on 31 May 1992. The latter's death, however, resulted in his becoming the twenty-third CJI on 13 December 1991 and he held that post for eleven months until he reached retirement age on 18 November 1992.

He returned to Bombay and engaged in chamber practice and served as an arbitrator. In March 2002, he was named by the Securities and Exchange Board as chairman of a committee to facilitate the process of corporatization and demutualization and to advise on the consolidation and merger of the stock exchanges. Two years later, he was appointed chairman of an 'expert group' charged with the task of suggesting improvements to the Securities and Exchange Board of India Act, 1992. Both reports resulted in significant changes in the stock exchanges.

He was also among the retired SCI judges who served on the advisory board of the Indian Legal Information Institute. He was a member of the

---

[8] (1976) 78 *Bombay Law Reporter* 125.

panel of arbitrators of the Indian Merchant Chamber and a member of the board of trustees of the Deutsche Trustee Services India Pvt. Ltd.

83. Kalmanje Jagannatha Shetty (1987–91)

K. Jagannatha Shetty was born on 15 December 1926 at Ambalapady, a small hamlet located in what is now the Udupi town and district of Karnataka.[9] He was the son of A. Boodha Shetty, an agriculturist who owned a small amount of land. By the standards of the day the family was of modest means.

He was both the first lawyer and first university graduate in his family. He earned a BSc in chemistry from St. Aloysius College in Mangalore in 1951. As a youngster, he aspired for a career as a mining engineer but he was unable to secure a seat in an engineering institute. He then turned to law, went to Hyderabad where he had a friend who helped him financially, and received an LLB from the Government Law College of Osmania University in 1954.

He was twenty-seven when he started practising law as a pleader in the then Part B High Court of Hyderabad on 14 July 1954, and on 16 August 1955 became an advocate of this court. During his first two years of practice he pursued the LLM degree, receiving it in 1956 from Osmania University.

After the reorganization of states in 1956, he was twenty-nine when he relocated to Bangalore and enrolled as an advocate of the Mysore High Court. After just fourteen years in Bangalore and at age forty-three, very early given his late start, he was appointed an additional judge of the Mysore High Court on 25 June 1970. This judgeship was made permanent on 10 February 1971.

During his years in private practice he served as a part-time professor of law for both the LLB and ML programmes from 1962 to 1970 at the Government Law College in Bangalore. He also was elected twice as a member of the state bar council and served from 1961 to 1970. Preferring the freedom of private practice, he declined an invitation to become a senior government advocate. Upon joining the high court bench, he severed all ties with off-the-bench activities, choosing a cloistered lifestyle. A believer in

---

[9] Formerly the South Kanara district, it also produced Sir Benegal N. Rao and K.S. Hegde.

the old-school definition of how judges should live, he said it 'was best to live like a hermit and work like a horse'.[10]

He ultimately served more than sixteen years on the Bangalore bench. Although not in line for the chief justiceship, when he was the seniormost associate judge and after V.S. Malimath's transfer to Kerala, he was named the acting chief justice on 25 October 1985. He remained in that status until 27 August 1986 when P.C. Jain of the Punjab and Haryana High Court was transferred to Karnataka as the permanent chief justice, meaning that he returned to the number two position. As per the prevailing practice at that time, he was transferred—to the Allahabad High Court in this instance—as its chief justice, effective 1 October 1986.

He was pleased to be transferred. Language was not a problem, for he had become proficient in Urdu and Hindi during his Hyderabad years. He quickly earned the respect of the Allahabad bar, was very happy there, and felt fortunate to have had that experience.

His sojourn at Allahabad was brief, for he was sworn in as an SCI judge on 1 May 1987 at age sixty. He reached retirement age on 15 December 1991.

He returned to Bangalore where he engaged in chamber practice and conducted arbitrations. He was among the retired judges who served as an arbitrator of the Indian Council of Arbitration. In 1992, he became the chairman of the Karnataka State Fourth Pay Commission for state government employees. His report was submitted in July 1993. In March 1996, he accepted the union law ministry's invitation to become chairman of the first National Judicial Pay Commission. His 'Shetty Commission Report' was submitted in November 1999. It attracted national attention because of its recommendation of a uniform pay structure for subordinate judicial officers throughout the country. During the course of this commission's work, the SCI directed him to examine the service conditions of the court staffs in each state. That report was submitted in 2003. The SCI directed that the recommendations, with some modifications, of both reports be implemented.[11]

He then returned to Bangalore where he resumed chamber practice and served as arbitrator in both domestic and international disputes.

---

[10] Interview with the author on 25 April 1988, in New Delhi, and correspondence dated 14 August 2009.

[11] All India Judges' Association v. Union of India (2002) 4 SCC 247.

84. Lalit Mohan Sharma (1987–93)

L.M. Sharma was born on 12 February 1928 at Gaya in the Gaya district of Bihar. He was the son of Lal Narayan Sinha, one of the nation's most prominent lawyers. He held the posts of Advocate General of Bihar, was Solicitor General of India from 1972 to 1977, was India's Attorney General from 1979 to 1983, and constitutional advisor to Prime Minister Rajiv Gandhi in the mid-1980s. Twice he declined an invitation to become an SCI judge. During British rule, three times he applied to become a munsif but the British refused to appoint him because he and his family members were active in the Indian National Congress.

Sharma grew up in an upper middle-class family and represented the third generation in the legal profession. Both his paternal and maternal grandfathers were lawyers.[12] He received a BA (honours) in mathematics from Patna College, Patna University in 1946. He had aspired to become a teacher of mathematics but his paternal grandfather persuaded him that the family tradition was law. He was only twenty years of age when he received his BL from Patna Law College in 1948.

After an apprenticeship year working with his paternal grandfather at the Gaya district court, he enrolled as an advocate of the Patna High Court on 6 February 1950 and commenced practice there with his father. During his Patna years, he was invited to become a Standing Counsel but declined because his father was the Advocate General.

After twenty-three years of private practice, he was offered a Patna High Court judgeship. His father, then Solicitor General of India, had declined a similar offer in the late 1940s and advised his son to remain in private practice, but Sharma was persuaded by his paternal grandfather to accept the invitation. On 12 April 1973, at age forty-five, he was sworn in as an additional judge. Confirmation as a permanent judge came on 1 January 1974.

After more than fourteen years on the Patna bench, by which time he was fifty-nine and second in seniority, he was sworn in as an SCI judge on 5 October 1987. On 18 November 1992, he became the twenty-fourth CJI. He served but three months until his own sixty-fifth birthday on 12 February 1993.

He was eighty when he died on 3 November 2008.

[12] Interview with the author on 24 April 1988, in New Delhi.

85. Manepalle Narayana Rao Venkatachaliah (1987–94)

M.N.R. Venkatachaliah was born into a prosperous family in Bangalore, Karnataka, on 25 October 1929. He was the son of Manepalle Narayana Rao, who early in his career was a teacher of philosophy, later a lawyer who practised at the Mysore High Court, and who was also the first principal of the Government Law College, Bangalore. Venkatachaliah's maternal grandfather, Balapur Subbanna, was also in the law profession and served as a judge of the Mysore High Court.[13]

He earned a BSc in natural science from Central College, Bangalore in 1948. He had considered a career in the Indian Administrative Service but the family tradition was law and, as the eldest son, he felt obliged to join that profession. When he received his BL from Government Law College, Bangalore in 1951, he stood first in the law examinations. A voracious reader throughout his life, he was at home in the sciences, the world's literature, psychology, and particularly English and American law.

He enrolled as a pleader in 1951, and practised in the Bangalore district courts for a year. On 7 July 1952, at age twenty-two, he enrolled as an advocate of the Mysore High Court, practising at first with his father. Ultimately he would spend twenty-four years in private practice, mostly in the city courts of Bangalore but with a noteworthy high court practice as well. During his years at the bar, he and his friend E.S. Venkataramiah can be credited with the establishment of the B.M.S. Law College. He served as a trustee of the B.M.S. Education Trust and, at various times, was a part-time professor at the college.

He was forty-six when he accepted appointment as a permanent judge of the Karnataka High Court on 6 November 1975. He did so reluctantly because he was unsure that he could be the type of judge he visualized—that he couldn't 'fill the bill'. Upon becoming a judge, believing that judges should live cloistered lives, he severed all ties with educational, cultural, and other institutions. Although asked to serve on commissions of inquiry, he declined, believing these were inappropriate for a sitting judge. While on the Karnataka bench, he initiated a series of innovative training courses for new members of the subordinate judiciary and refresher courses for veteran judges.

[13] Interview with the author on 1 September 1988, in New Delhi, and correspondence dated 9 September 2009.

After nearly a dozen years on the high court and when he was third in seniority, he was sworn at Delhi in on 5 October 1987 at age fifty-seven. On 12 February 1993, he became the twenty-fifth CJI. During his twenty-month tenure—he reached retirement age on 25 October 1994—he was successful in introducing many changes, including extending the Court's working hours, streamlining the listing of cases, connecting the SCI registry to a national computer network which enabled lower court judges to be aware of the status of cases, and taking steps to introduce a code of conduct for judges.

Having earned the reputation as one of the most distinguished SCI judges of his generation, he was asked to serve in important capacities after retirement. From November 1996 to October 1999, he held the post of chairman of the National Human Rights Commission and, from 2000 to 2002, he was chairman of the National Commission to Review the Working of the Constitution.[14] He served in the latter capacity for a token salary of one rupee per month, having chosen to forego the Rs 33,000 monthly salary provided for in the legislation.

He served as chairman of the ethics committee of the Centre of Psycho-Oncology for Education and Research. He was the founder of both the Society for Religious Harmony and Universal Peace, and the Sarvodaya International Trust. He was instrumental in the creation of the Centre for Standards in Public Life in Bangalore. He chaired the panel which chose the winner of the National Award for Excellence in Corporate Governance and was honorary chairman of the advisory board of the Institute of Company Secretaries of India Centre for Corporate Research. He helped launch the Initiatives for Change Centre for Governance in 2003. In 2005, he served as chancellor of the Central University of Hyderabad. His Tagore Law Lecture was published under the title of *Some Makers of Indian Law*. He was a contributor and member of the editorial advisory board for the 2008 reissue of *Halsbury's Laws of India*.

He served as chairman of the governing council of the Peepal Grove School in Andhra Pradesh, of the selection committee for the Ministry of Human Resources Development awards to scholars of Sanskrit, Pali/Prakit, Arabic, and Persian, and of the panel of judges to select the Nani A. Palkhivala Award for Civil Liberties.

Among the honours he received was an LLD (*honoris causa*) from H.N.B. Garhwal University in 2005. He was the recipient of the first Rotary India

---

[14] *Report of the National Commission to Review the Working of the Constitution*, 2 vols (Delhi: Controller of Publications, 2002).

Award on Human Rights in 2000. The Indian Institute of Arbitration and Mediation and the Hamline University School of Law (USA) annually awards the 'Chief Justice M.N. Venkatachaliah' trophy. He was among the few who have been named a distinguished fellow of the Indian Law Institute. The many contributions to his country by this self-effacing man were recognized in 2004 when he was awarded the Padma Vibhushan, the nation's second highest civilian award.

86. Srinivasachari Ranganathan (1987–92)

On 31 October 1927, S. Ranganathan was born in the city of Madras into a well-to-do family of professionals. He was the son of R. Srinivasa Chari who was an engineer in government service, and the grandson of a professor at the Madras Law College.[15]

He earned his BA (honours) in mathematics from Presidency College, Madras, in 1947, and his BL from the Madras Law College in 1949. In 1953, he received the ML degree from the University of Madras and was the recipient of the Sri Lakshmi Narasa Reddy Gold Medal.

On 21 July 1952, at the age of twenty-four, he enrolled as an advocate of the Madras High Court. Two years later, on 1 October 1954, he was appointed Junior Standing Counsel to the Commissioner of Income Tax, Madras, the first step in a career as an income tax specialist. In 1960, he was promoted to Senior Standing Counsel and held that title until 24 February 1964 when he was appointed as a judicial member of the Income Tax Appellate Tribunal. He was confirmed in that post on 4 August 1967. He was posted first in New Delhi, and then Hyderabad (1964–7), Calcutta (1967–9), Delhi again (1969–74), Madras (1975), and, finally, Delhi again (1976–7). He was vice-president of the southern and northern zones of this tribunal from 1975 to 1976 and president from 1976 to 1977.

Ranganathan was appointed an additional judge of the Delhi High Court on 14 November 1977 at age fifty, and this judgeship was made permanent on 19 March 1978.

A decade later, when he was fifty-nine and third in seniority, he was sworn in as an SCI judge on 5 October 1987. Having spent much of his

---

[15] Interview with the author on 24 October 1988, in New Delhi and correspondence dated 16 and 26 October 2009.

career associated with income tax tribunals, his path to the SCI was unlike any previous appointee.

Early in his career he was associated with the seventh revised edition of V.S. Sundaram's *Commentaries of the Law of Income-Tax in India* (Madras: Madras Law Journal Office, 1954). He was the author of *Corporate Taxation in India* (New Delhi: Documentation Centre for Corporate & Business Policy Research, 1983). He was the editor of the seventh (1981) and eighth (1990) revisions of A.C. Sampath Iyengar's *Commentary on the Income-Tax Act* (New Delhi: Bharat Law House). Published in 1999 were his *Megha-Dutam and Shri Hamsa Sandeshah: A Parallel Study* (Mumbai: Bharatiya Vidya Bhavan), and *Constitution of India: Five Decades, 1950–1999* (New Delhi: Bharat Law House).

Following his retirement from the SCI on 31 October 1992, he served for two years as a member of the Thirteenth Law Commission. Next, he was appointed chairperson of the Authority for Advanced Rulings, a quasi-judicial tribunal constituted under the Income Tax Act, 1961, and held that post until 30 October 1997. Thereafter, he conducted arbitrations and engaged in chamber practice.

87. Narain Dutt Ojha (1988–91)

On 19 January 1926, N.D. Ojha was born at Lilapur, Pratapgarh district, Uttar Pradesh. He was the son of Kuber Nath Ojha who was a zamindar with substantial landholdings.[16]

Ojha received his BA in English literature, Hindi literature, and political science from Allahabad University in 1943. His childhood aspiration had been to join government service but he had received his BA at age seventeen and eighteen was the minimum for entrance. He enrolled in law school and received the LLB from Allahabad University in 1945 at age nineteen. He then went to Varanasi, where for two years he studied Sanskrit. Ojha was both the first graduate and the first lawyer in his family.

Upon returning to Allahabad in 1947, he commenced practising law in the district courts. On 20 December 1951, he enrolled as an advocate of the Allahabad High Court. During his years at the bar, he 'scrupulously avoided other activities'.

---

[16] Interview with the author on 29 October 1988, in New Delhi.

At age forty-five, he was appointed an additional judge of the Allahabad High Court on 3 September 1971 and confirmation as a permanent judge came on 12 December 1972. Some fifteen years later, Ojha became the acting chief justice. That was on 18 August 1986, but he would serve in that capacity for only six weeks, until 30 September when K. Jagannatha Shetty came up from Bangalore to become the permanent chief justice and Ojha reverted to the number two position. Soon, however, Ojha himself was transferred. On 8 January 1987, he was sworn in as the chief justice of the Madhya Pradesh High Court. During his tenure there, he acted as governor from 1–29 December 1987. Although he had no previous involvement with legal aid, he was appointed a member of the National Committee for the Implementation of Legal Aid Schemes.

On the morning of 18 January 1988, President Neelam Sanjiva Reddy signed Ojha's warrant of appointment to be an SCI judge. He rushed to Delhi and was sworn in that evening at 10 p.m. at CJI Pathak's home, just two hours before his sixty-second birthday.[17] He retired from the Court on 19 January 1991.

Ojha died on 4 May 2009, at age eighty-three.

88. Subbiah Ratnavel Pandian (1988–94)

S. Ratnavel Pandian, the first of the Other Backward Classes to reach the SCI, was born on 13 March 1929, at Thiruppudaimarudhur in the Tirunelveli district of Tamil Nadu. He was the son of K. Subbiah who was a financially comfortable landlord and farmer.[18]

The first graduate and first lawyer in his family, he received his BA in economics from St. Xavier's College, Palayamkottai, Tamil Nadu, in 1952, and his BL from the Madras Law College in 1954.

In July 1955, at the age of twenty-six, he enrolled as an advocate of the Madras High Court. Three years later, he returned to Tirunelveli and practised at the district courts from 1958 to 1971. During his years at the bar, he was involved in both politics and the trade union movement. From 1959 to 1971, he was active in the Dravida Munnetra Kazhagam party and held the post of Tirunelveli district secretary of the DMK from 1968 to

---

[17] Had his swearing in been delayed one day, he would have been a retired judge with a break in service and his pension would have been reduced.

[18] Interview with the author on 19 November 1988, in Madras.

1970. During the 1955–70 years, he served at various times as president of three trade unions—the Indian Rayon Earth Company Trade Union, the Cooperative Spinning Mills Trade Union, and the Cement Factory Trade Union.

Pandian returned to Madras in 1971 and was appointed public prosecutor in the high court on 2 August 1971. He served briefly as acting advocate-general and government pleader until 27 February 1974 when, at age forty-four, he was appointed an additional judge of the Madras High Court. This judgeship was made permanent on 2 August 1975. In 1988, from 18–29 January and 13 March to 13 December, he was acting chief justice. While on the Madras bench, he was appointed a member of the executive council of the Indian Institute of Public Administration in 1985 and served as chairman of that institute's Legal Aid Society.

After almost fifteen years on the Madras bench, and second in seniority, he was sworn in at the SCI on 14 December 1988 at age fifty-nine. He reached retirement age on 13 March 1994.

A month later, he was appointed chairman of the Fifth Central Pay Commission, the report[19] of which was submitted in January 1997. In 2000, he accepted Jammu and Kashmir Chief Minister Farooq Abdullah's request that he investigate the killing by security forces of eight people in Brakpora, Anantnag district. He was also a member of the governing council of the National Judicial Academy in Bhopal. On 6 August 2006, he was appointed to a three-year term as chairman of the National Commission for Backward Classes.

89. Thamarappallil Kochu Thommen (1988–93)

The third member of the Christian community to serve on the SCI, T.K. Thommen was born at Kottayam in the Kottayam district of Kerala on 26 September 1928. He was the son of T.K. Thomas who operated a timber business.[20] All his forefathers were businessmen and his grandfather and great-grandfather were also members of the Travancore state legislature. Thommen was both the first graduate and first lawyer in his well-to-do family.

---

[19] *Fifth Central Pay Commission, 1997*, 3 vols (Delhi: Ministry of Finance, Controller of Publications).

[20] Interview with the author on 17 November 1988, in Ernakulam, Kerala.

No earlier judge received as extensive and cosmopolitan an education as Thommen. Over the course of eleven years, he earned four degrees and credentials as a barrister. He received a BA (honours) in history and political science from Presidency College, Madras, in 1951. While pursuing this degree, he won the election as president of the Presidency College Union and upon graduation, the Raja Sir Annamalai Chettiar Prize. From 1951 to 1952, he was a tutor in history and political science at Presidency College. In 1952, he earned an MA again in history and political science, from Presidency College. He then spent the 1953–6 years in England and in the latter year he was called to the bar from Lincoln's Inn. He signed the roll of barristers of the High Court of Justice, Queens Bench Division, on 28 November 1956, but did not practise there.

Thommen returned to India in 1956 and after an apprenticeship year, enrolled as an advocate of the Kerala High Court on 11 November 1957 and commenced practice there. From 1958 to 1960, he was a member of the bar council. In 1960, he returned to Europe, this time to the Netherlands where, as a Netherlands government research fellow, he earned an ML in 1960 and the LLD in 1962, both from the University of Leyden. He was the second SCI judge to have earned a doctorate.[21] Upon returning to India in 1962, he settled in Madras and practised law at the Madras High Court until 1965, when he again went to Europe and spent the 1965–6 academic year as a Rockefeller Foundation research fellow at the Institute of Advanced Legal Studies of the University of London, where he conducted research on the international unification of shipping law. A year earlier, he was named a fellow of The Hague Academy of International Law.

Returning to India again, he settled in Ernakulam–Cochin and resumed practise at the Kerala High Court. From 1967 to 1970, he served as a consultant in shipping law to the United Nations Conference on Trade and Development. He was also a United Nations advisor in port operation and admiralty law to the government of Jamaica in 1970.

The 1970–5 years were spent mainly in practice before the Kerala High Court. On 9 May 1975 and at age forty-six, he was appointed an additional judge of that court. He was reappointed on 9 May 1977, and again on 9 May 1979, and finally filled a permanent vacancy on 13 March 1980. During his thirteen-year tenure, he was twice acting chief justice.

[21] The first was B.K. Mukherjea.

Before his appointment to the SCI, Thommen had been very active in both teaching and university administration. He served as a part-time lecturer in international law at the Madras Law College in 1964–5, and in 1966–7 he served as a part-time honorary professor of law at the law college in Cochin. From 1974 to 1980, he was a member of the board of post-graduate studies in law of the University of Cochin. From 1976 to 1985, he was a member of the faculty of law at the latter institution and, from 1977 to 1978, he was a member of the board of studies in law of the University of Calicut. He served as dean of the faculty of law at the University of Cochin from 1980 to 1985 and in 1985 he was appointed chairman of the board of post-graduate studies in law at the University of Kerala. In 1988, he spent some time abroad again when he was a senior scholar at the Dean Rusk Center of International and Comparative Law at the University of Georgia (Athens, Georgia, USA).

In addition to this extensive involvement in education, Thommen was president of the Institute of Public Speaking in Madras from 1963 to 1965, was secretary of the Kerala branch of the Indian Law Institute from 1967 to 1971 and, beginning in 1977, served as a member of the governing body of the Indian Law Institute.

Thommen was also long involved with Congress party politics. During his student days, in 1946–7, he was secretary of the All-India Students Congress at Presidency College. In the early 1970s, shortly before being appointed to the Kerala bench, he was president of the Congress (I) Mandal committee in Chennur, Kerala.

International law, particularly shipping law, was an interest of Thommen all his adult life. Among his publications are *Legal Status of Government Merchant Ships in International Law* (The Hague: Martinus Nijhoff, 1962); *International Legislation on Shipping* (New York: United Nations, 1968); and *Bills of Lading in International Law and Practise* (Lucknow: Eastern Book Company, 1985).

When he was sworn in as an SCI judge on 14 December 1988, he was sixty and second in seniority on the Kerala bench. He retired on 25 September 1993. Because he was suffering from a malignant brain tumour, he was on leave during much of his last year on the Court. Immediately after his retirement, he was appointed a member of the National Human Rights Commission but illness prevented him from assuming this position. He was sixty-five when he died on 20 December 1993.

90. Aziz Mushabber Ahmadi (1988–97)

A.M. Ahmadi was born on 25 March 1932, at Surat in the Surat district of Gujarat. He was the son of Mushabber Imranali Ahmadi who was himself a judge. The elder Ahmadi served in the Bombay Presidency judicial service and after the creation of Gujarat in 1960 was allocated to the Gujarat judicial service. During his career, he was a civil judge, a small causes judge, a member of the Industrial Tribunal, and a member of the Sales Tax Tribunal.[22]

Ahmadi earned a law degree but not an undergraduate degree—it was possible in those days to go from the intermediate level to law school. After doing his first year at the Sir L.A. Shah Law College in Ahmedabad, he completed his legal education at the Sarvajanik Law College in Surat, receiving his BL in 1953.

He enrolled as a district pleader in the Bombay High Court on 15 June 1954 and began his law practice in Ahmedabad in the district, and the city civil and sessions courts. In 1960–1, he served as the law officer of the district court pleader's office, Ahmedabad. Shortly after the Gujarat High Court was created, he enrolled as an advocate on 21 February 1962. During his years at the bar, he was among the pioneers of the legal aid movement in Gujarat.

In 1964, he was invited to join the Gujarat judicial service and at the unusually young age of thirty-two he became a judge of the Ahmedabad City Civil and Sessions Court on 30 March 1964. He served in that capacity for a decade until 5 June 1974 when he was promoted to the post of secretary and remembrancer of legal affairs for the state government. Upon learning, in late 1975, that he was to be promoted to the high court, he returned to the post of civil and sessions judge on 1 January 1976.[23]

He was forty-four when he was sworn in as an additional judge of the Gujarat High Court on 2 September 1976. This judgeship was made permanent on 28 December 1977. During his dozen years of high court service, Ahmadi served as chairman of Gujarat's Third Pay Commission (1983–5), as chairman of the advisory board under the Conservation of Foreign Exchange and Prevention of Smuggling Activities Act (COFEPOSA),

---

[22] Interview with the author on 1 January 1989, New Delhi.

[23] It was the tradition in Gujarat that after a law secretary was recommended for promotion to the high court he returned to the bench until the promotion was cleared.

as chairman of the advisory board under the Prevention of Black Marketing and Maintenance of Supplies of Essential Commodities Act, and from 1986 to 1987 as a member of the Ravi and Beas Waters Disputes Tribunal.

Ahmadi was fifty-six when he was sworn in as an SCI judge on 14 December 1988. The ninth Muslim to serve on the SCI, he was the most senior associate judge on the Gujarat High Court and the second most senior of the nation's twenty-two Muslim high court judges. On the Court, he was president of the SCI's Legal Aid Committee from 19 June 1989 to 31 October 1990 and executive chairman of the SCI's Committee for Implementing Legal Aid Schemes from 1 November 1990 to 24 October 1994. In 1993, Ahmadi, at the CJI's request, accepted the chairmanship of a committee which looked closely at the deteriorating standards of legal education in the country and recommended measures for improvement.

On 25 October 1994, he became the twenty-sixth CJI and held that post for nearly two and a half years, retiring on 25 March 1997.

He remained very active during his retirement years. In June 1998, he was appointed chairman of an advisory panel to review the provisions of the 1993 Protection of Human Rights Act and the first five years of the National Human Rights Commission.[24] In 1999, the United Nations Commissioner for Human Rights appointed him a member of an international commission which investigated possible violations of human rights in East Timor. He was a member of an International Commission of Jurists committee which provided assistance to the judiciary in Liberia, and served on a committee of the International Bar Association that looked into charges of human rights violations in Zimbabwe. He was also chairman of the working group which deliberated on matters relating to the special status of Jammu and Kashmir within the Indian union and recommended methods to strengthen democracy, secularism, and the rule of law in the state. In 2003, he was elected chancellor of Aligarh Muslim University and, in 2007, was re-elected. In 1998, he became chairman of the Union Carbide-funded Bhopal Memorial Trust Hospital and held that post until he resigned in July 2010. He also served as chairman of the Centre for Corporate Governance and of the jury which selected the Golden Peacock award winner. He spoke frequently of the need to improve the quality of

---

[24] *Addendum to the summary of submissions to the High Level Committee created to review the Protection of Human Rights Act, 1993 and headed by the former chief justice of India, Justice A.M. Ahmadi, collated by the Commonwealth Human Rights Initiative* (New Delhi: Commonwealth Human Rights Initiative, 1998).

legal education and on many occasions of the need for Muslims to avail themselves of a modern education.

He received honorary LLDs from the University of Kurukshetra in 1994; the Maharishi Dayanand University and the University of Kanpur in 1995; and the University of Leicester in 1998. In 1996, he was named an honorary bencher of Middle Temple. He was the author of *A Guide to Uplift Minorities* (New Delhi: Jamate Islami-e-Hind, 2008). In 1997, the Andhra Pradesh Judicial Academy in Secunderabad published *Thoughts and Reflections of Sri Justice A.M. Ahmadi, Former Chief Justice of India*. On the occasion of his seventy-fifth birthday, he was the recipient of the Lifetime Achievement Award from the Institute of Objective Studies. On this occasion, the latter published *Flow of Thoughts: Selected Speeches, Lectures, and Writings of Justice A.M. Ahmadi* (New Delhi, 2008).

91. Khagendra Nath Saikia (1988–91)

The first of Mongolian lineage to be appointed to the SCI, K.N. Saikia was born on 1 March 1926 at Simaluguri Bharalula Gaon in the Sibsagar district of Assam. He was the son of Mileswar Saikia, a subsistence farmer. The Saikias are members of the Ahom community,[125] which is officially designated as Backward Class.[26]

The first graduate and the first lawyer in his family, Saikia earned four degrees. In 1947, he received a BCom degree from J.B. College, Jorhat, Assam, graduating in the first class. In 1949, he received an MA in commerce in the first class first position from Calcutta University. In 1954, he received the LLB and in 1959 the LLM, again securing the first class ranking, from Gauhati University. After passing the requisite examinations in 1956, he was admitted as an associate member of the London-based Corporation of Certified Secretaries.

An unusual feature of Saikia's background, one that sets him apart from other SCI judges, was that he managed to pursue successfully and simultaneously two different careers, that of a teacher/scholar specializing

---

[25] Interview with the author on 11 December 1988, in New Delhi and correspondence dated 10 October 2009.

[26] According to M.J. Akbar, *Nehru: The Making of India* (London: Penguin Books Ltd., 1988), p. 514, the Ahoms are a semi-Mongoloid people from Burma who conquered the Assam region in the thirteenth century.

in commerce, banking, commercial, and company law on the one hand, and that of a lawyer and ultimately a judge on the other. His first career was as a teacher. He was twenty-four when he began teaching as a lecturer in commerce at Gauhati University on 21 July 1950. He was promoted to reader in 1957 and to professor in 1964. He held that post until 13 December 1966 when he accepted appointment as professor and head of the department of law at Dibrugarh University in Guwahati and continued in that capacity until he resigned in February 1970. Later he was awarded an LLD (*honoris causa*) from that university.

It was not until 18 April 1955, at age twenty-nine, that he enrolled as an advocate of the Assam High Court and began practising law. Another fifteen years would pass before he practised law full-time. In May 1976, he returned to teaching as a part-time professor in the LLM classes at Gauhati University and that continued until his appointment to the Gauhati bench three years later. On 27 May 1978, the Assam government appointed him chairman of the Assam Land Reforms Commission.

In 1977, Saikia made an unsuccessful venture into electoral politics when he stood as a Janata Party candidate for the Assam Legislative Assembly. Both he and the Congress (I) candidate were defeated by a candidate of the Congress (O) Party.

On 12 February 1979, at age fifty-two, he was the first member of the Ahom community to be appointed a judge of the Gauhati High Court. On 20 December 1986, he became the acting chief justice, was confirmed as chief justice on 16 July 1987, and served in that capacity until his sixty-second birthday on 1 March 1988. While on the Gauhati bench, he served as a one-man commission of inquiry into the Moirang (Manipur) Students Firing.

When he was sworn as an SCI judge on 14 December 1988 at age sixty-two, he became the eldest ever appointed.[27] Less than twenty-seven months later he reached retirement age on 1 March 1991.

Saikia was the author of five publications: *Foreign Banking Systems* (Guwahati: privately published, 1959); *Studies in the Law of Banker-Customer Relationships* (Guwahati: privately published, 1959); *The Assam (Temporarily Settled Districts) Tenancy Act, 1935* (Guwahati: New Book Stall, 1965); *Commentary on Assam Fixation of Ceilings on Land-Holdings Act* (Guwahati:

[27] Just a few days older than his former Gauhati High Court colleague, Baharul Islam.

privately published, 1966); and *The Assam Land and Revenue Regulation, 1886*, second edition (Guwahati: Lawyer's Book Stall, 2003). He was also a vice-president of the India Council of Jurists and a fellow of the Indian Council of Arbitration.

Shortly after he left the Court, he was appointed by the central government to probe the election-related violence in Meham (Haryana) and inquire into the circumstances which led to the death of Amir Singh, an independent candidate for the May 1990 by-election.[28] In 1991, he was appointed chairman of the Committee on Vehicular Pollution, constituted under orders of the SCI, to assess and recommend solutions to the problems of vehicular pollution in Delhi. In 1996, he was appointed director-general of the National Judicial Academy and chairman of the Legal Education committee of the Bar Council of India. Also in 1996, he was appointed by CJI Ahmadi to head the study group which undertook a national assessment of the needs and solutions to the backlog and delays that have long plagued Indian courts. He was appointed, in 2005, by the Assam government to probe into charges of 'secret killings' in Assam between 1998 and 2001. Known as the 'Justice Saikia Commission', his 2007 report attracted national attention when it indicted former chief minister Prafulla Kumar Mahanta and the police hierarchy.

92. Kuldip Singh (1988–96)

The second member of the Sikh community to serve on the SCI and only the third SCI judge to accept appointment directly from the bar, K. Singh was born into well-to-do circumstances on 1 January 1932 at Dhudial, Jhelum district, in what today is located in Pakistan's Punjab province. He was the son of Sardar Harnam Singh Patwalia, a businessman who dealt with motor spare parts.[29]

The first graduate and first lawyer in his family, he was educated in both India and England. He earned his BA in political science, Punjabi, and English in 1952 from Punjab University[30] in Patiala. Next he received the

[28] *Report of Justice Saikia Commission of Inquiry on Meham Incidents* (New Delhi: Government of India Press, 1994).

[29] Interview with the author, 1 January 1989, New Delhi and correspondence dated 7 September 2009.

[30] Now Punjabi University.

LLB from Punjab University Law College in 1955. He then proceeded to England where he earned an LLM degree in 1958 from the University of London, majoring in international relations, constitutional law, and Hindu and Muslim law. He was called to the bar at Lincoln's Inn in absentia in 1960. He was the first Asian to be elected president of the Inns of Court student union.

In November 1959, he enrolled as an advocate of the Punjab High Court and practised at the district courts of Patiala for a year before commencing practice at the high court in Chandigarh. From 1960 to 1971, he was a part-time lecturer at the Punjab University College of Law. In 1966–7, he served as president of the Punjab and Haryana High Court bar association. In 1971, he was appointed Senior Standing Counsel for the central government, holding that post until 1982, when he returned to full-time private practice. During his years at the bar, he served as Standing Counsel in the High Court for Punjab University; Guru Nanak University; Punjab Agriculture University; the Post-Graduate Medical Institute; the Marketing Board; and several other public undertakings, corporations, local bodies, and cooperative institutions. In the early 1980s, he declined an invitation to become a judge of the Punjab and Haryana High Court. In May 1987, Singh was appointed the Advocate General for Punjab, but held that post only briefly, for in August 1987, he began serving as one of the three additional solicitors general of India, which meant moving to Delhi.

On 14 December 1988, at age fifty-six, he was sworn in as an SCI judge. In June 1989, he was appointed to head a central government commission of inquiry to investigate land transactions which took place in Karnataka when Ramakrishna Hegde was Chief Minister. His controversial report[31] a year later led to the resignation of Hegde from the post of deputy chairman of the Planning Commission. During his years on the SCI, he acquired a reputation as a leader of environmental preservation jurisprudence, earning him the sobriquet 'green judge'. Always colourful and often controversial, his SCI tenure ended when he reached retirement age on 1 January 1997.

Shortly after he left the Court, he became the founder-president of the World Sikh Council, and played a key role in the establishment of a 'people's commission', the purpose of which was to investigate human rights violations by the security personnel and by the militants during the years of terrorism in Punjab.

---

[31] *Report of the Justice Kuldip Singh Commission of Inquiry*, 2 vols (New Delhi: Ministry of Finance, 1990).

From 2002 to 2008, he served as chairman of the Delimitation Commission of India and presided over the redrawing of the boundaries of the nation's parliamentary and legislative assembly constituencies.[32] He was also a member of a citizens' panel which named Lok Sabha candidates believed to be involved in crimes ranging from bribery and corruption to moral turpitude and murder charges.

He served as chairman of the governing body of Sri Guru Tegh Bahadur Khalsa College. In 1995, he received an LLD (*honoris causa*) from Guru Nanak Dev University. In 1997 Pawan Chaudhary published *Justice Kuldip Singh: Vision and Mission, a Bouquet on the Eve of his Retirement* (New Delhi: Vidhi Sewa).

93. Jagdish Sharan Verma (1989–98)

J.S. Verma was born on 18 January 1933, at Satna in the Satna District of Madhya Pradesh. He was the son of Ram Sevak Verma who was in government service, retiring in 1948 as a divisional officer with the old G.I.P Railway.[33]

After receiving his early education in Satna and Lucknow, he earned the BSc degree in physics, chemistry, and mathematics from Allahabad's Ewing Christian College in 1952. In his youth, he had aspired to join the armed forces but his mother objected and, following his father's wishes he decided on a career as a lawyer. He received the LLB degree from the University of Allahabad in 1954. He was the first of this financially comfortable family to enter the legal profession.[34]

Returning to what is today Madhya Pradesh, Verma was twenty-two when he enrolled as a pleader at the Vindhya Pradesh judicial commissioner's court at Rewa in January 1955. From then until June 1967, although he had enrolled as an advocate of the Madhya Pradesh High Court on 19 August 1959, he practised at the district courts in his hometown of Satna. He served as a part-time law lecturer at the local law college from 1958 to

---

[32] *Changing Face of Electoral India: Delimitation 2008*, 2 vols (New Delhi: Delimitation Commission of India, 2008).

[33] Correspondence with the author dated 26 August 1990, and 14 and 28 August 2009.

[34] All his six brothers earned advanced degrees and achieved professional success in the fields of surgery, veterinary medicine, mathematics, and engineering.

1962. In June of 1967, he shifted to Jabalpur where he practised thereafter at the Madhya Pradesh High Court.

At the uncommonly young age of thirty-nine, he was appointed an additional judge of that high court on 12 September 1972. This judgeship was made permanent on 3 June 1973. During the early stage of the Emergency, he was one of the first judges to order the release of Maintenance of Internal Security Act detainees. While on the high court, he served as the company judge on the Indore bench from 1974 to 1976 and in the same capacity on the Jabalpur bench from 1978 to 1985. During these years, he was also chairman of the advisory boards constituted under the National Security Act and the Conservation of Foreign Exchange and Prevention of Smuggling Act, and was a member of the court's administrative committee, and served as the administrative judge in 1984–5.

Thirteen years after joining the court, he was appointed acting chief justice on 27 October 1985 and was confirmed as permanent chief justice on 14 June 1986. Shortly thereafter, he was transferred to the Rajasthan High Court as its chief justice, effective on 1 September 1986. He twice served as acting governor—from 15 October 1987 to 20 February 1988 and from 3 to 20 February 1989.

After nearly three years in Rajasthan, at age fifty-six and one of the longest-serving high court judges in the country, he was sworn in as an SCI judge on 3 June 1989. Less than a week after the assassination of former Prime Minister Rajiv Gandhi on 21 May 1991, Verma was chosen to head the commission of inquiry which was charged with determining the nature of the security lapses that led to the assassination. Among his conclusions was that the Intelligence Bureau had information of a possible assassination attempt but failed to share it with the Tamil Nadu police. The report of what came to be known as the Verma Commission was submitted in June 1992.[35]

He headed the SCI bench which dealt with the Jain Hawala case, the biggest political scandal of the mid-1990s. The unprecedented manner in which he handled this case attracted national attention.[36]

[35] J.S. Verma, *Report of the One-Man Commission of Inquiry Headed by Justice J.S. Verma, Judge, Supreme Court of India to Enquire into the Assassination of Shri Rajiv Gandhi, Former Prime Minister of India on 21st May 1991 at Sriperumbudur*, 2 vols (New Delhi: s.n., 1992).

[36] 'Mr Justice', the cover story in the 15 March 1996 issue of *India Today*, pp. 90–101. The Jain Hawala case is reported as *Vineet Narain* v. *Union of India*, AIR 1998 SC 889.

On 25 March 1997, Verma became the twenty-seventh CJI and held that post until he reached retirement age on 18 January 1998.

In 1998, he was appointed by the central government to head the committee for the selection of the next vice-chairman of the University Grants Commission. During 1998–9, he was chairman of the committee to suggest operationalization of the Fundamental Duties.[37] His most important post-retirement activity was serving as chairman of the National Human Rights Commission from 4 November 1999 to 18 January 2003. In that capacity, he personally investigated the murder of Muslims following the 2002 Godhra incident in Gujarat and concluded that the Gujarat government was complicit in the violence.[38]

In 1998, he delivered the first Justice P.K. Goswami Memorial Law Lecture, published under the title of *Independence of Judiciary: Some Latent Dangers*.[39] He was the author of *New Dimensions of Justice* in 2000 and *The New Universe of Human Rights* in 2004, both being collections of his speeches and articles.[40]

Among the many honours he received were LLDs (*honoris causa*) from Banaras Hindu University and the Universities of Allahabad and Jabalpur. From the Central Institute of Higher Tibetan Studies he received the honorary degree of Vakpati (DLittt.), and from the G.B. Pant University of Agriculture & Technology a DSc (*honoris causa*). He received the Gulzarilal Nanda Birth Centenary (Naitik Diwas) Award in 1998; the National Law Day Award in 2001; and the Dr B.R. Ambedkar National Award for Social Justice in 2008.

A man of indefatigable energy, he lectured abroad in the United States, Sri Lanka, Malaysia, the Philippines, Nepal, Bangladesh, England, and the Netherlands, in addition to participating in many international conferences. When not otherwise occupied, he provides legal advice and conducts arbitrations, both pro bono.

---

[37] Art. 51A of The Constitution.
[38] 'Letter of the Chairperson of the Commission, Justice Shri J.S. Verma, to the Prime Minister of India, dated 3 January 2003', Annexure 1 of the 2002–2003 *Annual Report of the National Human Rights Commission*, www.nhrc.nic.in.
[39] Guwahati, Law Research Institute, Eastern Region, 1998.
[40] Both published by Universal Law Publishing Company Pvt. Ltd., New Delhi.

Part Two
A COLLECTIVE PORTRAIT

I

Father's Occupation

Among the criteria employed for the attribution of social origin or class, father's occupation is widely considered the most trustworthy indicator.

Father's Occupation	1950–70 (per cent)	1971–89 (per cent)	1950–89 (per cent)
Lawyer	28.2	24.5	26.1
Lower Court Judge	7.7	3.8	5.4
High Court Judge	5.1	7.5	6.5
Supreme Court Judge	0.0	3.8	2.2
Landowner/Agriculturist	12.8	26.4	20.7
Businessman/Banker	7.7	17.0	12.0
Engineer or Physician	10.3	5.7	7.6
Scholar/Teacher	15.4	3.8	8.7
Government Service	12.8	7.6	9.8
Total	100.0	100.1	99.0

The fathers of 40 per cent were lawyers and judges, with virtually no change between the two periods. Lawyer-fathers often encouraged a son to become a lawyer and the offspring would inherit the father's law library and law practice.[1] For some, the practice of law had become a family

[1] Samuel Schmitthener, 'A Sketch of the Development of the Legal Profession in India', *Law & Society Review* vol. III, nos 2 and 3 (November 1968–February 1969), pp. 375–6.

tradition. This table does not distinguish between lawyers in the modern and more traditional sectors. A barrister practising at the Calcutta High Court would be a world apart from a country lawyer practising at a rural district court.

Of the known occupations of grandfathers, half had been lawyers and judges. For many, it was not just the father and grandfather who had been lawyers, but others from earlier generations as well. It was not uncommon to marry into another judicial family. Of those who spoke of their wife's antecedents, two-thirds reported that there were lawyers on her side as well.

Moving ahead to the present generation, about two-thirds of their children followed their fathers into the legal profession. This was twice (55 per cent) the case in the first period than the second (25 per cent). Many of these sons would rise to high positions in the superior judiciary. The sons of at least five SCI judges—P.N. Bhagwati, S.M. Fazal Ali, B.P. Singh (grandson of B.P. Sinha), N. Santosh Hegde, and B.N. Agrawal—became SCI judges themselves and at least another dozen became high court judges.[2] Several reported being offered high court judgeships and preferring to remain at the bar, but accepting the judgeship because of pressure from their fathers. Others reported accepting judgeships because it was the family tradition. A number of the post-1970 judges reported that for a variety of reasons, including the low salaries and the declining status of lawyers and judges and the increasing number of more attractive opportunities, they had discouraged their children from following them in the profession.

Forty-one per cent of the judges were the first lawyers in their extended families.[3] For the first generation, the figure was 34 per cent, and for the second 44 per cent, perhaps an indication that the law profession became more open over time and the number of law colleges had increased. Not unexpected is the fact that twice as many of the fathers of second-generation judges had been high court and SCI judges.

---

[2] Sons of SCI judges who became high court judges include A.K. Mookerji, son of B.K. Mukherjea; D.K. Kapur, son of J.L. Kapur; D.K. Mahajan and C.K. Mahajan, son and grandson of M.C. Mahajan; Bisheshwar Prasad Singh and Rameshwar Prasad Singh, son and grandson of B.P. Sinha; Ajoy Nath Ray, son of A.N. Ray; Dhananjay Chandrachud, son of Y.V. Chandrachud; Anil Dev Singh, son of Jaswant Singh; Ramprakash Misra, son of R.B. Misra; Paramjit Singh Patwalia, son of K. Singh; and K.M. Joseph, son of K.K. Mathew.

[3] Defined as parents, siblings, uncles, cousins, and other earlier antecedents.

There are noteworthy differences in fathers' occupations during the two periods. About 80 per cent of the first generation was raised in an urban westernized milieu where they had substantial contact with modernity. More than twice as many post-1970 judges than the pre-1971 ones came from landowner/agriculturist, businessmen/banker backgrounds. The fathers included a number of zamindars or owners of substantial landholdings, and the bankers were mainly traditional moneylenders. Those identified as businessmen were mostly owners of large businesses, not small shopkeepers. The second generation was more likely to have risen from rural backgrounds but few of these had to make a quantum leap to the modern field of law. If the teachers, most in government schools, and those identified as being employed by the government are combined, nearly three times as many of these parents are found in the first generation.

II

Caste

Caste, the most important differentiator in Indian social life, is a better indicator of social origin and class than parental occupation. Seventy-seven of the ninety-three judges were Hindus. The most striking thing about these tables is that brahmins, one-nineteenth of the nation's population, held thirty-three[1] of the judgeships. This is not the place to enter into the controversies concerning the sizes of the forward caste and OBC categories. Estimates of the latter depend on how they are defined and range from less than 25 per cent to more than 50 per cent of the Hindu population. The figures used here are census ones from the 1980s.

The caste identities of the judges were collected in almost every instance from the judges themselves. A delicate question, it occasionally elicited strongly expressed responses. Brahmins, many very emphatically, said that their caste was not only irrelevant in their own appointment but that caste had nothing to do with the selection of any other judge. A few of the non-brahmin judges and a few from minority communities were no less adamant

[1] 1950–70: M.P. Sastri, B.K. Mukherjea, N. Chandrasekhara Aiyar, B. Jagannadhadas, T.L. Venkatarama Ayyar, P.B. Gajendragadkar, K.N. Wanchoo, N. Rajagopala Ayyangar, J.R. Mudholkar, Vaidyanthier Ramaswami, J.M. Shelat, V. Bhargava, C.A. Vaidialingam, and A.N. Ray.
1971–89: D.G. Palekar, S.N. Dwivedi, A.K. Mukherjea, Y.V. Chandrachud, V.R. Krishna Iyer, P.K. Goswami, V.D. Tulzapurkar, D.A. Desai, R.S. Pathak, E.S. Venkataramiah, V. Balakrishna Eradi, R.B. Misra, S. Mukharji, R.N. Misra, G.L Oza, L.M. Sharma, M.N.R. Venkatachaliah, S. Ranganathan, and N.D. Ojha.

Caste Representation on the SCI	1950–70 (per cent)	1971–89 (per cent)	1950–89 (per cent)
Brahmins	40.0	45.2	42.9
Other Forward Castes	57.1	42.9	49.4
Scheduled Castes	0.0	4.6	2.6
Scheduled Tribes	0.0	0.0	0.0
Other Backward Classes	2.9	6.8	5.2
Total	100.0	100.1	100.1

Caste Distribution of Population	Hindu Population (per cent)	Indian Population (per cent)
Brahmins	6.4	5.3
Other Forward Castes	36.0	29.7
Scheduled Castes	17.7	14.6
Scheduled Tribes	8.4	6.9
Other Backward Classes	31.6	26.1
Total	100.1	82.6

in expressing the view that caste and class were criteria.[2] An unexpectedly large number of judges, even some who bristled at the caste queries, knew the castes of other judges, both past and present.

Caste was an important reason for the appointment of three, perhaps four, of the judges. In 1980, A. Varadarajan, from the Madras High Court, was the first member of the Scheduled Castes to become an SCI judge. Both the CJI[3] and the law minister[4] said that he was selected because the Scheduled Castes needed to be represented on the court. Two months after Varadarajan's retirement, B.C. Ray of the Calcutta High Court, of the same community, replaced him. He acknowledged that he was chosen because

[2] Without referring specifically to brahmins, P.B. Sawant, then a Bombay High Court and later an SCI judge, said in 1987 that: 'Whether it is appointment or promotion of the judges to the High Courts or the Supreme Court—along with political considerations, the class, caste, community, and region have played dominant roles. In particular, there is a genuine feeling in this country that unless one belongs to the proper class or caste, one cannot rise in any walk of life. The feeling is more pronounced in the higher judiciary where the posts are limited. ...' *Judicial Independence: Myth and Reality* (Pune: Pune Board of Extra-Mural Studies, 1988), p. 36.

[3] Interview with Chandrachud, 3 May 1983, in New Delhi.

[4] See Law Minister P. Shiv Shankar's claims expressed in Parliament quoted in *The Hindustan Times*, 4 December 1980.

of his caste.[5] The OBCs also gained representation in the 1980s. The first
was S.R. Pandian of the Madras High Court. The second was K.N. Saikia,
a retired chief justice of the Gauhati High Court. He acknowledged that
his Ahom community's OBC status was a factor in his appointment.[6] K.S.
Hegde, appointed in 1967, and A.N. Alagiriswami, appointed in 1972, were
members of castes later designated as OBC. It is possible that other judges
would today be counted among the OBCs, but were not when they were
appointed.

The usual explanation for the overrepresentation of brahmins is that they
were the privileged group before the British arrived, that they were the first
to learn English and take advantage of modern education, and as a result,
quickly secured high positions in the professions, law in particular, where
English was the language of the courts. Very few of the Scheduled Castes
and Tribes had received any education in English until after Independence.
Those who would come to be designated OBC were hardly much better off.
In 1983, the then law minister told Parliament that of the nearly 400 high
court judges, six were members of the Scheduled Castes and there were
none from the Scheduled Tribes.[7]

Whether the above is sufficient explanation for the extent to which the
brahmins have dominated the SCI's membership for four decades, and
particularly because the extent of their dominance increased during the
second generation, is a matter of dispute in some circles. During most of
1988, for the first time, a majority of the SCI's judges was brahmins. There
were only seventeen judges during that year and nine were brahmins.[8] But
in the middle of the same year, all of the following were also brahmins:
President R. Venkataraman, Vice-President S.D. Sharma, and Prime
Minister Rajiv Gandhi. During the four decades, every prime minister
was a brahmin. So brahmin dominance on the SCI was in keeping with
their overrepresentation elsewhere. It is noteworthy that the brahmin CJIs
were *less* likely than the others to see brahmins appointed during their
stewardships.

As the forty years drew to a close, there began a major change in the
caste composition of the Court. Following the appointment of N.D.

[5] Interview with Ray, 22 April 1988, in New Delhi.
[6] Interview with Saikia, 11 December 1988, in New Delhi.
[7] *The Hindustan Times*, 17 August 1983.
[8] R.S. Pathak, E.S. Venkataramiah, S. Mukharji, R.N. Misra, G.L. Oza, L.M. Sharma,
S. Ranganathan, M.N.R. Venkatachaliah, and N.D. Ojha.

Ojha in January 1988, there was not a brahmin among the next dozen appointees. The explanation for this turnaround was the fact that B. Shankaranand of the Scheduled Caste community, and P. Shiv Shankar of the OBC community, were law ministers in 1988 and 1989. By the end of 1989, a spate of appointments had increased the number of judges to twenty-five. Only seven of these were brahmins. These appointments are evidence of caste being a selection criterion. Evidence that it was a criterion earlier when the first Scheduled Caste and OBC judges were appointed is unimpeachable. But convincing evidence that brahmins over the years were preferred because of their caste is lacking. Judges of the highest rank in all or nearly all nations will not be representative of the social make-up of their country.

III

Economic Status

This table needs to be viewed with abundant caution, for the author's judgment played a large role in deciding the category in which to place the judge. The determinations were made from discussions with the judges about their family backgrounds and from unobtrusive indicators. The wealth of a judge's family was estimated relative to that of the other judges. None of the judges rose from poor backgrounds by Indian standards.

Economic Status of Different Classes	1950–70 (per cent)	1971–89 (per cent)	1950–89 (per cent)
Wealthy	69.0	56.6	62.0
Upper Middle	26.0	39.6	34.0
Lower Middle	5.0	3.8	4.0
Total	100.0	100.0	100.0

Because of the amount or arbitrariness in distributing the judges into the three categories, one cannot say that the differences among the degrees of wealth are especially meaningful. The difference in relative wealth between the first and second generation judges was not significant, but the sources of that wealth was, with the fathers of the first generation judges more likely to be from the more modern professional classes.

An illustration of a judge from an economically privileged family was S.J. Imam. He spent nearly a decade in England attending public schools, earned his undergraduate degree from Trinity College, and was called to the bar from Middle Temple. Another was Jaswant Singh, the son of a wealthy banker. P. Jaganmohan Reddy would be another—his father was a rich industrialist and philanthropist, and he, too, was educated in England. Indeed, every judge who could afford to travel to England for education was regarded as being a product of a family of substantial means,

Examples of families classified as upper middle-class include D.A. Desai's. His father was a revenue officer in the subordinate judicial service. S.K. Das's father was a secondary school headmaster.

Classified in the lower-middle category was E.S. Venkataramiah, whose father was school teacher in a rural part of Karnataka who farmed a small plot of land to supplement his income. Another was N.H. Bhagwati, whose father was also a poorly paid school teacher. K.N. Saikia's father was a subsistence farmer.

There are several examples of where economic class and social class do not coincide. K.N. Wanchoo was a Kashmiri brahmin whose father began his government service as a clerk. B.K. Mukherjea's brahmin family enjoyed little economic security—his father was a Sanskrit scholar and a district court lawyer, more the former than the latter. At the other end, B.C. Ray was a member of a Scheduled Caste community but his family was wealthy. None of those from the OBCs and Scheduled Castes rose from family backgrounds which could be considered economically underprivileged.

About half a dozen judges were described by the CJI who recommended them as men of 'impeccable breeding', as the offspring of 'prominent' or 'illustrious' families or being from 'distinguished' lineage. The intent of describing a judge in such terms was to underline that his background was high class and this usually meant wealthy also.

IV

Religion

Except for a relatively small under-representation of Muslims, the religious affiliations of the judges mirror the religious composition of the population at large to a remarkable degree. Religion has been a selection criterion—obviously this distribution cannot be a coincidence, and this extraordinary amount of proportional representation enhances India's secular foundation.[1] From the Court's inception in 1950, there has been a 'Muslim seat'. The convention of a Muslim seat dates back to the 1930s when the Federal Court began functioning. Of the three judges who comprised that Court until 1948 (when it increased in size), one was always a Muslim.[2] This convention carried over after Independence. Nine of the ninety-three were Muslims, and in most instances were the most senior Muslim High Court judges in the country.

[1] The classic *Fourteenth Report* of the Law Commission of India, completed in the late 1950s, was of a very different view: 'Though we call ourselves a secular State, ideas of communal representation, which were viciously planted in our body politic by the British, have not entirely lost their influence'. I, p. 34.

[2] Sir Shah Mohammad Sulaiman (1937–41), Sir Muhammad Zafrullah Khan (1941–7), and Sir S. Fazl Ali (1947–50).

Religion	Per cent of Judges	Per cent of Population[3]
Hindu	82.8	82.6
Muslim	9.7	11.4
Christian	3.2	2.4
Sikh	2.2	2.0
Other[4]	2.2	1.6
Total	100.1	100.0

It is easy to justify Muslim presence on the SCI. Muslims are not just one of India's many minority religious groups. They are a major minority that requires representation. Only two, perhaps three, other countries in the world have a larger Muslim population.

There were few Muslims on the high courts from which to choose. In 1980, only fifteen (4.3 per cent) of the 351 judges were Muslims.[5] By 1988, there was some improvement. The minister of state for law told Parliament that among the approximately 400 high court judges, twenty-seven (6.8 per cent) were Muslims.[6]

Because both Sikhs, two of the three Christians, and the Parsi were appointed after 1970, the Hindu representation fell slightly from the first to the second generation.

[3] The population figures are according to the 1981 census. The 2001 census figures are 80.5, 13.4, 2.3, 1.9, and 1.9 per cent, respectively.

[4] The two 'others' are O. Chinnappa Reddy who rejected any religious label, and the Zoroastrian D.P. Madon.

[5] *Judges of the Supreme Court and the High Courts* (New Delhi: Ministry of Law, Justice, and Company Affairs, 1980).

[6] *Indian Express*, 8 August 1988.

V

States of Birth

The ninety-three judges were born in sixteen of the twenty-five states[1] which existed in the 1980s. No judges were born in Haryana, Goa, Arunachal Pradesh, Tripura, Manipur, Meghalaya, Nagaland, Mizoram, and Sikkim. These states make up only about 3 per cent of the nation's population.

States	Number of Judges	Population Rank	States	Number of Judges	Population Rank
Andhra Pradesh	5	5	Madhya Pradesh	5	7
Assam	3	13	Maharashtra	6	2
Bihar	8	3	Orissa	2	11
Gujarat	9	10	Punjab	10	14
Himachal Pradesh	1	16	Rajasthan	1	8
Jammu and Kashmir	1	15	Tamil Nadu	11	6
Karnataka	5	9	Uttar Pradesh	7	1
Kerala	6	12	West Bengal	13	4

[1] R. Dayal, born in the Union Territory of Delhi, has been included in the Punjab total. Nine of the judges were born outside of the present boundaries of India. These are classified as born in the states where they 'belong'. Thus J.L. Kapur, S.M. Sikri, I.D. Dua, each born in what is today Pakistan, are in the Punjab total, as is Jaswant Singh, born in what is today Pakistan-occupied part of Jammu and Kashmir. A.N. Grover, A.P. Sen, and M.P. Thakkar, each born in Burma, are in the Punjab, Madhya Pradesh,

Uttar Pradesh and Maharashtra are especially underrepresented. This is largely because three[2] of the eleven judges who served on the Allahabad High Court were not born in Uttar Pradesh, and four of the Bombay High Court judges were born in today's Gujarat and a fifth in Karnataka.[3] Only one of them was born in Rajasthan. Punjab is overrepresented, largely because its ten include three who were born in today's Pakistan and another in Burma. The most notably underrepresented state is Rajasthan. There is no evidence that states controlled by a party different from the party that controlled the Centre received fewer judgeships.

In most instances, the judge was first appointed to the high court of his state of birth, and seventy-two came to the SCI directly from his home or parent high court. The remaining eighteen had been transferred to another high court, and fifteen of those arrived in Delhi from the high court to which they had been transferred. The other three—A.D. Koshal, O. Chinnappa Reddy, and A.P. Sen—had been punitively transferred during the 1975–7 Emergency but were back on their parent high court when the call came from Delhi.

---

and Gujarat totals, respectively. A.K. Sarkar and K.C. Das Gupta, born in today's Bangladesh, are among the West Bengal total. M.C. Mahajan is considered by all as a Punjabi but was born in what is today's Himachal Pradesh.

[2] G. Hasan (Punjab), K.N. Wanchoo (Madhya Pradesh), and R. Dayal (Delhi). K. Jagannatha Shetty served briefly at Allahabad but was a native of Karnataka.

[3] H.J. Kania, N.H. Bhagwati, J.C. Shah, and J.M. Shelat were born in Gujarat, and D.G. Palekar was born in Karnataka.

VI

Region

There is no constitutional mandate that the membership of the SCI must be representative of the nation but the table below shows clearly that the geographic composition of the Court has been an important selection criterion. The SCI's first four judges were representatives of the nation's four regions. In many instances, the judge selected to replace a retiring judge has been from either the same high court, or the same region as the man who stepped down. Shortly after H.J. Kania died in 1951, the next appointee was former Bombay High Court colleague N.H. Bhagwati. Shortly after V.R. Krishna Iyer retired in 1980, leaving Kerala without representation, another Kerala High Court judge, V. Balakrishna Eradi, was appointed.

Region	Judges (per cent)	Population[1] (per cent)
Northern (Uttar Pradesh, Punjab, Haryana, Rajasthan, Jammu and Kashmir, and Himachal Pradesh)	24.7	27.3
Southern (Tamil Nadu, Andhra Pradesh, Karnataka, and Kerala)	29.0	24.3
Western/Central (Maharashtra, Goa, Madhya Pradesh, and Gujarat)	20.4	22.2
Eastern (West Bengal, Bihar, Orissa, Assam, Tripura, Manipur, Meghalaya, Nagaland, Arunachal Pradesh, Mizoram, and Sikkim)	25.8	26.3
Totals	99.9	100.1

[1] The 1981 census figures have been used and the divisor excludes the union territories. Only the twenty-five states which existed in the 1980s are included.

The nature of the regional balance is clearly not a chance occurrence. Occasionally, a state is briefly over represented. Four Punjabis were once on the SCI at the same time.[2] In the late 1980s, three from the Karnataka High Court were serving simultaneously.[3] A few states were unrepresented for lengthy periods, none more so than Tamil Nadu. From 1964 to 1972, there was no judge from the Madras High Court on the SCI, but four judges whose pre-high court careers had been spent practising at that high court, came to the SCI from one of the new high courts created after the 1956 reorganization of states.

Those involved in the selection of the judges have paid close attention to the Court's geographic makeup. The ten appointees during S.R. Das's stewardship came from eight high courts. CJIs A.N. Ray and Y.V. Chandrachud, when asked to rank their selection criteria, mentioned geography first. The ten appointed during the Ray years came from nine states, and the fourteen appointed during Chandrachud's long tenure were chosen from thirteen high courts. In each instance, attention was paid to the region where the high court was located.

Given the fractious nature of Indian federalism and the linguistic and cultural differences among many of the states, the representation of individual states is more important than being from the same region. Assam would hardly feel represented by Orissa, though both are in the eastern region. Similarly, Rajasthan would not feel represented by Jammu and Kashmir, though both are considered northern states. The premium placed on geographic representation—on the membership of the SCI being a veritable map of India—means that the Court is an institution that has enhanced the unity of India.

Working closely with men from throughout the country was difficult for some of the judges. One said that 'we are a bunch of strangers, disparate elements from distant parts of this vast subcontinent. We have nothing in common, can't make friends, there is no sense of brotherhood. We come from different states and we don't have mutual respect for each other'. A judge from the north said that if he was on an airplane and seated between a European and a judge from the south, he would be more comfortable conversing with the European.

[2] S.M. Sikri, A.N. Grover, I.D. Dua, and H.R. Khanna in 1971–2.
[3] E.S. Venkataramiah, K. Jagannatha Shetty, and M.N.R. Venkatachaliah in 1987–9.

VII

Education

The judges received their baccalaureate degrees from about three dozen colleges in India, ranging from the oldest and most prestigious—Presidency College, Madras (twelve); Elphinstone College, Bombay (nine); Presidency College, Calcutta (five); and Ewing Christian College, Allahabad (five)—to the relatively unknown with modest reputations such as Holkar College in Indore and St. Andrews College in Gorakhpur. Well over half of the colleges can claim only one of its graduates as an SCI judge.

Baccalaureate (pre-law) Degrees	1950–70 (per cent)	1971–89 (per cent)	1950–89 (per cent)
India	72.5	98.0	86.8
England	12.5	2.0	6.6
Both	15.0	0.0	6.6
Totals	100.0	100.0*	100.0

* Neither M.P. Thakkar nor A.M. Ahmadi earned undergraduate degrees prior to beginning their law college education.

The differences between the two generations are significant. A dozen received an undergraduate degree in England, most from a college affiliated with Cambridge University, and all but one (M.H. Beg) of these was a pre-1971 appointee. Second generation judges remained at home for their baccalaureate degrees. Significant also is the fact that second generation judges were twice as likely as the first to be the first college graduate in their extended families.

Sixteen earned MA or MSc degrees, again more often those who served before 1971.

Law Degrees

Three-quarters of the judges earned an LLB or BL from one of nearly two dozen different law colleges in India. Almost all (twenty) of the South Indian judges were graduates of the Madras Law College. Next were Government Law College, Bombay (seven); University Law College, Calcutta (seven); Government Law College, Lahore (six); and five from Allahabad University. The list also includes many unfamiliar law colleges—Sarvajanik Law College in Surat and Earle Law College in Guwahati, being examples. There is a major divide between the two generations, for example, the eight who earned LLBs from universities in England were all first generation judges.

Advanced law degrees were uncommon but two of these were earned doctorates—B.K. Mukherjea's from Calcutta University in 1923 and T.K. Thommen's from the University of Leyden, Netherlands, in 1962.

Barristers

Two dozen had been called to the bar from one of the four Inns of Court in London. Again, the generational differences are significant. Seventeen (42.5 per cent) of the pre-1971 appointees had barrister credentials and only seven (13.2 per cent) of the post-1970 judges were so credentialed. There were years in the 1960s when a majority of the sitting judges were barristers. It was not uncommon for future SCI colleagues educated in England to have become acquainted there. P. Jaganmohan Reddy, A.N. Grover, and M.H. Beg were there at the same time.[1]

Ten of the barristers came to the SCI from Calcutta. That city had been the nation's capital until 1905 and many English barristers practised before the Calcutta High Court. Only barristers could practise on the more prestigious and remunerative 'original side' and be members of the

[1] Jaganmohan Reddy, *Down Memory Lane: The Revolutions I Have Lived Through* (Jaipur: Printwell and Rupa Books, 1993; revised edition, Hyderabad: Booklinks Corporation, 2000). There he also met S. Mohan Kumaramangalam.

exclusive Bar Library Club. To compete and enjoy the same status, Indians had to become barristers themselves. Two factors have resulted in barristers becoming virtually a vanishing breed. Soon after Independence the Reserve Bank of India refused to sanction foreign exchange for travel to England to seek barrister credentials, and the Advocates Act, 1961 put home-grown advocates and barristers on the same footing.

As was the case with baccalaureate degrees, many who earned law degrees or were called to the bar won recognition and prizes and medals for having demonstrated academic excellence. Both B.K. Mukherjea and R.N. Misra won gold medals for having stood first in their universities in the LLB and LLM examinations. Y.V. Chandrachud earned a first class first in the LLB examination at the Poona Law College. S.C. Roy passed the LLB and the bar final from Lincoln's Inn with a double first. A smaller percentage of second generation judges were recognized for superior academic achievement but the differences were not significant. Not once was a judge's academic record or reputation of the undergraduate or law college from which he graduated mentioned by a CJI as something that had any bearing upon on his appointment to the SCI.

VIII

Indian Civil Service Officers

Six[1] of the judges were officers of the storied ICS—the elite civil service trained during the colonial years. Entry was the ambition of nearly every student of outstanding merit. Acceptance was extremely competitive and there was not a more prestigious position for an Indian. There was no shame in failing and at least a half dozen other SCI judges had tried but failed to gain acceptance, remained in England to be called to the bar, and began their trek to the SCI as practising lawyers.[2] Four[3] of them had neither a law degree nor barrister credentials. The two years of probationary training in England included very little attention to law—what little there was dealt with criminal law. Upon returning to India, they worked their way up the judicial ladder. None had practised law but all brought decades of practical experience to the SCI, particularly in criminal law, an area that few SCI judges could claim much experience. One of them, K.N. Wanchoo, served as CJI in 1967–8. The six served during the 1956–71 years. The ICS ended in 1947 and its successor, the Indian Administrative Service, has no 'judicial side'.

[1] S.K. Das, K.N. Wanchoo, K.C. Das Gupta, R. Dayal, Vaidyanthier Ramaswami, and V. Bhargava. A seventh, A.K. Mukherjea had served in the ICS but resigned, became a barrister and practised at and reached the SCI from the Calcutta High Court. An excellent account of the ICS by an ICS judge is G.D. Khosla, *Memory's Gay Chariot: An Autobiographical Narrative* (New Delhi: Allied Publishers Pvt. Ltd., 1985). He served on the Punjab High Court.

[2] Most preferred that this matter be off-the-record.

[3] Das Gupta and Ramaswami, on leave, returned to England and qualified as barristers.

IX

Professional Careers

The average age at which these men had completed their education and commenced their professional careers was twenty-four. All, except the six ICS officers, began as practising lawyers, usually before the high court of the state where they were born and to which they would later be appointed.

An average of thirty-four years later, they were SCI judges. For P.N. Bhagwati, the journey took just twenty-eight years. For A.D. Koshal, the trip took forty-two. Because appointment to a high court preceded appointment to the SCI for all except the three appointed directly from the bar, serving on a high court was a rite of passage, so their paths to the high courts merit attention.

The private practice of five was very brief—they would join their state's judicial service soon after receiving their law degree. R.S. Sarkaria, for example, was twenty-seven when he joined the Patiala state judicial service. Twenty-four years later he was appointed to the Punjab and Haryana High Court, and seven years later to the SCI.

Another thirteen left private practice at mid-career, after about a dozen years, to accept appointment usually as a district and sessions judge or an equivalent post. An average of eight years later, they were promoted to their state's high court. Typical of this group was D.A. Desai who, after fifteen years of private practice, accepted appointment as an additional judge and assistant sessions judge at age forty. Eight years later, he was a member of the Gujarat High Court.

Thirty-four, in addition to private practice, had some experience as lawyers for the state or union governments. Illustrations of these posts are junior or senior standing counsel, government pleader, public prosecutor, and advocate general. Most of these posts were part-time and permitted simultaneous private practice, though the rules were not the same in every state. Some were, or once were, considered stepping stones to the high court.

The remaining thirty-two engaged only in private practice. No one spent longer in private practice before a high court than T.L. Venkataramana Ayyar. His appointment to the Madras High Court did not come until he was fifty-seven, thirty-four years after his private practice commenced.

Immediately prior to appointment to the high court, forty-four were engaged solely in private practice and another twenty were also in private practice but also serving in some capacity as lawyers for the government. Twenty held judicial service posts—twelve as district and sessions judges, five as high court registrars, and three as judicial secretaries. Three were serving as commission or tribunal members. S. Ranganathan, for example, resigned from the Income Tax Appellate Tribunal to accept appointment as a judge of the Delhi High Court. The remaining two—K.S. Hegde and B. Islam— resigned Rajya Sabha seats to become judges of the Mysore (Karnataka) and Gauhati High Courts, respectively.

X

Participation in Politics

Participation in politics prior to high court or SCI appointment was more common than most realize. The late Professor S.P. Sathe, a leading student of the SCI, wrote in 2006: 'With a few exceptions, the judges have lacked political experience. ... Only two judges have been active in politics before joining the judiciary, namely Krishna Iyer and PB Sawant JJ. Both were leftists'.[1] In fact, more that a quarter of the judges had engaged in political activities before their high court appointments. Active participation in the Freedom Struggle was the most common. Almost all these were post-1970 SCI appointees who were students during those years. Four reported that they were jailed by the British—J.L. Kapur during the Salt Satyagraha in the early 1930s, and the other three during the 1942 Quit India Movement—B. Jagannadhadas, S.N. Dwivedi, and P.N. Bhagwati.

Nature of Activity	Number of Judges*
Nationalist Movement Participant	14
Nationalist Movement Jailed	4
Held Elective Office	5
Defeated Legislative Assembly Candidate	3
Political Party Activist	6
Union Leader	2
Other	6

Note: *Several reported more than one type of activity.

[1] 'India from Positivism to Structuralism', in Jeffrey Goldsworthy (ed.), *Interpreting Constitutions: A Comparative Study* (New Delhi: Oxford University Press, 2007), pp. 215–65, especially, p. 263.

Five held elected office: one at the city level (B. Jagannadhadas), two at the state level (G. Hasan and V.R. Krishna Iyer), and two at the national level (K.S. Hegde and B. Islam). B.C. Ray stood as a Congress party candidate in West Bengal in 1955 but lost to the Communist Party candidate. G.L. Oza stood as the Socialist Party candidate in the 1952 Madhya Pradesh state election and was defeated by the Congress candidate. K.N. Saikia was an unsuccessful Janata Party candidate for a seat in the Assam Legislative Assembly. Both S. Mukharji and A.N. Sen were offered but declined Congress tickets for West Bengal legislative assembly elections. Those identified as party workers/activists included K.N. Singh, who held Congress Party posts in Uttar Pradesh for more than a decade, and D.A. Desai who for a decade was closely associated with the Congress Socialist Party in Gujarat. Illustrative of the union leader category were M.P. Thakkar who served as president of four trade unions in Gujarat and J.L. Kapur who was no less active in Punjab. Among the unclassified was M.C. Mahajan who, on leave from the East Punjab High Court, served as prime minister of Jammu and Kashmir immediately after Partition.

Almost all of those who were active in politics of any stripe were among those appointed after 1970. For almost all, by the time they reached the SCI, their earlier participation in political activities had long been buried and forgotten. The notable exception was Krishna Iyer who had been a minister in Kerala's first communist-led government and who arrived in Delhi carrying well-known leftist political baggage. There were two instances where the judge went directly from politics to a high court. These were Hegde who resigned from the Rajya Sabha in 1957 to accept an appointment to the Mysore (Karnataka) High Court, and Islam, who in 1972 resigned from the Rajya Sabha to become a judge of the Gauhati High Court.

XI

Arrival on the High Court

Appointment to the high court came at an average age of 46.4. The difference between the two periods was fractional—less than one per cent. The youngest, at thirty-seven, were S.M. Fazal Ali and R.S. Pathak. The eldest was T.L. Venkatarama Ayyar at fifty-seven.

There was some variation among the high courts concerning the age for appointment. Those who came to the SCI from the Bombay High Court averaged forty-five years when appointed, while the average age at the time of high court appointment of those from the Madras High Court, who came to the SCI, was fifty-one.[1]

Those who were promoted to the SCI arrived with an average of 12.4 years of high court experience. The generational differences are significant—10.9 years for the first and 13.6 for the second. S. Fazl Ali's 19.2 years of service on the Patna High Court was the lengthiest, and T.L. Venkatarama Ayyar, with only 2.4 years, the least. He and B. Jagannadhadas were the only two SCI judges whose high court service totalled less than five years. Thus, they qualified for appointment to the SCI not on the basis of their high court

---

[1] These late high court appointments were the main reason why Madras judges were older than the norm when they arrived in Delhi. Because of their advanced age and the convention of the seniormost associate judge becoming CJI, none ever reached the seniormost position, and the only Madras judge who became CJI did so only because of the premature death of H.J. Kania.

tenure, but because they had been 'for at least ten years an advocate of a High Court or of two or more such Courts in succession'.[2]

XII

High Court Seniority

Nearly half of those promoted to the SCI were high court chief justices. More than 80 per cent (85.2 per cent during the first period, 82.4 per cent during the second) were fourth or higher in seniority. For almost all of the eighteen judges who were fifth or lower, there is an explanation. Two illustrations will suffice. A.K. Sarkar was sixth on the Calcutta High Court. He was selected by CJI S.R. Das, whom he had known for decades, had worked as a junior in his chambers, and later sat with him on the Calcutta High Court. B.C. Ray was eighth in seniority at Calcutta. He was appointed because the SCI needed a Scheduled Caste judge and he was the most senior one in the country when appointed in 1985.

Seniority	1950–70 (per cent)	1971–89 (per cent)	1950–89 (per cent)
Chief Justice	46.2	47.1	46.7
Second	20.5	9.8	14.4
Third	12.8	11.8	12.2
Fourth	5.1	13.7	9.9
Fifth	2.6	3.9	3.3
Sixth	2.6	3.9	3.3
Seventh	0.0	2.0	1.1
Eighth	0.0	3.9	2.2
Retired	10.3	3.9	6.7
Totals	100.1	100.0	99.8

Seniority and length of experience relative to chief justices of other high courts are not always the same thing. One can rise to the chief justiceship quickly on a small high court. P.K. Goswami, for example, became chief justice of the Gauhati High Court just two and a half years after his appointment to that small court. After a total of only just over six years, he was sworn in as a judge of the SCI. CJI Bhagwati in 1985 pressed strongly for the appointment of P.B. Sawant of the Bombay High Court. Sawant had the lengthy experience—a dozen years—but he was eighth in seniority and the executive refused to appoint him.

The premium placed upon seniority is not simply to assure that seasoned high court judges reach the SCI. It also reduces the possibly of 'extraneous considerations'—political or caste considerations are examples—being promotion criteria. One CJI made the point that when he is looking for a high court judge to bring to the SCI, he felt that he must take the senior-most chief justice unless the next most senior is 'head and shoulders' a better choice.

XIII

Age and Tenure

The average age of appointment to the SCI was 58.5. The difference between the two generations was negligible—58.1 for the first and 58.8 for the second. The youngest was P.N. Bhagwati at fifty-one, and the eldest, on the cusp of his sixty-third birthday, was K.N. Saikia. Twenty-nine were sixty or older, and twenty were fifty-five or under.

The age of appointees depended to some extent on who was the CJI. S.R. Das clearly looked for relatively young men. The average age of his ten was 56.6 years, and six would go on to become CJIs. The five P.N. Bhagwati succeeded in getting appointed averaged 60.3 years and none were in line to become CJI.

There is, of course, some relationship between age and high court seniority when appointed, but the older appointees are quite often not the most senior on their high courts. One can be very young and very senior—the two youngest appointees, Bhagwati and Hidayatullah, were both chief justices of their high courts when they took their seats on the SCI. Conversely, one could be in his sixties and have more high court experience than the norm but be below the norm in seniority. This was true of S. Natarajan of the Madras High Court. When sworn in, he was sixty-one, had been a Madras High Court judge for thirteen years, but was third in seniority.

The age of appointees has not been a matter of much public concern. And to the extent that concern has been expressed, it has been directed most at appointments of men at the younger end. There has been little criticism over the appointment of septuagenarians.

The most obvious result of tenures averaging six and a half years is frequent turnover. Welcoming handshakes and goodbye's were routine. There were only five years when there was no fresh appointment, and five when there was not a single retirement.

The average expected tenure was six and a half years. But the actual average tenure was slightly lower because of deaths and resignations. Nine[1] died while on the bench and eleven[2] resigned.

---

[1] H.J. Kania (1951), G. Hasan (1954), P.G. Menon (1957), P.S. Raju (1966), S.C. Roy (1971), A.K. Mukherjea (1973), S.N. Dwivedi (1974), S.M. Fazal Ali (1985), and S. Mukharji (1990). A medical certificate is required before one is appointed but this didn't prevent several from arriving in Delhi in very poor health.

[2] B.K. Mukherjea (1956), B. Jagannadhadas (1958), S.J. Imam (1964), J.R. Mudholkar (1966), K. Subba Rao (1967), J.M. Shelat (1973), K.S. Hegde (1973), A.N. Grover (1973), H.R. Khanna (1977), B. Islam (1983), and R.S. Pathak (1989).

XIV

After Retirement

After being forced to leave the bench at sixty-five, less than half a dozen went quietly into the night and spent the evenings of their lives completely retired. For the remainder, retirement was often just a brief pause in their careers. Their average age at death was close to eighty and some remained active literally until the end. If retirement from the Court had not been mandatory, more than a few acknowledged that they would have continued.

A judge's pension was unattractive and, in the absence of substantial savings, inherited wealth, or other sources of income, his standard of living would likely diminish. In the mid-1980s, a judge whose combined high court and SCI service totalled twenty years, was entitled to a pension of about Rs 2,000 per month. At the then exchange rate, this amounted to the equivalent of about US $160. And that was before taxes. Their salaries on the Court were about double the amount of the pension. Several told the author that in order to maintain a respectable standard of living during their years as high court and SCI judges, they had depleted much of their savings. One was compelled to sell half of his library to raise funds for the marriage of his first daughter, later the remainder for the wedding of the second. By the 1980s, leading lawyers earned more in one day than a judge earned in a month. One judge said that some lawyers mocked them because of their 'small pay packets'.[1]

---

[1] Low salaries have deterred top advocates from accepting high court judgeships for decades. This was a concern expressed during the debates in the Constituent Assembly

As judges they were provided a furnished rent-free house, servants, and other allowances and perks, but all of that ended when they retired. Two of those who chose to remain in Delhi, and many did, said it was necessary to commute half of their pension to purchase a home. Some judges said they simply had to supplement their pensions in order to live at least reasonably comfortably and with the dignity appropriate to the high office they had held.

For nearly three-quarters of them, the most common activity was serving as chairman of one or more of the ubiquitous national or state commissions, tribunals, and committees. The nomenclature of the bodies varied and is not important for our purposes. Hereafter, the generic term 'commission' will be used for all. The point to be made here is that such work meant that the judge was back on the government payroll. His SCI salary was effectively restored, and again he was provided a rent-free accommodation, staff, and other amenities. Such posts also meant the retention of high status, especially important in India.

India is a land of commissions—a 'commission culture' was the term used by one CJI. Commissions are a highly institutionalized tradition, a deeply ingrained feature of the political culture. The British made occasional use of judge-staffed commissions, but after Independence they have exploded in number. At any one time dozens are functioning, providing many job opportunities for retired SCI and high court judges.

These bodies vary widely in purpose, importance, and prestige. Some of the more prized ones carry a fixed term and are 'owned' by retired SCI judges—the Law Commission and Press Council of India are prime examples. A few require that the head be a retired SCI judge—the National Consumer Disputes Redressal Commision is one of them. Most, however, are appointed for a specific purpose and usually in response to a demand from a segment of the public for a 'judicial inquiry'. The latter has long been a familiar phrase of the lexicon of Indian politics and public life. Retired

---

in the 1940s. The old tradition of accepting an invitation to become a high court judge eroded rather quickly after 1950, first in the old Presidency high courts and later in the newer ones, and the low salaries were often cited as the major reason. The problem of getting the best from the bar onto their high court was expressed by several SCI judges who had been high court chief justices. Few high court judges invited to become SCI judges declined. Some said that the increased pension was an important attraction, but less so than the higher status and prestige of serving on the nation's highest court. Salaries are set in the Constitution and improvements require a constitutional amendment.

judges are almost invariably demanded to head such inquiries *because* they have been judges, and are perceived to be more detached, unbiased, honest, and impartial than others. An excellent illustration was former CJI Y.V. Chandrachud's investigation of allegations of match-fixing by Indian cricket players which attracted national and international attention.

Retired SCI judges have headed inquiries into dozens of matters, including communal riots, deaths resulting from poisoned liquor, the slaughter of cows, the murder of public figures, the crash of a train or airplane, disturbances on a university campus, and strikes by workers and government employees. Alleged corruption by holders of high political office has been the subject of many judge-led investigations. Others examine matters such as state boundary disputes, the sharing of inter-state waters, the criteria for defining the OBC, and the working of India's federal system. Indeed, there are few matters that have escaped investigation by judges.

Not all commissions are established for noble purposes. Retired judges have acknowledged that some they headed were politically motivated witch hunts aimed at harassing political rivals. Often, the government appoints a commission to get a hot issue off the agenda, to mollify public opinion, or to satisfy opposition demands, and hands the matter to a judge to buy time, hoping that by the time the report is completed, the crisis will have been diffused, if not forgotten. Some, disputes over the sharing of inter-state waters being a good example, continue for decades. Often, the judge is given a deadline for his report but it is not uncommon for him to request extensions. Few seem in a hurry to complete their work.

Some judges move from one to another, occasionally heading more than one simultaneously. P.B. Gajendragadkar headed six different official bodies, J.L. Kapur, five. Some judges seem willing to accept any commission invitation, even ones that would seem to need no more than a district judge as chairman. Others accepted only national-level ones, feeling it was below their station to head a state-level one. A few refused to accept any commission assignments because they viewed them as either inappropriate for a retired SCI judge or as a 'waste of time'. These bodies are unlike courts in that they can offer only findings and make recommendations. Some are abruptly terminated when a new government is elected. The fact that their reports are often ignored, or otherwise not acted upon, seemed not to diminish the enthusiasm of retired judges for such work.

The reports of some have had important consequences, including the resignations of union cabinet ministers and state chief ministers. Former

CJI R.S. Pathak investigated allegations that External Affairs Minister Natwar Singh benefited financially from lucrative contracts from the United Nations Oil-for-Food Program. His 2006 report resulted in the resignation of Singh. S. Fazl Ali headed the States Reorganization Commission in the 1950s. His report established the blueprint for the massive reorganization of the Indian states. R.S. Sarkaria's review of the workings of Indian federalism in the 1980s precipitated a national seminar on the subject and is still cited frequently, though most of its recommendations have not been accepted. The reports of some have remained controversial decades later. What is invariably referred to as the Mahajan Commission failed to settle a boundary dispute between the states of Karnataka and Maharashtra in the 1960s. That dispute continues to fester today.

Putting retired judges back on the public payroll has been criticized. As early as 1958, the *Fourteenth Report* of the Law Commission recommended that such re-employment be banned because sitting judges desiring such work may be less independent of the executive. Three CJIs said that it was apparent that some judges, hoping for post-retirement employment, revealed a tendency to be more pro-government as their retirement dates drew near. One of the sitting judges acknowledged that less well-off judges like him have an 'inevitable tendency' towards the end of their tenure to become more 'executive-minded'.

There is ample evidence that judges whose decisions have not pleased the government have not been invited to chair commissions. Neither K. Subba Rao nor M. Hidayatullah was called upon to head a commission during Mrs Gandhi's first regime, nor were most of the seven who were in the *Kesavananda* majority, until after Mrs Gandhi was defeated in 1977 and the succeeding Janata government offered all of the latter jobs of one kind or another.

The second most common activity of retired judges was 'chamber' or 'consultation' practice. About one-quarter of the judges acknowledged engaging in such activity. Here the judge provides advice to clients for a fee and the fees were often substantial. Retired judges could double their monthly pension by one brief consultation. Very quickly retired SCI judges were engaging in such activity. Most of those who engaged in such activity were forthright in admitting it. Others were defensive about cashing in on their status as retired SCI judges in this manner, usually offering the justification that they simply needed the money. New Delhi was the best location for such activity. Bombay offered opportunities too, but Calcutta and Madras judges reported that there was little scope for chamber practice in those cities.

The Constitution prohibits a retired SCI judge from returning to the practice of law in any court or before any authority but is silent about chamber practice. The latter dates to the 1950s, and the *Fourteenth Report* expressed 'grave doubts' whether chamber practice is consistent with the dignity of these retired judges and consistent with the high traditions which retired judges observe in other countries'.[2] Some judges felt strongly that such activity was unconstitutional. Chamber practice became more common in the 1970s and 1980s.

Another relatively common post-retirement activity of the judges was serving as an arbitrator. About one-fifth served in this capacity. Some did so at the request of the CJI, but more often it was quarrelling private parties who sought the intervention of judges. More than a dozen devoted considerable time to the field of education, particularly educational administration. Four went directly from the bench to become vice-chancellors of universities. Riding the lecture circuit—delivering memorial or endowment lectures—was another common activity. Some became authors of books or editors of revised editions of standard law commentaries. There was sameness to their lectures and publications—the Constitution and the rule of law were common topics. Few of the judges could fairly be labeled as scholars and very little of their writings can be considered important contributions. There are exceptions, of course, the most notable one being B.K. Mukherjea's *The Hindu Law of Religious and Charitable Trusts*, still regarded, more than a half century later, as the definitive work on the subject. Another likely to stand the test of time is O. Chinnappa Reddy's recent *The Court and the Constitution of India: Summits and Shadows*.

Seven entered or returned to the political arena. Three (K. Subba Rao, H.R. Khanna, and Krishna Iyer), each in opposition to the ruling party candidate, made failed attempts to win the presidency of India. At least two

[2] Vol. 1, p. 45. Later the members of this law commission used more ominous language. After quoting an unnamed 'leading counsel in Bombay' who said that retired judges have been charging '...Rs. 10,000 or Rs. 15,000 or even Rs. 20,000' for advice after they retired, the members warned that 'The possibility of their being able to advise rich clients after their retirement may tend to affect their independence on the Bench. In any event, if judges are to be permitted to practise by giving advice after retirement, the public would be apt to think that in dealing with the cases of rich litigants whom they may hope after retirement to be asked to advise, the judges may not act impartially'. vol. 1, pp. 87–8.

others wanted the presidency, but were not nominated. K.S. Hegde, who had been a Member of Parliament before becoming a high court judge, won election to the Lok Sabha after resigning from the SCI, and was elected to be its Speaker. M. Hidayatullah was elected Vice-President and, as such, became the leader of the Rajya Sabha. B. Islam returned to the Rajya Sabha and R.N. Misra won a seat in the Rajya Sabha as well.

For some, their post-retirement activities constituted another career and some are remembered more for their post-superannuation activities than their years on the Court.

The Archetypal Judge

He was the son of a lawyer, often born into a family where the practice of law had been a tradition for generations. He was a Hindu and, more likely than not, a brahmin. He was born in an urban area into a wealthy or upper middle-class family. His state and region of birth could have been anywhere in the nation—the SCI is a national institution and states containing nearly 97 per cent of the Indian population have been represented on the Court.

He received both his baccalaureate and law degrees in India. He was a high achiever, often the recipient of prestigious academic awards. He began his professional career at age twenty-four when he commenced the practice law before the high court of his home state. He may have been among the two dozen who was active in politics during these years. Twenty-two years later, after having reached the front rank of the bar of his high court, he was appointed to that court. A dozen years later, by which time he was very senior, usually its chief justice, he was appointed to the SCI. It was his seniority that raised him to the recruitment plateau, but to get to the SCI, he usually needed to be from a particular high court or geographic region. He was no younger than fifty-one and no older than sixty-two. He may have met the usual criteria of merit—integrity, professional competence, incorruptibility, and neutrality towards litigants—but was not selected for that reason. His religion, seniority, state and region of origin, among other considerations, were more weighty than merit as traditionally defined. He was selected for appointment by the CJI but after 1970, the CJI had to share this power of selection with the executive.

He was 58.5 years of age when he arrived in Delhi and served for six and a half years until mandatory retirement forced his departure at age sixty-five. He remained active after leaving the bench. Serving on officially appointed commissions or tribunals and chamber practice were the most common post-retirement activities. He died when he was on the threshold of his eightieth year.

Of course, this brief description of the life and career of an SCI judge masks many significant differences among them. In particular, it overlooks the fact that eighteen had been lower court judges before reaching a high court. It also does not capture significant generational differences. Judges appointed during the first twenty years were more likely to have had substantial contact with a westernized life style and western values. A majority of the first generation had travelled to England for higher education. Almost all of the second received all of their education at home. Of the two dozen barristers, nearly two-thirds were appointed prior to 1971. The first generation was more cosmopolitan in background. The second generation rose from more traditional family backgrounds and was more likely to have attended second-tier and less urban-based colleges. They were, in a word, more Indian, and this was increasingly reflected in the outlooks they brought to Delhi and in the decisions they handed down from the bench.

Background differences nothwithstanding, all brought to the SCI a reputation for integrity and rectitude and left with that reputation intact. They served their nation well. India would not be the vibrant democracy it is without them.

Appendices

Appendix I Judges of the Supreme Court of India, 1950–89

No.	Judge	From	To	Tenure Shortened Because of
01	H.J. Kania	26 Jan. 1950	06 Nov. 1951	Death
02	S. Fazl Ali	26 Jan. 1950	19 Jan. 1951	
		15 Oct. 1951	30 May 1952	
03	M.P. Sastri	26 Jan. 1950	04 Jan. 1954	
04	M.C. Mahajan	26 Jan. 1950	23 Dec. 1954	
05	B.K. Mukherjea	26 Jan. 1950	31 Jan. 1956	Resignation
06	S.R. Das	26 Jan. 1950	01 Oct. 1959	
07	N. Chandrasekhara Aiyar	23 Sep. 1950	24 Jan. 1953	
		05 Oct. 1955	31 Oct. 1955	
		01 Dec. 1955	11 May 1956	
08	V. Bose	05 Mar. 1951	09 Jun. 1956	
		09 Sep. 1957	30 Sep. 1958	
09	G. Hasan	01 Aug. 1951	05 Nov. 1954	Death
10	N.H. Bhagwati	08 Sep. 1952	07 Aug. 1959	
11	B. Jagannadhadas	09 Mar. 1953	08 Sep. 1957	Resignation
12	T.L. Venkatarama Ayyar	04 Jan. 1954	25 Nov. 1958	
		01 Mar. 1961	30 Apr. 1961	
		20 Dec. 1961	06 May 1962	
13	B.P. Sinha	03 Dec. 1954	31 Jan. 1964	

No.	Judge	From	To	Tenure Shortened Because of
14	S.J. Imam	10 Jan. 1955	31 Jan. 1964	Resignation
15	S.K. Das	30 Apr. 1956	03 Sep. 1963	
16	P.G. Menon	01 Sep. 1956	16 Oct. 1957	Death
17	J.L. Kapur	14 Jan. 1957	13 Dec. 1962	
18	P. B. Gajendragadkar	17 Jan. 1957	16 Mar. 1966	
19	A.K. Sarkar	04 Mar. 1957	29 Jun. 1966	
20	K. Subba Rao	31 Jan. 1958	11 Apr. 1967	Resignation
21	K.N. Wanchoo	11 Aug. 1958	25 Feb. 1968	
22	M. Hidayatullah	01 Dec. 1958	17 Dec. 1970	
23	K.C. Das Gupta	24 Aug. 1959	03 Jan. 1965	
24	J.C. Shah	12 Oct. 1959	22 Jan. 1971	
25	R. Dayal	27 Jul. 1960	26 Oct. 1965	
		04 Apr. 1966	07 May 1966	
		08 Aug. 1966	10 Sep. 1966	
26	N. Rajagopala Ayyangar	27 Jul. 1960	15 Dec. 1964	
27	J.R. Mudholkar	03 Oct. 1960	03 Jul. 1966	Resignation
28	S.M. Sikri	03 Feb. 1964	26 Apr. 1973	
29	R.S. Bachawat	07 Sept. 1964	01 Aug. 1969	
30	Vaidyanathier Ramaswami	04 Jan. 1965	30 Oct. 1969	
31	P.S. Raju	20 Oct. 1965	20 Apr. 1966	Death
32	J.M. Shelat	24 Feb. 1966	30 Apr. 1973	Resignation
33	V. Bhargava	08 Aug. 1966	05 Feb. 1971	
		06 Feb. 1971	07 May 1971	
34	G.K. Mitter	29 Aug. 1966	24 Sep. 1971	
		25 Sep. 1971	07 May 1972	
35	C.A. Vaidialingam	10 Oct. 1966	30 Jun. 1972	
		23 Oct. 1972	06 May 1973	
36	K.S. Hegde	17 Jul. 1967	30 Apr. 1973	Resignation
37	A.N. Grover	12 Feb. 1968	31 May 1973	Resignation
38	A.N. Ray	01 Aug. 1969	29 Jan. 1977	
39	P. Jaganmohan Reddy	01 Aug. 1969	23 Jan. 1975	
40	I.D. Dua	01 Aug. 1969	04 Oct. 1972	
		05 Oct. 1972	06 May 1973	
41	S.C. Roy	19 Jul. 1971	12 Nov. 1971	Death
42	D.G. Palekar	19 Jul. 1971	04 Sep. 1974	

No.	Judge	From	To	Tenure Shortened Because of
43	H.R. Khanna	22 Sep. 1971	12 Mar. 1977	Resignation
44	K.K. Mathew	04 Oct. 1971	03 Jan. 1976	
45	M.H. Beg	10 Dec. 1971	22 Feb. 1978	
46	S.N. Dwivedi	14 Aug. 1972	08 Dec. 1974	Death
47	A.K. Mukherjea	14 Aug. 1972	23 Oct. 1973	Death
48	Y.V. Chandrachud	28 Aug. 1972	12 Jul. 1985	
49	A.N. Alagiriswami	17 Oct. 1972	17 Oct. 1975	
50	P.N. Bhagwati	17 Jul. 1973	21 Dec. 1986	
51	V.R.A. Krishna Iyer	17 Jul. 1973	15 Nov. 1980	
52	P.K. Goswami	10 Sep. 1973	01 Jan. 1978	
53	R.S. Sarkaria	17 Sep. 1973	16 Jan. 1981	
54	A.C. Gupta	02 Sep. 1974	01 Jan. 1982	
55	N.L. Untwalia	03 Oct. 1974	01 Aug. 1980	
56	S.M. Fazal Ali	02 Apr. 1975	20 Aug. 1985	Death
57	P.N. Shinghal	06 Nov. 1975	15 Oct. 1980	
58	J. Singh	23 Jan. 1976	25 Jan. 1979	
59	P.S. Kailasam	03 Jan. 1977	12 Sep. 1980	
60	V.D. Tulzapurkar	30 Sep. 1977	09 Mar. 1986	
61	D.A. Desai	30 Sep. 1977	09 May 1985	
62	R.S. Pathak	20 Feb. 1978	18 Jun. 1989	Resignation
63	A.D. Koshal	17 Jul. 1978	07 Mar. 1982	
64	O. Chinnappa Reddy	17 Jul. 1978	25 Sep. 1987	
65	A.P. Sen	17 Jul. 1978	20 Sep. 1988	
66	E.S. Venkataramiah	08 Mar. 1979	18 Dec. 1989	
67	B. Islam	04 Dec. 1980	13 Jan. 1983	Resignation
68	A. Varadarajan	10 Dec. 1980	17 Aug. 1985	
69	A.N. Sen	28 Jan. 1981	01 Oct. 1985	
70	V. Balakrishna Eradi	30 Jan. 1981	19 Jun. 1987	
71	R.B. Misra	30 Jan. 1981	15 Jun. 1986	
72	D.P. Madon	15 Mar. 1983	07 Apr. 1986	
73	S. Mukharji	15 Mar. 1983	25 Sep. 1990	Death
74	M.P. Thakkar	15 Mar. 1983	04 Nov. 1988	
75	R.N. Misra	15 Mar. 1983	26 Nov. 1991	
76	V. Khalid	25 Jun. 1984	01 July 1987	
77	G.L.Oza	29 Oct. 1985	12 Dec. 1989	
78	B.C. Ray	29 Oct. 1985	01 Nov. 1991	

No.	Judge	From	To	Tenure Shortened Because of
79	M.M. Dutt	10 Mar. 1986	30 Oct. 1989	
80	K.N. Singh	10 Mar. 1986	13 Dec. 1991	
81	S. Natarajan	10 Mar. 1986	29 Oct. 1989	
82	M.H. Kania	01 May 1987	18 Nov. 1992	
83	K. Jagannatha Shetty	01 May 1987	15 Dec. 1991	
84	L.M. Sharma	05 Oct. 1987	12 Feb. 1993	
85	M.N.R. Venkatachaliah	05 Oct. 1987	25 Oct. 1994	
86	S. Ranganathan	05 Oct. 1987	31 Oct. 1992	
87	N.D. Ojha	18 Jan. 1988	19 Jan. 1991	
88	S.R. Pandian	14 Dec. 1988	13 Mar. 1994	
89	T.K. Thommen	14 Dec. 1988	26 Sep. 1993	
90	A.M. Ahmadi	14 Dec. 1988	25 Mar. 1997	
91	K.N. Saikia	14 Dec. 1988	01 Mar. 1991	
92	K. Singh	14 Dec. 1988	01 Jan. 1997	
93	J.S. Verma	03 Jun. 1989	18 Jan. 1998	

Appendix II   Chief Justices of India, 1950–89*

Chief Justice	From	To
H.J.Kania	26 Jan. 1950	06 Nov. 1951[a]
M.P. Sastri	07 Nov. 1951	03 Jan. 1954
M.C. Mahajan	04 Jan. 1954	22 Dec. 1954
B.K. Mukherjea	23 Dec. 1954	31 Jan. 1956[b]
S.R. Das	01 Feb. 1956	30 Sep. 1959
B.P. Sinha	01 Oct. 1959	31 Jan. 1964
P.B. Gajendragadkar	01 Feb. 1964	15 Mar. 1966
A.K. Sarkar	16 Mar. 1966	28 Jun. 1966
K. Subba Rao	29 Jun. 1966	11 Apr. 1967[c]
K.N. Wanchoo	12 Apr. 1967	24 Feb. 1968
M. Hidayatullah	25 Feb. 1968	16 Dec. 1970
J.C. Shah	17 Dec. 1970	21 Jan. 1971
S.M. Sikri	22 Jan. 1971	25 Apr. 1973
A.N. Ray	26 Apr. 1973	28 Jan. 1977
M.H. Beg	29 Jan. 1977	21 Feb. 1978
Y.V. Chandrachud	22 Feb. 1978	11 Jul. 1985
P.N. Bhagwati	12 Jul. 1985	20 Dec. 1986
R.S. Pathak	21 Dec. 1986	18 Jun. 1989[d]

Notes:

Had Kania not died, neither M.P. Sastri nor M.C. Mahajan would have become CJI. Had P.S. Raju, S.C. Roy, S.N. Dwivedi, and A.K. Mukhjerjea not died, each would have served as CJI. Had S.J. Imam, J.M. Shelat (who could expect to become CJI only after Raju's death), K.S. Hegde, A.N. Grover, and H.R. Khanna not resigned, each would have had a spell as CJI. Ray was never in line to become CJI—he became such only because of the 1973 supersession. So had there been no deaths or resignations, there would have been twenty-two CJIs during the four decades.

[a] Date of death
[b] Date of resignation for health reasons
[c] Date of resignation to enter the political arena
[d] Date of resigntion to become a judge of the International Court of Justice

Glossary

Additional judge
>   Many who became permanent high court judges were first appointed as additional judges for a period not exceeding two years. An additional judge is not in a probationary status.

Bank Nationalization
>   *Rustom Cowasjee Cooper* v. *Union of India* [1970] 3 SCR 530. SCI declared unconstitutional Prime Minister Indira's Gandhi's effort to nationalize the nation's banks.

Brahmin (Brahman)
>   A member of the priestly-scholarly class in the Hindu caste system. The highest of the four orders into which society is divided by Hindu tradition.

District and Sessions Judge
>   Presides over the highest court in each district. Deals with both civil and criminal cases. The level of judiciary just below a high court and is under latter's administrative and judicial control.

Diwan (Dewan)
>   The chief minister of a state ruled by an Indian prince.

Emergency
>   State of Emergency declared by Prime Minister Indira Gandhi in June 1975 which enabled her to rule by decree. Elections were suspended, the press was censored, tens of thousands, including leaders of the opposition, were jailed, and a citizen's right to move any court for the

enforcement of any Fundamental Right were suspended. Ended when Mrs Gandhi was defeated at polls in March 1977.

Fourteenth Report

The Law Commission of India's classic and frequently-cited two volumes *Reform of Judicial Administration* published in 1958.

Golaknath

I.C. *Golaknath & Ors v. The State of Punjab* [1967] 2 SCR 762. By a six-to-five majority the SCI overruled precedents to the contrary and denied Parliament the right to amend the Constitution to take away or abridge a Fundamental Right.

Habeas Corpus

Additional District Magistrate, Jabalpur v. Shivkant Shukla, [1976] Supp SCR 172. SCI ruled that during a declared emergency, citizens could be deprived of life or liberty without the authority of law.

Indian Civil Service (ICS)

The elite civil service during British rule.

Kesavananda

His Holiness Keshavananda Bharati Sripadagalavaru v. State of Kerala [1973] Supp SCR 1. Often referred to as the 'Fundamental Rights' case. The majority ruled that SCI could strike down amendments to the Constitution which conflict with the Court's definition of the 'basic structure' of the Constitution.

Lok Ayukta

Anti-government corruption institution in states for the redressal of citizen grievances.

Mukhtar

Lowest grade of lawyers

Munsif

A judge of the lowest rank

Other Backward Classes (OBC)

Groups who, because of their low social and economic position, are singled out for special preferential treatment in education, recruitment to government employment, and the like. Composition varies from state to state.

Pleader

A name for a lawyer lower in rank than an advocate.

Privy Purses

H.H. *Maharaja Dhiraja Madhav Rao Jiwaji Rao Scindia Bahadur & Ors*

v. *Union of India* [1971] 3 SCR 9. SCI struck down a presidential order which sought to 'de-recognize' the former rulers of the princely states and enable the government to end the payment of privy purses to the ex-princes.

Puisne
A judge inferior in rank or junior to the chief justice. The term 'associate' is used in its place in this book.

Scheduled Castes (Dalits)
Those social groups designated by the government to receive educational, employment, housing, and other concessions and privileges. Castes or communities traditionally looked upon by orthodox Hindus as impure or 'untouchable'.

Scheduled Tribes (Adivasis)
Those tribal groups designated by the government to receive special concessions and privileges in education, employment and other areas in order to hasten their integration into Indian society.

Supersession
Mrs Gandhi's government in April 1973 violated the convention that the most senior associate judge of the SCI succeed the retiring chief justice. The fourth most senior judge was made chief justice and the three by-passed judges resigned. There was a second supersession in 1977.

Vakil
A grade of the legal profession lower than advocates but higher than pleaders practising in the subordinate courts.

Zamindar
A landlord, owner of a large agricuiltural estate (*zamindari*).

Bibliography

Books

Akbar, M.J. 1988. *Nehru: The Making of India*. London: Penguin Books Ltd.

Allahabad High Court Centenary Commemoration Volume Committee. 1968. *Centenary of the High Court of Judicature at Allahabad, 1866–1966*. Superintendent, Printing and Stationary, 2 vols, Allahabad Uttar Pradesh: Allahabad High Court Centenary Commemoration Volume Committee.

Amani, Sajid Zaheer. 1982. *Justice Hidayatullah on Commercial Laws*. Delhi: Deep & Deep Publications Pvt. Ltd.

Antulay, A.R. 1973. *Appointment of a Chief Justice: Perspectives on Judicial Independence, Rule of Law and Political Philosophy underlying the Constitution*. Bombay: Popular Prakashan.

Austin, Granville. 1966. *The Indian Constitution: Cornerstone of a Nation*. London: Oxford University Press.

———. 1999. *Working a Democratic Constitution: A History of the Indian Experience*. New Delhi: Oxford University Press.

Babu, I. Sharath and Rashmi Shetty. 2007. *Social Justice and Labour Jurisprudence: Justice V.R. Krishna Iyer's Contributions*. New Delhi: Sage Publications Pvt. Ltd.

Baum, Lawrence. 1998. *The Supreme Court*, sixth edition. Washington DC: CQ Press.

Baxi, Upendra (ed.). 1978. *K.K. Mathew on Democracy, Equality and Freedom.* Lucknow: Eastern Book Company.

———. 1980. *The Indian Supreme Court and Politics.* Lucknow: Eastern Book Company.

———. 1985. *Courage, Craft and Contention: The Indian Supreme Court in the Eighties.* Bombay: N.M. Tripathi Pvt. Ltd.

Bhardwaj, H.R. 1997. *Law, Lawyers and Judges.* Delhi: Konark Publishers Pvt. Ltd.

Bhushan, Prashant. 1978. *The Case That Shook India.* New Delhi: Vikas Publishing House Pvt. Ltd.

Chagla, M.C. 1978. *Roses in December: An Autobiography with Epilogue,* eighth enlarged edition. Bombay: Bharatiya Vidya Bhavan.

Chandavarkar, G.L., A.N. Kothare, and D.N. Marshall (eds). 1973. *Law, Society and Education.* Bombay: Somaiya Publications Pvt. Ltd.

Chander, Shailja. 1992. *Justice V.R. Krishna Iyer on Fundamental Rights and Directive Principles.* New Delhi: Deep & Deep Publications Pvt. Ltd.

Chinnappa Reddy, O. 2008. *The Court and the Constitution of India: Summits and Shallows.* New Delhi: Oxford University Press.

Choudhury, Ram Kishore and Tapash Gan Choudhary (eds). 2008. *Judicial Reflections of Justice Bhagwati.* Kolkata: Academic Foundation & Publication Pvt. Ltd.

Council of Ministers. 2004. *Names and Portfolios of the Members of the Union Council of Ministers (From 15 August 1947 to 25 May 2004).* New Delhi: Lok Sabha Secretariat.

Das, Gobind. 1987. *Supreme Court in Quest of Identity.* Lucknow: Eastern Book Company.

Department of Justice, Ministry of Law and Justice. Various years. *Judges of the Supreme Court and the High Courts.* Delhi: Controller of Publications.

Deshmukh, C.D. 1974. *The Course of My Life.* New Delhi: Orient Longman.

Deshpande, V.S. (ed.). 1985. *A Chandrachud Reader: Collection of Judgements with Annotations.* New Delhi: Centre for Corporate & Business Policy Research.

Dhavan, Rajeev. 1977. *The Supreme Court of India: A Socio-Legal Critique of its Juristic Techniques.* Bombay: N.M. Tripathi Pvt. Ltd.

———. 1978. *The Supreme Court Under Strain: The Challenge of Arrears.* Bombay: N.M. Tripathi Pvt. Ltd.

Dhavan, Rajeev and Alice Jacob. 1978. *Selection and Appointment of Supreme Court Judges: A Case Study.* Bombay: N.M. Tripathi, Pvt. Ltd.

—— (eds). 1978. *Indian Constitution: Trends and Issues*. Bombay: N.M. Tripathi, Pvt. Ltd.

——. 1980. *Justice on Trial: The Supreme Court Today*. Allahabad: A.H. Wheeler & Company Ltd.

——, R. Sudarshan, and Salman Khurshid (eds). 1985. *Judges and the Judicial Power: Essays in Honour of Justice V.R. Krishna Iyer*. London and Bombay: Sweet & Maxwell and N.M. Tripathi Pvt. Ltd.

——. 2000. *Supreme Court of India: Sentinel of Freedom*. New Delhi: Supreme Court of India.

Douglas, William O. 1956. *We the Judges: Studies in American and Indian Constitutional Law from Marshall to Mukherjea*. Garden City, New York: Doubleday and Company Inc.

Engineer, Asghar Ali. 1983. *The Bohras*. New Delhi: Vikas Publishing House Pvt. Ltd.

Gajendragadkar, P.B. 1983. *To the Best of My Memory*. Bombay: Bharatiya Vidya Bhavan.

Gauhati High Court. 1974. *Gauhati High Court, 1948–1973: Silver Jubilee Commemoration Volume*. Gauhati: Souvenir Committee.

Gokhale, B.N. 1963. *The Story of the High Court of Judicature at Bombay after Independence (1947–1962)*. Nagpur: The Maharashtra Law Journal.

Goldsworthy, Jeffrey (ed.). 2007. *Interpreting Constitutions: A Comparative Study*. New Delhi: Oxford University Press.

Gopal, Ram. 1986. *India under Indira*. New Delhi: Criterion Publications.

Gopalratnam, V.C. c. 1962. *A Century Completed: A History of the Madras High Court, 1862–1962*. Madras: Madras Law Journal Office.

Government of India, Ministry of Law, Justice, and Company Affairs. 1963. *Constitution of India, Fifteenth Amendment Act*. New Delhi: Controller of Publications.

Grover, A.N. 1973. 'Questions That Must Be Answered', in Kuldip Nayar (ed.), Supersession of Judges, pp. 55–68.

Gupta, O.N. 1980. *A Gandhi in the Supreme Court*. Delhi: Legal Literary Society.

Gupta, Vijay K. 1995. *Decision Making in the Supreme Court of India*. Delhi: Kaveri Books.

Hamid, Abdul. 1992. *Constitutional Law: A Profile of Justice M. Hidayatullah*, 2 vols, Jaipur: Printwell and Rupa Books.

Hegde, K.S. 1973. *Crisis in Indian Judiciary*. Bombay: Sindhu Publications Pvt. Ltd.

Hegde, Ramakrishna. 1986. *The Judiciary Today: A Plea for a Consortium*, Bangalore: Government of Karnataka.

Hidayatullah, M. 1972. *A Judge's Miscellany*. Bombay: N.M. Tripathi, Pvt. Ltd.

———. 1980. *My Own Boswell*. New Delhi: Arnold-Heinemann Publishers.

High Court at Calcutta: Centenary Souvenir, 1862–1962. 1962. Calcutta: High Court Buildings.

High Court of Judicature at Bombay: Post-Centenary Silver Jubilee, 1862–1987. 1988. Bombay: Government Central Press.

High Court of Judicature at Madras, 1862–1962, Centenary Volume. 1962. Madras: Madras High Court.

Hindustan Year-Book and Who's Who. Various years. edited by S. Sarkar, Calcutta: M.C. Sarkar & Sons Pvt. Ltd.

India Who's Who. Various years. New Delhi: INFA Publications.

Indian Judges: Biographical & Critical Sketches. Madras: G.A. Natesan & Co., 1932. A reprint entitled *Eminent Indian Judges* was published by Mittal Publications, Delhi, in 1988.

Jaganmohan Reddy, P. 1984. *We Have a Republic: Can We Keep It?* Tirupati: Sri Venkateswara University.

———. 1999. *The Judiciary I Served*. Hyderabad: Orient Longman.

———. 2000. *Down Memory Lane: The Revolutions I Have Lived Through*. Jaipur: Printwell and Rupa Books; revised edition, Hyderabad: Booklinks Corporation.

Joseph, E.X. 2005. *V.R. Krishna Iyer: Splendour of Humanism and Justice*. Delhi: Konark Publishers Pvt. Ltd.

Katju, Kailash Nath. 1961. *The Days I Remember*. Calcutta: New Age Publishers Pvt. Ltd.

Khan, Sheeraz Latif A. 1996. *Justice Bhagwati on Fundamental Rights and Directive Principles*. New Delhi: Deep & Deep Publications.

Khanna, Hans Raj. 1985. *Neither Roses Nor Thorns*. Lucknow: Eastern Book Company.

Khosla, G.D. 1985. *Memories Gay Chariot: An Autobiographical Narrative*. New Delhi: Allied Publishers Pvt. Ltd.

Kirby, Michael (ed.). 1998. *Collected Writings and Speeches of Justice P.N. Bhagwati: An Australian Appreciation*. Sydney, Australia: Law and Justice Foundation of New South Wales.

Kirpal, B.N., Ashok H. Desai, Gopal Subramanium, Rajeev Dhavan, and Raju Ramachandran (eds). 2000. *Supreme But Not Infallible: Essays in*

Honour of the Supreme Court of India. New Delhi: Oxford University Press.

Krishna Iyer, V.R. 2003. *Death and After*. Delhi: Konark Publishers Pvt. Ltd.

———. 2003. *Legally Speaking*. New Delhi: Universal Law Publishing Company Pvt. Ltd.

———. 2004. *Leaves from My Personal Life*, New Delhi: Gyan Publishing House.

———. 2009. *Wandering in Many Worlds: An Autobiography*, Noida, UP: Dorling Kindersley (India) Pvt. Ltd.

Krishna, Swamy. 2005. *V.R. Krishna Iyer*. New Delhi: Universal Law Publishing Company Ltd.

Krishnaswamy, P. 2000. *Justice V.R. Krishna Iyer: A Living Legend*. New Delhi: Universal Law Publishing Company Ltd.

Kulshreshtha, Abha and Sushna Kulshreshtha (eds). 2006 *Sriranganathsrih: Gems of Law & Dharmasastra: Justice Ranganath Misra*. New Delhi: Sanjay Prakashan.

Kumar, Raj and K. Chockalingam (eds). 2007. *Human Rights, Justice and Constitutional Empowerment: Essays in Honour of Justice V.R. Krishna Iyer*. New Delhi: Oxford University Press.

Kumaramangalam, S. Mohan. 1973. *Judicial Appointments: An Analysis of the Recent Controversy over the Appointment of the Chief Justice of India*. New Delhi: Oxford and IBH Publishing Co.

Law Commission of India, Ministry of Law. 1958. *Reform of Judicial Administration, Fourteenth Report*, 2 vols, New Delhi: Government of India Press.

———, Ministry of Law, Justice, and Company Affairs. 1980. *The Method of Appointment of Judges, Eightieth Report*, New Delhi: Government of India Press.

———. 1986. *A New Forum for Judicial Appointments, One Hundred Twenty-First Report*. New Delhi: Government of India Press.

———. 1988. *The Supreme Court: A Fresh Look, One Hundred Twenty-Fifth Report*. New Delhi: Government of India Press.

Lok Sabha Secretariat. *Lok Sabha Debates*. New Delhi.

Lok Sabha Secretariat. 1946–50. *Constituent Assembly Debates*, 12 vols, Reprinted by Lok Sabha Secretariat, New Delhi, 1985.

Mahajan, Mehr Chand. 1963. *Looking Back: The Autobiography of Mehr Chand Mahajan, Former Chief Justice of India*. Bombay: Asia Publishing House.

Mahajan, Vidya Dhar. 1966. *Chief Justice Gajendragadkar: His Life, Ideas, Papers and Addresses*. Delhi: S. Chand & Co.

——. 1967. *Chief Justice K. Subba Rao: Defender of Liberties*. Delhi: S. Chand & Co.

——. 1969. *Chief Justice Mehr Chand Mahajan: The Biography of the Great Jurist*. Lucknow: Eastern Book Company.

Manor, James (ed.). 1994. *Nehru to the Nineties: The Changing Office of Prime Minister of India*. Vancouver: University of British Columbia Press.

Mavalankar, G.V. 1955. *My Life at the Bar*. New Delhi: The Hindustan Times Press.

Mirchandani, G.G. 1977. *Subverting the Constitution in India*. New Delhi: Abhinav Publications.

Ministry of Law, Justice and Company Affairs, Government of India. *The Constitution of India (as modified up to the 1st August, 1977.)* New Delhi.

Misra, B.B. 1961. *The Indian Middle Classes: Their Growth in Modern Times*. London: Oxford University Press.

Muhammad, V.A. Seyid. 1975. *Our Constitution for Haves or Have-nots?* Delhi: Lipi Prakashan.

Munshi, K.M. 1963. *The Bombay High Court: Half a Century of Reminiscences*. Bombay: Bharatiya Vidya Bhavan.

Nair, M.P.R. (ed.) and Vinod Sethi (associate editor). 2005. *Justice Krishna Iyer at 90*, Delhi: Universal Law Publishing Company Ltd.

National Commission to Review the Working of the Constitution, 2 vols 2002. Delhi: Controller of Publications.

Nariman, Fali S. 2010. *Before Memory Fades: An Autobiography*. New Delhi: Hay House Publishers (India) Pvt. Ltd.

Nayar, Kuldip. 1973. *Supersession of Judges*. New Delhi: India Book Company.

——. 1975. *India After Nehru*. New Delhi: Vikas Publishing House Pvt. Ltd.

——. 1977. *The Judgement: Inside Story of the Emergency in India*. New Delhi: Vikas Publishing House Pvt. Ltd.

Noorani, A.G. 1970. *India's Constitution and Politics*. Bombay: Jaico Publishing House.

——. 2002. *Citizen's Rights, Judges and State Accountability*. New Delhi: Oxford University Press.

Palkhivala, N.A. (ed.) 1973. *A Judiciary Made to Measure*. Bombay: M.R. Pai.

——. 1975. *Our Constitution, Defaced and Defiled*. New Delhi: Macmillan.

——. 1984. *We the People: India: The Largest Democracy*. Bombay: Strand Book Stall.

Paul, John J. 1991. *The Legal Profession in Colonial South India*. New Delhi: Oxford University Press.

Prasad, Anirudh. 1983. *Democracy, Politics and Judiciary in India*. New Delhi: Deep & Deep Publications Pvt. Ltd.

Sathe, S.P. 2003. *Judicial Activism in India: Transgressing Borders and Enforcing Limits*. New Delhi: Oxford University Press.

Savant, P.B. 1988. *Judicial Independence: Myth and Reality*. Pune: Pune Board of Extra-Mural Studies, University of Poona.

Schmidhauser, John R. (ed.). 1987. *Comparative Judicial Systems: Challenging Frontiers in Conceptual and Empirical Analysis*. London: Butterworths.

Schubert, Glendon and David J. Danelski (eds). 1969. *Comparative Judicial Behavior: Cross-Cultural Studies of Political Decision-Making in the East and West*. New York: Oxford University Press.

Seal, Anil. 1968. *The Emergence of Indian Nationalism*. Cambridge: Cambridge University Press.

Seervai, H.M. 1968. *The Position of the Judiciary under the Constitution of India*. Bombay: University of Bombay.

——. 1983, 1984, and 1988. *Constitutional Law of India: A Critical Commentary*, third (edition), 2 vols and Supplement. Bombay: N.M. Tripathi Pvt. Ltd.

Setalvad, M.C. 1970. *My Life: Law and Other Things*. Bombay: N.M. Tripathi Pvt. Ltd.

Shah, Ghanshyam (ed.). 1998. *D.A. Desai: Social Justice, a Dialogue*. Jaipur: Rawat Publications.

Sharma, A.K. 1985. *Independence of Judiciary and Selection and Appointment of Judges in the Supreme Court of India*, a dissertation submitted in partial fulfilment for the award of the degree of Master of Laws, Faculty of Law, University of Delhi, Delhi.

Sharma, Ram Avtar (ed.). 1984. *Justice and Social Order in India*. New Delhi: Intellectual Publishing House.

Shiva Rao, B. (ed.). 1966–8. *The Framing of India's Constitution*, 5 vols, Bombay: The Indian Institute of Public Administration/N.M. Tripathi Pvt. Ltd.

Shourie, Arun. 1980. *Institutions in the Janata Phase*. Bombay: Popular Prakashan Pvt. Ltd.

——. 1983. *Mrs Gandhi's Second Reign*. New Delhi: Vikas Publishing House Pvt. Ltd.

Shukla, B.M. (ed.). 1998. *Law and Social Justice: A Critical Review of Justice D.A. Desai's Important Judgements*. Jaipur: Rawat Publications.

Singh, Karan. 1982. *Heir Apparent: An Autobiography*. New Delhi: Oxford University Press.

Singh, Mool. 1993. *Justice Iyer's Jurisconscience*. Jaipur: RBSA Publishers.

Sinha, B.P. 1985. *Reminiscences and Reflections of a Chief Justice*. Delhi: B.R. Publishing Corporation.

Sivamohan, M.V.K. (ed.). 1986. *Law & Society: Lectures and Writings of P. Jaganmohan Reddy*. Delhi: Ajanta Publications.

Siwach, J.R. 1986. *Sinking Indian Judicial Pyramid*. Pilani/Delhi: Chinta Prakashan.

Subba Rao, T.V. 1992. *Constitutional Development in India: Contribution of Justice K. Subba Rao*. New Delhi: Deep & Deep Publications Pvt. Ltd.

Supreme Court (Number of Judges) Act, 1956.

Supreme Court (Number of Judges) Amendment Act, 1960.

Supreme Court (Number of Judges) Amendment Act, 1977.

Supreme Court (Number of Judges) Amendment Act, 1986.

Swarup, Hari. 1981. *For Whom the Law is Made: Mind and Faith of Justice V.R. Krishna Iyer*. New Delhi: Veena Publications.

The Times of India Directory and Year Book Including Who's Who, various years, Bombay: Bennett, Coleman & Co. Ltd.

Tiruchelvam, Neelan and Radhika Coommaraswamy (eds). 1987. *The Role of the Judiciary in Plural Societies*. New York: St. Martin's Press.

Venkatarami, R. 1989. *Judgments of O. Chinnappa Reddy: A Humanist*. New Delhi: International Institute of Human Rights Society.

Venugopal K.K., et al. 2005. *Justice Bachawat's Law of Arbitration & Conciliation, including Commercial, International & ADR*, fourth edition, revised and enlarged. Nagpur: Wadhwa and Company.

Verma, S.K. and Kusum (eds). 2000. *Fifty Years of the Supreme Court of India: Its Grasp and Reach*. New Delhi: Oxford University Press.

Law Reporters and Journals

Allahabad Law Journal
All India Reporter
Andhra Law Journal

Andhra Law Times
Banaras Law Journal
Bihar Law Journal
Bihar Law Journal Review
Bombay Law Reporter
Calcutta Weekly Notes
Cuttack Law Times
Delhi Law Review
Gujarat Law Reporter
Indian Bar Review
Indian Journal of Public Administration
Jabalpur Law Journal
Jaipur Law Journal
Jammu & Kashmir Law Journal
Journal of Constitutional and Parliamentary Studies
Journal of the Bar Council of India
Journal of the Indian Law Institute
Karnataka Law Journal
Kerala Law Times
Madhya Pradesh Law Journal
Madras Law Journal
Madras Law Times
Madras Law Weekly
Mysore Law Journal
Nagpur Law Journal
National Law Review
Oudh Weekly Notes
Patna Law Journal
Punjab Law Reporter
Supreme Court Cases
Supreme Court Reports

Newspapers and Periodicals

Economic and Political Weekly
Frontline
The Hindu
The Hindustan Times

India Abroad
India Today
The Overseas Hindustan Times
The Times of India
Tribune, Chandigarh

Articles

'A Bad Decision'. *The Times of India*, 18 January 1983.

'A Controversial Appointment', *The Hindustan Times*, 27 April 1973.

'Address Presented to Hon'ble Shri Justice V.R. Krishna Iyer on his Retirement from the Supreme Court of India' [1981] 1 *Supreme Court Cases (Journal)*.

Baxi, Upendra. 1980. 'Appointment of the Chief Justice of India and Justices of the Supreme Court of India: How Long Shall We Evade *Real* Questions?' Mimeo, paper delivered at the Bar Council of India Trust Seminar on Judicial Appointments and Transfers. 17–19 October.

——. 1987. 'Au Revoir, Justice Bhagwati', *Lex Et Juris*, I, no. 9, January.

——. 1987. 'On the Shame of Not Being an Activist: Thoughts on Judicial Activism', in Neelan Tiruchelvam and Radhika Coomaraswamy (eds), *The Role of the Judiciary in Plural Societies*. New York: St. Martin's Press.

——. 1993. 'Remembering Justice Hidayatullah', [1993] 1 *Supreme Court Cases (Journal)*.

Beaumont, Sir John. 1946. 'The Indian Judicial System: Some Suggested Reforms'. *Bombay Law Reporter (Journal)*, vol. XLVIII.

'Beg is named chief justice; Khanna quits'. *The Times of India*, 29 January 1977.

Bhanot, Harish. 1986. 'I have been looking for grain in mounds of chaff'. *The Overseas Hindustan Times*, 1 November.

Bhatnagar, Rakesh. 1988. 'A-G's view on judicial panel may open a debate'. *The Times of India*, 13 April.

'Bombay Lawyers on Strike', *The Hindustan Times*, 27 April 1973.

'Cabinet Reshuffle: Wheel of Confusion'. *India Today*, 15 March 1988.

Chakravartti, P.B. 1969. 'Appointment to the Supreme Court'. *Calcutta Weekly Notes*, vol. LXXIII.

'Chandrachud to have longest spell as C.J.' *The Times of India*, 8 February 1978.

Chaudhuri, Amiya K. 1977. 'Appointment of a Chief Justice: The Study of a Controversy in a New Perspective'. *Journal of Constitutional and Parliamentary Studies*, vol. 11, no. 4, October–December.

Chawla, Prabhu. 1999. 'Courting Controversy'. *India Today*, 25 January.

'Chief Justice: govt move queried'. *The Times of India*, 7 January 1978.

Chinappa Reddy, O. 1983. 'Socialism under the Constitution: Promise and Performance'. *Indian Bar Review*, vol. X, no. 1.

'CJ to have final say on judges' appointments'. *The Times of India*, 7 October 1993.

'CJ's appointment by consensus, says PM'. *Indian Express*, 21 February 1978.

'Communists stall move on judges' appointments'. *India Abroad*, New York, 28 March 1997.

'Contempt Notice to Shiv Shankar'. *The Times of India*, 11 February 1988.

Daphtary, C.K. 1969. 'Editorial'. *The Indian Advocate*, vol. IX , nos 1 and 2, January–June.

Devadas, David. 1988. 'Thakkar urged to reject offer'. *The Indian Express*, 8 October.

———. 1988. 'Law Commission: Clouds of Controversy'. *India Today*, 15 November.

Desai, P.D. 1992. 'Full Court Reference in Memory of the Late Justice Mohammad Hidayatullah' [1992] 4 *Supreme Court Cases (Journal)*.

Dhavan, Rajeev and Balbir Singh. 1979. 'Publish and Be Damned: The Contempt Power and the Press at the Bar of the Supreme Court'. *Journal of the Indian Law Institute*, vol. 21, no. 1, January–March.

———, Lindsay Harris, and Gopal Jain. 1990. 'Whose Interest? Independent India's Patent Law and Policy'. *Journal of the Indian Law Institute*, vol. 32, no. 4, October–December.

———. 1992. 'The Constitution as the Situs of Struggle: India's Constitution Forty Years On' in Lawrence Beer (ed.), *Constitutional Systems in Late Twentieth Century Asia*, Seattle, WA, USA: University of Washington Press.

Diwan, Anil. 2008. 'A Profile in Judicial Courage'. *The Hindu*, 7 March.

Doshi, Anjali. 2004. 'Fading Away'. *India Today*, 27 September.

'Fading Hope in India'. *The New York Times*, 30 April 1976.

Gadbois, George H. Jr. 1964. 'The Federal Court of India, 1937–1950'. *Journal of the Indian Law Institute*, vol. 6, nos 2 and 3, April–September.

———. 1968–9. 'Indian Supreme Court Judges: A Portrait'. *Law & Society Review*, vol. III, nos 2 & 3, November–February.

——. 1970a. 'Indian Judicial Behaviour'. *Economic and Political Weekly*, vol. 5, nos 3, 4, & 5, Annual Number, January.

—— 1970b. 'The Supreme Court of India: A Preliminary Report of an Empirical Study'. *Journal of Constitutional and Parliamentary Studies*, vol. IV, no. 1, January–March.

——. 1982a. 'Participation in Supreme Court Decision-Making: From Kania to Vaidialingam, 1950–1967'. *Journal of the Indian Law Institute*, vol. 24, no. 1, January–March.

——. 1982b. 'Judicial Appointments in India: The Perils of Non-Contextual Analysis'. *Asian Thought & Society*, vol. VII, no. 7, July.

——. 1984. 'The Decline of Dissent on the Supreme Court', in Ram Avtar Sharma (ed.) *Justice and Social Order in India*. New Delhi: Intellectual Publishing House.

——. 1987. 'The Institutionalization of the Supreme Court of India', in John Schmidhauser (ed.), *Comparative Judicial Systems: Challenging Frontiers in Conceptual and Empirical Analysis*. London: Butterworths.

——. 2004. 'The Selection of Indian Supreme Court Judges', mimeo, paper presented at the annual meeting of the International Political Science Association's Research Committee on Comparative Judicial Studies. London, England: London School of Economics, January.

Gadgil, N.V. 1962. 'Appointment of Judges'. *AIR Journal*.

Gokhale, H.R. 1973. 'Government's Case', in Kuldip Nayar (ed.), *Supersession of Judges*. New Delhi: India Book Company.

Gopalakrishnan, I. 1993. 'Impeachment Fails: Judge Quits'. *Indian Abroad*, New York, 21 May 1993.

'Govt told to appoint judges by Dec. 7'. *The Times of India*, 18 November 1988.

'He lived a full life until the end'. *The Times of India*, 20 September 1992.

'Hegde could have been President', CoastalDigest.com, quoting from blog. lkadvani.in. (Last accessed 10 July 2010).

Hidayatullah, M. 1972. 'Justice Vivian Bose', in M. Hidayatullah, *A Judge's Miscellany*. Bombay: N.M. Tripathi Pvt. Ltd.

Honorary Editor. 'The Re-Shaping of the Supreme Court' [1970] 1 *Supreme Court Cases (Journal)*.

Jacob, Alice. 1977. 'Nehru and the Judiciary', *Journal of the Indian Law Institute*, vol. 19, no. 2, April–June.

Jacob, Alice and Rajeev Dhavan. 1978. 'The Appointment of Supreme Court Judges and Contemporary Politics in India'. *Cochin University*

        Law Review, vol. 2.

'Judiciary still has vitality: Pathak'. *The* Indian *Express*, 27 November 1988.

'Justly incensed'. *The Indian Express*, 21 November 1998.

Kalbag, Chaitanya. 1982. 'A Battle Supreme'. *India Today*, 15 December.

———. 1983. 'Ends of Justice'. *India Today*, 31 January.

Kania, M.H. 'Full Court Reference in the Memory of Late Justice M. Hidayatullah on 22nd September, 1992' [1992] *Supp*. 1 *Supreme Court Reports*.

Kondaiah, Challa. 1980. 'Late Dr P.V. Rajamannar'. *AIR* 1980 *Journal*.

Krishna Iyer, V.R. 2008. 'A Courageous Voice of Dissent'. *The Hindu*, 19 March.

Kumaramangalam, S. Mohan. 1973. 'Chief Justice: Criteria of Choice', in Kuldip Nayar (ed.), *Supersession of Judges*. New Delhi: India Book Company.

'Late Mr Justice K.K. Mathew'. (1992) 3 *SCC Journal*.

'Law Day Speech Delivered by Shri P.N. Bhagwati, Chief Justice of India, on November 26, 1986' (1987) 1 *SSC Journal*.

'Legal Causerie'. *The Hindustan Times*, 23 December 1951.

Library of Congress (United States). http://www.loc.gov. (Last accessed 3 October 2010).

Mahajan, Krishan. 1983. 'Legal Perspectives: Political Judges'. *The Hindustan Times*, 1 February.

Mitra, Sumit. 1985. 'Chief Justice P.N. Bhagwati: Age of Activism'. *India Today*, 15 August.

———. 1986. 'Supreme Court: Tug of War'. *India Today*, 15 January.

———. 1993. 'The Verma Commission: A Cover-Up Job?'. *India Today*, 15 August.

———. 1997. 'Legal Eagles'. *India Today*, 31 March.

———. 1997. 'Chief vs Lordships'. *India Today*, 10 August.

———. 1997. 'Judicial Dissensions'. *India Today*, 6 October.

———. 1997. 'A Benchmark for Bench Brawls'. *India Today*, 24 November.

———. 1998. 'Punchhi at Last'. *India Today*, 19 January.

Mitta, Manoj. 1990. 'Ramaswamy not in CJ's list'. *The Times of India*, 17 May.

———. 1993. 'Justice V. Ramaswami: A Career Spent in Controversy'. *India Today*, 15 June.

'More Than a Green Judge'. *Outlook India*, 22 January 1997, online at www. OutlookIndia.com.

'Mr Justice'. *India Today*, 15 March 1996.

'Mr Justice Syed Murtaza Fazal Ali' [1985] 3 *Supreme Court Cases (Journal)*.

Mukherjea, B.K. 1955. 'Retirement of Shri Mehr Chand Mahajan' [1955] *SCR*.

Mukherjea, Sisir Kumar. 1973. 'In Memoriam: The Late Justice Arun. K. Mukherjea'. *Calcutta Weekly Notes*, vol. LXXVIII, 26 November.

Nagarajan, Rema. 1998. 'Three Generations of Judges'. *The Hindustan Times*, 2 March.

Narayan, Hemendra. 1983. 'Baharul says he did not resign to become MP'. *The Indian Express*, 28 February.

Nariman, Fali S. 1987. 'The Judiciary and the Role of the Pathfinders' [1987] 3 *Supreme Court Cases (Journal)*.

National Law School of India University Library. www.nls.ac.in. (Last accessed 3 October 2010).

Nayar, Kuldip. 1973. 'An interview with former Chief Justice S.M. Sikri: Consequences of Supersession', in Nayar, *Supersession of Judges*. New Delhi: India Book Company.

———. 1978. 'New Chief Justice may be outsider'. *The Indian Express*, 21 February.

———. 1984. 'Chief Justices of States Need Their Day in Court'. *India Abroad*, 14 December.

'New CJ according to statute'. *The Hindustan Times*, 12 January 1978.

Noorani, A.G. 1973. 'The Bar Protests', in N.A. Palkhivala (ed.), *A Judiciary Made to Measure*. Bombay: M.R. Pai.

———. 1973. 'The Chief Justice of India'. *The Indian Express*, 2 May.

———. 1982. 'The Twilight of the Judiciary'. *Debonair*, February.

———. 1983. 'Extra-judicial activity of judges'. *The Indian Express*, 15 February.

———. 1983. 'Our Judiciary: An Insider's Account'. *Opinion*, vol. XXIV, nos 3-4, March-April.

———. 1986. 'Crisis in Judiciary'. *The Indian Express*, 30 April.

———. 1994. 'The Prime Minister and the Judiciary'. in Manor (ed.), *Nehru to the Nineties, The Changing Face of Prime Minister of India*. Vancouver: University of British Columbia Press.

———. 2000. 'Courts and Contempt Power'. *Frontline*, vol. 17, issue 8, 15-28 April.

'Ordinance to increase judges' salary proposed'. *India Abroad*, 19 December 1997.

Palkhivala, N.A. 1977, 'Salute to Justice Khanna'. *The Indian Express*, 30 January.

———. 1982. 'The Supreme Court Judgment in the Judges' Case'. *Journal of the Bar Council of India*, vol. IX, no. 2.

Pathak, Rahul. 1990. '"I feel like an animal in a zoo" says Meham judge'. *Indian Express*, 24 November.

———. 1990. 'Judge sends in resignation, inquiry is dead: Meham probe gets decent burial'. *The Indian Express*, 12 December.

Prakash, A. Surya. 1998. 'Ombudsman or Bogeyman'. *The Indian Express*, 18 December.

'Recruitment of Judges'. 1968. *Calcutta Weekly Notes*, vol. LXXXII, 26 June.

'Reserving Judgement, the delay in naming the new chief justice is a situation India could have done without'. *India Today*, 5 January 1998.

'Retirement of Shri Mehr Chand Mahajan, Chief Justice of India: Judges' Farewell Dinner' [1955] *Supreme Court Reports*.

Rudolph, Lloyd and Susanne Hoeber Rudolph. 1965. 'Barristers and Brahmans in India: Legal Cultures and Social Change'. *Comparative Studies of Society and History*, vol. VIII, no.1, December.

Sachar, Rajinder. 2008. 'Justice H.R. Khanna: When others crawled, he stood tall'. *The Tribune*, Chandigarh, 3 March.

Sahay, S. 1981. 'The Role and Status of the Judiciary in Indian Government'. *Journal of the Bar Council of India*, vol. VIII, no. 3.

Sathe, S.P. 1978. 'Limitations on Constitutional Amendment: "Basic Structure" Principle Re-examined', in Rajeev Dhawan and Alice Jacob (eds), *Indian Constitution: Trends and Issues*. Bombay: N.M. Tripathi Pvt. Ltd.

———. 2006. 'India from Positivism to Structuralism', in Jeffrey Goldsworthy (ed.), *Interpreting Constitutions: A Comparative Study*. New Delhi: Oxford University Press.

Schmitthener, Samuel. 1968–9. 'A Sketch of the Development of the Legal Profession in India', *Law & Society Review*, vol. III, nos 2 and 3, November 1968–February 1969.

Sethi, Vinod. 'Life's Long Voyage of Justice V.R. Krishna Iyer'. www.vrkrishnaiyer.org/article1.htm.

———. 'Participation in Social Organizations and Professional Bodies'. www.vrkrishnaiyer.org/achievements.htm.

———. www.vrkrishnaiyer.org/awards.htm.

———. 'The Living Legend'. www.vrkrishnaiyer.org.

——. www.vrkrishnaiyer.org/books.htm.

(All the above were accessed in October 2010.)

Sharma, R.D. 1992. 'Need for National Judicial Commission'. *The Times of India*, 21 October.

Singh, Khushwant. 1986. 'Good Man dee Laltain: H.R. Khanna'. *The Overseas Hindustan Times*, 22 March.

Singh, N.K. 1983. 'MP Govt, CJ row over new judges'. *The Indian Express*, 14 January.

'S.K. Das Commences Investigation of Serajuddin Affair'. 1963. *The Times of India*, 13 May.

'Speeches Delivered at a Farewell Dinner in Honour of Shri S.R. Das, the Retiring Chief Justice, on September 30, 1959, in the Supreme Court Building' [1959] *Supreme Court Reports*.

Sridhar, V. 2001. 'Railway Safety: A Poor Record'. *Frontline*, vol. 18, issue 15, 21 July–3 August.

Subba Rao, K. 1975. Constitutional Despotism, *Swarajya* (Annual Number), 6, pp. 42–4, 47–8.

'Supreme Choice'. *India Today*, 31 May 1986.

'Tribunal to Investigate Meerut Riots'. *The Indian Express*, 29 February 1988.

'Three Supreme Court Judges Quit: Protest Against Supersession'. *The Hindustan Times*, 27 April 1973.

Tulzapurkar, V.D. 1977. 'Inaugural Address'. *AIR 1977 Journal* (also published in *Bombay Law Review Journal*, LXXIX).

——. 1983. 'Judiciary: Attacks and Survival'. *AIR 1983 Journal*.

——. 1984. 'Threats to the Independence of the Judiciary', *AIR 1984 Journal*.

'Uproar in Lok Sabha'. *The Indian Express*, 27 April 1973.

Verma, J.S. 2003. 'Letter of the Chairperson of the Commission, Justice Shri J.S. Verma, to the Prime Minister of India, dated 3 January 2003'. Annexure 1 of the 2002–2003 *Annual Report of the National Human Rights Commission*, www.nhrc.nic.in.

Vettath, Balakrishna Eradi. www.supremecourtcaselaw.com/jus_vberadi.com. Last accessed 3 October 2010.

Wright, Theodore P. 1978. 'Kinship Ties among the Muslim Elite in India since Independence', mimeo, paper presented at the annual meeting of the Association for Asian Studies, Chicago, USA.

Index

About the Author

George H. Gadbois, Jr was born in Boston, Massachusetts, USA in 1936. After serving in the U.S. Army for three years, he received his BA degree in Political Science and History from Marietta College (Ohio), graduating with high honours. He received his PhD in political science from Duke University (North Carolina) in 1965. He was a graduate student when he spent the year 1962–63 in India. Supported by fellowships from the American Institute of Indian Studies, he continued his research in India during 1969–1970, 1982–1983, and 1988–1989. He was a political scientist at the University of Kentucky, USA.